AFTER
"Happily Ever After"

Contemporary Approaches to Film and Media Series

A complete listing of the books in this series can be found online at wsupress.wayne.edu.

GENERAL EDITOR
Barry Keith Grant
Brock University

AFTER "Happily Ever After"

Romantic Comedy in the Post-Romantic Age

Edited by
MARIA SAN FILIPPO

Foreword by
TAMAR JEFFERS MCDONALD

WAYNE STATE UNIVERSITY PRESS
DETROIT

Copyright © 2021 by Wayne State University Press, Detroit, Michigan, 48201. All rights reserved. No part of this book may be reproduced without formal permission.

Three essays appearing in this volume have been previously published and are reprinted here by permission of Taylor & Francis, www.tandfonline.com:

Mary Harrod, "'Money Can't Buy Me Love': Radical Right-Wing Populism in French Romantic Comedies of the 2010s," *New Review of Film and Television Studies* 18, no. 1 (2020): 101–18, DOI: https://doi.org/10.1080/17400309.2019.1664055.

Sueyoung Park-Primiano, "The Awkward Truth: Failure to Romance and the Art of Decoupling in the Films of Hong Sang-soo," *New Review of Film and Television Studies* 18, no.1 (2020): 49–64, DOI: https://doi.org/10.1080/17400309.2019.1664054.

Maria San Filippo, "Breaking Upwards: The Creative Uncoupling of Desiree Akhavan and Ingrid Jungermann," *Feminist Media Studies* 19, no. 7 (2019): 991–1008, DOI: https://doi.org/10.1080/14680777.2019.1667064.

ISBN (paperback): 978-0-8143-4674-7
ISBN (hardcover): 978-0-8143-4673-0
ISBN (ebook): 978-0-8143-4675-4

Library of Congress Control Number: 2020948734

Cover art © Mascha Tace / Shutterstock
Cover design by Laura Klynstra

Wayne State University Press
Leonard N. Simons Building
4809 Woodward Avenue
Detroit, Michigan 48201-1309

Visit us online at wsupress.wayne.edu

Contents

Foreword: Romantic Comedy Today:
Making Progress *Always* or Only *Maybe*?　　　　ix
Tamar Jeffers McDonald

Introduction: Love Actually:
Romantic Comedy since the Aughts　　　　1
Maria San Filippo

Act 1.
What's New Is Old: Regenerating Romcom

1. We Found Love in a Hopeless Place:
   Romantic Comedy in the Post-Romantic Age　　　　27
   Beatriz Oria

2. Comedy and Melodrama from *Sunrise* to *Midnight*:
   Genre and Gender in Richard Linklater's *Before* Series　　　　47
   James MacDowell

3. From Jane to Mindy: The Politics of Narrative
   Control in the Contemporary Romantic Comedy　　　　67
   Alice Guilluy

4. "Third-Act Romances" in Contemporary American
   Film and Television　　　　85
   Betty Kaklamanidou

5. Queer Romance in *Take My Wife*: How the Television Rom-Sitcom Gives New Life to the Genre   101
Ash Kinney d'Harcourt

Act 2.
Love in a Time of Precarity: Romcom Realism

6. In Love and Up in Smoke: *Harold & Kumar* and the Romantic Turn of the Post-9/11 Stoner Comedy   123
Maya Montañez Smukler

7. Romance as Business in the Capitalist Metropolis: Johnnie To's *Don't Go Breaking My Heart 1* and *2*   145
Tom Cunliffe

8. *Obvious Child*, Bookshops, and Postcrisis Romcom Urbanism   163
Martha Shearer

9. Connecting with Strangers: Cosmopolitanism, Romance, and Hospitality in Transnational Romantic Comedy   179
Manuela Ruiz

10. "Money Can't Buy Me Love": Radical Right-Wing Populism in French Romantic Comedies of the 2010s   197
Mary Harrod

Act 3.
Reimagining "Happily Ever After"

11. The Radical Middle: *Jane the Virgin*, *Crazy Ex-Girlfriend*, and the Subversive Potential of the Television Post-Romcom   219
Elizabeth Alsop

12.	The Awkward Truth: Fractured Romance and the Art of Decoupling in the Films of Hong Sang-soo Sueyoung Park-Primiano	241
13.	Addicted to Love: The Productive Pathology of the Romantic Comedy in the Netflix Series *Love* John Alberti	257
14.	Breaking Upwards: The Creative Uncoupling of Desiree Akhavan and Ingrid Jungermann Maria San Filippo	275
15.	"I fantasize sometimes about being alone . . . being in a quiet room, by myself, with no one touching me": "Wrong-coms" and the End of Marriage in Contemporary Romantic Comedy Deborah Jermyn	301

Acknowledgments   319
Selected Bibliography   321
Contributors   345
Index   351

Foreword

Romantic Comedy Today: Making Progress *Always* or Only *Maybe*?

Tamar Jeffers McDonald

At the end of January 2017, pop culture site Vulture spent a week looking at the contemporary romantic comedy under the banner "The Romcom Lives!"[1] This feature, celebrating old favorites like *When Harry Met Sally...* (1989), asserted that texting was "a rich narrative tool for the modern" romcom and listed "The 34 Best Romantic Comedies of the Past Decade"[2] in an attempt to defend the premise that "The Romantic Comedy Is Not Dead—It's Just Not the Same as You Remember."[3] In mounting this defense, Vulture was responding to murmurs of the genre's demise circulating since at least 2013, when National Public Radio tentatively inquired, "Are Romcoms Dead?"[4] Subsequent media outlets agreed that the genre had indeed expired, with the *Washington Post* not only concurring, but also kicking the corpse: "The Romcom is dead. Good."[5] Despite Vulture spiritedly championing the genre, by August 2017 the general view—based on a widely syndicated article by Jason Guerrasio—was that "The Big Hollywood Romantic Comedy *Is* Dead."[6]

Looking at the titles and box office figures gathered by Box Office Mojo reveals that these comments were made in the context of a very definite fall in the numbers of romantic comedies being released in Hollywood, from an average of ten per year in the 2000s to just two in 2013 and one in 2017.[7] Yet announcing the romcom's passing is not a new occurrence. The celebrated piece by Brian Henderson from 1978, "Romantic Comedy Today: Semi-Tough or Impossible?," declared not only the genre's contemporary malaise but the impossibility of its recovery, given its then-current developments. Henderson used the 1977 film *Semi-Tough* as his test case, finding this and all 70s romantic comedies falling woefully short of the 30s screwball comedies he also examined. What did Henderson find so troubling about the romantic comedies of his own period? Examining this, and then considering how subsequent products of the genre might have assuaged or confounded his doubts about its continued validity, helps to illuminate why the genre has subsequently been deemed to have perished.

Brian Henderson raised many points of interest in his important article, but three of the most germane for this foreword were his assertions about subgenres, the heroine, and the role of sex in the romcom. First, noting that "definition, even delimitation, is difficult or impossible because all Hollywood films (except some war films) have romance and all have comedy,"[8] Henderson suggested that examining a smaller unit within the main romantic comedy genre might perhaps help to capture its essential qualities: "It may be that subdividing romantic comedy into its component types or genres will further analysis of it. The definition that is elusive might be easier to accomplish at a level of greater particularity. Let us take 'screwball comedy,' a term one finds in critical contexts of all sorts."[9]

Henderson's chosen example, however, only led him into deeper despair. Comparing the romantic comedies of the '70s with the sophisticated, wordy, rapid-fire screwball comedies of the '30s made Henderson lament the decline of the genre in his own time. Further, he explicitly located the deterioration in the genre within what he viewed as the then-contemporary enfeeblement of the heroine, in comparison to her shrewd, active, and gutsy 30s counterpart. As noted, he took as his case study the example of Michael Ritchie's *Semi-Tough*, a film that culminates in the heroine's last-minute rescue from a wedding to the wrong partner. While noting that this trope was inherited from screwballs such as *It Happened One Night* (1934), Henderson denounced it with respect to *Semi-Tough*'s Barbara Jane (Jill Clayburgh) as woefully ineffectual: "In *Semi-Tough* the heroine does nothing after the rescue except to be catatonic."[10] Although he had initially invoked the screwball to show how close examination of smaller units of the overall genre could aid definition, he ended despondent that the screwball's power, and that of its compelling heroines, had entirely vanished, starkly asserting that the 70s film's conclusion "marks the collapse of the filmic Barbara Jane—[and] reveals that there never was a character at all. With her collapse, the film collapses. There can be no romantic comedy without strong heroines."[11]

Perhaps most significantly, a section of Henderson's article engages with the then-innovative filmic acknowledgement of sex, as reflected in *Semi-Tough*, and specifically blamed this for the demise of the romcom: "At one point in *Semi-Tough*, the heroine says to the hero, 'How come we never fucked?' It is arguable that romantic comedy depends upon the suppression of this question and that with its surfacing romantic comedy becomes impossible. The question always circulates in romantic comedy, it is its utterance that is forbidden."[12] Henderson here posited that all romantic comedy had this question at its center, but, for the genre to survive, the "utterance" must never be allowed to "surface"; instead, it must be kept subterranean. Henderson would presumably lament even more the *visualization* of the act referred to, since he believed it was the very frustration of desire that gave romantic comedy its frisson: "[Sex] can never be said or referred to directly. This is perhaps the fascination of the romantic comedy. It implies a process of perpetual displacement, of euphemism and indirection at all levels, a latticework of dissembling and hiding laid over what is constantly present but denied, unspoken, unshown."[13]

To examine these useful points in order, I find Henderson's notion of subdividing the romcom provocative, because, like him, I have charted the changes in Hollywood products of this genre and have been interested in differentiating the films of the time he was writing from those of the 1980s, 1990s, 2000s, and more recent developments. While "romantic comedy" as a whole remains a large genre, various trends within it have held sway for up to a decade or so—namely, the screwball, the sex comedy, and, from Henderson's own time, what I have called the "radical romcom": a film that seems revolutionary by explicitly dealing with sex, and in being prepared to end the film without the couple together.[14] With the end of this realistic cycle, the more conservative "Neo-Traditional romcom" became dominant in the late 80s; crucially, it abandoned the elements Henderson found problematic and returned the treatment of sex to the "latticework of dissembling and hiding" previously mandated by the Production Code, even though the industrial justifications for such coyness had ended.[15] The reversal of the realistic trend of the 70s and the resultant hegemony of its sexless successor eventually led to the short-lived appearance of the collection of films I have called the "hommecom" (2008), which took over cinema screens and attained dominance and influence for about a five-year period in the mid-90s.

Films in this group rehearsed all of the major elements of the romantic comedy but centered them around a male, rather than a female, lead character, thus making the tropes fresher and generating comedy from them in a self-reflexive way, as with scenes where, in a supposed gender reversal, men worried about what to wear on dates or asked their best friends for romantic advice. Seeming—at least superficially—so different, these films were for a time both very prevalent and very lucrative. Although the hommecom could be traced back at least to 1996's *Swingers*, the real watershed moment came in 2005, when *Wedding Crashers* and *The 40-Year-Old Virgin* generated over $315 million between them in theatres. After the financial success of these two films, entries in the cycle inevitably snowballed: the next few years produced *Good Luck Chuck*, *The Heartbreak Kid*, *I Now Pronounce You Chuck and Larry*, and *Knocked Up* (all 2007); *Made of Honor* and *Forgetting Sarah Marshall* (both 2008); and many more. Arguably, however, the cycle had begun to wane by about 2009, with that year's *I Love You, Man* both a high point and a concluding one.

The hommecom's undoubted if short-lived popularity with audiences, if not critics, is perhaps explained less because of the novelty of men concerned with clothing options and more because of dissatisfaction with the alternative form of the genre: the more usual female-centered romcom. This had become over time, generally, sexless and staid; though ironically returning to the reticence on sex that Henderson advocated, such films seemed thoroughly to justify Henderson's other fear that "there can be no romantic comedy without strong heroines," since its central females were usually portrayed as clumsy, tearful, weak-willed career women desperate to trade their jobs for a man. Ultimately, however, the hommecom, too, proved problematic, as it *also* tended to downgrade the importance of the heroine, marginalizing her and also tending to deny her the meaningless hedonistic erotic encounters that made up the comedic material for the hero, thus recreating the sexual double standard.

The chapters in this edited collection follow, with erudition and invention, in Henderson's footsteps, investigating the *current* state of the romcom, forty years after his survey of the genre. In some cases the contributors to this anthology concentrate on discovering what happened after the waning of the hommecom and the seeming disappearance of the staid female-centered alternative, but, throughout, they are all intent on widening the usual ambit of investigation. Each of the chapters adds to the scholarly literature on the genre by taking its study of romantic comedy *beyond* the usual: beyond Hollywood, either in the sense of concentrating on independent production (MacDowell, Shearer), racially or geographically outside the traditional Anglo-Saxon, North American focus (Smukler, Cunliffe, Ruiz, Harrod, Park-Primiano); beyond the standard heterosexual couple (Oria, d'Harcourt, San Filippo); beyond film as the medium under inquiry (Guilluy, Alsop, Alberti); and beyond the common age of protagonists (Kaklamanidou, Jermyn). Together these pieces demonstrate that Henderson's fears for the genre's continued survival as a relevant form of film entertainment have not been realized.

In discussing the very recent resurgence of the romantic comedy, it is hard to avoid acknowledging the importance of streaming giant Netflix, as Betty Kaklamanidou, Ash Kinney d'Harcourt, Elizabeth Alsop, and John Alberti do. While the genre never entirely went away after Guerrasio's reading of its burial rites, as indie directors did continue to develop such pictures during the moribund years, the romantic comedy does seem to have resuscitated and been brought back into the mainstream, somewhat due to the support of Netflix's original content filmmaking. The streaming company's different financial model—which means that its films do not appear in box office listings unless released theatrically as well—on top of its reluctance to give hard data to support its announced viewing figures, however, make it difficult to ascertain the actual popularity of its films. While for most mainstream fare using Box Office Mojo's account of domestic and international grosses can be problematic (it counts monies earned rather than tickets sold), the site can be used to compare, with caveats, the performance of films in their theatrical runs. Netflix's alternative model complicates this by entirely moving consumption from the big screen to a variety of small screens, or by releasing its films simultaneously in theaters as well as on its own platform.

Accounting for the importance of Netflix as a generator of, as well as a viewing place for, romantic comedies means the romcom scholar needs to examine both the available data like box office returns as well as more subjective information, such as film reviews, critical think pieces on the genre, cultural roundups, and perhaps even memes, in order to track popularity. Despite the methodological torsions required to do all this, it is worth it:

Netflix has repeatedly been credited with resurrecting the romcom, although studying its slate of recent original movies does not show the dominance of the genre among its original content, despite what some seem to believe.[16] If the number of romcoms commissioned or purchased by Netflix is not as high as has been suggested, many of its films have, nevertheless, attracted much media and internet attention. A closer exploration of one of them, *Always Be My Maybe* (2019), shows how the parameters of the genre are being extended, at least apparently, while underneath much of the genre's status quo is still being maintained.

Always Be My Maybe tells the story of Sasha and Marcus, who grew up together in San Francisco and experienced their first partnered sex together as teenagers. Having drifted apart, the two meet again when Sasha, now a famous chef, moves back to the Bay Area to open a new restaurant, and Josh, still working for and living with his dad, comes to fix the air conditioning in her rented house. Although Sasha has a fiancé and Marcus acquires a girlfriend during the running time of the movie, it is immediately clear to the audience that both of these others represent the "wrong partner" that Steve Neale identified as one of the traditional tropes of the romcom.[17] Sasha's intended is withdrawn both emotionally and, soon, geographically, as he decides to go traveling for six months before settling down with her, and, once away, discovers that marriage is not what he wants at all. Marcus's girlfriend is represented as a "hippy-dippy" caricature who may seem to fit with his current "slacker" or alternative lifestyle but does not actually understand his personal and career aspirations. Eventually—after an interlude in which Marcus's attempts to tell Sasha how he feels about her have been frustrated by her new passionate affair (with Keanu Reeves, playing an exaggeratedly awful version of himself)—the right couple gets together and enjoys a brief period of romantic calm before the plot machinations determine the inevitable breakup at the end of the third quarter. With the rote aid of two Embarrassing Public Gestures later, however, Sasha and Marcus are of course back together by the end credits.

If this narrative account seems instrumentalist, it is because the film, though not without its amusing moments, displays its plot structure too overtly and bows to narrative exigencies that have been made to seem important through their sheer repetition in the genre. The writers thus mistake generic inevitability for generic significance—for example, with the breakup, which seems motivated not by genuine character conflict or

Sasha (Ali Wong) and Marcus (Randall Park) with their "wrong partners" (including Keanu Reeves playing himself) in *Always Be My Maybe*.

misunderstanding, but by being the next event on a romcom checklist. That the writers include Ali Wong and Randall Park, who themselves play Sasha and Marcus in the film, does not make such decisions easier to excuse. The importance of these cast members, who have worked together along with the film's director, Nahnatchka Khan, on the TV series *Fresh Off the Boat* (ABC, 2015–2020), resides largely in their being Asian Americans. As most of the reviews of the film have noted, it is still rare to have nonwhite actors cast as central characters and love interests in mainstream American movies, although this claim does overlook the large number of successful romcoms made with Black casts for Black audiences, such as *Breakin' All The Rules* (2004) and *Think Like A Man* (2012).[18]

The ethnicity of its leads is one of the ways in which *Always Be My Maybe* appears to be doing something different with the romcom. But "appears to be" is the significant factor here: reversing the usual phrase "the same but different," this film actually is "different but the same," since the changes are only superficial. For example, while the film may seem to be more realistic in acknowledging that relationships can start with, rather than build up to, sexual relations, it still eschews *showing* the sex, thus conforming to the avoidance of such displays I have previously noted as one of the hallmarks of the neotraditional romcom and mentioned above.[19] Furthermore, while the protagonists are not white, they are still heterosexual—again, consistent with the majority of romcoms. Gay characters do exist in the diegesis, but are firmly relegated to supporting roles. Sasha's best friend and business manager, Veronica, is engaged to a woman and pregnant with their child, but these facts seem to have been included to score cool points: the film downplays their relationship to the extent that Veronica's fiancée, Denise, is only seen once. In this respect the film's emphasis on gay people has not evolved beyond that evinced twenty years ago in *My Best Friend's Wedding* (1997), which has been subsequently criticized for advancing the trope of the gay best friend.[20]

Perhaps the most noticeable way in which *Always Be My Maybe* shows itself to be a different type of romantic comedy is in the fact that Sasha's job is seen to be important to her, but she is not encouraged to view her commitment to her career as unhealthy or to abandon it, as some 90s romcom career woman heroines were—for example, in *Kate & Leopold* (2001) and *The Proposal* (2009). Instead she encourages Marcus to be more ambitious and commit his energies to making his band a success while he supports her business ventures. In all, while innocuous, the film does not justify the claim that Netflix is "saving" or rebooting the romantic comedy genre by permitting it, finally, to grow up and reflect contemporary reality.[21] As the rehearsal of its common tropes above indicates, *Always Be My Maybe* commits to hitting the usual romcom beats with gusto rather than originality, other than in the nonwhite casting of its leads.

While Netflix and other nontraditional commissioning agents like Amazon and Hulu seem set to continue to develop and release romantic comedies, the genre is likely to need support from both TV and mainstream film production companies if it is to reclaim a prominent place in contemporary generic output. Nevertheless, as the provocative and enjoyable chapters in this edited collection indicate, both Henderson and Guerrasio's pronouncements of the death of the genre seem unfounded: in many different forms, the romcom *does* live.

Notes

1 "The Romcom Lives!," Vulture, January 30, 2017, https://www.vulture.com/news/the-romcom-lives/.

2 "The 34 Best Romantic Comedies of the Past Decade," Vulture, January 31, 2017, www.vulture.com/2017/01/best-romantic-comedies-streaming-past-decade.html.
3 Jen Chaney, "The Romantic Comedy Is Not Dead—It's Just Not the Same as You Remember," Vulture, January 30, 2017, www.vulture.com/2017/01/romantic-comedy-is-not-dead.html.
4 Linda Holmes, "Are Romcoms Dead?" National Public Radio, March 4, 2013, www.npr.org/2013/03/04/173424536/are-romantic-comedies-dead?t=1562956633023.
5 Emily Yahr, "The Romcom Is Dead. Good." *Washington Post*, October 8, 2016, www.washingtonpost.com/lifestyle/style/the-romcom-is-dead-good/2016/10/06/6d82a934-859c-11e6-ac72-a29979381495_story.html?utm_term=.a0fcdbcde9c1.
6 Jason Guerrasio, "The Big Hollywood Romantic Comedy Is Dead," Business Insider, August 8, 2017, www.businessinsider.com/why-movie-studios-no-longer-make-romantic-comedies-2017-8?r=US&IR=T.
7 It should be noted that I am counting only films included in Box Office Mojo's list of Top 100 Box Office films; see www.boxofficemojo.com/genres/chart/?id=romanticcomedy.html (accessed September 4, 2020).
8 Brian Henderson, "Romantic Comedy Today: Semi-Tough or Impossible?," *Film Quarterly* 31, no. 4 (Summer 1978): 12.
9 Henderson, "Romantic Comedy," 12.
10 Henderson, 18.
11 Henderson, 18.
12 Henderson, 21.
13 Henderson, 22.
14 Tamar Jeffers McDonald, *Romantic Comedy: Boy Meets Girl Meets Genre* (London: Wallflower, 2007), 10.
15 Jeffers McDonald, *Romantic Comedy*, 84.
16 See Rachel Aroesti, "Can Netflix Save Us from the Great Romcom Shortage of 2018? I Watched 11 Films to Find Out," *Guardian*, August 24, 2018, www.theguardian.com/film/2018/aug/24/can-netflix-save-us-from-the-great-romcom-shortage-of-2018-i-watched-11-films-to-find-out; Lisa Bonos, "Netflix Knows We Need an Escape, So It Built a Romcom Factory," *Washington Post*, July 26, 2018, www.washingtonpost.com/news/soloish/wp/2018/07/26/netflix-knows-we-need-an-escape-so-it-built-a-rom-com-factory/.

17 Steve Neale, "The Big Romance or Something Wild?: Romantic Comedy Today," *Screen* 33, no. 3 (1992): 289.
18 For example, of *Set It Up* (2018) Rachel Aroesti asserts that it is "refreshing to have a blossoming relationship between an Asian-American woman and African-American man as the focus of a romcom, a genre hitherto populated almost exclusively by white people." See Aroesti, "Can Netflix Save Us?"
19 See Jeffers McDonald, *Romantic Comedy*, 97–98; and Tamar Jeffers McDonald, "Hommecom," in *Falling in Love Again: Romantic Comedy in Contemporary Cinema*, ed. Stacey Abbott and Deborah Jermyn (London: I. B. Tauris, 2008), 146–59.
20 Baz Dreisinger, "The Queen in Shining Armor: Safe Eroticism and the Gay Friend," *Journal of Popular Film & Television* 28, no. 1 (Spring 2000): 2–11.
21 Guy Lodge, "Netflix Has Picked Up Where Hollywood Left Off, with a Handful of Cute, Smart, and Genuinely Relevant Date Movies," *Guardian*, September 3, 2018, www.theguardian.com/film/2018/sep/03/new-netflix-romcoms-streaming-new-dvds-guy-lodge.

Introduction

LOVE ACTUALLY:
ROMANTIC COMEDY SINCE THE AUGHTS

Maria San Filippo

"The romantic comedy is dead." Or so pronounced critic Amy Nicholson in a 2014 article in *L.A. Weekly*, after noting that in the previous year not one romcom appeared among the top 100 films at the U.S. box office.[1] The numbers for 2013, as tallied by the revenue-tracking website Box Office Mojo, largely confirm Nicholson's pronouncement; the only film among the top 100 that clearly belongs to the romcom category is Spike Jonze's *Her*, which just snuck in at one-hundredth place. A half-decade later, *Entertainment Weekly* devoted its entire 2019 Valentine's Day issue to celebrating bygone Hollywood romcoms, nostalgia being another sure sign that the genre has stalled. And yet, as Nicholson goes on to concede, romcom refuses to *actually* die; as relatively inexpensive films aimed primarily at adults—and women to boot—romcoms serve as reliably if not massively profitable counterprogramming to the animated family fare and superhero franchises that dominate the postmillennial multiplex and, since Nicholson's writing, romcoms have gone on to become a staple of Netflix's streaming platform. As Tamar Jeffers McDonald, author of this book's foreword, persuasively claims in surveying the genre's history from the 1930s–40s screwball era to the "Neo-Traditionalism" that took hold in the late 1980s and remained ensconced in 2007, when her study concludes, romantic comedy may well be Hollywood's most consistently popular genre.[2] And bona fide blockbusters do occasionally emerge; *Trainwreck* topped the $100 million mark in 2015, and as recently as 2018 *Crazy Rich Asians* cracked the all-time top ten for romantic comedy at the U.S. box office, with Box Office Mojo reporting $238.5 million in estimated worldwide grosses. These top-performing titles are telling, both for being, perhaps, the (two) exceptions that prove the rule that romcoms don't possess superhero earning power, and for bearing vivid markers of the neotraditionalist turn that Jeffers McDonald notes, which in its obsessive drive to reassure itself (and us) of "the possibility of lasting love in contemporary society . . . betray[s] its own lack of faith in such an outcome."[3] As appealing as audiences found both films, it's a tough call which requires a greater suspension of disbelief: the fantasy wish fulfillment of *Crazy Rich Asians*'s Singaporean restaging of *Cinderella*, or Amy Schumer's transformation from the titular trainwreck who heckles Laker Girls ("You're going to lose us the vote!") into an eager-to-please girlfriend who abandons her "monogamy is unrealistic" motto and teams with those same cheerleaders to win over the staid suitor proffering those very shackles of monogamy. Even recent romcoms that claim to take a knowing stance succumb to these neotraditional impulses, with *Slant*'s critic noting of *Isn't It Romantic* (2019)—in which a concussed Rebel Wilson awakens to find her "life's become a [bleep] romantic comedy" (a PG-13 rated one at that)— that it "evolves into the very thing it set out to parody."[4] Similarly, the 2019 documentary *Romantic Comedy*, billed as a self-examination of creator Elizabeth Sankey's own long-term love affair with the genre, advertises itself with a trailer featuring nostalgia-inducing iconic movie moments worthy of a romcom flashback montage.

Apart from those high-earning outliers of the last decade, the modest box office performance of romcoms reveals less about contemporary romantic comedy and more about the current entertainment industry's production, distribution, and exhibition models. With movie studios preoccupied with churning out superhero sequels, family-friendly animation, and horror reboots, the peak TV era of proliferating niche programming and "quality television" has given romcom a much-needed makeover, with television's key attribute, seriality, providing an invaluable resource for explorations that go beyond "happily ever after." So too have internet-based producers and distributors (from behemoths Amazon, Facebook, and Netflix to independent web series creators) taken up the slack, administering our romcom fix via the small screen, through digital delivery systems and streaming platforms. Contemporary romcoms are as, or possibly more, likely to have their initial release online rather than theatrically, with what we might call "post-theatrical romcom"—works that bypass theatrical release, whether they be film, TV, or web series—having propagated to the point that cultural critic Lisa Bonos proclaimed in 2018 that Netflix's glut of original romcom content had left her in a "rom-coma."[5] Whether romcom has benefited or suffered from these developments is debatable, but romcom is assuredly more diverse, in all senses of the term, than ever. Ultimately Nicholson's investigation concludes that, in fact, romcom isn't dead—it's different. It's indie, it's queer, it features (if still too rarely) lead characters of color or (as in the case of 2017's *The Big Sick*) interracial couplings, it diverts focus from the romantic couple to platonic buddies (as in the bromance and the momcom), and it's now as often as not about *un*coupling.

Beyond Creating the Couple

This last development threatens traditional and contemporary notions of romantic comedy as lighthearted narratives about couple formation. These new-ish traits and tones—for romcom's diversification dates back to the 1970s, as will be discussed below—make it increasingly challenging to define the parameters of a genre that has always been hard to isolate, given the ubiquity of romantic story lines in (especially Hollywood) narrative cinema. This trend toward genre hybridity and rebranding, "creating films with greater depth and breadth of setting, storyline, and character," while retaining the all-important element of romantic affirmation/wish fulfillment, is noted by Ashley Elaine York as a key factor driving the success of the contemporary "women's blockbuster," with releases such as *Mamma Mia!* (2008) and *Bridesmaids* (2011) finding enormous success with a "bigendered, worldwide audience."[6] Elżbieta Ostrowska (drawing on the foundational work of Betty Kaklamanidou, one of this volume's contributors) connects the generic and textual inclusiveness of contemporary romantic comedies to the neoliberal logic of both their and their creators' emphasis on the accumulation of wealth, concluding that "the genre has become an aesthetic nomad wandering from one generic convention to another, hoping to accumulate ideological and aesthetic capital in order to secure a maximised financial return."[7] This high concept, global-marketed model issuing from studio boardrooms might be said, then, both to have saved the romcom and diluted its brand by blurring its generic parameters. Meanwhile, romcom's valence and viewership have been revived through its dissemination via Netflix algorithms and in the online/fan discourse devoted to cataloging its tropes (the "manic pixie dream girl"; the grand gesture; the airport confrontation), repurposing its motifs as memes (Feminist Ryan Gosling; *The Graduate*-inspired "Hello Darkness My Old Friend"), and exposing its normalization of such questionable behavior as that diagnosed by a sociological study as "persistent pursuit" and satirized by the *Onion* under the headline "Romantic-Comedy Behavior Gets Real-Life Man Arrested."[8]

The tensions and transformations always involved in the construction and dissemination of genre concepts have cemented genre theorists' conviction that it is unproductive to police any given genre's boundaries, even as demarcations remain legible, of practical use, and in need of parsing.[9] Heeding critic Adrian Martin's recommendation regarding contemporary romantic comedy ("We need to chase the genre's self-definition in flight, as it happens") this collection delineates a grouping of texts bound together by a shared idiom, recurrent tropes, and industrial-cultural positioning, while recognizing that such groupings are subject to change and must be productively stretched to encompass modified and hybridized strains.[10] In another foundational work by one of our contributors, John Alberti joins cultural critics such as Hanna Rosin and Laura Kipnis in noting the contemporary crisis surrounding masculinity and argues that it "opens up new imaginative possibilities for the idea and ideal of The Couple, but the expanded possibilities equally mean the radical destabilization of existing genres of both narrative and gender."[11] The "anxious romance"—Alberti's nomenclature for a significant emergent romcom subgenre symptomatic of this (post-9/11, postrecession, perhaps even postpatriarchal) crisis of masculinity—is one of several such designations that our contributors devise in appraising the brave new world of post-2000s romcom. In a ten-year span that has seen Hollywood studios' hegemony toppled by Amazon and Netflix, moviegoing ceding the way to streaming and (at current writing) hobbling back from hiatus due to COVID-19, and the progressive policies of Barack Obama's two-term presidency torn asunder by rollbacks in civil and reproductive rights, environmental and immigration crises, and resurgent white supremacy (to name but a few), it is no surprise that romcom has experienced considerable whiplash as its industrial and ideological chakras realign in response.

This collection encompasses, therefore, narratives that deviate from romcom formula (by centering on same-sex couplings both platonic and romantic, for example, or by combining in roughly equal measure comedy and melodrama) and that adapt Hollywood-centric romcom's cinematic conventions and national-industrial positionalities to fit serialized, cross-platform formats and indie and non-U.S./transnational production contexts. Such an approach reflects transmedia and transnational practices within not only romcom production and consumption but throughout the screen media industries, *and*, moreover, within the field of media studies. Beyond an openness to generic indeterminacy and affirmation of romcom renewal and dispersal, what further unites this collection is its contemporaneity, with each chapter presenting case studies from the last decade. This period-specific approach follows the model of such classic studies of romantic comedy as Stanley Cavell's exploration of the 1930s–40s "comedy of remarriage" cycle in *Pursuits of Happiness* (1984) onward and follows the precepts articulated by Celestino Deleyto, who posits that romantic comedy comprises "not so much, or at least not only, tales of the consolidation of a heterosexual couple as series of narrative events representing assorted forms of desire within particular historical contexts."[12] The recognition, increasingly prevalent within romcom studies, that the genre's teleological drive has been overemphasized at the expense of its negotiation—over the course of what Deleyto terms the film's narrative "middle"—of "interpersonal affective and erotic relationships" comedically treated and culturally inscribed, additionally supports our historically defined scope and aligns with our locally informed yet globally attuned perspectives.[13]

The development of the genre over the last decade offers unassailable evidence, we believe, that romcom is alive and well—and, in some quadrants, better than ever, on account of the generic revisions, representational inclusions, and critical reorientations it has undergone. As our chapters cumulatively aim to demonstrate, the genre's key attribute since the 2000s may be the impulse to couple romcom and realism. Unlike the illusory wish fulfillment of neotraditional romantic comedies such as the one referenced in the title of this volume's introduction, the works singled out by our contributors reflect the genre's recent reactivation as a means for regarding love, sex, and relationships in all their actuality—even at further risk of rendering romcom difficult to disambiguate. Thinking back to Amy Nicholson's mystery of the murdered romcom, maybe the culprit is romcom itself, insofar as the more complex and anti-illusory romcom becomes—the more it reflects the realities of coupling and relationships—the less likely it is to be called romcom. As noted in a 2017 *Glamour* article titled "Why Is It So Wrong to

Love Romantic Comedy?," romcom's stigmatization perpetuates its generic illegibility, as "the warped logic applied to romantic comedies goes so far as to strip the genre label from anything the critics decide is good . . . dramas about love are allowed to have quality—just don't call them romcoms."[14] Whether because the creators and promotional campaigns for these diverse new works showing up on screens big and small are understandably reluctant to brand them explicitly as romcoms, given the derision heaped on the genre and its fans; or because the feminist-minded critics and scholars operating in romcom studies have so often opted (justifiably) to critique neotraditional romcom, regrettably the most innovative, idiosyncratic, and inclusive (and thus most interesting) works of romantic comedy, however creatively and expansively defined, have not yet received serious, sustained analysis of the type this collection aims to perform.[15] Collectively, my co-contributors and I seek to reorient romcom scholarship by confronting the actual contours of what constitutes romcom since the 2000s, as the genre has been reshaped in response to two pervasive forces: the "digital era" of screen media production, distribution, and exhibition; and the reconfiguration of social relations and practices linked to romance as a result of neoliberalism, globalization, civil rights legislation (e.g. marriage equality), social media, and other cultural factors that characterize what we will call, and consider below, the "post-romantic age."

The question may well arise whether "romantic comedy" is any longer a viable generic designation, given the dissents and divergences from classic genre forms my contributors and I trace in the works we study. The term "romantic comedy" retains its relevance, and appeal, for a number of reasons. Given that romantic comedy is typically stigmatized in both popular and critical discourse, in terms that link the low value placed on the form to its feminization—its orientation toward and consumption by female audiences—retaining that label is precisely a protest against the pejorative attitude toward women-oriented media that has long prevailed in the genre's reception. The label continues to play an important role in industrial and promotional contexts; witness the huge output of boy-meets-girl narratives that Netflix has bought up and pumped out in recent years and proudly labels in their database taxonomy "Romantic Comedies." Even as contemporary radical romcoms torque, tweak, and overturn the classic patterns, they nevertheless pay homage and foreground their connection to the works that preceded them, and whose power and interest they acknowledge precisely through their efforts at subversion. These historical and allusive linkages make an argument for transformation, rather than rupture. Indeed, a number of contributors to this volume see the romcoms of the "post-romantic age" less as rejecting the legacy of earlier eras than as extending and bringing to the fore tendencies already implicit in pre-existing romcom; revisionist works thus encourage us to read classic romcoms with greater sensitivity and alertness to their ambivalence about and questioning of the regime of heteronormative coupling and happy endings.

"The same old story of a boy and a girl in love..."

Before examining how things have changed, it bears assessing the ways romcom has remained the same—neotraditional, in the parlance of previous romcom scholarship—even as it has migrated into "post-theatrical" industrial and "post-romantic" cultural contexts. As Billie Holiday's lyrics attest, the romance narrative has proven remarkably resistant to modernizing influences while simultaneously accommodating the need of any genre to adapt in response to changing times and flagging formulas; the observation that genres follow cyclical rather than linear paths of (re)development points to romcom's projected lifespan as perennial rather than moribund. Yet reading romcom its last rites is nothing new; as Jeffers McDonald observes in the foreword, Brian Henderson's 1978 article "Romantic Comedy Today: *Semi-Tough* or Impossible?" notably—and, it turns out, wrongly—predicted that traditional romcom's dependence on sexual innocence and its delay of coupled consummation spelled its doom in the era of the sexual revolution.[16] Henderson's rather narrow definition of romantic comedy failed to anticipate the possibility of narratives of queer desire, which would increasingly be seen in the decades that followed his essay, or the neotraditional romcoms that sidelined questions of sex as they sought a return to earlier genre conventions; at the extreme, as in Nora Ephron's *Sleepless in Seattle* (1993) and *You've Got Mail* (1998), extraordinarily contrived situations ensure that couple formation precedes sexual contact (in *Sleepless*, couple formation precedes *physical* contact). Perhaps we might see these neotraditional narratives as the cinematic equivalent of the born-again virgin movement that gained momentum among evangelical Christians in the 90s, in which Christian youth who had "slipped" were able to regain their status as virgins, and thus their marriageability, by rigorously abstaining from sex for an extended period before marriage. What's certain is that, contrary to Henderson's gloomy prognosis, after a period of turbulence in the 70s and 80s generated by the women's movement's critique of romantic myths, romcom came back strong in the 1990s and 2000s, with hits like *Pretty Woman* (1990), *Four Weddings and a Funeral* (1994), and *Notting Hill* (1999), and the brand-name recognition built by romcom auteurs Nancy Meyers and the aforementioned Ephron purveying what Michele Schreiber describes as "postfeminist nostalgia": a relapse into an ostensibly outmoded desire for romantic fulfillment as a reassuring escape from the contradictions between feminist ideals and the realities of the labor and mating markets.[17] This neotraditionalism reflects that era's antifeminist backlash, but was also a response to the economic precarity and social insecurity of neoliberal capitalism. Neotraditional romcoms paper over the dawning disillusionment provoked by the recognition that feminism's promise of women's professional and sexual fulfillment was stymied by systemic barriers, persistent inequality, and the impossibility of "having it all."

So, while feminism did not kill the romcom—indeed, romcom became a prominent locus of postfeminist backlash and retreatist discourses—feminism stimulated a renewed interest in self-reflexivity, though one distinct from that of 1970s "radical romantic comedy," as Jeffers McDonald designated that era's genre upheaval.[18] The radical romcoms of the 1970s (1977's *Annie Hall* being the exemplar) married form and content by employing "denarrativizing" devices and distanciation effects (direct address, split screen, nonlinear editing) that exposed the impossibility of the romantic illusions they wistfully grieved rather than wishfully embraced.[19] The persistent nostalgic allusions in neotraditional romantic comedies, on the other hand, as Jeffers McDonald notes, "do not seem to be seeking to improve upon their inspirations in terms of increased realism, but merely to evoke them to share any left-over romantic charge they may carry."[20] This ironic disavowal around genre and gender manifests the neotraditional romcom's stubborn attempt to have it both ways: maintaining the fantasy of women's fulfillment through heteronormative coupling (though apparently only nostalgically and playfully) while simultaneously displaying feminist revisionism, or at least an awareness of the wish-fulfilling nature of the fantasy.

To take a recent post-theatrical romcom as an example, the 2018 Netflix original production *Ibiza* appears in its marketing and narrative first act to subordinate romantic coupling to what Alison Winch names the "girlfriend flick," playing up the "girl tripping" misadventures that occur when a work trip for Harper (Gillian Jacobs) is hijacked by her party-hearty gal pals Nikki (Vanessa Bayer) and Leah (Phoebe Robinson), who entice her into an MDMA-fueled hedonistic holiday in Spain.[21] Yet the film settles into a fairly conventional "boy meets girl" (or "girl meets boy") narrative trajectory upon the arrival of Prince Charming—in the person of EDM DJ Leo (played by *Game of Thrones* heartthrob Richard Madden), who singles Harper out of a nightclub crowd and cajoles her into playing hooky on Ibiza. After an idyllic interlude, the film's final sequence finds Harper back at home (and fired from her job), reporting to her girlfriends about informing Leo that, rather than follow him to his next gig, she plans to focus on getting her new business venture off the ground.

> HARPER: Leo asked me to meet him in Tokyo. I said no. I told him he had to come to me.
> LEAH: Yasss feminism! [*clinks glasses*] But, you know, you should've gone.
> NIKKI: The feminism is too much in this situation. Being too feminist is antifeminist.
> LEAH: Let's just stop it at wearing pants.
> HARPER: If he wants to see me, he has to come to me. I'm not going to keep flying around the world to see him.
> NIKKI: We'll go to Tokyo with him and then we'll come back here and *then* we'll make him come to you.
> HARPER: Noooo!
> LEAH & NIKKI: YASSS!

Apart from superficial signs of romcom revisionism—making one of the sassy sidekicks a woman of color; having Harper abandon corporate America for (the assurance of even greater success in) creative entrepreneurship—*Ibiza* essentially updates the postfeminist neotraditional romcom *Working Girl* (1988), in which an ambitious yet reassuringly feminine woman achieves professional *and* romantic triumph at the cost of her bitchy, sex-starved boss. Rather than nostalgically reference classic romances like *An Affair to Remember* (1957) and *Casablanca* (1942), as Schreiber notes of neotraditional romcom's first wave, *Ibiza* uses irony to wink at the audience,

Ibiza's "throuple" (Phoebe Robinson, Gillian Jacobs, and Vanessa Bayer) don't need Prince Charming to have a good time—or do they?

acknowledging our desire for the fantasy ending (Harper whisked into the Tokyo sunset) even as it resists, on feminist grounds, capitulating to that fantasy. This poke at feminism's penchant for raining on romance permits the film *and* viewers to have their wish fulfillment and disavow it too, delivering Prince Charming and the possibility of globe-trotting and work-shirking while reassuring us of its feminist bona fides: a feminist veneer assuages the guilty pleasure of retrograde romcom fantasy. Compare this use of irony to that of the 2004 revisionist romcoms *Before Sunset* and *Eternal Sunshine of the Spotless Mind* that Leger Grindon singles out as "taking romantic comedy seriously," in which he finds irony operating as an indication "that the couple accepts the dissonance that may be inevitable in all but the most blessed of human relationships." Whereas a postfeminist romcom like *Ibiza* exhibits ironic self-awareness precisely in order to subdue skepticism regarding romantic fantasy, *Before Sunset* and *Eternal Sunshine* follow 1970s radical romcoms in "portray[ing] our doubts about romance without abandoning a commitment to its fulfillment."[22]

In Love, Out of the Closet, and Online

The last decade's proliferation of web series production, catalyzed by funding mechanisms such as Kickstarter, self-distribution hosting services such as

Vimeo, and self-promotion courtesy of social media platforms, has led to a veritable cottage industry of romcom web series featuring queer and/or people of color protagonists. Many such series use a quasi-detached self-awareness of the genre's conventions to sustain its emotional affects while accommodating the jaded spectatorial sensibilities of a viewing constituency long accustomed to seeing their on-screen surrogates sidelined on romcom's representationally exclusive playing field. It would be misleading, however, to trace an entirely causal relationship between these technological-industrial changes and these recent romcoms' increased attentiveness to the genre's habitual blind spots around its own heteronormativity, whiteness, and Hollywood-centrism; indeed, a key aim of this collection is to redress romcom's persistent reinforcement of culturally normative coupling and its attendant marginalization of sexual and racial minorities. In underscoring the importance of taking romantic comedy seriously, these chapters employ perspectives drawn from feminist, queer, critical race, and postcolonial studies to critique the genre's residual homogeneity and social-sexual conservatism and to focus attention on works created by and focused on LGBTQ+ people and people of color. Just as seriality has proven a rejuvenating force for romcom, the gradual queering and dewhitening of the genre (and its attendant scholarship) has helped to relegitimate and even politicize romcom, even as it becomes incumbent on the genre to navigate assimilationist ideologies, universalizing (and thus dequeering and deracializing) narratives, and debates that instrumentalize (or weaponize) individual works to exaggerated effect and in service to predetermined agendas.

As a case in point, season 1 of *Strangers*, created by Mia Lidofsky and distributed in 2017 through Facebook Watch, features (like *Ibiza*) another professionally striving but romantically distracted twentysomething woman, struggling writer Isobel (Zoë Chao), who plays host to a series of Airbnb guests while navigating the challenges of being newly single and bisexual. *Strangers*' identity-minded but politically muted content bears the imprint of its corporate distributor Facebook and producer Refinery29, the young women-focused but male-owned media company whose mission statement vows to "deliver optimistic and diverse storytelling, experiences, and points of view to our audience of smart, curious, passionate women,"[23] a sensibility that aligns with Lidofsky's ambition, as her coproducer and wife Celia Rowlson-Hall describes it, "to become the Nancy Meyers of gay content."[24]

In an episode titled "Hot Set" (1.5), after an ill-timed appearance by her ex-boyfriend seems to have sabotaged her blossoming romance with aspiring filmmaker Hailey (Isabelle McNally), Isobel gets another chance when a production crew rents her apartment to make a film about (as a quick glance at the script reveals) "straight white people falling in love." Drafted into service as the lead actress's stand-in to run lines with the self-important lead actor, Isobel seizes the moment and veers off script to address Hailey:

> ISOBEL: Shouldn't you be able to love the parts of me that are afraid? Shouldn't you be able to love the ugly and difficult parts?
> ACTOR: Hey, guys, are there revisions I don't know about?
> ISOBEL: Look, I am just a person like you, struggling to get through each day, and I'm really scared, because I thought I was supposed to be more at this point in my life; I thought I was supposed to know more and understand more about how it all works, maybe have a job that I actually really like, with health insurance. But I don't. I don't have any of it. And I'm still really trying to figure out who I am. I do know that I like you. I think you like me too. I think that's worth something. I think this is worth something. I feel like we owe it to ourselves to give it a chance.
> ACTOR: That is so much better than the script!

Whereas *Ibiza* employs irony to evade feminism's killjoy demands, here irony enables us to appreciate the moment's sincerity as being "so much better" than "straight" romcom's hackneyed, heteronormative scripts—the reference to Julia Roberts's "I'm just a girl, standing in front of a boy, asking him to love her" speech in *Notting Hill* is unmistakable. Isobel's public declaration similarly revises Hollywood romcom's typical obliviousness to real-world struggles, while the scene's self-reflexivity pulls back the curtain to reveal "the work" of movieland fantasy in another sense, further distancing itself from neotraditional romcom by referencing the professional/financial insecurity of its precariously employed millennial protagonist. If these references to socioeconomic struggle strain against Nancy Meyers–style illusion, that *Strangers* salvages Hollywood romance with a rewrite—one conceived and performed by queer women, though with the watchful straight white cisgender man (or corporate overlords) hovering close at hand—makes visible how neotraditional romcom is alive and well, adapted for (and co-opted

Isobel's (Zoë Chao) neotraditional declaration of love to Hailey (Isabelle McNally) on set in *Strangers*.

by) post-2000s audiences and the advertising revenue-oriented protocols of media platforms that benefit from their consuming, circulating, and commenting on these series. In *Ibiza* and *Strangers*, ironic self-reflexivity addressed to the knowing yet still desiring spectator enables the expression of ambivalence over relinquishing romcom fantasy in favor of a romantic narrative more grounded in the lived realities of the neoliberal order.

Learning to Love (Romcom) Again

Alongside the constant, if exaggerated, reports of its death, romantic comedy is also persistently cast as a (at best) guilty pleasure and (at worst) shameful vice. As a young teen in the early 1990s, I was excited when my favorite female relative, also a film buff, indulged my desire to watch my latest favorite, the recently released *Pretty Woman*; afterward she admitted she enjoyed it but wouldn't want her (then-preadolescent) daughter to see it, concerned that she would take its Cinderella fantasy too much to heart. My own heart sank at hearing her clear-eyed feminist assessment, both because—I would eventually realize—I was stung by having my taste disparaged, however gently, by someone I fiercely admired, and because I feared I had already bought into the movie's message. It was my own feminist consciousness-raising moment where romcom was concerned, and, though I hardly went cold turkey from that day forward, in my eagerness to embrace the perspective of my own nascent feminism I overcorrected and grew utterly contemptuous of a genre that I increasingly viewed as having a default setting misaligned with progressive gender politics. As critic Emily VanDerWerff, speaking in a recent Vox roundtable devoted to assessing the genre's limits and possibilities, noted of its ideologically high stakes, "A bad rom-com too often isn't just a bad movie; it's also propping up some pretty toxic worldviews."[25]

Yet, many years later, in the wake of a relationship's breakup, I found some semblance of (however masochistic) comfort in watching, and rewatching, romcoms. When I got the chance to teach a film genre course at my graduate institution, I impetuously proposed a class on romantic comedy, thinking that subjecting such films, and the concept of romantic love, to critical scrutiny would open some distance on my still-raw sensibilities. I likely overcorrected there too, having prompted the teaching assistant to ask tentatively, after one of my more stringent lectures, "Do you really think *all* love is socially constructed?" Like my sensibilities, my syllabus has stabilized over the past decade, as I have continued teaching the course at multiple institutions; the impetus for this book emerged from that teaching and is inspired by my class discussions with students through the years. As a genre that is both critically and academically held in low esteem, yet one to which many college- and university-aged viewers hold substantial emotional attachments, romantic comedy manifests with particular intensity the challenge that all teachers of popular culture encounter in encouraging students toward critical examination of texts still widely perceived as "mere entertainment." Precisely because romantic comedy typically cloaks an exclusionary vision of love and relationships inside works that are so viewed and consumed, this collection—like my courses on romcom—aims to model serious scrutiny of the genre through rigorous engagement with both canonical and noncanonical works.

It is a familiar observation that romcom has for decades been stigmatized as a female-oriented genre, both in terms of audiences (the derisive term "chick flick") and of creators; female directors and (especially) writers have been far more numerous in romcom than in most other genres. And yet other women media creators appear to steer clear of the genre for fear that it will taint their artistic sensibilities or imperil their auteur credibility; the esteemed Argentine filmmaker Lucrecia Martel pronounced in 2018, "Romantic comedies are my enemy."[26] This stigmatization is also reflected in a long tradition of critical and scholarly inattention or dismissal. Robert Warshow's seminal essays of the late 1940s took the gangster and the cowboy ("the Westerner"), men with guns, as the central figures in American cinema, while Alexander Walker's account of the 1950s sex comedy cycle, "The Last American Massacre," written at the cycle's tail end, connects his disdainful account of these films to the female audiences they served.[27] As Lili Loofbourow points out in her 2018 article "The Male Glance," knowing a work is by a woman—or, I would add, is aimed toward a female audience—still tends to encourage problematic habits of response, discouraging us from ascribing to it artistic intentionality and complexity.[28] While understanding the impulse toward critical dismissal that typifies much writing on romantic comedy, it gives away the game too early by offering concessions that work against the kind of open-minded response and appreciation we should bring to the work of women filmmakers and to films oriented toward female audiences. Clearly it is time to think and write about romantic comedy unapologetically, to assume the value and importance of cinema about women, by women, and for women, in the way that the value of cinema made by and about (and largely for) men has long been assumed. This by no means entails an uncritical celebration of romantic comedy, but it does mean taking the genre as seriously as it deserves.

As the personal anecdote recounted at this section's start reveals, my own blind infatuation-turned-tainted love for romcom has subsided into a more sensible recognition that, regardless of how they are commonly perceived, these are complex works that express our own conflicting desires and flawed impulses. To view them as inherently bad objects is to overlook their inherent humanism—how, in conjoining "romance" with "comedy," their creators and audiences imagine an ideal of human connection through love and laughter. As Deleyto regards it, "[Romantic comedy] looks for the underlying humanity in people's behavior and . . . magically transforms hostility into affinity, or perhaps affirms that hostility and affinity are, if properly managed, part of the same positive feeling, part of the fun of being alive."[29] And, as the aforementioned article "Why Is It So Wrong to Love Romantic Comedy?" more cheekily contends, "Watching people try to get their shit together for long enough to have a relationship is truly a tale as old as time. Done right, it can be mightily entertaining, funny, heartbreaking, and even artful."[30] Just as the pain and havoc that it sometimes causes should not drive us to abandon the possibility of human connection, we have an enduring need for romantic relationships *and* narratives. Or, as that still profoundly resonant romcom *Annie Hall* puts it, "we need the eggs."

Keeping (Actual) Love Alive

It has often been observed that the "happily ever after" conclusion of so many romantic comedies enables the genre to avoid addressing the challenges posed by coupled life: long-term monogamy (and the possibility of adultery or sexual dysfunction), child-rearing or fertility challenges, career setbacks, aging and illness, and other vicissitudes of life. While the neotraditional romcoms that flourished in Hollywood in the 1990s and 2000s, from *Pretty Woman* to *The Ugly Truth* (2009), reverted to the genre's atavistic, idealizing strategies for representing romance, romantic comedy of the past decade has increasingly opted for a sobering appraisal of the labors and letdowns of love and the compromises involved in coupling. This collection focuses on works that explore what happens when the honeymoon is over, that dispense with fairy-tale wish fulfillment to end ambivalently or even unhappily, and that, most radically of all, disengage romantic coupling from happiness and self-actualization. In looking past, and through, the "happily ever after," the authors of these chapters collectively confront how recent romantic comedy contends with what cultural critic Pamela Haag terms the "post-romantic age," a contemporary cultural mood of romantic disillusionment and seismically shifting affective and relational bonds. As Haag characterizes this 21st-century paradigm of coupling, "It doesn't abide by either the romantic or the traditional scripts for marriage that came before it; it dismantles romantic premises and ideals around career, work, lifestyle, childbearing, or sex in marriage, to different effects and with different degrees of mindfulness." In borrowing Haag's simple but telling formulation, this collection finds reflected in contemporary romcom a range of culturally pervasive symptoms that simultaneously signal the malady for (mainly) women carried by the romance narrative ("with its notions of chronic dependency and emotional fulfillment") but also present—as does Haag's treatise—some potential remedies.[31]

Beyond the foundational studies of classical romantic comedy that underlie the arguments made in the chapters to come, the past two decades have seen the burgeoning of contemporary romantic comedy studies, from the landmark 1998 collection *Terms of Endearment: Hollywood Romantic Comedy of the 1980s and 1990s* to the equally notable anthology *Falling in Love Again: Romantic Comedy in Contemporary Cinema*, coedited by Deborah Jermyn, who provides this collection's closing chapter.[32] I am pleased to have among this volume's contributors some of those books' authors: in addition to Jermyn and Jeffers McDonald, who provides our foreword, John Alberti, Mary Harrod, Betty Kaklamanidou, James MacDowell, and Manuela Ruiz have all authored important monographs on the genre.[33] Knowing just how substantially the chapters to come rely on these and other key works, and having revealed my own debt at a number of points above, rather than obtrusively insert a literature review I leave it to my co-contributors to inform us in context of the ongoing importance and enduring influence of previous scholarship for contemporary understandings of the genre. In addition, the selected bibliography at the book's end serves as more than a relisting of works cited within, having been curated for use as a compendious resource for scholars, teachers, and students of romantic comedy, with the aim of fostering further recognition of and for the genre and its interlocutors.

While my romcom courses and students have more than sustained my faith in the genre's urgency, the precise impetus for this collection developed more recently out of the "Radical Romantic Comedy" special issue of *New Review of Film and Television Studies* (18, no. 1, Winter 2020) that I guest edited. Having received many outstanding proposals in response to my call for papers—far more than a single special issue would accommodate—and noting that most of them focused on romantic comedy of the past decade, I was inspired to spin off a larger grouping of essays focused exclusively on recent trends and transformations, whether radical or more traditional, in the genre. Together the resulting fifteen chapters defy the romcom doomsayers by attesting to romantic comedy's continuing vitality, in new modes and forms that reimagine and rejuvenate the genre by representing romance in ideologically and artistically innovative ways. Having noted that romcom is perhaps the most consistently popular and profitable of film genres yet critically underappreciated, academically underexamined, and still largely defined within parameters of Hollywood and heteronormativity, this collection conceptualizes romantic comedy *and* romantic coupling more broadly by focusing on those unconventional, updated treatments of romcom tropes and traditions to (re)emerge since the 2000s. These "post-romantic comedies" resist the genre's romanticizing tendencies while also defying its perception as escapist entertainment and stigmatization as "chick flicks," instead disrupting and subverting romcom fantasy and formula in ways that reflect on the realities and complexities of intimacy.

Our timeline aligns with the end of the most recent spate of studio-produced, theatrically released romcom features around 2009—the perceived "death of romcom" that this volume challenges—and so sets out to scrutinize romcom trends of the last decade, as the genre has migrated away from the fantasy factory of Hollywood (and into indie, international, and online realms) and has responded to cultural transformations in affective relationships and intimacy. Taking up where *Falling in Love Again* left off a decade ago, we contemplate (and coin names for) emergent cycles such as the "romsitcom" and the "wrong-com," examine new approaches in genre hybridity and serial narrative, and assess how recent romcom deals with divisive topical issues and changes in sexual mores (including reproductive politics, hookup culture, friends with benefits, and pharmaceutical- and technology-enabled sex). Our explorations focus particularly on ways that romantic comedies reflect and negotiate shifting cultural discourses around gender roles, relations between the sexes and within the same sex, and issues of race, class, ethnicity, religion, age, work, friendship, family, and citizenship. Fairy tales no more, yet far from unremittingly grim, the most sensitively humane and compellingly iconoclastic (and, we predict, most memorably enduring) of these recent romantic comedies demonstrate their commitment to opening eyes alongside hearts. And, whereas much of the scholarship on recent romantic comedy has focused on neotraditional works created within the postclassical Hollywood production system, our collection is grouped around three more recent and now more pervasive trends, each of which reflects a distinctive post-romantic sensibility that crosses screen media platforms and acknowledges the diverse constituencies invested in contemporary romcom production and consumption.

The collection opens on act 1: "What's New Is Old: Regenerating Romcom." In defiance of the persistent proclamations about romcom's demise, these chapters explore ways that romantic comedy has been revived through genre mixing and narrative recalibration, by transgressing media categories and finessing aesthetic techniques, and in welcoming novel voices and stories through more inclusive authorship and representation. Yet, even as these strategies offer romcom renewed life, these chapters consider the ongoing conflict between regenerative romcom's anti-illusory, demythologizing potential and the persistence both of nostalgia for traditional romance and of gendered and social inequities. As a result, these romcom revisions make moderate rather than radical maneuvers, finding it challenging to condone *or* condemn the compromised values and comforting narratives necessitated in a world in which romcoms, like women, are expected to "have it all."

Act 2, "Love in a Time of Precarity: Romcom Realism," maps romcom's transnational migrations and cross-cultural interactions, assessing how romcom's rules of attraction have been reconfigured in the wake of neoliberalism, neoconservatism, globalization, and gentrification. This section's chapters examine works that deromanticize romcom, rupturing its idyllic yet hermetic world(view) by bringing socioeconomic and geopolitical realities to bear and confronting how romcom's lessons in love are employed for a combination of ideologically progressive and reactionary ends. Undetached from the contemporary climate of struggle and uncertainty and hierarchies of power and privilege, the feature films analyzed within amply indicate how recent romantic comedy proves increasingly willing to exchange its traditional idealism for clearer-eyed realism.

The third and final act, "Reimagining 'Happily Ever After,'" contemplates ways we might restore romcom's hopefulness without falling back on idealized representations and retrograde fantasies. Pointing the way to alternative relationship formations and constructive means of partnering *and* unpartnering, these final ruminations on romance gesture at the way the genre's enduring appeal is transformed through an expansion of its representational borders and emotional logics, offering up reimagined possibilities for a post-romantic age. This section focuses on works that most pointedly turn away from the neotraditional romcom to take back up with the legacy of 1970s radical romcom, which Jeffers McDonald praises for its reckoning with "the possibility of revealing that life continues after the final clinch."[34]

Writing on the heels of a global lockdown following COVID-19's shock to social networks, I perceive the urgency for revitalizing romcom as a defense against cultural and generational pessimism. As Kate Julian, who sounded a call for reinvigorating millennials' faith in committed coupling (and, on connected terrain, in carnal relations) in her 2018 *Atlantic* article "The Sex Recession" puts it, "As American social institutions have withered, having a life partner has become a stronger predictor than ever of well-being."[35] Hardly confined to the U.S., the disenfranchisement, division, and disintegration that plagues populations within the sphere of neoliberal capitalism will scarcely be resolved by romantic partnering (much less by romantic comedy), but, as film scholar B. Ruby Rich contends, in the landmark 1993 collection *Queer Looks*, "the advantage of romance as a launching pad for political engagement is that it carries built-in optimism, just possibly enough to move ahead in these times of race-hatred and scapegoating."[36] Clearly, Rich's words resonate all too powerfully today, encouraging us to reassess the imaginative potential of romantic comedy in a world roiled by racial injustice and human exploitation, entrenched militarism and wealth inequality, escalating radicalism and fascism, environmental emergency and inhumane health care, and now a once-in-a-century pandemic. We might even take our lead from romantic comedy itself, for this eminently adaptable genre has once again sought and found rejuvenation, and the means by which it has done so resides both in the enabling mechanisms of contemporary media technologies and cultures, and in the facts and factors influencing modern love. Far from the solipsism and sanguinity presupposed of a genre perceived to be about soul mates and sunsets, romantic comedy models on an interpersonal scale the reconciliation and collaboration we are in dire need of on the intercultural world stage.

Notes

1. Amy Nicholson, "Who Killed the Romantic Comedy?" *L.A. Weekly*, February 27, 2014, www.laweekly.com/news/who-killed-the-romantic-comedy-4464884.
2. Tamar Jeffers McDonald, *Romantic Comedy: Boy Meets Girl Meets Genre* (London: Wallflower, 2007).
3. Jeffers McDonald, *Romantic Comedy*, 92.
4. Derek Smith, "Isn't It Romantic Cheekily Sends Up the Romcom, But Only Up to a Point," Slant, February 13, 2019, https://www.slantmagazine.com/film/review-isnt-it-romantic-cheekily-sends-up-the-rom-com-but-only-up-to-a-point/.
5. Lisa Bonos, "Netflix Knows We Need an Escape, So It Built a Romcom Factory," *Washington Post*, July 26, 2018, www.washingtonpost.com/news/soloish/wp/2018/07/26/netflix-knows-we-need-an-escape-so-it-built-a-rom-com-factory/.

6 Ashley Elaine York, "From Chick Flicks to Millennial Blockbusters: Spinning Female-Driven Narratives into Franchises," *Journal of Popular Culture* 43, no. 1 (2010): 12.

7 Elżbieta Ostrowska, "Corporations of Feelings: Romantic Comedy in the Age of Neoliberalism," in *Contemporary Cinema and Neoliberal Ideology*, ed. Ewa Mazierska and Lars Kristensen (New York: Routledge, 2018), 201. Betty Kaklamanidou notes that these films posit that "love conquers all" provided that financial/professional success are similarly guaranteed. See Kaklamanidou, *Genre, Gender, and the Effects of Neoliberalism: The New Millennium Hollywood Rom Com* (New York: Routledge, 2013).

8 See Julia R. Lippman, "I Did It Because I Never Stopped Loving You: The Effects of Media Portrayals of Persistent Pursuit on Beliefs About Stalking," *Communication Research* 45, no. 3 (2018): 1–28; "Romantic-Comedy Behavior Gets Real-Life Man Arrested," *Onion*, April 7, 1999, local.theonion.com/romantic-comedy-behavior-gets-real-life-man-arrested-1819565117.

9 See, for example, Barry Langford, *Film Genre: Hollywood and Beyond* (Edinburgh: Edinburgh University Press, 2005). See also Raphaëlle Moine, *Cinema Genre*, trans. Alistair Fox and Hilary Radner (Oxford: Blackwell, 2008).

10 Adrian Martin, "In the Mood for (Something Like) Love: The Situation of the Rom-Com Today," *Cineaste* 39, no. 1 (Winter 2013): 17.

11 John Alberti, *Masculinity in the Contemporary Romantic Comedy: Gender as Genre* (New York: Routledge, 2013), 88. See also Hanna Rosin, *The End of Men: And the Rise of Women* (New York: Penguin, 2012); and Laura Kipnis, *Men: Notes from an Ongoing Investigation* (New York: Metropolitan, 2014).

12 Stanley Cavell, *Pursuits of Happiness: The Hollywood Comedy of Remarriage* (Cambridge, MA: Harvard University Press, 1981). For two additional key readings of classical romantic comedy's prehistory in silent cinema divorce comedies, see Charles Musser, "Divorce, DeMille and the Comedy of Remarriage," in *Classical Hollywood Comedy*, ed. Kristine Brunovska Karnick and Henry Jenkins (New York: Routledge, 1995), 282–313; and Leslie H. Abramson, "Evidence to the Contrary: Matrimony and Legal Interventionism in Silent Divorce Comedies," in

"Radical Romantic Comedy," special issue, *New Review of Film and Television Studies* 18, no. 1 (2020): 8–27.

13 Celestino Deleyto, "Humor and Erotic Utopia: The Intimate Scenarios of Romantic Comedy," in *A Companion to Film Comedy*, ed. Andrew Horton and Joanna E. Rapt (Malden, MA: Wiley-Blackwell, 2013), 175–76. See also Celestino Deleyto, *The Secret Life of Romantic Comedy* (Manchester: Manchester University Press, 2009).

14 Elizabeth Logan, "Why Is It So Wrong to Love Romantic Comedies?" *Glamour*, February 14, 2017, www.glamour.com/story/why-is-it-so-wrong-to-love-romantic-comedies.

15 Important examples of feminist readings of neotraditional romantic comedy include Charlotte Brunsdon, "Post-feminism and Shopping Films," in *The Film Studies Reader*, ed. Joanne Hollows, Mark Jancovich, and Peter Hutchings (London: Bloomsbury, 2000), 289–99; Angela McRobbie, "Postfeminism and Popular Culture: Bridget Jones and the New Gender Regime," in *Interrogating Postfeminism: Gender and the Politics of Popular Culture*, ed. Yvonne Tasker and Diane Negra (Durham, NC: Duke University Press, 2007), 27–39; and Catherine L. Preston, "Hanging on a Star: The Resurrection of the Romance Film in the 1990s," in *Genre 2000*, ed. Wheeler Winston Dixon (Albany: SUNY Press, 2000), 227–44.

16 Brian Henderson, "Romantic Comedy Today: Semi-Tough or Impossible?" *Film Quarterly* 31, no. 4 (Summer 1978): 11–23.

17 Michele Schreiber, "'Misty Water-Colored Memories of the Way We Were . . .': Postfeminist Nostalgia in Contemporary Romance Narratives." In *Reclaiming the Archive: Feminism and Film History*, ed. Vicki Callahan (Detroit: Wayne State University Press, 2010), 364–83. See also Michele Schreiber, *American Postfeminist Romance: Women, Romance, and Contemporary Culture* (Edinburgh: Edinburgh University Press, 2014).

18 Jeffers McDonald, *Romantic Comedy*, 59–84.

19 See Frank Krutnik, "Love Lies: Romantic Fabrication in Contemporary Romantic Comedy." In *Terms of Endearment: Hollywood Romantic Comedy of the 1980s and 1990s*, ed. Peter William Evans and Celestino Deleyto (Edinburgh: Edinburgh University Press, 1998), 15–36.

20 Jeffers McDonald, *Romantic Comedy*, 94.

21 Alison Winch, "We Can Have It All: The Girlfriend Flick," *Feminist Media Studies* 12, no. 1 (2012): 69–82.

22 Leger Grindon, "Taking Romantic Comedy Seriously in *Eternal Sunshine of the Spotless Mind* (2004) and *Before Sunset* (2004)," in *A Companion to Film Comedy*, ed. Andrew Horton and Joanna E. Rapt (Malden, MA: Wiley-Blackwell, 2013), 215.

23 "Who We Are," Refinery29, accessed August 25, 2020, corporate.r29.com/about#about-intro (accessed August 25, 2020).

24 Kerensa Cadenas, "The Bighearted Drama of Facebook's *Strangers*," Vulture, August 9, 2018, www.vulture.com/2018/08/strangers-mia-lidofsky-celia-rowlson-hall-interview.html.

25 Emily VanDerWerff, "Why Romantic Comedies Matter," Vox, August 29, 2018, www.vox.com/culture/2018/8/29/17769168/romantic-comedies-crazy-rich-asians-all-the-boys-set-it-up.

26 J. Hoberman, "Lucrecia Martel: A Director Who Confounds and Thrills," *New York Times*, April 13, 2018, www.nytimes.com/2018/04/13/movies/lucrecia-martel-zama-argentina.html.

27 Robert Warshow, *The Immediate Experience. Movies, Comics, Theatre, and Other Aspects of Popular Culture*, exp. ed. (Cambridge, MA: Harvard University Press, 2001); Alexander Walker, *Sex in the Movies* (London: Penguin, 1966).

28 Lili Loofbourow, "The Male Glance," *Virginia Quarterly Review* 94, no. 1 (Spring 2018): www.vqronline.org/essays-articles/2018/03/male-glance.

29 Deleyto, "Humor and Erotic Utopia," 193.

30 Logan, "Why Is It So Wrong to Love Romantic Comedies?"

31 Pamela Haag, *Marriage Confidential: Love in the Post-Romantic Age* (New York: Harper Perennial, 2012), xiv, 12.

32 Peter William Evans and Celestino Deleyto, eds., *Terms of Endearment: Hollywood Romantic Comedy of the 1980s and 1990s* (Edinburgh: Edinburgh University Press, 1998); *Falling in Love Again: Romantic Comedy in Contemporary Cinema*, ed. Stacey Abbott and Deborah Jermyn (London: I. B. Tauris, 2008).

33 Alberti, *Masculinity in the Contemporary Romantic Comedy*; Mary Harrod, *From France with Love: Gender and Identity in French Romantic Comedy* (London: I. B. Tauris, 2015); Kaklamanidou, *Genre, Gender*; James MacDowell, *Happy Endings in Hollywood Cinema: Cliché, Convention, and the Final Couple* (Edinburgh: Edinburgh University Press, 2013); Manuela Ruiz, *Hollywood Romantic Comedies of the Fifties: A Critical Study of a Film Genre* (Lewiston, NY: Edwin Mellen, 2013).

34 Jeffers McDonald, *Romantic Comedy*, 90.
35 Kate Julian, "The Sex Recession," *Atlantic*, December 2018, 94.
36 B. Ruby Rich, "Authenticating the Goldfish: Re-Viewing Film and Video in the Nineties," in *Queer Looks*, ed. Martha Gever, John Greyson, and Pratibha Parmar (New York: Routledge, 1993), 336.

Act 1

What's New Is Old
Regenerating Romcom

1

We Found Love in a Hopeless Place

Romantic Comedy in the Post-Romantic Age

Beatriz Oria

Romantic comedy is in a permanent state of crisis. In its long history as one of Hollywood's oldest genres, it has gone through countless "deaths" and "rebirths." This tendency has continued into the new millennium: the 21st century inaugurated a period of renewed turmoil for the Hollywood studio romcom, whose output followed a steadily declining path during the 2000s. Its fall from grace became even steeper in the 2010s: from 2012 to 2017 the number of romcoms widely released oscillated between two and zero.[1] By the end of the 2010s these figures had increased slightly, with the success of *Crazy Rich Asians* (2018) timidly hinting at a possible revival for the genre at the box office, but in general terms it still remains in a slump, commercially speaking.[2] The raunchy, often sexist, male-dominated romcom popularized by Judd Apatow during the 2000s seems to be on the wane, but it has not been replaced with a clearly identifiable single trend. Arguably, it is precisely a lack of homogeneity that characterizes contemporary romantic comedy, challenging perhaps this sort of pronouncement about its commercial performance. The genre has developed a range of strategies for reinventing itself in the so-called "post-romantic age," a context defined by a cynical attitude toward romance that has rendered the traditional romantic plot increasingly suspect for media-savvy millennials. The prefix "re-" is key here, as none of these formulas is really new, but a reworking of ideas previously tested in the genre's long history that have been adapted to the contemporary zeitgeist.

These formulas include the rise of multiprotagonist films such as the five-part *Cities of Love* (2006–) franchise, *He's Just Not That Into You* (2009),

Happythankyoumoreplease (2010), *The Romantics* (2010), *Valentine's Day* (2010), *Crazy, Stupid, Love* (2011), *Friends with Kids* (2011), *New Year's Eve* (2011), *To Rome with Love* (2012), *What to Expect When You're Expecting* (2012), *The Big Wedding* (2013), *The Little Death* (2014), *She's Funny That Way* (2014), *Love the Coopers* (2015), *That's Not Us* (2015), *How to Be Single* (2016), *Mother's Day* (2016), *I Do . . . Until I Don't* (2017), and *Book Club* (2018), which provide multiple iterations of the fantasy of "the One," perhaps to overcompensate for people's loss of faith in soul mates.[3] These films suggest that this trope is wearing thin, as they replace a single grand romantic narrative with a mosaic of relationships that, together, present a complex, more nuanced picture of contemporary intimacy and dating.

Similarly, the increasing visibility of queer characters—in, for example, *I Love You Phillip Morris* (2009), *Is It Just Me?* (2010), *The Kids Are All Right* (2010), *Your Sister's Sister* (2011), *Gayby* (2012), *Appropriate Behavior* (2014), *Boy Meets Girl* (2014), *Date and Switch* (2014), *Life Partners* (2014), *Me Him Her* (2015), *Naomi and Ely's No Kiss List* (2015), *That's Not Us* (2015), *The Feels* (2017), *Alex Strangelove* (2018), *Hearts Beat Loud* (2018), *Love, Simon* (2018), and *The Half of It* (2020)—points to a hopeful future for the genre in terms of representation, and the success of films with protagonists of color, such as *Just Wright* (2010), *Jumping the Broom* (2011), *Think Like a Man* (2012), *Baggage Claim* (2013), *The Best Man Holiday* (2013), *About Last Night* (2014), *Top Five* (2014), *The Big Sick* (2017), *Crazy Rich Asians*, *To All the Boys I've Loved Before* (2018) and its sequel *To All the Boys: P.S. I Still Love You* (2020), *Always Be My Maybe* (2019), *Falling Inn Love* (2019), *Last Christmas* (2019), *Yesterday* (2019), *The Half of It*, and *Love, Guaranteed* (2020) may help resurrect the romcom at the box office. As the popularity of these films suggests, one key to romantic comedy's rebirth may lie in the particularization of sexual and racial experience: increasing the genre's specificity may wind up, paradoxically, encouraging its expansion.

Contemporary romantic comedy is also diversifying by wooing the "gray dollar," meeting the needs of an aging audience that had been overlooked. The recent cycle of "mature love stories"[4] such as *Last Chance Harvey* (2008), *Mamma Mia!* (2008), *It's Complicated* (2009), *The Best Exotic Marigold Hotel* (2011), *Larry Crowne* (2011), *Darling Companion* (2012), *Love Is All You Need* (2012), *At Middleton* (2013), *The Big Wedding* (2013), *Enough Said* (2013), *The Love Punch* (2013), *And So It Goes* (2014), *Learning to Drive* (2014), *The Rewrite* (2014), *Hello, My Name Is Doris* (2015), *I'll See You In*

My Dreams (2015), *The Intern* (2015), *Finding Your Feet* (2017), *Hampstead* (2017), and *Book Club* is challenging romantic comedy's ageism by featuring "older" women as both desirable and desiring subjects.[5]

This chapter explores some additional new directions that have not received as much attention in recent years—namely, unexpected genre mixing, an increased emphasis on friendship as an alternative to heteronormative coupling, and a focus on the individual instead of the couple. These formulas are not exclusive to the post-romantic comedy, having been previously deployed at different points in history, but the specificity of the context in which they are being resurrected at the beginning of the 21st century imbue some of these familiar tropes with new meanings that are worth exploring.[6]

The ability of film genres to express the zeitgeist is one of their most compelling attributes and, arguably, what helps them stay fresh, culturally and commercially relevant. As Diane Negra and Yvonne Tasker state, "Genre cinema has long been understood as revealing both cultural anxieties and fantasized solutions which emerge in response to them."[7] The directions being taken by contemporary romantic comedy seem to constitute a response to a crisis of intimacy closely linked to millennials' pessimistic attitude toward romantic love. So too may these new generic inflections be symptomatic of cultural anxiety about the future of romantic love in an increasingly individualistic society fueled by a neoliberal ethos. This sociosexual context threatens to throw the shared project of the couple off-center and compels the post-romantic era romcom to imagine possible solutions.

For Lauren Berlant, the historical present is always hard to grasp, as it is perceived "affectively": it is "a thing that is sensed and under constant revision, a temporal genre whose conventions emerge from the personal and public filtering of the situations and events that are happening in an extended now."[8] Film genre mediates the perceived "affect" of the present so as to help us make sense of it. For this reason, genres are in constant flow, continually evolving to keep current. As Berlant argues, "Older realist genres are on the wane because their conventions of relating fantasy to ordinary life and their depictions of the good life now appear to mark archaic expectations about having and building a life."[9] In the romantic realm, Berlant's concept of the "good life" translates to the traditional fantasy of lively, durable intimacy, complete with marriage, a family, and financial security.[10] Arguably, one reason for the decline of the traditional romcom formula may lie in its apparent incapacity to faithfully represent the reality of contemporary experience: the fantasy of the "good life" has become unsustainable in the face of today's romantic and socioeconomic turmoil. Hence, the need for a significant "repackaging" of the genre.

This romantic turmoil is inextricably linked to the cynical attitude toward romance that is said to characterize U.S. millennials. According to a 2011 Pew Research Center study, only 28 percent of Americans aged 18 and older believed in the idea of "one true love." Among those believers, about half (54 percent) of 18- to 29-year-olds thought themselves to have found theirs, compared with nine in ten adults aged 50 and older.[11] Unsurprisingly, people's loss of faith in traditional romance is also reflected in record low rates of marriage among the young, as only 20 percent of 18- to 29-year-olds were married in 2011, compared with almost 60 percent in 1960.[12] These figures seem to explain the obsolescence of the trope of marriage as traditional romantic comedy's telos and viewer skepticism regarding its ideological pillars of "the One," "love at first sight," and "happily ever after." For instance, in the era of Tinder, the lovers' "meet cute" is more likely to happen online, which limits its dramatic and representational possibilities. As Emily Yahr posits, "Romantic comedies are fueled by an idealized version of love, while modern sensibilities about gender roles and romance have increasingly caused audiences to see these films through a much different lens."[13] This new lens prevents 21st-century audiences from buying into the sincerity that the genre has traditionally assumed. Spectator engagement with iconic romcoms such as *When Harry Met Sally . . .* (1989), *Pretty Woman* (1990), or *Sleepless in Seattle* (1993) crucially depends on their capacity to believe in the mighty power of romantic love, capable of sweeping human beings off their feet and lasting forever. Contemporary viewers, however, appear reluctant to suspend disbelief about romantic relationships. These neotraditional movies are revisited with nostalgia and ironic knowingness, but, if made today, they would be considered hackneyed and hard to relate to.[14] Furthermore, some of the tropes traditionally championed by the genre, such as the concept of the soul mate, are increasingly likely to be viewed as damaging for the unrealistic standards they put forward, and, in a context of growing gender equality and feminist awareness, the relationship models proposed by the traditional (or neotraditional) romcom read today as deeply imbalanced or even toxic.

Part of contemporary audiences' lack of engagement with traditional ideas of romance and the shared project of the couple lies in their inhabiting an increasingly individualistic ethos. Though attributed to neoliberalism's entrenchment more recently, this phenomenon is not new: Ulrich Beck and Elisabeth Beck-Gernsheim describe how this "individualization process" started in the second half of the 20th century in wealthy Western industrialized countries as a side effect of modernization.[15] Discussing the "age of narcissism" and a new ethic based on "one's duty to oneself," they posit that the individual came to feel the need to break with preconceived social roles and patterns in order to pursue one's own personal development.[16] As Barbara Ehrenreich and Deirdre English put it, "In the post-romantic world, where the old ties no longer bind, all that matters is *you*. . . . The old hierarchies of protection and dependency no longer exist, there are only free contracts, freely terminated. The marketplace, which long ago expanded to include the relationships of production, has now expanded to include *all* relationships."[17] This process of individualization, which started decades ago, is often considered to have reached its peak with the millennial generation,[18] which displays a degree of individualism that is "postpatriotic, postfamilial, disaffiliated."[19] As Ross Douthat points out, this development yields a series of questions: Is this kind of individualism sustainable across the life cycle? Can it become a culture's dominant way of life? And, in the specific case of romance, how can individuals protect and pursue the personal self-interests that the free market mandates while remaining part of a couple?

When Harry Met Siri

As the aforementioned figures show, the big studios have almost ceased to make generically "pure" romantic comedies, and those that are being made are not marketed as such. As Billy Mernit notes, "The smart romantic comedy writer of 2017 is writing a script that they aren't calling a romantic comedy. They have to have a fresh angle."[20] "Fresh angles" were not a must until the late 2000s, when the genre did not have to masquerade as something else to be marketable. Romantic comedy's decline in popularity has prompted strategies of innovative genre mixing in order to surmount its current stigma and target a broader range of viewers. Of course, this is nothing new or extraordinary; generic hybridity has characterized genre evolution since

Hollywood's inception, infusing new life into familiar formulas through a calculated combination of variation and repetition.[21] However, the commercial decline experienced by romantic comedy during the 2010s has pushed the genre one step further in the variety of elements that it is willing to integrate in its basic formula. For instance, contemporary romantic comedy has found a fruitful "marriage" with unlikely genres such as fantasy, science fiction, and even horror. Films like *Enchanted* (2007), *Ghost Town* (2008), *Over Her Dead Body* (2008), *Ghosts of Girlfriends Past* (2009), *The Invention of Lying* (2009), *TiMER* (2009), *Scott Pilgrim vs. the World* (2010), *When in Rome* (2010), *Midnight in Paris* (2011), *Ruby Sparks* (2012), *Seeking a Friend for the End of the World* (2012), *Safety Not Guaranteed* (2012), *About Time* (2013), *Warm Bodies* (2013), *Comet* (2014), *In Your Eyes* (2014), *Life After Beth* (2014), *The One I Love* (2014), *The Relationtrip* (2017), *Naked* (2017), *When We First Met* (2018), *Last Christmas, Isn't It Romantic* (2019), and *Yesterday* all include some kind of nonrealistic or supernatural element that puts a new spin on familiar romantic formulas. Despite the genre's best efforts to create a "magic space of romantic transformation," its realistic urban milieus have come to feel clichéd, and, more important, the kind of love stories usually presented in these films has become increasingly unrelatable to viewers skeptical of romance.[22] By contrast, incorporating conventions from fantasy and science fiction opens the door to the creation of parallel universes in which the rules of the romantic game have been altered, and love can develop in a more engaging and, paradoxically, believable way. Of course, romantic comedy has frequently incorporated nonrealistic genre elements in the past, but, in today's climate of post-romantic skepticism, such generic twists prove more proficient than ever at enlivening the genre, bringing a welcome poignancy to its inherently hopeful nature.

Another way in which recent romantic comedy intersects with other genres lies in its greater willingness to explore darker subjects. Whether set in the fantastical realm or not, the romcom has typically avoided dealing with weighty issues and extreme dramatic situations, considered a threat to the genre's light-hearted spirit. The neotraditional romantic comedy of the 1990s and 2000s was specially "disconnected" from its social context and unwilling to acknowledge issues that threatened to puncture the genre's escapist bubble.[23] This started to change in the 2010s—mostly in the independent sector—with films that addressed unconventional, uncomfortable, thorny, or potentially grave dramatic subjects, thus partly harking back to the more realistic romantic comedy of the 1970s. These subjects include issues such as abortion (*Greenberg* [2010], *Obvious Child* [2014], *Almost Friends* [2016]); mental illness (*Greenberg*, *It's Kind of a Funny Story* [2010], *Silver Linings Playbook* [2012]); death (*Seeking a Friend for the End of the World*, *The Pretty One* [2013], *Life After Beth*, *Tumbledown* [2015]); parenthood (*Happythankyoumoreplease*, *Life as We Know It* [2010], *Friends with Kids*, *Gayby*, *Begin Again* [2013], *Maggie's Plan* [2015], *People Places Things* [2015], *Juliet, Naked* [2018]); addiction (*Unlovable* [2009], *Don Jon* [2013], *Newlyweds* [2013], *The Spectacular Now* [2013], *Sleeping with Other People* [2015]); medical emergency (*Take Care* [2014]; *The Big Sick*; *Juliet, Naked*), economic instability and career prospects (*The Giant Mechanical Man* [2012], *Laggies* [2014], *Life Partners*), or simply the passing of time and the crushing routine of a long-term relationship (*Couples Retreat* [2009]; *Date Night* [2010]; *Crazy, Stupid, Love*; *The Five Year Engagement* [2012]; *This Is 40* [2012]; *I Give It a Year* [2013]; *While We're Young* [2014]; *I Do . . . Until I Don't*; *In a Relationship* [2018]).

A good example of a film featuring both dramatic and nonrealistic elements is Spike Jonze's *Her* (2013). Set in the near future, *Her* is a love story about introverted Theodore (Joaquin Phoenix) and his highly advanced AI operating system. With its melancholy tone, *Her* may not at first seem like a romcom, but it uses many of the conventions of the genre, updating them in the process. Theodore is mourning his breakup with his soon-to-be ex-wife when he meets Samantha (Scarlett Johansson, in a voice-only role). Slowly but surely, they fall in love, and, despite their obvious differences, Samantha seems to be the perfect partner for Theodore. Though we might assume that Samantha's lack of a physical body would constitute the most significant obstacle to their love, instead the couple's conflicts are primarily internal in nature and concern the characters' emotional arcs. Theodore and Samantha face a series of difficulties that have little to do with the human-machine pairing: his not being able to express his emotions (the reason for his previous relationship's end), and her "cheating" on him (she admits to being in love with 861 other people, a revelation that challenges contemporary notions of fidelity and monogamy by introducing the possibility of polyamory as a viable option for contemporary relationships). The ultimate obstacle between the couple ends up being Samantha's process of self-development, which extends to the point of her acquiring an actual "human" consciousness. In the end, she leaves him not because she lacks

Her's final shot: a new relationship for Theodore (Joaquin Phoenix)?

a body or because she loves others, but because she changes and outgrows their relationship ("I love you so much, but this is where I am now, and this is who I am now").

Her deliberately avoids the feel-good happy ending of traditional romantic comedy. In the final scene Theodore writes a letter to his ex-wife, but it seems to be addressed to Samantha, or maybe to both. In it, he explains what he has learned: "You helped make me who I am. I just wanted you to know . . . that there will be a piece of you in me, always. And I'm grateful for that." Even if couple (re)formation does not take place, Theodore has undergone his own growing process, learned valuable lessons from his relationships, and hopefully will be able to use this newfound knowledge in the next one—perhaps (the film hints) with best friend Amy (Amy Adams).

Arguably, the bittersweet ending, together with the film's melancholic tenor and pensive protagonist, paints a more touching and real picture of love than many conventional romcoms, and the sci-fi backdrop does not detract from this impression—quite the opposite, as it paradoxically grounds the story in reality more successfully than "purer" examples of the genre. Seeking fresh scenarios for depicting romance believably, the generic twists deployed by *Her* and the other films mentioned above can be viewed as a response to a cultural loss of faith in the idealistic perspective of the traditional romcom. These scenarios stand on the opposite ends of the realism spectrum: romantic love today seems plausible only if represented in fantastical fictional worlds governed by different rules or, on the contrary, when firmly anchored in reality through the inclusion of serious dramatic elements—or, as in the case of films like *Her*, both at the same time.

Friends with Benefits?

Friendship has consistently been an important element of romantic comedy, with many films placing it at plot's center with an eye to exploring its limits. Partly fueled by a budding feeling of disenchantment with romance, the genre started to search for alternatives to heterosexual coupling at the end of the 20th century. In his analysis of the role of friendship in romantic comedy of the 1990s, Celestino Deleyto points out that same-sex bonds tend to represent a threat to the heterosexual couple in these films, but, while male friendship must often be forsaken by the end (*White Men Can't Jump* [1992], *We're No Angels* [1989], *Much Ado about Nothing* [1993]), female relationships are more easily incorporated into the happy ending (*Clueless* [1995], *The Truth about Cats & Dogs* [1996], *Walking and Talking* [1996]). Cross-sex friendship, on the other hand, proves to be more "subversive," as it is directly opposed to the traditional ideology of the romantic comedy, which explains the genre's struggles to accommodate this trope.[24]

As one of the best-known examples of movies dealing with cross-sex friendship, *When Harry Met Sally . . .* is a landmark both of the genre and in its treatment of a topic that remains the focus of contemporary films such as *Made of Honor* (2008), *Zack and Miri Make a Porno* (2008), *The Switch* (2010), *Friends with Kids*, *Just Go with It* (2011), *Something Borrowed* (2011), *What's Your Number?* (2011), *Cavemen* (2013), *What If* (2013), *Love, Rosie* (2014), *Slow Learners* (2015), *Almost Friends* (2016), *When We First Met* (2018), *Long Shot* (2019), *Tall Girl* (2019), and *Yesterday*, all of which pose a key question: Is it possible for a man and a woman to be *just* friends? In an attempt to modernize this trope, two films of the early 2010s, *Friends with Benefits* (2011) and *No Strings Attached* (2011), introduced into the romcom the concept of the "fuck buddy," adding sex to the equation and so prompting the new question of whether a relationship can be sustained sans romance, based only on sex and friendship. Traditionally, romantic comedy's answer to all of these questions has been negative, as films dealing with this topic tend to require the alignment of love, friendship, and sex to guarantee the happily ever after.

One of the recent films to deal with this issue in a sexually frank manner, Leslye Headland's *Sleeping with Other People* (2015), is the story of Lainey (Alison Brie) and Jake (Jason Sudeikis), who lose their virginity to each other in a one-night stand in college, then reconnect at a sex addiction support group more than a decade later. Their shared problem maintaining healthy monogamous relationships—he is a womanizer, she is a commitment-phobe obsessed with her ex—prompt them to keep their relationship platonic despite their mutual attraction. The characters' fidelity issues form a modern obstacle that keeps the protagonists believably apart until the end. The film explores the boundaries between friendship and love in a dialogue-driven dissection of modern relationships, with frank sex talk that is refreshing after the prudish wave of neotraditional romances in the 1990s and early 2000s. The protagonists' raunchy conversations cement their friendship while increasing the sexual tension between them and raising everyone's eyebrows: "Where is the fucking in all this? . . . Men and women can't be friends. It's like Life 101. Stop lying to yourself," Lainey's friend admonishes her. The familiar will-they-or-won't-they trope receives a twist at the end, when Lainey and Jake decide to get married before having sex for the first—or, actually, second—time. Even if they break their "chastity vow" minutes before the wedding, the film offers a fantasy of "revirginization" that feels both old and new: well rooted in the genre's traditional conventions but consistent with the sexually frank tone of the movie and in sync with contemporary dating protocols.

Frank sex talk: Jake (Jason Sudeikis) giving Lainey (Alison Brie) a masturbation lesson in *Sleeping with Other People*.

Sleeping with Other People's convenient conjunction of friendship, love, and sex constitutes the most common recipe for romantic comedy's happy ending but, despite its endurance, the 21st century has witnessed a more thorough exploration of the dynamics created by friendship in romantic relationships. In the new millennium, the boundaries of cross-sex friendship have been widely examined, but it is same-sex friendship that has gained greater visibility, thanks to the popularity of two new cycles of films: the "bromance" and the "womance." The former experienced a boost in the mid-2000s with films such as *Wedding Crashers* (2005), *I Now Pronounce You Chuck & Larry* (2007), *Superbad* (2007), *Role Models* (2008), *Humpday* (2009), and *I Love You, Man* (2009) and continued in the 2010s with *Dinner for Schmucks* (2010), *Due Date* (2010), *Get Him to the Greek* (2010), *The Dilemma* (2011), *Hall Pass* (2011), *The Internship* (2013), *That Awkward Moment* (2014), *The Night Before* (2015), and *Tag* (2018). Judd Apatow is usually credited with the creation of this subgenre of romantic comedy: a film that involves a romantic interest(s) for the male protagonist(s) but that actually revolves around the relationship between its male leads. These films push women to the margins of one of the few women-centric genres in Hollywood, renegotiating the nature of male friendship on-screen as a response to increasing awareness of the constructedness and instability of conventional straight masculinity. Walking a fine line between homophobia and homophilia, bromances feature male characters perpetually stuck in adolescence whose romantic relationships rarely seem as fulfilling as their homosocial bonds.

Despite the criticism some of these films received for their construction of men as funny and charming and women as humorless scolds, they contributed to a healthy destabilization of codes of gender identity, proposing a "softer," more complex model of masculinity in tune with contemporary discourses of gender equality and creating a new kind of romantic hero for the 21st century.[25] Unlike the 1990s movies analyzed by Deleyto, these new bromances do not generally require the abandonment of the male bond for the heterosexual couple to exist, which is symptomatic of the heightened status enjoyed by male friendship in the new millennium.[26]

The popularity of the bromance started to wane in the early 2010s, which coincided with the success of the *Sex and the City* franchise (1998–2004 [HBO], 2008, 2010), and, especially, *Bridesmaids* (2011). The latter, produced by Apatow, seemingly replicates the bromance formula, but from a female perspective. This "womance" brought women back to the center of the genre; it also reminded audiences that women could be funny, using the kind of scatological humor previously reserved for male-driven movies. Strikingly, despite including romantic comedy's emblematic iconography and themes (the film is about a wedding, after all), *Bridesmaids* features little romantic love. Instead, it focuses on the importance of female friendship as a foundation for personal happiness, with heterosexual love subordinated to sisterhood.

The success of *Bridesmaids* seemed to herald the birth of a new kind of raunchy women-centric comedy, but it was not until the mid-2010s that a number of films following in its steps emerged, such as the *Pitch Perfect* franchise (2012, 2015), *Bachelorette* (2012), *For a Good Time, Call . . .* (2012), *The Heat* (2013), *Hot Pursuit* (2015), *Sisters* (2015), *Bad Moms* (2016), *Mike and Dave Need Wedding Dates* (2016), *A Bad Mom's Christmas* (2017), *Girls Trip* (2017), *Rough Night* (2017), *Blockers* (2018), *Dude* (2018), *Ibiza* (2018), *The Spy Who Dumped Me* (2018), *The Hustle* (2019), *Wine Country* (2019), and *Like a Boss* (2020). These movies often make use of a sort of broad humor virtually unheard-of in female-centered narratives, relegating romance to a subplot or disposing of it altogether in order to focus on their protagonists' sisterly bonds. It is worth noting that, when these films venture more heavily into romance, bawdy situations and language are usually curtailed, as is the case in *Laggies, Life Partners, The Other Woman* (2014), *How to Be Single, Lady Bird* (2017), *Half Magic* (2018), *Someone Great* (2019), and *Book Club*. These "tamer" womances draw more heavily on the conventions of romantic comedy than do those lewder womances, suggesting that the recent marriage between romance and raunch feels awkward when the latter is performed by women. In any case, the emphasis on female friendship in the womance might be read as emerging out of a social climate characterized by Hollywood's growing feminist awareness and an increased sense of women's solidarity fueled by the Time's Up and #MeToo movements, updating the genre in a way that is in tune with today's heightened ideals of sisterhood.

Finally, a third tendency—especially in the independent sector—presents cross-sex friendship as a fully viable alternative to romantic love, an option that had rarely been seriously contemplated in previous decades, maybe because to exclude heterosexual desire from the equation would mean omitting the genre's main ingredient. In the 1990s, *My Best Friend's Wedding* (1997) and *The Object of My Affection* (1998) were pioneers in challenging the meaning of the "happily ever after" by leaving their heroines uncoupled at the end and rewarding them with the company of their (gay) male best friends instead. In the 2010s, the possibility of replacing romance with cross-sex friendship for the happy ending is more thoroughly explored in films such as *The Dish & the Spoon* (2011), *Liberal Arts* (2012), *Begin Again, Drinking Buddies* (2013), *Learning to Drive, Nobody Walks in L.A.* (2016), *Tramps* (2016), *Hearts Beat Loud* (2018), *The Kissing Booth* (2018), and *Unlovable* (2018). In these movies, couples with romantic potential never actually take it further and seem content with this decision. Other films, like *Celeste & Jesse Forever* (2012) and *People Places Things*, feature troubled couples who end up as friends after a painful breakup. In both scenarios, friendship is presented as a preferable option—being far more dependable, placid, and stable—to romantic attachment. The increasing incidence of this motif signals the genre's willingness to adapt to a new climate of gender equality that has devalued heterosexual desire in favor of other models of intimacy. It may also be connected to the "sex recession" millennials are apparently experiencing: surprisingly, young people are having much less sex than previous generations, which may be related to a decline in couplehood.[27] In any case, whether cross-sex or same-sex, the renewed relevance of friendship rewrites one of romantic comedy's main scripts, dovetailing with a waning cultural belief in the possibility of everlasting love. In today's "hookup culture," friendship seems to constitute the only kind of reliable long-term relationship available to the individual, to the extent that it has come to modify the meanings attached to what may be romantic comedy's most solid convention: the happily ever after.

Me, Myself, and I

If the previous section highlighted the importance of one's friendship network for the romantic heroine or hero of the 21st century, this one seems to point in the opposite direction, as it deals with romantic comedy's growing inclination to focus on the individual rather than on the couple. These two tendencies seem to be at odds, but in fact are intimately connected. In an increasingly individualized society, millennials tend to prioritize individual pursuits such as friends and careers over shared projects including committed, long-term relationships. This is reflected in the rise of the "self-centered romcom," which revolves around the protagonist's negotiation of their sense of self.²⁸ This usually involves some kind of romantic endeavor, but one that is secondary to the real issue at stake: the construction of the character's self-identity, which is represented as being more multifaceted and less dependent on romantic fulfillment or coupled self-definition than traditional romantic comedy has led us to believe. In the quest for self-identity, love is put on equal footing—or even subordinated to—not only friendship, but also other aspects of selfhood such as parenthood, professional accomplishments, family ties, or simply self-discovery. As a result, these characters become highly self-centered, no longer concerned with "us" but with "I." Examples of this tendency include *Greenberg, It's Kind of a Funny Story, Arthur* (2011), *The Dish & the Spoon, The Giant Mechanical Man, Hello I Must Be Going* (2012), *Liberal Arts, Lola Versus* (2012), *The Perks of Being a Wallflower* (2012), *Begin Again, Don Jon, In a World . . .* (2013), *The Pretty One, Appropriate Behavior, Big Stone Gap* (2014), *Life Partners, Obvious Child, Top Five, Maggie's Plan, People Places Things, Trainwreck* (2015), *Almost Friends, How To Be Single, Humor Me* (2017), *The Incredible Jessica James* (2017), *Alex Strangelove, I Feel Pretty* (2018), *Isn't It Romantic*, and *Nappily Ever After* (2018).

This tendency is reminiscent of the "radical" romantic comedies of the late 1960s and 1970s such as *The Graduate* (1967), *An Unmarried Woman* (1978), and Woody Allen's "nervous romances" (*Annie Hall* [1977], *Manhattan* [1979]), which also exhibit a heightened preoccupation with the individual. Characterized by introspection and self-absorption, the 1970s was known as the "Me decade,"²⁹ a term that is inevitably brought to mind when 21st-century social commentators herald the arrival (or, rather, the return?) of what now is referred to as "Generation Me," a self-centered social cohort whose penchant for navel-gazing feels old and new at the same time.³⁰

These two generations seem to be linked by their narcissism, but their sociocultural circumstances are significantly different. Millennials are said to prefer pursuing individual projects to settling down with a romantic partner during "the best years of their lives."³¹ This period of life (the twenties, mainly), which previous generations had devoted to the search for a suitable partner to marry and start a family with, is termed by sociologists as "emerging adulthood." This new stage extends from the late teens to the late twenties (but is most pronounced between ages 18 to 25), and in some cultures it allows young people "a prolonged period of independent role exploration."³² This period typically involves instability in love and work, self-centeredness, freedom for identity exploration, and a sense of inbetweenness or limbo.³³

The representation of relationships in these films reflects the stretching of this "emerging adulthood" stage, which often extends into the early thirties.[34] By delaying adulthood proper, millennials may spend more than two decades of their lives focusing on individual projects of the self, trying to become full-fledged individuals before committing to serious relationships and, possibly, starting families.[35] Most of the films previously mentioned convey the "excitement and uncertainty, wide-open possibility and confusion, new freedoms and new fears" of this period in a positive way, but what happens when individuals overstay their welcome in the "emergent adulthood" stage?[36] This question informs many of these films, but it is directly addressed in Lynn Shelton's *Laggies*, a movie whose very title suggests the idea of a generation falling behind in achieving the markers of adulthood. Its protagonist, Megan (Keira Knightley), a woman in her late twenties, has lagged behind since high school, both romantically and professionally. Faced with the scary possibility of accepting adult responsibility when her boyfriend proposes, she hides for a week in the house of Annika (Chloë Grace Moretz), a teen she randomly befriends, attracted by her apparently simpler life. She ends up falling for Annika's father, Craig (Sam Rockwell), which gives Megan the final push to eventually leave her long-time partner.

The movie follows the familiar romantic comedy convention of new love replacing old, but fundamentally this is a movie about the self: it deals foremost with Megan's need to find herself and to find direction in her life.

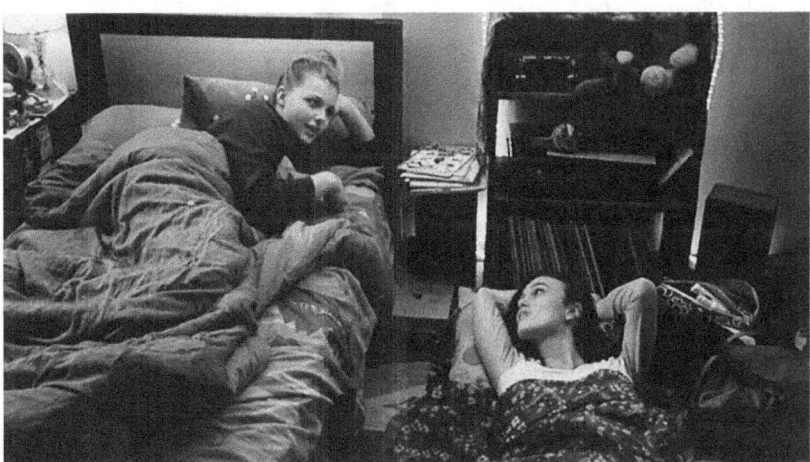

Megan (Keira Knightley) postponing adulthood in Lynn Shelton's *Laggies*.

In the course of the film, she realizes she has avoided making real choices, letting other people make decisions for her. Ending her relationship is the first step toward taking control of her life, and starting a new one marks the beginning of the process of constructing her adult self—but not the raison d'être of her new life, as is often the case in conventional romantic comedy. On the contrary, the hedonistic enjoyment and development of her "emergent adult" self is privileged. At one point in the film, Annika asks Megan to act as her mother for a meeting with her teacher, a conversation that forces Megan to assume a grown-up role and to reflect, "As her mom, I'd say that . . . I'm sure it does seem kind of stupid to make some sort of rigid plan for the future. But . . . It's stupider not to start paying attention to who you are and what makes you happy. Otherwise, you just float." This quotation—and the movie as a whole—reflects millennials' ethos of self-fulfillment, which is perceived as more important than following socially sanctioned life goals and preconceived notions of heterosexual coupledom. In the film, the process of becoming an adult is equated with chasing your dreams. Like *Laggies*, many of these movies acknowledge the importance of fully exploring life's options during the emergent adulthood phase, while constantly wondering about its expiry date. The moment when it is finally time to settle down is uncertain, and this constitutes a new source of anxiety for new generations, who are faced with a dilemma their parents never had to deal with.

Conclusion

In a historical moment in which the romcom (once again) finds itself in dire straits, the genre needs to reinvent itself to remain current because, as director Michael Sucsy says, "audiences aren't tired of romance; they're tiring of formulas."[37] This chapter has explored some of the new directions taken by contemporary romantic comedy, including unexpected generic mixing, the newfound centrality of the trope of friendship, and the increased prominence of the self over the couple. None of these innovations is really new, having been previously deployed in the genre's long history, but their reactivation feels particularly apt in the new millennium's climate of romantic cynicism and acute individualism.

These new tendencies are by no means the only variations that characterize the era of the post-romantic romcom. The increasing variety in characters' sexual orientation, race, background, age, and even number constitute one of the keys to the genre's revitalization. Such generic twists are frequently interconnected: the multiprotagonist film lends itself well to presenting friendship as a valid alternative to romantic love, and the expansion of romantic comedy's boundaries in terms of characterization may open the door to new generic twists and the representation of dramatic or thorny issues rarely addressed by previous romcoms. The proclivity to feature mature love stories is particularly remarkable, not only because of their popularity, but also because this trend may be viewed as the natural consequence of the self-centered romcom: when earnest young love has become unbelievable, these films suggest that true romance can happen only at later stages in life, when all of the big marks—such as career and children—have already been hit. Once the project of the self is complete, it is finally time to focus on "us." But might it be too late? The history of the genre suggests that it is never too late for the romcom. Despite critics' general distaste for it, this is one of the most vibrant, popular, malleable, and socially aware of genres: always in tune with its cultural context, it continues to display the ability to capture the anxieties, joys, and pains that shape our romantic experiences, both mirroring and (re)writing their scripts, and always with unfaltering optimism. For this reason alone, romantic comedy will always be a hopeful place.[38]

Notes

1. Jason Guerrasio, "The Big Hollywood Romantic Comedy Is Dead—Here's What Happened to It," Business Insider, August 8, 2017, www.businessinsider.com/why-movie-studios-no-longer-make-romantic-comedies-2017-8?IR=T.
2. In 1999 romantic comedy reached its highest commercial peak in its recent history with a 9.85-percent market share. Twenty years later, in 2019, it registers one of its lowest points, with only 1 percent. "Box Office History for Romantic Comedy," The Numbers, www.the-numbers.com/market/genre/Romantic-Comedy (accessed September 14, 2020).
3. María del Mar Azcona, *The Multi-Protagonist Film* (Malden, MA: Wiley-Blackwell, 2010).
4. Alex Hobbs, "Romancing the Crone: Hollywood's Recent Mature Love Stories," *Journal of American Culture* 36, no. 1 (March 2013): 42–51.

5 See Deborah Jermyn, "Unlikely Heroines? 'Women of a Certain Age' and Romantic Comedy," *CineAction* 85 (2011): 26–33.
6 These changes figure more prominently in the independent sector, where the genre enjoys greater vitality than in the mainstream. Therefore, many of the films this chapter discusses are not wide releases, but independently produced movies with limited distribution. For more on romantic comedy and independent cinema, see Beatriz Oria, "Love on the Margins: The American Indie Romcom of the 2010s," *Atlantis: Journal of the Spanish Association for Anglo-American Studies* 40, no. 2 (2018): 145–67.
7 Diane Negra and Yvonne Tasker, "Neoliberal Frames and Genres of Inequality: Recession-era Chick Flicks and Male-centred Corporate Melodrama," *European Journal of Cultural Studies* 16, no. 3 (2013): 350.
8 Lauren Berlant, *Cruel Optimism* (Durham, NC: Duke University Press, 2011), 4.
9 Berlant, *Cruel Optimism*, 6.
10 Berlant, 2–3.
11 "The Decline of Marriage and Rise of New Families," Pew Research Center, November 18, 2010, www.pewsocialtrends.org/2010/11/18/iii-marriage/.
12 D'vera Cohn, Jeffrey S. Passel, Wendy Wang, and Gretchen Livingston, "Barely Half of U.S. Adults Are Married—A Record Low," Pew Research Center, December 14, 2011, www.pewsocialtrends.org/2011/12/14/barely-half-of-u-s-adults-are-married-a-record-low/.
13 Emily Yahr, "The Romcom Is Dead. Good," *Washington Post*, October 8, 2016, www.washingtonpost.com/lifestyle/style/the-romcom-is-dead-good/2016/10/06/6d82a934-859c-11e6-ac72-a29979381495_story.html?utm_term=.d635325b91b2.
14 Chandra Johnson, "As Romcoms Decline So Do Conventional Ideas About Love," *Deseret News*, July 26, 2014, https://www.deseret.com/2014/7/26/20545085/as-rom-coms-decline-so-do-conventional-ideas-about-love#friends-eating-fast-food-posing-to-camera.
15 Ulrich Beck and Elisabeth Beck-Gernsheim, *The Normal Chaos of Love* (Cambridge: Polity, 2004), 8.
16 Beck and Beck-Gernsheim, *Normal Chaos of Love*, 43.

17 Barbara Ehrenreich and Deirdre English, *For Her Own Good: 150 Years of the Experts' Advice for Women* (New York: Anchor House, 1979), 276.

18 Jean M. Twenge, *Generation Me: Why Today's Young Americans Are More Confident, Assertive, Entitled—and More Miserable Than Ever Before* (New York: Atria, 2014).

19 Ross Douthat, "The Age of Individualism," *New York Times*, March 15, 2014, www.nytimes.com/2014/03/16/opinion/sunday/douthat-the-age-of-individualism.html.

20 Guerrasio, "Big Hollywood Romantic Comedy Is Dead."

21 Rick Altman, *Film/Genre* (London: BFI, 1999), 25; Steve Neale, *Genre* (London: BFI, 1980), 84.

22 Celestino Deleyto, *The Secret Life of Romantic Comedy* (Manchester: Manchester University Press, 2009), 36.

23 Tamar Jeffers McDonald, *Romantic Comedy: Boy Meets Girl, Meets Genre* (London: Wallflower, 2007), 88.

24 Celestino Deleyto, "Between Friends: Love and Friendship in Contemporary Hollywood Romantic Comedy," *Screen* 44, no. 2 (2003): 167–82.

25 Claire Mortimer, *Romantic Comedy* (London: Routledge, 2010); John Alberti, *Masculinity in the Contemporary Romantic Comedy: Gender as Genre* (New York: Routledge, 2013).

26 Deleyto, "Between Friends."

27 According to Kate Julian, "People now in their early 20s are two and a half times as likely to be abstinent as Gen Xers were at that age; 15 percent report having had no sex since they reached adulthood." This sex decline is linked with a decrease in the number of young people in relationships: "About 60 percent of adults under age 35 now live without a spouse or a partner." Kate Julian, "Why Are Young People Having So Little Sex?" *Atlantic*, December 2018, www.theatlantic.com/magazine/archive/2018/12/the-sex-recession/573949/ (accessed September 4, 2020).

28 Beatriz Oria, "'I'm Taken . . . by Myself': Romantic Crisis in the Self-Centered Indie Romcom," *Journal of Film and Video* 73, no. 1 (2021): forthcoming.

29 Tom Wolfe, *Mauve Gloves and Madmen, Clutter and Vine* (New York: Farrar, Straus & Giroux, 1976).

30 Twenge, *Generation Me*.

31 Twenge.

32 Jeffrey Jensen Arnett, "Emerging Adulthood: A Theory of Development from the Late Teens Through the Twenties," *American Psychologist* 55, no. 5 (2000): 469.

33 Frank D. Fincham and Ming Cui, *Romantic Relationships in Emergent Adulthood* (Cambridge: Cambridge University Press, 2011), 3–4.

34 Jeffrey Jensen Arnett, *Emerging Adulthood: The Winding Road from the Late Teens through the Twenties* (New York: Oxford University Press, 2004); Arnett, "Emerging Adulthood."

35 Millennials tend to wait longer than previous generations to marry, with only 26 percent of this generation presently married. When they were the age that millennials are now, 36 percent of Generation X, 48 percent of baby boomers, and 65 percent of the members of the Silent Generation were married ("Millennials in Adulthood," Pew Research Center, March 7, 2014, www.pewsocialtrends.org/2014/03/07/millennials-in-adulthood/). By 2017, the median age for first marriage reached its highest point on record: about 27 for women and 29 for men (Gretchen Livingston and Andrea Caumont, "5 Facts on Love and Marriage in America," Pew Research Center, February 13, 2017, www.pewresearch.org/fact-tank/2017/02/13/5-facts-about-love-and-marriage/).

36 Arnett, "Emerging Adulthood," 3.

37 Tatiana Siegel, "R.I.P. Romantic Comedies: Why Harry Wouldn't Meet Sally in 2013," *Hollywood Reporter*, September 26, 2013, www.hollywoodreporter.com/news/rip-romantic-comedies-why-harry-634776.

38 Research toward this article was funded by the Spanish Ministerio de Economía, Industria y Competitividad (research project no. FFI2017–82312-P), Diputación General de Aragón (re. H23–17R), and Universidad de Zaragoza/Obra Social Fundación Ibercaja (research project no. JIUZ-2017-HUM-02). Thanks are also due to Celestino Deleyto, for his careful revision of the manuscript.

2

Comedy and Melodrama from *Sunrise* to *Midnight*

Genre and Gender in Richard Linklater's *Before* Series

James MacDowell

Richard Linklater's *Before* series—*Before Sunrise* (1995), *Before Sunset* (2004), and *Before Midnight* (2013)—revisits a Franco-American[1] couple, Céline (Julie Delpy) and Jesse (Ethan Hawke), every nine years.[1] *Sunrise* depicts the pair meeting as early-twentysomethings on a cross-European train and impulsively beginning a day-long romantic relationship while exploring Vienna, culminating in a rushed plan to reunite there in six months' time. *Sunset* sees the couple (now in their early thirties), having failed to achieve their planned rendezvous, remeeting in Paris; this film ends with Jesse—now an unhappily married father—on the verge of deciding to remain with Céline. In *Midnight* they are a long-term fortyish couple, and parents to twins, holidaying in the southern Peloponnese. The pair argue about their past, present, and future, and the film concludes with a hint that they *may* be able to salvage this embattled relationship, which we have seen coming dangerously close to dissolution.

Resolutely indie and "realist" in style, certainly unconventional in several respects, the *Before* films have tended to be defined critically in terms of their opposition to Hollywood's conventional generic frameworks, particularly romantic comedy.[2] I suggest, however, that we should view this series not as rejecting, but rather engaging in a more ambivalent dialogue with longstanding generic (and ideological) conventions—not only those of romantic comedy, but also of romantic melodrama. Relating Linklater's series to these genres may help us to explore the implications of one thing about the *Before* movies that *is* undeniably unconventional: they offer sequels within a generic field—romance—that "do[es] not usually provide fertile ground for spawning sequels."³ We can begin to reflect on the significance of this by revisiting the opening of the first film as viewed from the vantage point of the last.

After *Before Sunrise*

Sunrise's first words are spoken by an arguing middle-aged Austrian couple who are clearly tired of each other's company, each intentionally testing the other's nerves. After Céline has changed seats to escape the couple's escalating bickering, Jesse uses her quizzical look at the pair as they loudly exit the train carriage as an excuse to ask her: "Do you have any idea what they were arguing about?" The primary resonance created by this older couple in *Sunrise* is the contrast it establishes between them and our protagonists' burgeoning relationship. The look Jesse gives them as they storm agitatedly back into the carriage is one of amused mock bafflement—suggesting how distant from this couple and their ways of behaving Jesse currently views himself as being.⁴ The rest of the film then proceeds indeed to demonstrate the gulf between this image of heterosexual coupledom and the one embodied by Céline and Jesse. Whereas the arguing Austrians seem unable even to listen or exchange words civilly, Céline and Jesse's delightfully verbose

Before Sunrise: Céline (Julie Delpy) and the arguing Austrian couple.

hours together in Vienna will be characterized by almost nothing else *other* than an open, generous, and egalitarian (in Stanley Cavell's phrase) "meet and happy conversation"—an eagerness to engage and hear one another, unburdened by the pent-up resentments and power games apparently gripping the older pair.[5]

It is this egalitarianism—combined with the fact that *Sunrise* "systematically and rigorously resists identification with one character above or against the other"[6]—that prompts Robin Wood to argue of Céline and Jesse that, unlike so many fictional heterosexual romantic couples, "[they] meet and negotiate on a level of equality. . . . That the film seems so inspirational and life-giving is surely because, within a cultural situation that often seems incorrigibly and fathomlessly discouraging, it reminds us that there *have* been advances, and important ones."[7] However, what is striking about rewatching *Sunrise*'s opening scene today is, firstly, that this arguing middle-aged couple are probably about the same age as Jesse and Céline will be by the time of *Midnight*; and, secondly, viewed from the perspective of *Midnight*, we might regard the fact that their arguing brings *Sunrise*'s couple together as something of a cruel cosmic irony. After *Midnight*, the poignant quality of *Sunrise*'s opening now lies in how different from the Austrian couple they once seemed, and how like them they appear eighteen years later. And, suddenly, the apparent "advances" in gender relations to which Wood alludes seem not nearly so great.

We can account for this trajectory, partly, by considering these films in relation to the genres of romantic comedy and romantic melodrama. By taking the radical decision to append sequels to *Sunrise* after the way that first film ends—with its hope of at least a *possible* happy future—it seems that the *Before* movies have effectively transformed what might have been a stand-alone (relatively unconventional, but still passingly familiar) romantic comedy into merely the first act in what has become an ongoing romantic melodrama, climaxing (for now) in the bitterness and recrimination of *Midnight*. This chapter will consider this possibility in terms of both the films' generic identities and their gender politics.

Between Comedy and Melodrama: From *Sunrise* to *Sunset*

In popular cinema, a romance focused on courtship will most usually be comedic, while marriage or long-term coupledom will tend to be treated as melodramatic. The former kind of film typically deals with only the *promise* of a couple, ending happily at a moment which is in truth only a "happy *beginning*," the start of the relationship.[8] Romantic melodrama, meanwhile, more often depicts what romantic comedy only hints at: what a couple's future looks like following its formation. In this sense, it represents the "sequel" to such courtship tales, telling "the story of what *follows* that happy ending."[9]

Deborah Thomas suggests that love in romantic comedy tends to feel liberating, since the couple's "benevolent and safe" fictional world is geared toward securing a positive outcome for shared romantic desires.[10] In melodramatic worlds, however, love tends to feel "repressive and full of danger"[11]—perhaps manifesting in unhealthy, obsessive ways (say, *Vertigo* [1958]); or being experienced as "fantasies of escape," often via desire for a third party (*Intermezzo* [1939], *September Affair* [1950]); or simply being left ultimately unfulfilled (*Now, Voyager* [1942]).[12] Regarded generically, the *Before* series can certainly be seen as charting a gradual journey away from the comedic and toward the melodramatic.

At one moment in *Sunset*, Céline cautions Jesse against assuming that the pair's lives "might've been so different" if they had managed to reunite in Vienna. "Maybe not," she offers with a rueful smile. "Maybe we would have hated each other eventually. . . . Maybe we're only good at brief encounters . . . in a warm climate." Viewed generically, this "warm climate" might bring to mind the generous and accommodating mood and world of romantic comedy as critics have long conceptualized it—from Northrop Frye's identification of Shakespearean comedy's pastoral "green world" to what Celestino Deleyto calls romantic comedy's protective "magic space."[13] Characteristically, this genre, in Thomas's words, "transform[s] the world into something more spontaneous and, at the same time, safe, providing a home (as opposed to a battleground) for reciprocal erotic desire."[14] It also, importantly, usually encourages the audience to desire and anticipate this union almost as much as its protagonists do.

True to comedic convention, the Vienna of *Sunrise* appears extremely welcoming toward Céline and Jesse's burgeoning love: the barman who self-lessly gifts them a free bottle of wine; the harpsichord player whose music floats up magically from a basement and allows for a brief dance at dawn; the record store that provides the right soundtrack and space for one of their most romantically charged moments; the Prater Ferris wheel that offers a picturesque view and privacy for their first kiss. And, while *Sunrise*'s ending

Before Sunrise: Céline and Jesse's (Ethan Hawke) romantic-comedic egalitarianism.

only *hints* at a reunion, given how obliging the film's world has thus far been toward this couple's relationship, we could certainly be forgiven—despite the film's realist trappings—for making unrealistically romantic predictions.

The series' movement in the direction of melodrama, however, is soon gestured toward in *Sunset*, when we learn that the pair failed to remeet: Jesse showed up in Vienna, while Céline (because of her grandmother's funeral) did not. This twist is immediately suggestive of a melodramatic world: Jesse's fate recalls the many melodramatic lovers left abandoned on train platforms (*Casablanca* [1942], *Letter from an Unknown Woman* [1948]), while Céline's impediment is reminiscent of the kind of unforeseeable tragedy that prevents, for example, a planned reunion in *An Affair to Remember* (1957), as well as that film's own dying grandmother. In such filmic worlds, Thomas suggests, romantic love "finds itself embattled and at constant odds with the requirements of melodrama."[15] This sense is only increased by the fact that in *Sunset* Jesse is married; by the looming deadline represented by his impending flight home; and, especially, by the shocking revelation that Céline and Jesse both lived in New York for several years but never crossed paths. Jesse's pained recounting of the moment he thought he spotted Céline from a taxi window while en route to his wedding is paradigmatically melodramatic in its sense of tragically/ironically near-missing—what Steve Neale calls this genre's characteristic feeling of "if *only*. . . ."[16]

Jesse and Céline's interactions in *Sunset* do respark some of the romantic-comedic mood of the first film, and they do *just* manage to wrest something like a happy ending from the jaws of melodramatic circumstance: "Baby, you are gonna miss that plane. . . ."[17] This ending—Céline dancing subtly seductively for Jesse as he smiles—is ecstatically alive with the assurance of an imminent passionate union and romantic comedy's characteristically reassuring promise of "time laid up in store."[18] Of course, this conclusion is also burdened by the very *un*promising consequences of the forthcoming moment of passion, due mainly to the fact that it must be (lest we forget!) adulterous, which firmly suggests again the realm of melodrama. Nonetheless, *Sunset*'s poignancy lies precisely in its hovering precariously between moods of desperation and hope, tension and ease, melodrama and comedy.

By *Midnight*, however, the bleaker forecasts available to us at *Sunset*'s conclusion are quickly confirmed by the reportedly acrimonious relationship Jesse now has with his ex-wife: "She just hates you so much," his (now-)thirteen-year-old son reminds him in the very first scene. And—despite the literal "warm climate" of *Midnight*'s Peloponnesian setting—there are many further ways in which melodrama permeates this third film's representation of its (now-)long-term couple.

Midnight, Melodrama, and Gendered Conflict

Most obviously, this is the first film in which we have seen Céline and Jesse truly fight. The instigating argument in *Midnight*—beginning in the couple's first scene together—concerns Jesse's fear that he is missing his son's formative years, and his resultant desire to relocate from France to the U.S. to be closer to him. Céline believes both that moving back to the States would negatively affect her career,[19] and that for Jesse even to make the request reveals something troubling about the way he *regards* her career—a concern that sparks much of the conflict besetting the pair's exchanges hereafter. *Midnight* thus feels melodramatic, because the couple's relationship is represented as more like (in Thomas's words) a conflict-riven "battleground." Yet, as the subject of their central argument suggests, the melodramatic character of the couple's relationship in *Midnight* also has ideological dimensions.

Melodramas typically depict "a hierarchical social setting whose privileges are heavily dependent upon markers of difference based on such things as . . . gender."[20] Indeed, classical romantic melodramas persistently explore the seemingly intractable conflicts involved in pursuing romantic love, marriage, and parenthood within a culture that invariably consigns women to various forms of explicit and implicit subordination. They depict, for instance, the frequently challenging nature of (particularly female) parenthood (in maternal melodramas such as *Stella Dallas* [1937] or *That Certain Woman* [1937]); the conflict between domesticity and work (*Mildred Pierce* [1945], *Imitation of Life* [1959]); and—very often—the ways in which the roles of husband and wife can in practice be far from egalitarian (in authoritarian-husband melodramas like *Gaslight* [1944] and *Caught* [1949]). Usually, as befits their status as so-called "women's films," these melodramas tend, broadly speaking, to be sympathetic to the woman's predicament, even when ultimately dramatizing her defeat by social pressures. In short, they often present "a recognizable picture of woman's ambivalent position under patriarchy."[21]

Given the dates of all the films cited above, we might hope that a 2013 romantic melodrama would not necessarily need to cover the same territory. This hope might be further bolstered both by our memories of the seemingly democratic nature of Céline and Jesse's interactions in previous installments, as well as by the stated intentions of Linklater, who has said of the third film that "you can see both their points of view—it's not seen more from the male or the female side."[22] However, the influence of age-old gendered hierarchies—so familiar from classical romantic melodramas—certainly still haunt *Midnight*. The question to consider now is its treatment of this conventional material.

Important to note is that, in a first for the series, *Midnight* ensures that the goals of its protagonists are—as in much romantic melodrama—significantly at odds. Jesse claims at one moment that he is "still that same guy who asked [Céline] to get off that train with him." And he is indeed largely represented as being driven by broadly the same romantic hopes as in the preceding films, remaining ostensibly committed throughout to the aim of overcoming the couple's conflicts. "I love you," he proclaims during one fight, "and I'm not in conflict about it." Céline, on the other hand, is now cast as a veritable thorn in the side of the possibility that the film might move past its couple's conflicts and achieve the desired end of most romance narratives: a happy ending. As Kathleen Rowe [Karlyn] notes, even melodrama "depends on a belief in the possibility of romantic comedy's happy ending, a belief that heightens the pathos of its loss."[23] Yet, from their first conversation, Céline is already anticipating this relationship's end: "This is how people start to break up . . ." Later, it will be she who resists visiting the romantic hotel retreat their friends have organized for them; she who opposes the romantic mood Jesse desires to create there (a desire we likely share); and she who will twice storm out. Finally, it will be she who ultimately utters the words that are surely designed to sound devastating to any long-time fan of the series: "I just don't love you anymore."

However, it is not just Céline who stands in the way of this film offering something like the benevolent comedic climate of the first two films, but, more specifically, the feminist—or at least gendered—critique she hopes to offer on the couple's relationship. At dinner, Céline accuses Jesse of being a "closet macho"—a shoe that perhaps fits, given, say, how aroused he is by her parodic performance of an ego-flattering bimbo, his pressuring Céline to sign a book for a fan, or his anxiety that his son can't throw a baseball ("a father is supposed to teach you that"). This begins to recall those melodramas in which "the romantic couple is under siege both from the outside and, to the extent that the couple have internalized [their society's] values and commitment to gendered roles . . . , from within."[24] Céline, by contrast, tries always to place their relationship in a more critical, sociopolitical light. She repeatedly frames her arguments in ways that imply that she constantly feels the inescapable context of a millennia-old history of female subjugation, whether the topic be what she sees as Jesse's dismissive attitude toward her career (her "secret fear" being that men ultimately want to make her into a housewife who "sews the drapes"); her anxieties about motherhood (the postnatal depression she says she experienced due to cultural expectations concerning women's instinctively "nurturing" natures); or her accusation that Jesse always attempts to win arguments by claiming to be "rational" rather than "emotional" ("The Final Solution was a *very* 'rational' plan," she spits). "This," she claims at one point, "is bigger than me."

Having established an irreducibly gendered conflict, *Midnight* occasionally provides us with chances to see validity in Céline's side of that conflict. For instance, Jesse shares one of his most explicitly philosophical discussions (about the nature of time, and his latest novel), not with Céline, but instead with the other men with whom the couple are holidaying. At this moment these men's female partners are absent, only to be revealed (by a pointed cut) to be in the kitchen preparing food for the forthcoming dinner scene. Céline obliquely brings this up during the hotel argument, speaking of the "fairies" men think take care of such household labor, and of the indulgently long wanderings Jesse often takes with their (male) host, which, she implies, her work makes possible. This complaint is thus implicitly supported by the film through this subtle sketch we receive of the kinds of unquestioned gender roles often unconsciously slipped into by long-term couples. We also learn that Céline still desires to be making music, but cannot find the time—amid, that is, the combined demands of work and (what she suggests are) unbalanced child-rearing duties.

The parentheses I am required to use in this last example, though, are indicative of a troubling possible limit placed on the extent to which *Midnight* can consistently encourage us to take Céline's side of its gendered conflict—or even to frame the conflict evenhandedly. This limit is created not only by constructing Céline as the character who resists the development of a comedic-romantic mood, but due also to the film's approach to storytelling and form.

A Conflict of Form and Content?

Midnight, of course, follows the storytelling model established by *Sunrise* and *Sunset*: it represents only one short period of time (here probably around twelve hours) that is made to feel as if it is unfolding in a heightened present tense. This form made obvious sense for the content of the first two films, whose scenarios both came with built-in deadlines. In *Midnight*, though, the highly restricted time frame might appear more arbitrary. I suggest that its more troubling side effect is also to tip the scales of the film's point of view in Jesse's favor.

It is crucial to recognize that, until *Midnight*, we had spent almost as much time with these characters as they had with each other. By the third film this situation has radically changed; the approach to the storytelling, however, has not. How well does this approach fit with the new things this film is attempting—namely, its dramatization of a highly gendered conflict between a long-term romantic couple?

Any romance film is likely to, implicitly, ask its audience to hazard ongoing judgments about the dynamics and health of its central relationship. If a film is interested in allowing us to make judgments about the overall nature of a nine-year relationship, then this might seem to necessitate a relatively broad time frame—one permitting a wide-ranging overview of

Before Midnight: Céline and Jesse's melodramatic gendered conflict.

the ups, downs, and intricacies of a couple's life span.²⁵ Instead, *Midnight* again applies the device of the restrictive time frame, which now creates problems that neither *Sunrise* nor *Sunset* faced. In those films we did not need to see beyond their brief temporal windows in order to amply fulfill the spectatorial requirement of assessing the dynamics of the couple's relationship. By contrast, within the dramatically altered narrative circumstances of *Midnight*, the tight time frame now ensures that we are necessarily denied the chance to see a great deal of what has passed between Céline and Jesse, which here affects our ability to evaluate them as a couple. Specifically, we have no access to the voluminous evidence Céline must cite to support her arguments: for instance, the impact on her of moving to New York; her sense of abandonment by Jesse in their children's early years; the matter of whether Jesse ever arranges a babysitter; even whether Jesse's loquacious holiday walks with their host have typically taken two hours (Jesse's claim) or three (Céline's).

This fact, moreover, plainly has greater significance for our view of Céline, as the one required to resist happy reconciliation, than of Jesse, as the one seemingly still merely trying to forge it. The film's structure means that so many of her critiques—contested by Jesse at every turn—refer to parts of the couple's life to which we cannot be granted access. *Do* the majority of household responsibilities usually fall to her? How *do* Jesse's prolonged absences affect his partner? What *is* his typical attitude toward Céline's career? The answers to such questions would be crucial to assessing how much *Midnight* encourages us to sympathize with Céline's resistance to the establishment of the desired romantic-comedic mood, and none of them can be known, thanks to the form of storytelling adopted. Jesse therefore seems to be assisted by the film in at least two ways: first, his most basic putative desire for the relationship aligns with the most basic generic desire the series has instilled in its audience from the first film onward; and, second, most of the questionable, unthinking actions Céline accuses him of, which might cause us to look askance at his claims to be simply a romantic trying to "make things work," must remain forever unseen.

This is all to say that the film's point of view often seems more closely aligned with Jesse than Céline. That sense is never stronger than in the moment following Céline's final departure from the hotel room. Breaking the habit of a lifetime for this series, which has largely divided its perspective so equally, at this moment Linklater elects not to cut between Céline and Jesse to convey both their emotional states upon her momentous exit; rather, we stay in the hotel room with Jesse alone, even receiving a series of what seem to be point-of-view shots as he surveys the room: the bed, the bottle of wine, and so on. These point-of-view shots are highly unusual in the stylistic vocabulary of the *Before* films, and it is very tempting to see them as indicative of the extent to which *Midnight* effectively (begins and) ends as Jesse's film, rather than his *and* Céline's together.[26] It now seems that our hero—and this moment suddenly makes him feel more like one than ever before—must pursue the passionate, "difficult" woman he loves if this narrative is going to end in anything like the way we are surely being encouraged to hope that it still might.

He ultimately follows her out to the veranda, and (given the history invested in this couple) there are unlikely to be many viewers who aren't ardently willing him to do whatever it takes to win Céline back, to convince her to assent to fulfilling Jesse's and our desires for one more—provisional, always only provisional—happy ending. Their final conversation does hint that Céline may be prepared to forgive Jesse, and the film effectively ends poised at another moment of imminent lovemaking. Yet my concern is with the terms on which this conclusion is reached—terms that have established *Midnight* as being predicated on a gendered conflict between Céline and

Jesse, that then stacked the deck of the conflict in favor of one member of the couple, ultimately resulting in Céline and her feminist perspectives being cast as problems that must be overcome by Jesse in his quest to keep alive the romantic hopes of the series and its fans.

Perhaps it would be worse if *Midnight* chose not to address gendered hierarchies at all, especially given the series' self-identification as "realistic": after all, as Thomas notes, "the world in which we live has a kinship with the melodramatic—in being hierarchical, gendered, class-based, and so on."[27] Equally, perhaps we witness enough of Céline and Jesse's daily, moment-by-moment interactions to extrapolate a fuller picture of the relationship's gendered hierarchies. Nonetheless, the question remains whether *Midnight* has found the form most appropriate to that aim—if, that is, it hopes to ensure the conflicts it depicts are "not seen more from the male or the female side," as Linklater avows. The most disheartening aspect of *Midnight*, however, may be simply that it must be constructed around gendered conflicts and hierarchies in the first place. I say this, ultimately, because of where this series began.

Before Sunrise after *Before Midnight*

In his aforementioned essay (published in 1998, before either of the sequels), Robin Wood raises an unexpected question about *Sunrise*'s ending: "The question of 'Will they or won't they [meet again]?' may be a simple (and sentimental) evasion of the real question posed by the film's ending, which is far more radical and disturbing: Would it be better if they did or if they didn't?"[28] Wood poses this question for two reasons. Firstly, there is his great appreciation for the resolutely equal nature of the relationship as depicted in the first film. Its couple's stated belief that "it's a healthy process to rebel against everything that's come before" seems to extend promisingly to their thinking about romantic relationships. Pulled between skepticism regarding "romantic projections" and the hope that "if there's any kind of magic in this world it must be in the attempt of understanding someone, sharing something," Céline and Jesse appear prepared to question and reconsider familiar assumptions.[29] "Maybe we should try something different," Céline suggests when they hatch their initial plan to treat that night in Vienna as both the beginning *and* end of their relationship—a proposition met by Jesse with the probing question, "Why do you think everybody thinks relationships are supposed to last forever anyway?" While they ultimately renege on this plan, the fact that they even raise such questions and *desire* to "try something different" suggests something hopeful and progressive about the character of the hypothetical relationship they could eventually construct. "My one clear wish for the project," cowriter Kim Krizan has said of *Sunrise*, "was that it attempt some kind of optimism and hope regarding human connection. . . . Cynicism is cheap, safe, and easy. Could we possibly move beyond it?" This wish to try different things, move beyond old models, seems to represent—in Krizan's words—a hope that "perhaps we can forge a *new* romanticism," whatever that might ultimately look like.[30]

The second strand feeding into Wood's question about the end is his observation that, against the democratic backdrop of Céline and Jesse's relationship, *Sunrise* also subtly invokes various reminders of a far less utopian cultural history of heterosexual romantic love—away from which advances assuredly need to be made. Along with the arguing married Austrian couple in the first scene, Wood suggests two important cultural reference points: Henry Purcell's 17th-century opera *Dido and Aeneas*, whose overture features in *Sunrise*'s opening credits, and whose depiction of the death-by-broken-heart of a woman abandoned by her lover certainly does foreground "the subordinate position of women in patriarchal culture";[31] and Max Ophüls's melodrama *Letter from an Unknown Woman*, set in early 1900s Vienna, one of cinema's most poignant dramatizations of a woman's destruction by internalized ideological forces associated with the concept of romantic love.[32] Victim of a romantic ideal of self-sacrifice and obsessively committed to a self-abnegating belief in fated love, this film's titular character convinces herself that a notorious but charming womanizer is her destined true love, sleeps with him, then proceeds to refrain from imposing herself upon him following his abandonment of her—even after she discovers she is pregnant by him. Perhaps this film's most heart-rending moment comes with Lisa's (Joan Fontaine) response to being told that "you have a *will*—you can do what's best for *you*." "No," she counters. "I've had no will but *his*, ever."

It is the gulf *Sunrise* establishes between such melodramatic depictions of unequal romantic love under patriarchy and the thrilling equality of Jesse and Céline's brief meeting that prompts Wood's question about the end of the movie. "If we *want* them to form a relationship (as surely we do)," he writes, "then it must be of a quite different order than anything offered by the familiar models," ensuring the film's open ending becomes "a signpost to an unknown destination."[33] And perhaps, Wood wonders, the risk that their love will lose its vital egalitarianism if pursued further is simply too great: "If a relationship must lead either to the tragic waste and desolation offered by past concepts of romantic love, or to the stagnation and bitterness into which so many contemporary marriages seem to degenerate, would it not be better if Jesse and Céline were left at least with indelible memories of one magical night?"[34] What is so dispiriting about *Midnight* is that it tempts us to answer this question with "Yes." When the most recent *Before* movie is placed alongside the first it creates a feeling of deep loss: a loss of the hope that Jesse and Céline might have somehow been able to escape the familiar traps that long-term heterosexual romantic relationships can so routinely set for lovers. Once *Midnight* has shown the couple reenact and clash so bitterly over (contemporary variations on) some of the most persistent gender binaries constructed by Western culture—and dramatized in so many melodramas—the degree of ease, mutuality and equality the lovers embodied in the first film feels even more valuable, and more utopian.

Relevant again here is how the series' comedic and melodramatic modes relate to the treatment of gender. "It is a central aspect of comedic films," writes Thomas, "that the social space within them is transformable into something better than the repressive, hierarchical world of melodramatic films."[35] Contrary to popular belief, the sense of liberation and freedom that can accompany comedic films may extend to a movie's politics—even the politics of a romantic comedy.[36] The comedic "magic space" of *Sunrise* thus was important not only for how it helped bring Céline and Jesse together, but also for how it allowed them initially to escape the kind of intractable gendered hierarchies represented in a melodrama like *Letter from an Unknown Woman*, or a high tragedy like Purcell's *Dido and Aeneas*—or even simply the daily bitterness and anger of an average middle-aged couple. Retrospectively, this can now be felt especially at those moments in *Sunrise* when gendered conflict arises explicitly as a topic in the couple's meandering conversation. Of particular note is the moment when a discussion about the differences between men and women threatens momentarily to turn sour. Céline is becoming slightly upset about the subject of whether men or women have the greater power to "destroy" the other, stumbling over her words and trailing off into: ". . . It's depressing. Ah—you know what . . . ?" Jesse immediately intuits her desires correctly: "What? You want to stop talking about this?"

"Yeah." And they do—walking away from camera, down Vienna's cobbled streets, laughing, completing each other's sentences in the characteristically free-flowing and democratic style of the first film in general:

> CÉLINE: You know, men, women: there's no end to it, it's like—you know . . .
> JESSE: It's like a skipping record . . .
> CÉLINE: [*Laughing*] Yeah . . . !
> JESSE: Every couple's been having this conversation forever . . .
> CÉLINE: And nobody came up with an answer.

The gendered conflict here is deferred rather than solved, but that is precisely the point. At this moment in the series and the relationship, this couple were able to convince themselves that they could move the needle past the skip—past this treacherous inherited cultural argument, with its ignoble history of patriarchal power relations, which informs so much of our present. At this privileged point in time, protected by the impervious idealism of youth and the "warm climate" of romantic comedy, they—and perhaps we—could momentarily be seduced into believing that they were somehow *beyond* this.

Before Sunrise: the comedic couple escapes a gendered argument.

Of course in fact they, and we, were not—as *Midnight* so forcefully demonstrates. What makes the third film feel as desolating as it does is the way that—rather than fulfilling *Sunrise*'s promise of "something different," of a "new romanticism"—it falls back into old grooves so resolutely: a happy, egalitarian comedic couple can still only precede the long-term relationship, while a conflicted, gender-stratified melodramatic couple is still created *by* the relationship. What's more, as I have suggested, *Midnight* arguably goes further still by doing at least a minor disservice to Céline and her feminist-influenced arguments—making it not only a melodrama, but a melodrama that may actually be less sympathetic to the exploration of gender inequalities than many of its classic precursors.

Nothing now prevents us from returning to *Sunrise* whenever we wish to reexperience its inspirational promise of a more mutual and equal romantic future than many romances offer. We can still revisit the couple's first meeting, forged in the shadow of the arguing Austrians, and that playful initial exchange about men and women's hearing:

CÉLINE: Have you ever heard that, as couples get older, they lose their ability to hear each other?
JESSE: No . . .
CÉLINE: [*Smiling*] Well, supposedly, men lose their ability to hear higher-pitch sounds and women eventually lose their hearing at the low end. I guess they sort of nullify each other or something.
JESSE: [*Laughing*] Yeah, I guess: nature's way of allowing couples to grow old together without killing each other.

On first appearance playfully cynical, this supposition now seems to contain the seed of something impossibly, comedically, hopeful: a proposition that "nature" might somehow be committed to magically easing the process of heterosexual lovers remaining together into their dotage. The pity of *Midnight* is that the same man and woman who once laughed and bonded over the notion that a couple should need to be spared the ability to "hear each other" now seem to require just such magical assistance—but also that their world now appears far less accommodating toward their needs and desires than it did eighteen years ago. The only hope, perhaps, is the possibility ("if *only* . . .") that it could yet seem a little more so another nine years hence.

Notes

1. Henceforth referred to simply as *Sunrise*, *Sunset*, and *Midnight*.
2. See, for instance, Joanna Di Mattia (2018) calling *Sunrise* "so much more than [a] trifling 'Gen X' romantic comedy" ("Thinking about Celine and Jesse: Traveling through Time with the *Before* trilogy," *Senses of Cinema*, 87 [2018]: sensesofcinema.com/2018/stardust-memories/thinking-about-celine-and-jesse-travelling-through-time-with-the-before-trilogy [accessed September 8, 2020]); Koresky (2005) stressing that *Sunset* resists "generic reduction" ("Before Sunset," Reverse Shot, January 4, 2005, www.reverseshot.org/reviews/entry/1078/before-sunset [accessed September 8, 2020]); and Alexander Huls (2014) recruiting *Midnight* to his argument that "The Romantic Comedy is Dying" ("The Romantic Comedy Is Dying, but Cinematic Romance Is Thriving," *Atlantic*, Jan 24, 2014, www.theatlantic.com/entertainment/archive/2014/01/the-romantic-comedy-is-dying-but-cinematic-romance-is-thriving/283252). Notable exceptions, which appreciate the *Before* films' generic dimensions, include Celestino Deleyo, *The Secret Life of Romantic Comedy* (Manchester: Manchester University Press, 2009), and Leger Grindon, "Taking Romantic Comedy Seriously in *Eternal Sunshine of the Spotless Mind* [2004] and *Before Sunset* [2004]," in *A Companion to Film Comedy*, ed. Andrew Horton and Joanna E. Rapf, 196–216. Oxford: Wiley-Blackwell.
3. Kathrina Glitre, *Hollywood Romantic Comedy: States of the Union* (Manchester: Manchester University Press, 2006), 20.
4. Later, in the "telephone" scene, he will describe the Austrian pair as "this very weird couple."
5. Stanley Cavell, *Pursuits of Happiness: The Hollywood Comedy of Remarriage* (Cambridge, MA: Harvard University Press, 1981), 146.
6. Robin Wood, *Sexual Politics and Narrative Film, Hollywood and Beyond* (New York: Columbia University Press, 1998), 331.
7. Wood, *Sexual Politics*, 328.
8. James MacDowell, *Happy Endings in Hollywood Cinema* (Edinburgh: Edinburgh University Press, 2013), 57–97.
9. Kathleen Rowe [Karlyn], "Comedy, Melodrama, and Gender: Theorizing the Genres of Laughter," in *Classical Hollywood Comedy*, ed. Kristine Brunovska Karnick and Henry Jenkins (New York: Routledge, 1995), 51.

10 Deborah Thomas, *Beyond Genre* (Dumfriesshire: Cameron & Hollis, 2000), 9.
11 Thomas, *Beyond Genre*, 9.
12 Thomas, 14.
13 Celestino Deleyto, *The Secret Life of Romantic Comedy* (Manchester: Manchester University Press, 2009).
14 Thomas, *Beyond Genre*, 21.
15 Thomas, 22.
16 Steve Neale, "Melodrama and Tears," *Screen* 27, no. 6 (November/December 1986): 22.
17 See Deleyto's excellent analysis in *Secret Life of Romantic Comedy*.
18 MacDowell, *Happy Endings in Hollywood Cinema*, 62–65.
19 "*Back*" is worth stressing: at one point we learn—in dialogue that passes quickly enough to be missed—that Céline previously moved temporarily to New York with Jesse and the children.
20 Thomas, *Beyond Genre*, 14.
21 Linda Williams, "'Something Else Besides a Mother': *Stella Dallas* and the Maternal Melodrama," *Cinema Journal* 24, no.1 (Fall 1984): 23.
22 Andrea Cirla, "*Before Midnight* Press Conference, Berlin Film Festival," YouTube, February 16, 2013, https://www.youtube.com/watch?v=sFiq8LUGXD8&t=15m16s.
23 Rowe [Karlyn], "Comedy, Melodrama, and Gender," 49.
24 Thomas, *Beyond Genre*, 22.
25 This happens, for instance, in melodramas like *Penny Serenade* (1941) or *The Marrying Kind* (1950), or even Ingmar Bergman's epic television film *Scenes from a Marriage* (1973).
26 Céline is also absent from the first scene, in which Jesse says goodbye to his son at the airport. This echoes the opening of *Sunset*: the only other moment in the series that significantly privileges one partner over the other.
27 Thomas, *Beyond Genre*, 22.
28 Wood, *Sexual Politics*, 325.
29 On this oscillation in the film, see MacDowell, *Happy Endings in Hollywood Cinema*.
30 Kim Krizan, "Foreword," in *Before Sunrise: The Screenplay* (London: Faber & Faber), iv.
31 Wood, *Sexual*, 327.

32 Linklater confirmed to Wood that he showed this film to Hawke and Delpy before shooting began (1998, 328).
33 Wood, *Sexual Politics*, 327.
34 Wood, 324.
35 Thomas, *Beyond Genre*, 14.
36 Glitre, *Hollywood Romantic Comedy*, 41–64. This is not, of course, to say that romantic comedy is somehow an inherently progressive genre—merely that this represents one possibility open to it; as Deleyto puts it: "The 'better world' of romantic comedy [is] . . . an empty formal concept, not an ideologically charged one. Different texts . . . may associate it with different discourses on love and desire" (37).

3

From Jane to Mindy

The Politics of Narrative Control in the Contemporary Romantic Comedy

Alice Guilluy

In January 2013, to celebrate the two-hundredth anniversary of the publication of *Pride and Prejudice*, the BBC radio program *World Book Club* dedicated a full episode to the novel, which was introduced as "a romantic comedy; the original romcom one might say, but also *much more than that*" (my emphasis).[1] The influence of Jane Austen's novel on the contemporary romantic comedy (or "romcom") narrative, particularly the popular enemies-to-lovers trope—Nancy Miller calls this the "marriage plot," Kathrina Glitre the "battle of the sexes" plot—is indeed widely recognized.[2] Romcom screenwriter, showrunner, and actress Mindy Kaling defines this trope with specific reference to *Pride and Prejudice*'s central couple, and Mr. Darcy's disastrous first proposal to Elizabeth Bennet: "A man and a woman are very attracted to each other, but there still seem to be lots of reasons why they can't be together. Sometimes it's logistical (he goes off to war), sometimes it's situational (she's engaged to someone else), sometimes it's emotional *(he calls her family tacky and she thinks he's a dickhead)*. Whatever it is, the audience knows in the back of their heads that these two dum-dums will eventually figure it out and get together" (my emphasis).[3]

Indeed, scenarios of protagonists who begin by disliking each other but end up falling in love occur repeatedly in romantic comedy, extending far beyond direct adaptations of *Pride and Prejudice*. This is, of course, true of numerous entries in romcom's screwball cycle, which, under the constraints of the Production Code, displaced the representation of on-screen sex onto the lead couple's adversarial relationship.[4] Meanwhile, contemporary examples include Nora Ephron's *You've Got Mail* (1998), Nancy Meyers's *What*

Women Want (2000) and *Something's Gotta Give* (2004), Anne Fletcher's *27 Dresses* (2008) and *The Proposal* (2009), Kaling's own TV series *The Mindy Project* (Fox, 2012–2015; Hulu, 2015–2017), and, most recently, Nisha Ganatra's feature *Late Night* (2019).

Much of the discussion within the growing scholarly literature on romantic comedy has focused on the genre's gender representation and politics. And, while scholars are largely ambivalent in their assessment of the romcom's feminist potential, a more solid consensus holds around the genre's definition, which is constructed almost exclusively in narrative terms.[5] Simply put, romantic comedies are often defined as "love stories with happy endings."[6] Indeed, some scholars have even argued that the genre has no characteristic stylistic features.[7] One of the dangers of such a definition, however, is that it feeds into dismissive—and often patronizing—attitudes toward the genre as "uncinematic." On the contrary, this chapter explores a defining stylistic feature of the contemporary romantic comedy: the voice-over.

One of few scholars to have examined the use of voice-over in the contemporary romcom, Sarah Kozloff argues that it has become a key trope of the genre, serving as both a source of irony and as a way to create intimacy between audience and characters.[8] I want to expand on Kozloff's account here by drawing on some of the extensive scholarship on the work of Jane Austen—the so-called "great-great-grandmother" of the romcom[9]—with a particular focus on her use of free indirect discourse to create irony and undermine characters' narrative authority.[10] A similar tone, I argue, permeates the films and TV show examined in this chapter. This is particularly significant in the case of *The Mindy Project*, which has received critical acclaim for its regeneration of romantic comedy as an allegedly "dying" genre.[11] In an echo of the unreliable Austenian narrator, the show uses voice-over to blur the boundary between writer and creator Mindy Kaling and lead character Mindy Lahiri. Moreover, as in much of Austen's work, narration in *The Mindy Project* is a site of conflict, one in which the struggle for narrative control is actively gendered. In scrutinizing voice-over's importance in these texts, this chapter will suggest that a renewed focus on the romcom's formal elements reveals a more radical engagement with the politics of romance than is usually assumed.

Jane Austen is often credited as one of the earliest and most influential users of free indirect discourse, which consists of reporting a character's thoughts or feelings by voicing their perspective through third-person narration rather than quotation.[12] As Susannah Fullerton has noted, the discrepancy in Austen's novels between characters' inner thoughts and what might be termed more "objective" narration is often comical. Fuller uses as her example Elizabeth's reaction to Mr. Darcy's first proposal (referenced by Kaling in her previously cited definition of the marriage plot), which moves from third-person narration in the first sentence to free indirect discourse in the second: "Her astonishment, as she reflected on what had passed, was increased by every review of it. That she should receive an offer of marriage from Mr. Darcy! That he should have been in love with her for so many months!"[13]

Additionally, certain characters are more frequent targets of such humor than others.[14] In *Pride and Prejudice* Austen often uses free indirect discourse, for example, to poke fun at the Bennet family's pompous cousin Mr. Collins and his devotion to his patroness, Lady Catherine de Bourgh:

> [Mr. Collins] protested that he had never in his life witnessed such behavior in a person of rank—such affability and condescension, as he had himself experienced from Lady Catherine. She had graciously pleased to approve of both the discourses, which he already had the honor of preaching before her. She had also asked him twice to dine at Rosings, and had sent for him only the Saturday before, to make up the pool of quadrille in the evening. Lady Catherine was reckoned proud by many people he knew, but *he* had never seen any thing but affability in her.[15]

The sentence begins with indirect discourse, as the reporting verb "protested" introduces Mr. Collins's praise for Lady Catherine. The next sentences moves into free indirect discourse: while no speech marks are used, the exaggerations, repetitions, and overly polite turns of phrases ("had the honor"; "any thing but affability") clearly suggest that these sentences are Mr. Collins's own, rather than that of the narrator. By reproducing these through free indirect discourse, Collins's grandiloquence is highlighted and ridiculed.

As Nora Nachumi and Sarah M. Morrison have each demonstrated, free indirect discourse makes film adaptations of Austen's novels particularly difficult: How can the film medium "negotiate the space between the heroine's subjective experience, other characters' perspectives, and something that may be called 'objective reality?'"[16] Nachumi considers *Clueless* (1995) to be the most successful Austen adaptation in this regard, because the film frequently plays up the contrast between the main protagonist's self-centered voice-over and the visuals on screen. She points to its opening scene as a definitive example of Austenian irony: despite Cher's (Alicia Silverstone) insisting that "I actually have a *way* normal life for a teenage girl" via voice-over, we see her picking out her daily outfits on a computer.[17] For both James MacDowell and Sarah Kozloff, voice-over is indeed a central source of irony in film,[18] precisely because it allows for a dynamic or even dissonant "interplay between narration and scenic presentation."[19]

A more recent example of this can be found in the opening scene of Anne Fletcher's *27 Dresses*. Like a large number of contemporary romcoms, the film employs voice-over sparingly, featuring it in its opening and closing sequences only; this is the case in *Notting Hill* (1999), which is at the heart of Sarah Kozloff's analysis, but more recent examples include the ensemble films *He's Just Not That Into You* (2009) and *How to Be Single* (2016), as well as recent Netflix original releases *Nappily Ever After* (2018) and *To All the Boys I've Loved Before* (2018). This is of course not always the case, with both the *Bridget Jones's Diary* (2001, 2004, 2016) and *Sex and the City* (1998–2004 [HBO], 2008, 2010) franchises making recurrent use of voice-over throughout.[20] Meanwhile, *27 Dresses* aligns the audience with its heroine Jane (Katherine Heigl) from the outset, as it opens with her voice-over during a flashback of her eight-year-old-self attending a wedding: "Mozart found his calling at age five, composing his first minuet. Picasso discovered his talent for painting when he was nine. Tiger Woods swung his first club well before his second birthday. Me? I was eight when I discovered my purpose in life. . . . That's when I fell in love with weddings." The film plays on the opposition between sound and image, as the solemnity in Heigl's voice is undercut by the ridiculousness of the scene's visual elements: the film opens with long and medium shots of a busy church, and the frame is crammed full of big hairstyles and voluminous dresses associated with (outdated) 80s fashion. The irony here is also verbal, stemming from the contrast between the "seriousness" of artistic (or athletic) genius and the "frivolity" of wedding preparations. This opposition recalls that of *Pride and Prejudice*'s famous opening line: "It is a truth universally acknowledged, that a single man in possession of a good fortune, must be in want of a wife."[21]

Another significant effect of Austen's use of free indirect discourse is what Anne Waldron Neumann calls Austen's novels' "double voice." For Waldron Neumann, free indirect discourse "*welcomes* ambiguity," as it often makes it difficult to know for certain whether it is the character or the narrator who is speaking.[22] Once again, as scholars such as Nachumi, Morrison, or Hilary Schor have highlighted, this kind of ambiguity is usually difficult to transpose to film. Indeed, neither of the two most frequently used adaptation strategies retains the ambivalence of the double voice: using the voice of one of the cast members for the voice-over suggests that we are hearing their thoughts (as in *Clueless*); alternatively, using a disembodied voice (as in Douglas McGrath's *Emma* [1995]) signals the presence of an omniscient narrator.[23] Enter *The Mindy Project*, a TV show created by and starring Mindy Kaling, who also cites *Pride and Prejudice* as her inspiration.[24] As the remainder of this chapter will argue, *The Mindy Project* is perhaps the most radical of these contemporary romcoms in its leaning into this confusion between narrator and character. In doing so, the voice-over also foregrounds the heroine's struggle for narrative control.

The pilot episode of *The Mindy Project* combines two defining stylistic features of the contemporary romcom genre, as a montage is accompanied by voice-over to depict its heroine growing up. In the scene, protagonist Mindy Lahiri—who is played by Kaling—talks us through her childhood love of romantic comedies ("In high school, Tom Hanks was my first boyfriend"), her training as an obstetrician-gynecologist, and, finally, her meet cute with fellow doctor Tom (Bill Hader) when they get stuck in a hospital

Visual irony employed to poke fun at weddings in *27 Dresses*.

elevator together. The montage implies that the voice-over is a verbalization of Mindy's thoughts, a conclusion inferred by the show's opening with a black screen; we can hear Mindy before we even see her, which aligns us as viewers with her perspective (we are *in* her head). This alignment is supported by what Kozloff calls the "complementary" relationship between sound and image, as the whip pans match the pace of Kaling's screwball-fast delivery.[25] The punch line comes at the end of the montage, when it is revealed that Mindy has in fact been talking to another character the entire time. Her emotion-laden voice is suddenly interrupted by an unknown voice, which is revealed to belong to a policewoman, asking impatiently, "What does this have to do with the circumstances of your arrest?" The voice-over thus turns out to have been part of a dialogue between the officer and Mindy, who is trying to talk herself out of a public intoxication charge at the police station.

The slippage between interior monologue and dialogue here also creates comic effect through what James MacDowell terms "ironic pretense," as it subverts audience expectations of romantic comedy conventions.[26] As Lilian Furst and Rachel Brownstein have noted, irony as a rhetorical device relies on shared knowledge between the speaker and the addressed.[27] More specifically here, the irony is metatextual, as it relies on viewers' familiarity with the romcom genre and its tropes such as the montage and voice-over. This is played on throughout the show's run, where episodes will frequently open with a voice-over. This serves the practicalities of the serialized TV format by providing recaps of previous plotlines but, most important, it continually aligns the series with the romcom genre through one of its key stylistic tropes. The show will frequently superpose Mindy's voice-over and aerial shots of New York landmarks (e.g., the Empire State Building, Manhattan Bridge, yellow cabs). This taps into another of the romcom genre's iconographic features: its close relationship with the Big Apple, perhaps most famously represented in the *Sex and the City* TV series.[28] In *The Mindy Project*'s pilot and subsequent episodes, this strategy embodies what Sarah Kozloff terms "romantic irony . . . the deliberate calling into question or demolishing of a work's dramatic illusion."[29] Indeed, this playful confusion between narration and dialogue recurs repeatedly in the course of the show's first season and, to a lesser extent, in later seasons.[30] A number of episodes thus open with Mindy soliloquizing—with full orchestral accompaniment provided by the nondiegetic score—in a subway train (1.2, "Hiring and

Adolescent but already in love with romcom: Mindy Lahiri (Mindy Kaling) in the pilot episode of *The Mindy Project*.

Firing"), a carriage in Central Park (1.11, "Bunk Bed"), or in the middle of a busy restaurant (4.18, "Bernardo and Anita").

This ironic dissonance also underscores the unreliability of the narrator. In her analysis of Douglas McGrath's *Emma*, Hilary Schor argues that, while "in a novel, we rarely begin by questioning the person who is speaking to us," both Austen's novel and McGrath's adaptation undermine our trust in the narrator.[31] Schor also highlights the way in which the characters in both novel and film jostle with each other for control of the narration. This is particularly the case with the novel's central protagonist, Emma Woodhouse, who "wants . . . to believe that she sees the order behind the colorful events, that she can in some way both record and reorder the events of her shifting community. . . . It offers the relief of authority, a fiction of control which everyone in the novel longs for, and ultimately fails to achieve."[32] Rachel Brownstein, similarly, has argued that struggles for power are central to Austen's work and are often played out in courtship through characters' use of verbal irony.[33] The opening scene of *The Mindy Project* similarly foregrounds the lead character's (thwarted) attempt at narrative authority. In fact, this power struggle is frequently played for laughs. For example, the show's second episode (1.2, "Hiring & Firing") also begins with a voice-over: opening over a dark screen, a dulcet-toned Mindy informs us that "if you look hard enough, you can see love everywhere" as we fade into a close-up of her staring dreamingly screen right as she holds onto the railing of a crowded subway. The camera then cuts to point-of-view shots of several couples as she continues what seems to be an internal monologue ("take my commute to work, every stage of romance is on display"), before being interrupted by her colleague and future love interest Danny (Chris Messina), who brusquely asks her to "please stop narrating." Here again, the voice-over serves the show's ironic pretense, as it pays homage to the romcom genre while poking fun at Mindy's overromanticism. The opening line is a near-direct quote from Richard Curtis's *Love Actually* (2002), which also opens with a voice-over meditation on love spoken by the British prime minister, played by Hugh Grant: "If you look for it, I've got a sneaky feeling you'll find that love actually is all around." In doing so, the voice-over thus allows Mindy to gain control of the narrative and reappropriate a famous quote associated with a powerful white man—before she is rudely interrupted, by another man. Indeed, with the exception of the pilot, it is most often white men who interrupt Mindy's opening monologues, such as colleague and future-husband Danny, her boyfriend Josh (1.6, "Thanksgiving"), or an exasperated Christmas-tree vendor (2.11, "Christmas Party Sex Trap").

Like Austen's novels, *The Mindy Project* therefore enhances "the difficulty of locating the . . . narrator" and does so by blurring the line between voice-over and dialogue.[34] Furthermore, this struggle for narrative control is both extra- and intradiegetic: the series pilot ends with Mindy being interrupted by Danny while she watches *When Harry Met Sally . . .* (1989)—a romcom classic penned by Nora Ephron, whose own debt to Austen was widely acknowledged. "I always think that all romantic comedies can be traced to *The Taming of the Shrew* or *Pride and Prejudice.* . . . Jane Austen had more of an effect on me than *It Happened One Night* did," Ephron famously stated.[35] Before we see him appear, Danny's voice can be heard yelling, "Who would actually do that? Billy, don't run!," as the camera lingers on the TV screen where Harry (Billy Crystal) is running to reunite with Sally (Meg Ryan). "I'd be like, 'Hey, man, I'm just trying to party with my friends and kiss some strangers at midnight. Just leave me alone,'" jokes Danny, before Mindy orders him to "never speak for Meg Ryan again." Like *27 Dresses*, *The Mindy Project* privileges the subjectivity of its female protagonist through the voice-over, but makes more explicit the gendered politics of narrative control.

On the other hand, as a number of critics have noted, the show generally evades the politics of race (despite its star, an Indian American, being one of few women of color to helm and star in a U.S. TV series).[36] Thus, Janani Subramanian notes that, while "in many ways, Mindy writing herself as a romantic comedy heroine with a string of white, male love interests is a radical act," Kaling's star persona "acknowledges and disavows race and ethnicity at the same time."[37] This was also noted by reviews of Kaling's 2019 film *Late Night*, a comedy centered around a female late-night talk-show host (Emma Thompson) who hires a young woman of color (played by Kaling herself) to improve her flagging ratings. The film again plays up the conflation between Kaling and her character, Molly, and Kaling has underlined how much of the film was based on her own experiences of sexism and racism at the start of her Hollywood career.[38] While it is effectively a call for more diversity in U.S. television (particularly writers' rooms),[39] critics have suggested that the film eschews the complexities of issues around diversity and representation in Hollywood in favor of a retrograde romantic plot.[40] By contrast, for example, the intersection of race and gender is at the heart of Haifaa al-Mansour's *Nappily Ever After* (2018), whose opening voice-over highlights the marginalization of women of color in popular romance media and also emphasizes the issue of control, this time with regards to the racist beauty standards to which Black women's bodies (and specifically hair) are subjected: "No fairy tale ever ended with the words 'nappily ever after,'" concludes heroine Violet (Sanaa Lathan) after a flashback of her teenage self being discriminated against because of her natural hair.

However, both Kaling and *The Mindy Project* have become increasingly vocal about issues of representation in the last years of the show's run. In a much-commented-on episode released shortly after the 2016 U.S. presidential election (5.12, "Mindy Lahiri Is a White Man"), Mindy dreams of being a white man after being unfairly passed up for a promotion.[41] This is one of several episodes which fit into the romcom's fantasy subgenre, as it pays homage to films such as 1993's *Groundhog Day* (5.8, "Hot Mess Time Machine"), 1998's *Sliding Doors*, and 2004's *13 Going on 30* (both in 4.1, "While I Was Sleeping"). Once again, the comedy comes from the interplay between the image- and soundtracks, as Mindy's voiced thoughts are superimposed over the images of a white man (played by Ryan Hansen) who behaves and speaks in a similar manner to her. By retaining Mindy's voice-over, the show allows for a power reversal in which a woman of color effectively gains control over a white man's body, from commanding his morning routine to deciding to use his privilege to support another woman of color obtain a promotion.

Additionally, much of the episode's comedy centers on discursive control and hinges on the different ways in which white men and women of color are listened to: while Mindy is frequently criticized by other characters throughout the series for being overly loud, chatty, and confident, Mindy-as-a-white-man's odd comments are treated as a display of wit: "You're so funny, Dr. L!" exclaims one of the nurses as Mindy's alter ego marvels when her colleagues actually listen to her. This flips on its head one of the show's most frequent sources of humor: Mindy's exceedingly high view of herself, which is often played for laughs. Even though the show had previously alluded to how this might tap into problematic race and gender stereotypes ("I think of you as a white man. Largely because of your entitlement," one of her colleagues tells her in 4.18, "Bernardo & Anita"), the direct comparison enabled by the body-swap episode drives home the double standards faced by women of color: while a white man is expected to exude confidence, an Indian American woman is mocked for doing the same thing. This also applies to Kaling outside of the show: during a roundtable at the Sundance Film Festival in 2015, she used a very similar phrase to describe herself when stating that "my parents raised me with the entitlement of a tall, blonde, white man."[42]

Indeed, the slippage between thought and speech blurs the line between the series' lead character, narrator, and author, who are all one and the same. In doing so, it also blurs the line between Mindy Kaling, the screenwriter and showrunner whose passion for romcom's escapist fantasies is well documented, and the "gullible" diegetic Mindy Lahiri, who truly believes in the romantic fantasies offered up by the genre.[43] *The Mindy Project*'s opening sequence foregrounds this conflation, as identical whip pans are used to move between young Mindy's tearful face and the romantic comedies she is watching on TV, and between adult Mindy and two of her love interests. In this way, the show creates a clear association between the pleasure of falling in love and the pleasure of consuming romantic fiction. Similarly, the beginning of Susan Johnson's *To All the Boys I've Loved Before* opens with a voice-over narration of a forbidden love ("we knew that it was wrong, that he was betrothed to my sister") over shots of a couple in period costume walking toward each other in a field; the voice-over is abruptly stopped as the female protagonist receives a pillow to the face, and what appeared to be interior monologue turns out to have been heroine Lara Jean (Lana Condor) reading a romance novel out loud and inserting herself into the narrative. This blurring of boundaries fits into the broader "oscillation between awareness and ironic ignorance" that Subramanian identifies as central to Kaling's star persona.[44] This ambiguity is indeed cultivated outside of the show: on the one hand, in her 2014 commencement speech at Harvard's School of Law, Kaling referred to the romantic comedy *Legally Blonde* (2001), which is set at the institution, as a "trenchant documentary."[45] At the same time, she has also famously described the romcom genre as a "subgenre of sci-fi, in which the world operates according to different rules than [in the] regular human world."[46] This conflation of character and creator (who share the same first name) offers a novel way of adapting Austen's double-voiced utterances to the film medium.

I do not wish to overstate here the direct influence of Jane Austen on contemporary romantic comedy. While Kaling herself has openly declared her indebtedness to Austen and *Pride and Prejudice* in particular, it would be reductive to imply that this is the case for all of contemporary romcom. What I want to suggest, rather, is that romantic comedy scholars can use Austen's work to reappraise the convention of voice-over in the genre, and to explore how it draws us into the narrative through the eyes of one protagonist, often with more humor than one might think. Additionally, concepts such as free indirect discourse raise important questions about subjectivity and narrative control that, when adopted by the contemporary romcom, is perhaps more overtly feminist than is often assumed. Such criticisms of the genre are encapsulated in a sequence from Netflix's romcom parody *Isn't It Romantic* (2019). The film begins with heroine Natalie (Rebel Wilson) ranting against the genre's sexism and clichés and singling out the voice-over as a particularly nefarious trope: "They always have some stupid voice-over that comes on to tell you what you're supposed to think." Will Gluck's *Friends with Benefits* (2013), meanwhile, makes a similar point with regards to another aspect of the genre's nondiegetic soundscape, as Jamie (Mila Kunis) explains that romcoms have "terrible music . . . so that you know how to *feel* every single second." Instead, I wish to suggest that, rather than forcing viewers into a specific (and, it is often implied, harmful) viewership position, the romcom voice-over on the contrary opens up a space for its heroines to claim narrative control.

Writing in the *New Yorker* in 2011, Mindy Kaling admitted to being embarrassed about openly enjoying romantic comedies, saying, "The genre has been so degraded in the past twenty years that saying you like romantic comedies is essentially an admission of mild stupidity."[47] Similarly, despite Austen's status as one of the best-loved authors in the British literary canon, her work too has suffered from being associated with the critically undervalued romance genre. Even some of her most ardent supporters have tended to separate the romance narrative of her novels from her writing style, with praise for the latter regularly balanced by disparagement of the former. For instance, the crime novelist P. D. James—a self-professed fan of Austen, and one of the guests on the BBC radio program quoted at the start of this chapter—once referred to Austen's *Emma* as "Mills and Boon written by a genius," referring to the mass-market U.K. romance series.[48]

Nonetheless, as the scholars who have pored over the intricacies of Austen's writing have demonstrated, romance and style are intrinsically joined in her work. Obvious examples include Mr. Darcy's two proposals to Elizabeth Bennet in *Pride and Prejudice*, both of which start with an exclamation reported in direct speech, such as "In vain have I struggled. It will not do. My feelings will not be repressed. You must allow me to tell you how

An Austenian ending between Molly (Mindy Kaling) and Tom (Reid Scott) in *Late Night*.

ardently I admire and love you" before moving to free indirect speech.[49] This restraint, Janis Stout argues, stems from "a belief in . . . the inadequacy of language for the expression of strong feeling."[50] After all their witty banter, Elizabeth and Darcy are rendered speechless by the exchange of their true feelings, and Austen's stepping back, as if to give them privacy, is central to the scene's intimate romance. Therefore, critics of the romcom might follow in the footsteps of Austen scholars and explore further how the romcom's formal elements contribute to the genre's enduring appeal. For example, a similar strategy is employed in Nisha Ganatra's *Late Night*, which includes a romantic subplot evocative of *Pride and Prejudice*: although TV writer Molly is at first attracted to the charming Charlie (Hugh Dancy), who turns out to be a player, she ends by falling in love with her prickly colleague Tom (Reid Scott). At first rude and dismissive, Tom grows to respect and praise Molly's writing abilities. The film ends with the taping of a show the couple has written together: there is no lengthy declaration of love—instead, the nondiegetic pop track drowns out the couple's dialogue as they laugh and talk together. And, rather than the big kiss in close-up, the camera cuts away from a medium close-up to a wide as Tom places a quick kiss on Molly's shoulder. Belying frequent criticisms of the romcom as "uncinematic," the film's restrained use of framing and sound underlines the content intimacy of Molly and Tom's romance in a very Austenian manner.

Notes

1. "Jane Austen—Pride and Prejudice," *World Book Club*, BBC World Service, January 6, 2013.
2. Nancy K. Miller, *The Heroine's Text: Readings in the French and English Novel, 1722–1782* (New York: Columbia University Press, 1980); Kathrina Glitre, *Hollywood Romantic Comedy: States of the Union, 1934–1965* (Manchester: Manchester University Press, 2006), 19.
3. Mindy Kaling, *Why Not Me?* (London: Ebury, 2015), 24.
4. Glitre, *Hollywood Romantic*, 27.
5. See, for example, Suzanne Ferriss and Mallory Young, *Chick Flicks: Contemporary Women at the Movies* (New York: Routledge, 2008); Stacey Abbott and Deborah Jermyn, eds., *Falling in Love Again: Romantic Comedy in Contemporary Cinema* (New York: I. B. Tauris, 2009); Alison Winch, "We Can Have It All: The Girlfriend Flick," *Feminist Media*

Studies 12, no. 1 (2012): 69–82; and Mari Ruti, *Feminist Film Theory and Pretty Woman* (New York: Bloomsbury Academic, 2016).

6 Celestino Deleyto, *The Secret Life of Romantic Comedy* (Manchester: Manchester University Press, 2009), 24.

7 Claire Mortimer, *Romantic Comedy* (London: Routledge, 2010), 8; Hilary Radner, *Neo-Feminist Cinema: Girly Films, Chick Flicks, and Consumer Culture* (New York: Routledge, 2011), 39.

8 Sarah Kozloff, "About a Clueless Boy and Girl: Voice-Over Narration in Contemporary Romantic Comedy," *Cinephile* 8, no. 1 (Spring 2012): 5.

9 Jennifer Frey, "Jane Austen: A Love Story," *Washington Post*, August 22, 2004, www.washingtonpost.com/wp-dyn/articles/A22819-2004Aug21.html.

10 Hilary Schor, "Emma, Interrupted: Speaking Jane Austen in Fiction and Film," in *Jane Austen on Screen*, ed. Gina MacDonald and Andrew MacDonald (Cambridge: Cambridge University Press, 2003), 144–74.

11 Amy Nicholson, "Who Killed the Romantic Comedy?," *LA Weekly*, February 24, 2014, https://www.laweekly.com/who-killed-the-romantic-comedy/; David Canfield, "The Romantic Comedy Is Having a Revolution—And It's Happening on TV," IndieWire, July 6, 2015, www.indiewire.com/2015/07/the-romantic-comedy-is-having-a-revolution-and-its-happening-on-tv-60577.

12 Schor, "Emma, Interrupted," 151.

13 Susannah Fullerton, *Happily Ever After: Celebrating Jane Austen's* Pride and Prejudice (London: Frances Lincoln, 2013), 40.

14 Fullerton, *Happily Ever After*, 39–40; Anne Waldron Neumann, "Characterization and Comment in *Pride and Prejudice*: Free Indirect Discourse and 'Double-Voiced' Verbs of Speaking, Thinking, and Feeling," *Style* 20, no. 3 (Fall 1986): 377–81.

15 Jane Austen, *Pride and Prejudice*, ed. R. W. Chapman, 3rd rev. ed. (Oxford: Oxford University Press, 1982), 66.

16 Sarah R. Morrisson, "*Emma* Minus Its Narrator: Decorum and Class Consciousness in Film Versions of the Novel," Persuasions Online, Occasional Papers, no. 3 (Fall 1999), www.jasna.org/persuasions/on-line/opno3/morrison.html (accessed September 8, 2020).

17 Nora Nachumi, "'As If!' Translating Austen's Ironic Narrator to Film," in *Jane Austen in Hollywood*, ed. Linda Troost and Sayre Greenfield, 2nd ed. (Lexington: University Press of Kentucky, 2001), 136.

18 James MacDowell, *Irony in Film* (London: Palgrave Macmillan, 2016), 109.
19 Sarah Kozloff, *Invisible Storytellers: Voice-Over Narration in American Fiction Film* (Berkeley: University of California Press, 1988), 103.
20 It is noteworthy that both series' heroines are writers (columnist or diarist), and both series are adaptions of magazine columns, later published as novels. For an analysis of the significance of female authorship in contemporary women-centered popular cinema, see Marie-Alix Thouaille, "The Single Woman Author on Film Screening Postfeminism," PhD diss., University of East Anglia, 2018.
21 Austen, *Pride and Prejudice*, 3. For an analysis of irony in the opening sentence, see Lilian R. Furst, *Fictions of Romantic Irony in European Narrative, 1760–1857* (London: Palgrave Macmillan, 1984), 50.
22 Neumann, "Characterization and Comment," 366.
23 Morrisson, "Emma Minus Its Narrator."
24 Kaling, *Why Not Me?*, 75.
25 Kozloff, *Invisible Storytellers*, 106.
26 MacDowell, *Irony in Film*, 99, 106.
27 Furst, *Fictions of Romantic Irony*, 49–50; Rachel M. Brownstein, "Jane Austen: Irony and Authority," *Women's Studies* 15, nos. 1–3 (October 1988): 61.
28 Deborah Jermyn, "I Love NY: The Rom-com's Love Affair with New York City," in *Falling In Love Again: Romantic Comedy in Contemporary Cinema* (New York: I. B. Tauris, 2009), 9–24.
29 Kozloff, *Invisible Storytellers*, 112.
30 Perhaps less necessary once the heroine's control of the narrative has been firmly established?
31 Schor, "Emma, Interrupted," 146.
32 Schor, 149.
33 Brownstein, "Jane Austen," 57.
34 Schor, "Emma, Interrupted," 147.
35 Catherine Shoard, "Nora Ephron—a Career in Clips," *Guardian*, June 27, 2012, www.theguardian.com/film/filmblog/2012/jun/27/nora-ephron-career-clips.
36 Ayesha Siddiqi, Heben Nigatu, and Durga Chew-Bose, "A 'Mindy Project' Roundtable," Buzzfeed, April 1, 2014, www.buzzfeed.com/aasiddiqi/a-mindy-project-roundtable; Rebecca Nicholson, "Mindy Kaling: 'I Wasn't

Considered Attractive or Funny Enough to Play Myself,'" *Guardian*, June 1, 2014, www.theguardian.com/tv-and-radio/2014/jun/01/mindy-kaling-project.

37 Janani Subramanian, "*The Mindy Project*: South Asians and Television Multiculturalism," in *The Millennials on Film and Television: Essays on the Politics of Popular Culture*, ed. Betty Kaklamanidou and Margaret Tally (Jefferson, NC: McFarland, 2014), 72, 61.

38 Maureen Lee Lenker, "Mindy Kaling Fires Back at TV Academy for Being Singled Out during *The Office* Emmy Nominations," Entertainment Weekly, October 9, 2019, ew.com/tv/2019/10/09/mindy-kaling-fires-back-tv-academy-the-office-emmy-nominations; Daniel D'Addario, "Actors on Actors: Mindy Kaling and Constance Wu Talk About Their Craft," *Variety*, November 17, 2019, variety.com/2019/film/actors/actors-on-actors-mindy-kaling-constance-wu-1203406691.

39 The lack of diversity in writers' rooms, in particular, has received significant coverage and push back in the last year or so, as demonstrated via the #showusyourroomchallenge hashtag on Twitter.

40 Jourdain Searles, "In 'Late Night,' Comedy's Whiteness Is a Backdrop for a Love Story," Bitch Media, 2019, www.bitchmedia.org/article/late-night-love-story-review (accessed September 8, 2020).

41 Hanh Nguyen, "*The Mindy Project*'s Lang Fisher on Writing Mindy as a White Man in the Age of Trump," IndieWire, March 14, 2017, www.indiewire.com/2017/03/the-mindy-project-lang-fisher-white-man-ryan-hansen-1201793611; Kate Stanhope, "*The Mindy Project* White Privilege Episode," *Hollywood Reporter*, March 14, 2017, www.hollywoodreporter.com/live-feed/mindy-project-white-privilege-episode-983629.

42 Jarett Wieselman, "The Secret Behind Mindy Kaling's Success Is Incredible," BuzzFeed, January 24, 2015, www.buzzfeednews.com/article/jarettwieselman/mindy-kaling-shared-a-truly-amazing-secret-to-her-success.

43 Kaling has long been vocal about her appreciation for romantic comedy. A recent Buzzfeed article referred to her as the "queen of romantic comedy": Casey Rackham, "Mindy Kaling Has Written All Of Us A List Of Her Favorite Romcoms," BuzzFeed, https://www.buzzfeed.com/caseyrackham/mindy-kaling-knows-rom-coms; see also Emma Rosenblum, "Vulture Watches *You've Got Mail* With Mindy Kaling," Vulture,

September 23, 2010, www.vulture.com/2010/09/watch_youve_got_mail_with_mind.html; Mindy Kaling, "Flick Chicks," *New Yorker*, October 3, 2011, www.newyorker.com/humor/2011/10/03/111003sh_shouts_kaling.

44 Subramanian, "*Mindy Project*," 62.
45 Quoted in in Kaling, *Why Not Me?*, 207.
46 Mindy Kaling, "Flick Chicks."
47 Kaling, "Flick Chicks."
48 P. D. James, *Talking about Detective Fiction* (London: Faber & Faber, 2010), 17.
49 Janis P. Stout, "Jane Austen's Proposal Scenes and the Limitations of Language," *Studies in the Novel* 14, no. 4 (1982): 324.
50 Stout, "Jane Austen's Proposal Scenes," 325.

4

"Third-Act Romances" in Contemporary American Film and Television

Betty Kaklamanidou

The Third-Age Representation Trend of the 2010s

Imagine this film scene: a woman visits a male neighbor at night and, after exchanging the necessary pleasantries, she hesitantly yet decisively asks him, "Would you be interested in coming to my house sometime to sleep with me?" You might be slightly taken aback by the light gender subversion of the exchange; after all, such sexual proposals in cinema usually come from male characters—for example, Ned's (William Hurt) vulgar "Hey, lady, ya wanna fuck?" in *Body Heat* (1981), and Austin Powers's (Mike Myers) humorous "Shall we shag now or shall we shag later?" in *Austin Powers: International Man of Mystery* (1997). How would you feel, then, if you knew the phrase above is spoken by eighty-year-old female protagonist Addie (Jane Fonda) and addressed to octogenarian Louis (Robert Redford) during the film's establishing sequence in the recent romantic drama *Our Souls at Night* (2017)?

This film is one of the latest titles in an international trend that began in the early 2010s and gained momentum after 2015, including a number of films and TV shows starring well-known actors in their sixties, seventies, and eighties—the "third age," as it has come to be known. Titles such as *Hot in Cleveland* (TV Land, 2010–2015), *The Best Exotic Marigold Hotel* (2011), *Last Tango in Halifax* (BBC One, 2012–2016), *Unfinished Song/Song for Marion* (2012), *Last Vegas* (2013), *The Love Punch* (2013), *And So It Goes* (2014), *Elsa & Fred* (2014), *Love Is Strange* (2014), *45 Years* (2015), *Grace and Frankie* (Netflix, 2015–), *Grandma* (2015), *The Intern* (2015), *Lady in the Van* (2015), *The Second Best Exotic Marigold Hotel* (2015), *Youth* (2015), *Hello, My Name Is Doris* (2016), *Going in Style* (2017), and *Our Souls at*

Night not only bring together celebrated actors, but also offer multilayered and complicated narratives that have rarely appeared before on either the big or small screen.

Indeed, as some of the titles above reveal, older characters now abound in contemporary film and television. From buddy comedies and heist movies (*Last Vegas*, *Going in Style*) to ensemble pieces and "female friendship" sitcoms (*The Best Exotic Marigold Hotel*, *Grace and Frankie*), these productions deploy the familiar conventions of their respective genres, adapting them to the age of their protagonists. The interpretation of these audiovisual texts demands that we place each title within its larger generic cosmos in order to understand its distinctive revision of genre norms. Thus, *Grace and Frankie* can be situated in the sitcom tradition, especially those TV comedies that center on the adventures of two women, regardless of their age—for example, *Laverne & Shirley* (ABC, 1976–1983), *Kate & Allie* (CBS, 1984–1989), and *2 Broke Girls* (CBS, 2011–2017). Similarly, *Elsa & Fred* and *And So It Goes* belong in the "unlikely couple" tradition of film romance, from *The King and I* (1956) and *The Way We Were* (1973) to *Knocked Up* (2007), in which the formation of the heterosexual couple depends on the man and woman overcoming their inherent differences in personality and sociocultural background.

At this point, it is essential to define what I mean by "older characters." As concepts of stages of life are socially constructed to serve specific sociopolitical practices, "old age" has signified different things at different time periods. For instance, Chris Gilleard and P. Higgs reveal that in 1941 the U.S. National Institute of Health began "research in gerontology, . . . direct(ing) attention particularly upon the normal processes of late maturity, approximately the period between 40 and 60 years of age."[1] Almost 80 years later, this taxonomy sounds antiquated, if not outright amusing, as the threshold of old age has been placed much later, thanks to the advancement of technology, quality of life, medicine, and insights within the field of gerontology. For the last few decades, old age has been systematized, reevaluated, and segmented into specific age ranges. In fact, what we now call the "third age" can be further subdivided into the third and fourth ages. While the third age is associated with active "agency and choice,"[2] the fourth age is a state "beyond any possibility of agency, human intimacy, or social exchange."[3] This chapter adopts Gilleard and Higg's definition of the third age "as a cultural field," one characterized by "the development of generational lifestyles whose origins can be traced to 1960s youth culture with its emphasis upon choice, autonomy and self-expression. As this generation has grown older, it has carried these dispositions over into later life."[4] Therefore, my emphasis is on narratives whose characters have already celebrated their sixtieth, seventieth, or even eightieth birthdays and whose energy and activity levels, as well as financial status—whether in the form of pension or savings—allow them to enjoy their everyday lives and affords them substantial scope for "agency and choice."

A number of cultural and media sites have already noted this recent wave of third-age narratives.[5] As mentioned, these films and TV shows are a varied group and invite a series of queries on representation, production factors, and audience demographics: How has the representation of aging and the aged changed from the arguably stereotypical depictions of the past? Who are the filmmakers/TV creators? Who finances these texts? Why are they made in such numbers today? Is it that they satisfy a niche audience of baby boomers (the older ones being past their seventies and the younger ones reaching their sixties) and can therefore be economically viable because their majority are low-budgeted independent productions? Is it that in today's culture older performers retain the fan bases they built earlier on? Does the inevitability of death cast a cloud on these narratives? How do these works mediate gender, class, and race issues in a person's twilight years? Is it still the case, as Amir Cohen-Shalev and Esther-Lee Marcus note in their discussion of similar narratives before 2007, that "the filmmakers do not make an attempt to tackle the psychological and social realities of old age, but to protect viewers, most of them not old, from exposure to its harsher side," and that, while representations of old characters do exist, they are not "realistically satisfying pictures"?[6] Do the older men-driven films outnumber the older women-centered films? Do these titles bring anything new in terms of narrative structure or their use of genre conventions?

The questions above not only show how important and multifaceted this kind of visual representation is, but also merit book-length discussions. The aim of this chapter is necessarily much more modest. I focus my investigation on three U.S. produced and/or coproduced films and one TV show: *I'll See You in My Dreams, Hello, My Name Is Doris, Our Souls at Night,* and *Grace and Frankie.* These narratives predominantly star female characters, aged from their mid-sixties to their early eighties, who are active and may even be employed and who, despite acknowledging some limitations that come with age, still embrace love, companionship, and friendship, as well as sexual activities and fantasies. After initially situating the films in their industrial and sociopolitical context, I examine the distinctive characteristics of what I call "third-act romances." While scholarly monographs and journal articles on the subject of the representation of aging and the aged and the circulation of images of same in the media are also increasing in numbers, the literature on the representation of romance between older characters remains limited.[7] My goal here is to contextualize this particular group of films and TV shows centered on third-age romantic relationships by discussing their production, distribution, and reception and examining their place among contemporary screen narratives. My discussion of the narrative strategies deployed by these texts will reveal a set of tropes characteristic of the third-act romance and explore the function of these works as optimistic mediating stories for their viewers. Of the four texts under discussion, only *Our Souls at Night* gives equal narrative time to its male and female protagonists, although it is mainly the female protagonist's action that moves the plot forward. Although this narrative choice invites a gender discussion already taken up in the popular media, my analysis focuses instead on distinguishing the main narrative patterns of these texts and discussing the representation of the third-act romance as a powerful way to increase the visibility of sexual activity among older individuals.[8]

The Rise of the 50–60+ Viewers vs. the "Coveted" Teenage Audience

One of the truisms pervading film criticism regards Hollywood's insistence on catering to the desires and tastes of the male teenage viewer. It is true that ever since Hollywood discovered the youth market in the 1950s, it hasn't ceased to exploit it. In the blockbuster age, ushered in by *Jaws* (1975), studio filmmaking is still typically understood to target the coveted 18–24 demographic. But does it? The MPAA 2017 annual survey reveals some interesting results regarding the 43 million "frequent" moviegoers the researchers identified within the U.S. market and divided into seven age groups. The coveted 18–24 age group is actually in the penultimate place, with 5.2 million, ahead only of the 3–11 age group (with 3.3. million). The top three of frequent moviegoers is the 25–39 age group (11.1 million), the 40–49 age group (6.5 million), and the 60+ age group (6.2 million), while fourth and fifth place are occupied, respectively, by the 50–59 age group

(5.6 million) and the 12–17 age group (5.2 million). The numbers are clear and provided by the same trade association responsible for the continuing investment in youth-driven blockbuster franchises. Teenagers can no longer be depended upon as majority filmgoers, as they are surpassed by five age groups, four of which are older viewers. The 2017 MPAA statistics, which corroborate the impressive increase in older film viewers in the last two decades, also agree with a recent study showing that 50+ filmgoers have "increased by a striking 67% in the USA between 1995 and 2011."[9] The data explain to an extent the production, distribution, and exhibition of films and TV shows with older characters. Hollywood is a business, and, so long as it identifies a new and potentially viable niche audience (in our case, senior citizens who still regularly attend theatres and would be interested in seeing themselves represented on screen), it will try to satisfy that audience's needs and desires. In other words, as Josephine Dolan observes, "film makers are responding to a notable demographic shift in the composition of cinema audiences which are increasingly composed of older people."[10]

The overwhelming majority of films starring older characters are independent, low-budget productions, the distribution of which is typically confined to the United States.[11] Yet several of these titles have become both indie hits and critical darlings. For instance, *Hello, My Name Is Doris* won the Audience Award at the 2015 South by Southwest Film Festival, earned more than $14 million on a $1-million budget, and currently holds an 83-percent approval rating on Rotten Tomatoes. *I'll See You in My Dreams* and *Our Souls at Night* hold scores of 93 and 92 percent respectively on Rotten Tomatoes, while the former has also been nominated for a number of awards. The establishment of the Movies for Grownups Awards by the AARP (formerly known as the American Association of Retired Persons) in 2002—which celebrates "an array of actors, films and filmmakers whose work has particular relevance to a 50-plus audience," according to the official website—is further proof of the economic viability of the older audience.[12] In addition, this data can, in part, explain the adoption of this specific demographic as main characters of an impressive number of recent narratives by the U.S. film and TV industry, which now views productions about older characters, predominantly aimed at similar age groups, as a sound investment.

By slightly altering the grammar of cinematic romance, the narratives I examine here take the genre in new directions. The representation of romance has followed the same syntax since the invention of the film medium, and centuries more if we trace back the origins of romance to the French troubadours of the Middle Ages: two humans meet and fall in love, face an obstacle, and either overcome it and live happily—and, in most cases, heteronormatively—ever after (resulting in a romantic comedy) or not (resulting in a romantic drama). The innumerable variations of this simple pattern have produced countless romantic narratives that still move and engage viewers. The third-act film and TV romances alter only one aspect of this two-human pairing; instead of showing them in their teenage years or early to mid-adulthood, it presents them predominantly after their sixties and occasionally even beyond their seventies. It is exactly this seemingly trivial revision in the genre's semantic field that generates new variations in an already successfully elaborated syntax and drives the evolution of the genre. Therefore, the next section is dedicated to distinguishing those narrative traits (from actions to narrative atmosphere), assisted mainly by Roland Barthes's categorization of narrative's functions.

Semantic Changes to an Old Syntax: Loss and Sex

The first observation regarding the syntax of the screen romances under discussion is that the characteristic narrative structure of romance does not change simply because the characters are older: two people meet, become romantically involved, have to overcome obstacles, and either succeed or fail at couple-formation. Yet, even though there are actually no key alterations except for the central characters' age, the texts are not quite the romances we are used to. So, what is different about these third-act romances? Does the age of the protagonists transform the narrative, and, if so, in what ways?

In his seminal 1966 article "Introduction to the Structural Analysis of Narrative," Barthes distinguishes two main categories of units in any given narrative: "functions" and "indices." Functions are subdivided into "cardinal functions" (main plot actions) and "catalysers" (secondary actions that assist the development of the cardinal ones). The category of indices comprises the "informants" (pieces of information with direct meaning—e.g., names, places) and the "indices proper," which have to do with the narrative "atmosphere"—that is, information on characters' age, look, profession, psychology, and descriptive passages that set a certain mood. In Barthes's own words, "Indices involve an activity of deciphering; the reader is to learn to know a character or an atmosphere."[13] André Gardies notes that indices are fundamental during the establishing sequences of films: "The beginning of films . . . disperses the necessary information, but most importantly it confirms the narrative status quo and determines the rules of the game."[14] In what follows, I examine the beginnings of the aforementioned three films and TV show in detail to distinguish potential emerging patterns due to the change in the semantic side of the romantic narrative; in other words, I study the impact of the characters' age on the traditional syntax of romance.

Interestingly, all the introductory sequences of the three films consist of three parts/scenes. In the first sequence of *I'll See You in My Dreams*, we observe retiree Carol's (Blythe Danner) daily routine with her dog, Hazel. She wakes up at 6 a.m., feeds her companion, has some lunch, plays cards with three girlfriends at a retirement community where she socializes but refuses to live, and is back in bed by 11 p.m. The second part begins with the heroine in bed again at night, but this time Hazel seems to be ill, and Carol has to rush her to the vet and unfortunately say goodbye to her there. Despite the loss, the introduction's third part, which also serves as the initiation of the plot after the establishment of the place and central characters, shows Carol continuing with her daily routine. She soon befriends Lloyd (Martin Starr), the young man responsible for cleaning the pool at her complex, and she also starts dating the more age-appropriate Bill (Sam Elliott), a handsome guy from the retirement community, who happens to have the same name as her late husband. Both of Carol's relationships with these men develop organically, out of ordinary interactions. She meets Lloyd in her backyard and discovers that they share a love of music—they both used to sing in bands—while Bill flirts with her and asks her out after bumping into her a couple of times at the retirement community.

In *Hello, My Name Is Doris*'s first scene, we meet eccentric hoarder Doris (Sally Field) at her mother's funeral. The second scene comes immediately after the service, when Doris is met by her brother and his wife, and their conversation reveals that she was taking care of her mother for years, is single, and does not agree with her brother about selling the house and dividing the money between them. The third sequence follows Doris as she goes to work and sees a young man in a crowded elevator. She is instantly attracted to him and dares to steal a pencil from his bag. Surprisingly, she, along with all of her colleagues, is soon thereafter introduced to him at the office because he, John (Max Greenfield), has accepted a new executive position at the company. Doris is mesmerized and entertains a brief romantic fantasy until reality brings her back to her cubicle. The rest of the plot concerns Doris trying and succeeding at befriending John, but with the ultimate goal of making him fall in love with her.

Our Souls at Night opts for a slightly different approach, as the first scene spatially orients viewers with the use of an American folk melody and shots of a small town somewhere in Colorado around sundown during the credits, yet the three-scene/sequence structure remains. The second scene follows an older man having dinner alone in a modest house, washing his spoon and plate, and then reading the paper while listening to the weather on television. Louis (Redford) is initially surprised when his long-time neighbor Addie (Fonda) knocks on his door, but is completely astonished when the latter proposes they sleep together at night so that they both feel less lonely after the loss of their spouses in the third scene. Gradually, the two protagonists come to know each other and to develop intimate feelings, until Addie's grandson comes into the picture and her son's problems cast a shadow over their newfound relationship.

Finally, in *Grace and Frankie*, Grace (Jane Fonda) and Frankie (Lily Tomlin) are at a fancy California restaurant to celebrate what they think is the retirement of their husbands and law partners, Robert (Martin Sheen) and Sol (Sam Waterston), only to be confronted with the latter's revelation that they have been a couple for two decades, and that they have finally decided to leave their wives. Grace and Frankie not only have to recover from the shock of this revelation, but also need to actively restructure their lives. I could argue that the show's first episode, ironically titled "The End," also follows a three-part opening (Grace and Frankie meet, they have dinner with their husbands where the surprising announcement fundamentally upsets their reality, and the two couples return home), but only thematically because the third part involves two separate scenes (the two couples in their respective homes fighting, albeit at what seems the same time).

Regardless of differences in setting, actors, and mise-en-scène, the opening sequences described share a fundamental element: that of loss. As such, the atmosphere that is initially constructed—the indices proper, according to Barthes—is somber, touching, and affective, as viewers are immediately directed to care about the suffering character(s). A typical film romance revolving around young protagonists often begins with a "meet cute," a structural device that introduces the two protagonists in a humorous, unexpected, or surprising way. The third-act romances add a new ingredient in the genre's semantic field by beginning with the representation of a loss, predominantly death. Although loss can be either physical (the death of a loved one) or symbolic (losing one's job), the term is most closely linked to death, because "death is probably the only type of loss that can never be recovered."[15] Indeed, three of the four stories explored in this chapter use death as their narrative motivation, while only *Grace and Frankie* opts for a symbolic loss (divorce). Regardless of its nature, loss becomes the plot trigger, an event to be overcome but also a reason to move forward in life, instead of an event or situation that, as is typically the case in narrative, is negotiated in the middle of a story or constitutes its ending.

In the semantic spectrum of the third-act romance cycle, loss replaces a number of other romance-instigating possibilities, such as a change of jobs (*Friends with Benefits*, 2011), a trial separation (*Crazy, Stupid, Love*, 2011), or a mistaken identity (*You've Got Mail*, 1998). After all, most people in their seventies are retirees, so the obstacles they may face in a fictional narrative are vastly different from those devised by writers of romances that center on younger men and women. Of course, our characters are also without partners (they are widowed, separated, or, more rarely, single), which allows the quest for romance to become the narrative goal of the protagonist. Yet loss remains the sine qua non of entering the third-act romance universe.

A second key point regarding third-act romances revolves around their representation of sex. In their long history, romances and especially romantic comedies have had a rather unstable relationship with the depiction of sex, due to censorship issues and the surrounding sociopolitical context. Suffice it to say that, after a period in the late 1960s and 1970s when romantic comedies often addressed questions of sex and sexual satisfaction with directness, the majority of rom coms from the 1980s and 1990s "greatly de-emphasize[d] sexuality."[16] Yet again, the new millennium witnessed a change in the culture's sexual mores, which, along with the social context of Web 2.0, gave birth to a cycle I call the "romantico-sexual" romcom, including such titles as *Friends with Benefits* (2011), *No Strings Attached* (2011), and *Trainwreck* (2015)—in other words, romantic comedies in which sex is represented on-screen and the central couples are established well before the final scene.[17]

Sex is also prominent in third-act romances. Our female protagonists, as well as their male objects of desire (with the exception of Doris, whose relationship exists only in fantasy), treat sexual intimacy and intercourse with a timidity and anxiety that is often encountered in representations of much younger individuals, especially inexperienced teenagers and young adults. In *I'll See You in My Dreams*, before Carol kisses Bill in her living room after their first date, she confesses her apprehension about being "out of practice." Their kiss is immediately followed by a long shot of both of them in bed; the camera lingers in a medium shot while they laugh and talk about how pleasurable the experience was after such a long time. The same happens in *Our Souls at Night*: Louis has taken Addie to a fancy hotel, and, after they enjoy a lovely dinner and a sensuous dance, a cut moves us to their room. Addie is waiting in the bed—it appears she is naked underneath the sheets—and Louis gets out of the bathroom in his pajamas. Although both characters seem to want to consummate their relationship, their verbal and physical exchange, as Louis gently lies down next to Addie, is indicative of both their excitement and hesitation. The camera shows them in a medium close-up as Addie unbuttons Louis's pajama top, indicating her willingness to move forward. Louis seems more uncertain, and, after a few seconds, he confesses that "it has been a while" as he caresses Addie's bare arm. Addie comforts him by replying that they "don't need to rush" and "can take [their] time," and the scene ends with the couples' kiss, accompanied by Etta James's 1960 hit "A Sunday Kind of Love." The song provides the bridge between the kiss and the next scene, in which both protagonists drive home. We listen to the melody while we see both Addie's and Louis's stolen glances at each other and their smiles, connoting their satisfaction.

Finally, in episode 8 of *Grace and Frankie*'s first season, aptly titled "The Sex," Grace is getting ready to sleep with the man she has been dating, Guy (Craig T. Nelson). Although, once again, we hear that Grace is anxious because of her long "abstinence" period, the long-form TV narrative allows for a complex representation of both sexual activity and the description of it; as Grace describes her lovemaking with Guy to Frankie the next morning, insert scenes show the couple having sex and talking, in a cleverly revised *Annie Hall*-esque editing style. Grace tells Frankie that Guy "has a very gentle touch," while the insert shot reveals her screaming from pain; Grace adds, "It was a delicate dance, really," and the insert shot shows Guy on top of Grace asking, "Are you there yet?," which elicits the response "Where?

Making love in *Our Souls at Night*.

Oh, never mind." This humorous alternation between Grace's obviously inventive answers to her friend and the clearly unpleasant sexual experience revealed in the insert shots ends with Frankie asking her roommate about whether or not she climaxed, leading the conversation to the subject of female orgasm. In subsequent episodes, *Grace and Frankie* includes many more sex scenes and open discussions about sexuality after your seventies.[18] Season 3, for instance, finds both heroines enjoying sex and masturbation; in season 4, Grace enjoys a fulfilling romantic and sexual relationship with a much younger man. Although the differences between the long-form TV format and the limited time of a feature movie, as well as those changes that originate from generic conventions, in addition to specific industrial parameters, could account for the reasons behind the films' rather uncomplicated depiction of their older characters' sexual activity and television's much richer and nuanced representation, this discussion goes beyond the scope of this chapter and should be reserved for a detailed examination.

Taken together, these scenes are not only illuminating but also refreshing, tender, revealing, and even humorous. First, they allow viewers to see that senior citizens can also be sexually active. Second, even though the (re)introduction of sex as a semantic element, even in PG-rated fashion, does not alter the main syntax of third-act romances, it does enrich the indices proper (i.e., narrative atmosphere), by injecting the narrative with more intimacy, humor, and a sense of narrative completion as well as an endorsement of the healthfulness of late-life sexual activity. For the depiction of older characters' sexuality, while rare, can have a significant social impact. According to a 2019 study on late-life sexuality, the researchers found that one of three major themes that emerged from the 15 interviewed physicians and certified sexologists was how the lack of media visibility of sexuality in later life contributes to a host of continuing problems that surround this issue. One interviewee remarked:

> To increase social awareness, the subject needs to be presented in the media. But, if there is no financial interest, it won't be. For example, sexual function was brought up in the nineties, because they had Viagra . . . but for women's sexuality there is no solution . . . so then we have to wait for a star or a producer that will, once every ten years make a film about older adults' sexuality, like that beautiful movie with Diane Keaton and Jack Nicholson.[19]

This interviewee refers to *Something's Gotta Give* (2003), written and directed by Nancy Meyers, one of the first mainstream and widely popular romcoms to focus on the romantic entanglements of a woman in her late fifties (Keaton) with two men (Nicholson and Keanu Reeves). The authors fittingly note that media representation can help counter long-standing stereotypes, such as depicting "older adults as asexual and not interested in

Grace (Jane Fonda) and Nick (Peter Gallagher) in season 4 of *Grace and Frankie*.

sexual intimacy." They add that "the media have the power to promote the importance of sexuality in later life by presenting older adults expressing their sexuality in movies, shows, ads and campaigns."[20] Representation matters, and the commercial viability of films and TV shows depicting third-act romances suggests that this form will both flourish and continue to perform important cultural work going forward.

Third-act romances constitute a booming recent trend in both independent American filmmaking and television, especially in the 2010s. Their production is linked to the existence of a niche audience (mainly baby boomers) interested in these narratives, popular and still bankable older actors, and filmmakers and TV showrunners willing to subvert the stereotypical representations of older characters. For instance, *I'll See You in My Dreams*'s writer-director Brett Haley notes, "I think a lot of movies about older people are about looking back ... with regret ... and I wanted to make a movie about older characters where they're looking forward."[21] Marta Kauffman, cocreator of *Grace and Frankie*, reveals that one of the main narrative goals of the show was "to deal with ... sexuality in your 70s," because "once you get past a certain point, for women in particular, people dismiss you as a sexual being."[22] Finally, in 2016, Vulture's Mark Harris posted an article titled "Actresses Over 60 Are the New Box-Office Powerhouse,"[23] while three days later Flavorwire's Lara Zarum added old-age romance to her listing of recent TV trends.[24]

My discussion underscores how contemporary third-act romances in both film and television help the genres of romance and romantic comedy remain vital and even constitute a move forward for the romantic comedy genre, whose popularity—at least in mainstream releases since the 2010s—seems to have withered. Although the narratives I explore use a classic generic syntax, their semantic changes (age, loss, sexual intimacy among older people) bring a fresh perspective to viewers, while offering an optimistic tale bound to real-life circumstances. The message of these narratives is clear, whether their viewers' age coincides with that of the protagonists or whether the films are watched by younger audiences who get a glimpse of the unexamined potential third age can bring. Jane Fonda summarizes best the power of these third-act romances in an interview about *Our Souls at Night*: "Don't let yourself think into loneliness and sadness, even if you're close to the end of life. Always take a leap of faith and go for love, and go for closeness and relationships."[25]

Notes

1 Chris Gilleard and P. Higgs, "Aging without Agency: Theorizing the Fourth Age," *Aging & Mental Health* 14, no. 2 (2010): 121.
2 Gilleard and Higgs, "Aging without Agency."
3 Gilleard and Higgs, 125.
4 Gilleard and Higgs, 122.
5 See, for example, Jason Bailey, "How Senior Citizens Became Independent Film's Most Powerful Audience," Flavorwire, March 9, 2016, www.flavorwire.com/564907/how-senior-citizens-became-independent-films-most-powerful-audience; Lara Zarum, "Trendspotting: Old-Age Romance on TV," Flavorwire, August 4, 2016; www.flavorwire.com/584832/trendspotting-old-age-romance-on-tv; Mark Harris, "Actresses Over 60 Are the New Box-Office Powerhouses," Vulture, August 1, 2016, www.vulture.com/2016/08/actresses-over-60-are-now-box-office-powerhouses.html; and Jordan Crucchiola, "Building the Old-Guys-Gone-Wild Movie Dream Team," Vulture, April 7, 2017, www.vulture.com/2017/04/going-in-style-and-the-old-guys-gone-wild-movie-dream-cast.html.
6 Amir Cohen-Shalev and Esther-Lee Marcus, "Golden Years and Silver Screens: Cinematic Representations of Old Age," *Journal of Aging, Humanities, and the Arts* 1, nos. 1–2 (June 2007): 86.
7 See, among others, Amir Cohen-Shalev, *Visions of Aging: Images of the Elderly in Film* (Sussex: Sussex University Press, 2012); Pamela H. Gravagne, *The Becoming of Age: Cinematic Visions of Mind, Body, and Identity in Later Life* (Jefferson, NC: McFarland, 2013); Nicola Evans, "No Genre for Old Men? The Politics of Aging and the Male Action Hero," *Canadian Journal of Film Studies* 24, no. 1 (Spring 2015): 25–44; and Timothy Shary and Nancy McVittie, *Fade to Gray: Aging in American Cinema* (Austin: University of Texas Press, 2016).
8 See, for instance, Amber Heckler, "The 'Silver' Screen: Top TV Shows Starring Women Over 50," After55, August 22, 2016, www.after55.com/blog/tv-shows-starring-women-over-50/; and Rachel Simon, "Why Movies About Women Over 60 Are So Beloved by Millennial Women," Bustle, May 2018, www.bustle.com/p/why-movies-about-women-over-60-are-so-beloved-by-millennial-women-9092891.

9   Barnes and Cieply in Deborah Jermyn, "'Grey Is the New Green'? Gauging Age(ing) in Hollywood's Upper Quadrant Female Audience, *The Intern* [2015], and the Discursive Construction of 'Nancy Meyers,'" *Celebrity Studies* 9, no. 2 (2018): 2.

10 Josephine Dolan, *Contemporary Cinema and "Old Age": Gender and the Silvering of Stardom* (New York: Palgrave, 2017), 32.

11 All 16 films I refer to in the introduction are independent productions. The films that cost more than 20 million to produce are the following: *The Best Exotic Marigold Hotel* and its sequel *The Second Best Exotic Marigold Hotel*, which were released internationally and earned, combined, more than $223 million on a total budget of $20 million; *Last Vegas*, which returned around $135 million on a budget of $28 million; and, finally, *Going in Style*, which brought in almost $85 million on a $25-million budget. Yet these films are not romances, and I would argue their success is mostly due to their ensemble casts and the audience eagerness to watch a group of award-winning, bona fide stars—including Judi Dench, Richard Gere, Michael Douglas, and Robert De Niro—sharing the screen.

12 Bill Newcott, "Kathy Griffin to Host Her Second Movies for Grownups Awards," AARP, January 5, 2016, www.aarp.org/entertainment/movies-for-grownups/info-2016/kathy-griffin-celebrity-news.html.

13 Roland Barthes, "Introduction to the Structural Analysis of Narrative," in *Image—Music—Text*, trans. Stephen Heath (New York: Hill & Wang, [1966] 1977), 96.

14 André Gardies, *Le récit filmique* (Paris: Hachette, 1993), 45.

15 Eric D. Miller and Julie Omarzu, "New Directions in Loss Research," in *Perspectives on Loss: A Sourcebook*, ed. John H. Harvey (New York: Routledge, 1998), 6.

16 Tamar Jeffers McDonald, *Romantic Comedy: Boy Meets Girls Meets Genre* (London: Wallflower, 2007), 97.

17 Betty Kaklamanidou, "The Romantico-Sexual Narrative and Intertextuality in *Friends with Benefits* and *No Strings Attached*," in *The Millennials on Film and Television: The Politics of Popular Culture*, ed. Betty Kaklamanidou and Margaret Tally (Jefferson, NC: McFarland, 2014), 155–69.

18 In fact, one of the main arcs late in season 2 and continuing through all of season 3 sees Grace and Frankie start a business selling vibrators specifically designed to pleasure women their age.

19 Ateret Gewirtz-Meydan, Inbar Levkovich, Moshe Mock, Uri Gur, and Liat Ayalon, "Promoting a Discussion on Later Life Sexuality: Lessons from Sexologist Physicians," *Sexual and Relationship Therapy* 34, no. 2 (2019): 193–210.
20 Gewirtz-Meydan et al., "Promoting a Discussion."
21 In Hilary Lewis, "*I'll See You in My Dreams*: Blythe Danner, Writer-Director Brett Haley Talk Personal Connections to Loss, Karaoke," *Hollywood Reporter*, May 17, 2015, www.hollywoodreporter.com/news/ill-see-you-my-dreams-796308.
22 Marta Kauffman, "*Grace and Frankie* Boss on Older Women as 'Sexual Beings' and Those Vibrator Billboards," *Hollywood Reporter*, May 29, 2017, www.hollywoodreporter.com/news/grace-frankie-boss-older-women-as-sexual-beings-vibrator-billboards-guest-column-1006611.
23 Harris, "Actresses Over 60."
24 Zarum, "Trendspotting."
25 In Julie Miller, "Jane Fonda on the Joys of Reuniting with Robert Redford for One More Movie Romance," *Vanity Fair*, September 29, 2017, www.vanityfair.com/hollywood/2017/09/jane-fonda-robert-redford-netflix-our-souls-at-night.

5

Queer Romance in *Take My Wife*

How the Television Rom-Sitcom Gives New Life to the Genre

Ash Kinney d'Harcourt

Gender and Subversion through Comedy

In 1989, despite network pushback, executive producer and comedian Roseanne Barr's self-titled sitcom, *Roseanne* (ABC, 1988–1997), aired an episode in which her character's 11-year-old daughter experiences her first menstrual cycle, marking the first time a network TV show addressed the topic of menstruation. Jokes about Darlene's period that recur throughout the series foreground and explicitly name the physicality of the "cramps" and "blood stains" as part of the bodily experience of menstruation. This treatment of a taboo topic stands as part of the sitcom's larger project of unsettling social norms around women's bodies, gender inequality, and misogyny. In her analysis of the comedian's performative techniques and celebrity text, Kathleen Rowe [Karlyn] observes how Barr freely expresses anger and resistance to patriarchal constructions of gender through her comedy. Indeed, Barr's work in the 1990s was considered the vanguard of a generation of unruly women in comedy, either "unable or unwilling to confine herself to her proper place."[1] Writer Kate Clinton coined the term "fumerist" to designate humor that both intends to bring down the house and "burn the house down."[2] The fumerist's comedy criticizes social conventions and morality by drawing attention to the comedy in the "micropractices of every day life . . . that make up the normal and *normalizing* codes of gender and other sites of oppression" (my emphasis).[3] These everyday micropractices, I will argue, have been used by other comedians to surreptitiously center their marginalized identities in their TV series.

For the most part, scholarly treatment of gender in stand-up and television has focused on women's use of comedy conventions to "act out," in Mary Russo's words, the "dilemmas of femininity" through representations of the female form in popular culture.[4] For example, Joanne Gilbert lists among the oppositional identities women comics have historically enacted the kid, the bawd, the bitch, the whiner, and the reporter.[5] These roles continue to be performed by contemporary comedians on television; for instance, Abbi Jacobson and Ilana Glazer of *Broad City* (web, 2010–2011; Comedy Central, 2014–2019) portray their unruly characters as goofy, gross, and devoted to women friends above all else.[6] Meanwhile, Samantha Bee displays her bitchy refusal to accept and live by the status quo in her news satire TV show *Full Frontal with Samantha Bee* (TBS, 2016–). Amy Schumer and Sarah Silverman are heralded by Gilbert as the new bawds who "simultaneously reject and reinvent notions of female power through their unique performance of marginality, critiquing hegemonic structures through strategies of confrontation and celebration."[7] The edgy and explicit humor of these comedians—obscene, angry, and sexual—breaks the mold of patriarchal feminine ideals, to the point where they are sometimes perceived by some audiences as threatening or intimidating.

Normalizing Otherness in *Take My Wife*

Not all comedians bring their brash and bawdy stand-up humor to the screen. Comedians with marginalized identities face obstacles that many of the white, middle-class, cisgender, and heterosexual comedians described above do not. Particularly in the aftermath of Barr's racist tweet during the airing of ABC's *Roseanne* reboot in 2018, it is important to keep in mind that "unruly" comedy is not a feminist strategy that includes and is available to all women.[8] Created nearly three decades after the wildly successful *Roseanne*, the series *Take My Wife* (Seeso, 2016–2018) offers a case study of these tensions. In this series, writer-comedians and (then) real-life married couple Cameron Esposito and Rhea Butcher eschew graphic representations of their bodies in order to focus attention on their romantic and domestic life together. Instead of landing punch lines about menstruation like in *Roseanne*, they are simply two comedians who happen to menstruate. While Esposito does not hesitate to use the topic as comedy fodder in her stand-up, she and Butcher repackage their "unruliness"—most prominently their comedic takes on gender and queerness—into an everyday reality in their TV series.⁹

Esposito and Butcher nonetheless resist gender and sexual identity norms by centering queer characters and romance within familiar TV genre conventions; in doing so, they normalize LGBTQ+ identities for mainstream TV audiences.¹⁰ Stephen Tropiano observes how "gaycoms" (gay-centered situational comedies) such as *Ellen* (ABC, 1994–1998) and *Will & Grace* (NBC, 1998–2006, 2017–2020) changed the image of lesbians and gay men two decades earlier in a similar manner.¹¹ However, the treatment of the protagonists' identities in *Take My Wife* moves past the assimilationist and postqueer storytelling in many gaycoms. The two out lesbian characters in this series are not portrayed within a heteronormative televisual world or depicted as secondary to principal heterosexual characters.¹² Instead, the love story between Cameron and Rhea situates this series in a distinctly queer world and, in the process, reinvigorates the genre with their original and intimate narrative.

Promotion for Seeso's first season of *Take My Wife*.

The romantic comedy genre has migrated in recent years from film to television, occasionally blending with the established sitcom formula. This hybrid rom-sitcom combines the dramatic tension of the will-they-or-won't-they story line in romcom films with the episodic serialization of TV sitcoms. Esposito and Butcher's TV series, and the first season in particular, provides an opportunity to explore the potential of these genre conventions together to center the two lesbian protagonists and their relationship. For comparison, I also consider other media texts in which the comedians address their gender and queer identities from the margins in a more "unruly" manner. First, though, I examine the sociocultural and TV industry contexts in which representations of queerness have been produced.

Representing Queerness in a Changing Television Landscape

The couple's self-portrayal in *Take My Wife* recalls that of their most prominent comedy predecessor, Ellen DeGeneres. Similar to DeGeneres in *Ellen*, Esposito and Butcher perform charming, somewhat awkward versions of themselves on-screen. However, *Take My Wife* was produced in a markedly different industrial context than *Ellen*, which aired when only a handful of networks existed with programming oriented toward a broad "mass" audience. As technological and regulatory factors drove TV networks to target increasingly narrow niche audiences, media companies began to pursue more flexible production and distribution practices to attract these audiences. These shifting conditions, new financing models, and creative practices have led to an expansion in textual possibilities.[13] What was once considered outside or even oppositional to the mainstream has become commercially viable for media conglomerates. As Michael Curtin has suggested, "The mass audience no longer refers to one simultaneous experience so much as a shared, asynchronous cultural milieu."[14] So why, in this era of postnetwork niche audience targeting, would the show's creators be concerned with broadening the appeal of the series' characters?

Esposito and Butcher's queer identities—Esposito identifies as lesbian and Butcher has since the show come out as gender nonbinary—complicated the portrayal of their TV characters at a time when half of Americans elected a vice president with a record of staunch opposition to LGBTQ+ rights. Broadening the appeal of the characters they play may also be linked to society's embrace of postfeminism and backlash against feminism in the decades leading up to the show's production. The building tension between the prevalence of sexual assault and harassment of women and the failure of the entertainment industry to hold powerful men accountable resulted in the mainstream affirmation of the #MeToo movement one year after the production of the first season of *Take My Wife*. Thus, the series' first season was created in the historical moment between the aftermath of the 2016 presidential election, which set a decidedly pessimistic tone about the future status of women and queer people in the U.S., and the surge in #MeToo-fueled "popular feminism" that came the next year.[15]

For Esposito, performing her identity and critiques of mainstream (heteronormative) culture as lighthearted joking has been a necessary strategy from early in her stand-up career. She explains that this aspect of her stage presence stems in part from her sexual orientation: "I think that's one of my strengths as a comic. I'm tiny and smiley. I think a lot of it comes from creating safety for myself because as a queer person, I was just very unsafe."[16] Like DeGeneres twenty years earlier, Esposito has made herself and her comedy palatable to multiple audiences and at one time credited DeGeneres with paving the way: "Ellen has to exist in people's house during the daytime so that people aren't so scared, and then I can get married. That has to happen."[17]

Take My Wife was produced and distributed by Seeso, a comedy subscription streaming service owned by Comcast through NBCUniversal. Promoted as a "neighborhood restaurant" alternative to Netflix's "supermarket programmed by algorithms," Seeso launched in January 2016.[18] *Take My Wife* became the platform's first critical hit among the service's new programming, which included approximately thirty original series and specials. Seeso was subsequently shut down in 2017 as part of its parent corporation's move toward pursuing fewer and larger audience segments via other established channels. Though not all of Seeso's original series found new homes, the first and second seasons of *Take My Wife* that had already been produced were picked up by Starz and distributed by the network and on iTunes after a fan-driven social media campaign on Twitter to save the series (#TakeMyWife trended that week). The closure of Seeso reflects a general trend of precarity for original programming, as companies rapidly cycle through content acquisition and distribution strategies in search of economically viable models.

Thus, although the series was marketed as edgy comedy, financial incentives created pressure to broaden the targeted audience. Alexander Doty's analysis of *Glee* (Fox, 2009–2015) and *Modern Family* (ABC, 2009–2020) reveals the effects of such constraints on the representation of queer characters; as he states, these series "put the normative back into their homo(s)" with their emphasis on domesticity, monogamy, and the desexualization of their gay characters.[19] For example, Alfred L. Martin describes how the kissing of two gay male characters has been mitigated with camera angles and editing to avoid direct and prolonged shots of such affection in the single-camera sitcoms *Modern Family*, *The New Normal* (NBC, 2010–2013), and *Happy Endings* (ABC, 2011–2013).[20] Though cable-produced dramas such as Showtime's *Queer as Folk* (2000–2005)[21] and *The L Word* (2004–2009) expanded representations of LGBTQ+ romance, these series nevertheless emphasize domestic themes such as marriage and parenting, sometimes at the cost of depoliticizing queerness.[22]

With the exception of *The L Word*, most of the queer characters in the series described here are white cisgender gay men. The present moment has witnessed a relative increase in queer (and predominantly white) women characters and relationships, particularly in series on streaming platforms. Some of these shows, such as the Netflix Original comedy-drama *Orange Is the New Black (OITNB)* (2013–2019) and Amazon's *Transparent* (2014–2018), explore, if also sensationalize, lesbian sexuality on screen. The choice, by the creators of *Take My Wife*, of the romantic comedy sitcom over the comedy-drama format of *OITNB* and *Transparent* steers the show away from the more provocative portrayals of sexuality in this latter form. As a half-hour single-camera comedy series, *Take My Wife* more closely resembles Amazon's *One Mississippi* (2015–2017), another semiautobiographical series about a comedian. Created by and starring stand-up comic Tig Notaro, the two lead characters in *One Mississippi* are played by Notaro and her real-life wife and comedian, Stephanie Allynne. Both characters are likable and relatable to a general audience; the show has even been described as "not just for lesbians."[23] Similar to *Take My Wife*, *One Mississippi* was canceled in 2018 after two seasons, with Amazon reportedly abandoning its niche programming in favor of a more "mainstream" content strategy.[24]

When Romcom Met TV

Romantic comedy films have traditionally performed societal norms rather than introduce experimental themes and subject matter, making the genre a valuable tool for reading contemporary cultural values. For example, the genre's overwhelmingly heterosexual pairings since the first part of the 20th century reflect dominant cultural notions of gender and sexuality. In *The Hollywood Romantic Comedy: Conventions, History, Controversies*, Leger Grindon reviews how romantic comedies in the 1980s and 1990s reaffirm many early genre conventions;[25] these "neo-traditional romantic comedies" occasionally even transpose the plots of classical romantic comedies to a contemporary setting, as in Nora Ephron's film *Sleepless in Seattle* (1993).[26] The genre began to incorporate queer characters during this time as well, though as Kyle Stevens observes, usually for the purpose of comic relief and "outside claims to institutional, generic—and ultimately cultural—affirmation."[27]

Celestino Deleyto finds a greater range of political and ideological expression manifesting over time in romantic comedy as the genre evolves to reflect changing social practices. He notes, for example, that recent romcoms display an increased flexibility in gender roles and represent emerging alternative sexualities.[28] Deleyto explains that humor creates a space that insulates the characters from social rules and allows them to explore their affection and desires freely: "This comic, protective, erotically-charged space is the space of romantic comedy."[29] In addition, Betty Kaklamanidou has found that popular millennium romantic comedies expand the range of femininity and masculinity represented on-screen, as well as the age, race, and ethnicity of romcom protagonists.[30] Thus, the present moment is one in which a mainstream romantic comedy has the potential to decenter heteronormativity as well.

The popularity of the romantic comedy film has declined in recent years, leading culture and media websites to speculate on whether the romantic comedy is "dead."[31] This decline may be linked to the postmodern scrutiny and demystification of our culture's romantic script by contemporary audiences, the risks associated with relying on star capital, and the romcom's close-endedness, which restricts opportunities for sequels and franchising.[32] By integrating the romantic comedy structure with action, fantasy, and other narratives, the genre is adapting into new hybridized forms. Simultaneously, it has migrated from film to television, where it is restructured to fit the medium's serialized and open-ended context.

The flexibility of the sitcom in particular accommodates a variety of narratives. Media editor and reporter Claude Brodesser-Akner rhetorically asks, "What are sitcoms' 'will-they-won't-they' arcs other than long romantic comedies?" The appearance of what has been referred to as the "rom-sitcom" is, therefore, not surprising.[33] This hybrid form combines the dramatic tension of the will-they-or-won't-they story line of romcom films with the episodic serialization of TV sitcoms; essentially, it is "a happy ending that doesn't quite end."[34] The rom-sitcom format can be seen in hit series such as *Mad About You* (NBC, 1992–1999), *How I Met Your Mother* (CBS, 2005–2014), and, more recently, *The Mindy Project* (Fox, 2012–2015; Hulu, 2015–2017). These series are less dramatic than romcom films and incorporate the timeline of relationships leading up to and after the wedding. Discourse about rom-sitcoms in online media websites indicates the popularity of these series; in what she names the "golden age of television romcoms," Lauren Le Vine notes, "TV continues to kick movies' asses when it comes to presenting nuanced romantic storylines in a [sic] edgier, more realistic way that people clearly want to watch."[35]

The rom-sitcom affords extensive opportunities for reimagining the romantic comedy genre, often in ways that subvert the conservative values of their film predecessors—for example, by satirizing postfeminist messages of the romantic comedy (*The Mindy Project*) and problematizing the genre's rigid gender stereotypes (*Crazy Ex-Girlfriend* [The CW, 2015–2019]). This ideological and genre analysis explores how queer romance in *Take My Wife* is centered within the rom-sitcom through the characterization of the two leads as nonthreatening to the status quo, the episodic resolution of tensions in their romantic story line, and the eclipsing of the couple's sexuality by their domesticity.

"Set-up": Rom-Sitcom Conventions in *Take My Wife*

"Charming" was a word frequently used in critical reviews of *Take My Wife* during its first season in 2016. Neil Genzlinger of the *New York Times* praised its "D.I.Y. charm,"[36] and in the geek-girl culture site *The Mary Sue*, Molly Booth described the series as "feel-good," even as it tackled serious issues.[37] This lightheartedness, a defining feature of the rom-sitcom, is evident in many aspects of the series, beginning with the tongue-in-cheek title—a signature one-liner of comedian Henny Youngman and a reference that links the show reassuringly to 1950s-style domesticity.

Esposito and Butcher are relatively late to the trend of comics bringing their comedy to television. Esposito's personal history, in particular, has been deeply entrenched in the stand-up comedy world. She has prioritized the cultivation of the alternative stand-up scene through her weekly stand-up show at the Upright Citizens Brigade (UCB) Theatre and in her podcast with Butcher, *Put Your Hands Together* (2013–2019), in which they shared live stand-up shows from other comics as well as backstage interviews with their podcast audience. Esposito performs her unabashedly feminist perspective on being a woman and lesbian in a culture that is male- and hetero-dominant. Her "friendly yelling" style of comedy can be seen in guest appearances on several late-night talk shows and in her own stand-up specials.[38] Stand-up comedy typically engages in a direct and confrontational manner with contemporary topics; a similar spirit infuses TV stand-up comedy specials, as well as variety and sketch comedy, though somewhat less so the talk show format, and least of all the scripted sitcom. Where stand-up disrupts the social order, the sitcom tends to reinforce it; indeed, scholars have proposed that the sitcom format may limit the potential subversiveness of feminist humor.[39]

Neither the romantic comedy with its heteronormativity nor the sitcom with its tidy resolutions to complex problems would appear to be obvious venues for two queer, feminist stand-up comics. Nevertheless, these attributes invite mainstream audiences' emotional investment in Esposito and Butcher's on-screen characters and relationships. The familiar, lived-in structures of the rom-sitcom create a space for the intimacy that is portrayed in *Take My Wife*. Several sitcom aesthetic and narrative conventions are evident in the series, beginning with the opening scene in the pilot, "Set-up," which focuses on the couple's domestic life together. After a playful flashback scene in which Cameron proclaims, "Welcome to the rest of our lives!" and proceeds to carry and then drop Rhea across a metaphorical marriage threshold, the episode continues with a montage of scenes from their present-day home. These scenes include two toothbrushes in a cup with a single tube of toothpaste, two pairs of lace-up boots, a kitchen sink with dirty dishes, and photographs of the couple on their refrigerator. Cameron pours coffee into two mugs, one with "Sausage City" printed on the side, that were presumably acquired during one of her comedy tours. "Is it weird that we have these mugs?" she asks Rhea. "You mean, because we're lesbians or because we're vegetarians?" Jokes about sexual identity are casually introduced into their morning routine of drinking coffee. As they sip from mugs, chatting sleepily, the two protagonists give the impression of a contented domestic bliss.

Although the couple starts out in an established relationship, they face some generic obstacles during the series' first season that test their relationship. For example, disequilibrium arrives in the pilot episode when it becomes clear that, despite their domestic bliss, the characters are each experiencing a crisis in their lives. Rhea is dissatisfied with her day job as a graphic designer and yearns to be a comedian; Cameron feels lonely in the relationship because Rhea is routinely on call at work. At the end of the episode, the two reach a temporary solution to their problems in the process of performing stand-up together. While on-stage, Rhea decides to quit her day job and afterward pursue stand-up full time as Cameron's cohost at the Off Vermont comedy show, thus alleviating career frustrations and allowing the partners to spend more time together. Rhea bookends the episode with Cameron's earlier declaration: "Welcome to the rest of our lives!" This resolution in the pilot is echoed in the season finale with Cameron's formal marriage proposal to Rhea resolving the season arc of the romantic narrative. The familiarity of these generic-specific resolutions draws attention to

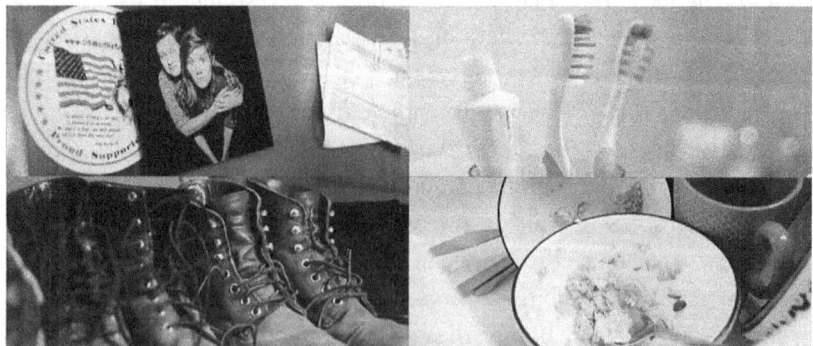

Images of Cameron and Rhea's domestic life together in the pilot of *Take My Wife*: the odds and ends displayed on their refrigerator door; the couple's toothbrushes, boots, and dirty dishes.

how the two main characters in *Take My Wife* conform to, rather than differ from, the status quo.

The series also includes short postepisode interviews with the two comedians during the first season that blur the on-screen narrative with the stars' real life relationship at the time. During these brief vignettes, which are interspersed with black-and-white shots of the theater and close-ups of the two comedians' hands (including one in which Esposito is playing with her wedding ring), Esposito and Butcher break the fourth wall to talk to viewers about making the episode. These scenes, filmed with a handheld camera, are less formal in style than the rest of the show; they include bloopers, the partners complimenting each other, and some playful riffing. The interviews effectively accomplish the hopes that Esposito expresses for the series to "kind of erase the boundary between us and the show." From the domesticity that permeates the episodes to the restoration of equilibrium that is reinforced by the intimacy of these postepisode interviews, the show depicts Cameron and Rhea's romance as a typical love story—"the only difference," noted in discourse prior to Butcher publicly identifying as nonbinary, "is that the couple at the center of the series is played by two women."⁴⁰

"Punchline": Romance and Sexuality in *Take My Wife*

Storytelling in many rom-sitcoms revolves around the day-to-day routines of the characters in their domestic and/or workplace settings. In keeping with this trend, *Take My Wife* focuses on the decisions the comedians face as a couple from how to set up their home—in one episode Rhea is tasked with finding the couple a sofa—to which career they should each pursue (spoiler: both choose stand-up). Also noteworthy are the topics this domestic- and career-focused content displaces, including their sexual relationship. Similar to other TV rom-sitcoms, there is no nudity in the series; the changing of clothes, as in the episode in which Rhea demands that Cameron return a Whitesnake t-shirt, either occurs off-screen or the camera strategically pans to avoid their undressed bodies. Reference to the body in general is limited to the occasional joke, as in the following on-stage exchange between the characters on parenthood:

> RHEA: I'm great dad material. I just don't have dad *materials*, you know.

CAMERON: You mean sperm?
RHEA: Yeah.
CAMERON: 'Cause we got baseball hats . . .

Even Esposito's graphic three-minute stand-up bit on menstruation is reduced to one line spoken by Rhea about how the couple cannot have a white sofa because "we're two women—periods."

Another topic the series does not address is the protagonists' coming out. In contemporary media, the happiness of LGBTQ+ characters often depends on revealing their identity to—and earning acceptance from—the straight characters. The two protagonists in *Take My Wife* are in an established relationship at the beginning of the series, and neither character is given a coming-out narrative. In contrast, the comedians have been frank about many of their personal experiences as lesbian and genderqueer, including coming out, in other media projects. Before the series was released, the two had become unofficial "spokeslesbians," hosting online series aimed at entertaining while simultaneously educating viewers. In the tongue-in-cheek Buzzfeed series *Ask a Lesbian* (2014–2016), Esposito fields questions about her sexual identity ("How do you know you're lesbian if you've never had sex with a man?") as well as about her coming out ("What were your parents' reactions when you told them?"). Esposito and Butcher cohosted the Amy Poehler's Smart Girls–produced web series *She Said* (2015), described as a "space where women talk about stuff" in which they discuss the female body, sexism, and feminism. In the short episode entitled "Coming Out!," the comics also discuss how they first knew they were (as each identified themselves) "gay" and how they were able to explore their developing queer identities through comedy.

The two masculine-of-center lesbian characters refreshingly avoid the femme stereotype ubiquitous on television, as in, for example, the first two seasons of *OITNB* and recent seasons of *Grey's Anatomy* (ABC, 2005–) that focus on the relationships of mostly white and/or femme characters while sidelining others.[41] Cameron and Rhea are both, however, noticeably desexualized in the series. The absence of sex in *Take My Wife* avoids the hypersexualized depictions of lesbian characters in many contemporary comedy-dramas; indeed, the comedians have gone to the opposite extreme. Sex is a punch line throughout the first season, in which comedy is used to divert attention from sexuality. As part of an interview for a podcast in the pilot of *Take My Wife*, Cameron and her interviewer have the following exchange:

> INTERVIEWER: [Being a comic] must make it pretty hard for dating, unless you're dating—god forbid—a comic.
> CAMERON: Actually, that's weird you would bring that up. I *am* dating someone who's trying to be a comic.
> INTERVIEWER: And succeeding?
> CAMERON: Yeah. The sex is hilarious.

The second episode, entitled "Punchline," begins with the couple in a postintimate moment ("Good job," one of them says). The two muse about what a TV show of their lives might look like. In discussing the possibility of sex scenes in such a show, Butcher asks, "So, on our TV show, will it show us having sex?" and Esposito responds, "Oh, yeah, like, a lot." This conversation, however, ends up serving as a humorous stand-in for the real thing; there are no sex scenes in either season of the series. Their kissing throughout the first season is cut short by playful gags such as the sound of an alarm clock and interjections of "I can't kiss you when your whole mullet is in my mouth!" and "Did you just have sushi?"

Kissing in the series then is part of the day-to-day reality of the couple's relationship, while their passion is channeled into their enthusiasm for working together and making their relationship official with a marriage proposal in the season finale—the ultimate romcom resolution. The overall downplaying of sexuality in this way is not necessarily a straightforward "breaking of a taboo and the rejection of a compulsory [heterosexual] way of life"; however, it successfully emphasizes intimacy over fetishization and expands the range of queer narratives on television.[42]

A Happy Ending?

The first season of *Take My Wife* conforms to several romantic comedy and sitcom conventions, with its romantic story line and happy endings, its focus on everyday domestic and work life, and its endearing albeit desexualized portrayal of the protagonists. Many of the tropes of the first season examined here are also evident in the second; in both seasons, familiar generic conventions subtly center and normalize the characters' gender and

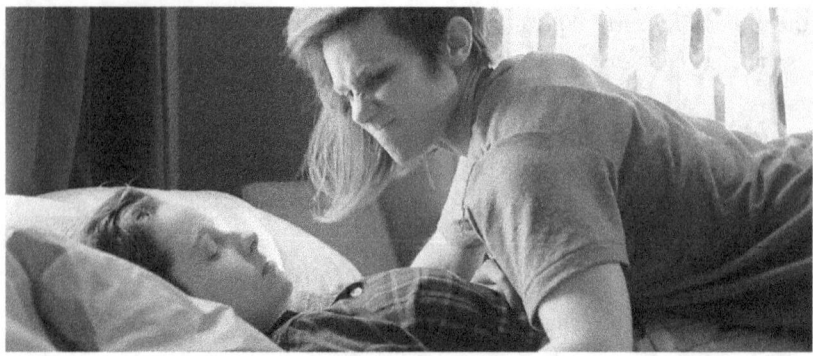

An alarm clock interrupts a frustrated Cameron while she kisses Rhea in episode three of *Take My Wife*.

LGBTQ+ identities, in a conspicuous departure from the more candid treatment of these topics in the comedians' other media projects. The show's creators have not ignored the social and political contexts in which the show was produced, however. From the point of view of its two protagonists, the series addresses struggles experienced by women and queer people that are often absent from scripted television, such as the prevalence and impact of rape culture on members of these groups, as well as the daily microaggressions directed at gender-nonconforming individuals living in a culture structured around a strict gender binary. *Take My Wife* should also be celebrated for its intimate portrayal of everyday aspects of queer existence after coming out, especially as such story lines remain rare in mainstream media.

The show's reliance on conservative genre devices is, however, a double-edged sword. For example, the framing of the two white, Midwestern lesbian characters in a domestic, middle-class life runs the risk of reifying homonormativity—a failure to contest dominant heteronormative assumptions—and of depoliticizing queer identity and culture.[43] Doty explains, with regard to the limits of TV liberalism in many popular contemporary series, the "'good' gays . . . keep their 'place at the table'" by striving to be just like their straight middle class counterparts"—only lacking in cultural permission to show each other physical affection or (pre-Obergefell v. Hodges) to marry.[44] Still, Esposito and Butcher's particular foray into queering the rom-sitcom is innovative and highly affecting. Most important, the show is a product of their own creative endeavor, setting it apart from most contemporary liberal narratives with LGBTQ+ characters. Also, the comics *were* married at the time the series was produced. Their characters' on-screen wedding takes place on the stage that they share in the Off Vermont theater, echoing the comedians' real-life wedding at the Hideout Theatre in Chicago.

This chapter has explored some of the ways in which these two comedian-showrunners offer more complex representations of queer characters in their rom-sitcom. Despite the inclusive casting of the show, *Take My Wife* focuses on the white-centered narrative of Cameron and Rhea's relationship.[45] Industrial and sociocultural shifts in the 2010s postnetwork era have created more opportunities for women of color in romantic comedy televisual spaces. Alongside questions of gender and sexuality, it is equally important to consider the representation of race and ethnicity in romantic comedy televisual spaces. A preliminary look at two series, *The Mindy Project* and *Insecure* (HBO, 2016–), reveals that these shows have also adopted several rom-sitcom conventions. For example, Mindy Kaling's hyperfeminine attire and performance in *The Mindy Project* is part of a distinctly gendered postfeminist romcom aesthetic. Moreover, both series incorporate familiar romantic comedy archetypes, most prominently in their first seasons.[46] These series warrant further critical examination of the ways in which established romantic comedy (and sitcom, in the case of *The Mindy Project*) conventions expand and confine representations of gender, race, and ethnicity.

The focus of this chapter has been on the intersection of gender and sexual identity in *Take My Wife*, which incorporates conventional formulas and tropes to alleviate mainstream fears of queer romance while also expanding on narratives that resist anti-LGBTQ+ ideologies. Five months after the second season of *Take My Wife* was released on iTunes, Esposito and Butcher announced to devastated but supportive fans that they were parting ways. Esposito tweeted: "Rhea & i are separating to live individual lives for a time. We care very much about each other & that's why we're doing this."[47] The comedian later published a poignant and revealing column about the pain of divorce and her fight for "the right to be queer and human, to have the privileges straight people enjoy, like the privilege to be imperfect and fail."[48] Both comedians have continued to perform stand-up and are working on their own podcasts,[49] and a joyful Esposito recently tweeted about her new relationship.[50] Though Esposito and Butcher's real-life story is messier, the series provides a neat and happy resolution for its viewers. We cannot know for certain whether the inclusion of two queer characters in this rom-sitcom will ultimately contribute to greater acceptance of diversity either on- or off-screen. However, the visibility and centralization of these characters as protagonists in their own happily-ever-after story has an indisputably positive impact on viewers, particularly those who see their lives and identities reflected in the show.

Notes

1. Kathleen Rowe [Karlyn], *The Unruly Woman: Gender and the Genre of Laughter* (Austin: University of Texas Press, 1995), 31.
2. Gina Barreca, *They Used to Call Me Snow White . . . But I Drifted: Women's Strategic Use of Humor* (Hanover, NH: University Press of New England, 1991), 178.
3. Cynthia Willett, Julie Willett, and Yael D. Sherman, "The Seriously Erotic Politics of Feminist Laughter," *Social Research* 79, no. 1 (Spring 2012): 230.
4. Quoted in Rowe [Karlyn], *Unruly Woman*, 225.
5. Joanne Gilbert, *Performing Marginality: Humor, Gender, and Cultural Critique* (Detroit: Wayne State University Press, 1994), 97–128.
6. Anne Helen Petersen, *Too Fat, Too Slutty, Too Loud: The Rise and Reign of the Unruly Woman* (New York: Plume, 2017), 51–72.
7. Joanne Gilbert, "'My Mom's a Cunt': New Bawds Ride the Fourth Wave," in *Transgressive Humor of American Women Writers*, ed. Sabrina Fuchs Abrams (London: Palgrave MacMillan, 2017), 204.
8. Lesley Goldberg, "*Roseanne* Canceled at ABC Following Racist Tweet," *Hollywood Reporter*, May 29, 2018, www.hollywoodreporter.com/live-feed/roseanne-canceled-at-abc-racist-tweet-1115412.
9. As illustrated by a video of a live performance that Esposito published on YouTube on February 9, 2015, "The Greatest Period Joke Of [sic] All Time #CHUNKS," www.youtube.com/watch?v=J1irAxNOHxs.
10. The word "normalize" here is only meant to indicate that queer-centered narratives are not common ("the norm") in mainstream television in this historical moment.
11. Stephen Tropiano, *The Prime Time Closet: A History of Gays and Lesbians on TV* (New York: Applause Theatre & Cinema, 2002), 245–53.

12 After the production of both seasons of the series, Rhea Butcher tweeted that they officially use they/them/their pronouns, though they continue to identify with women culturally and politically. In *Take My Wife*, Butcher portrays a lesbian character. The television character, Rhea, is referred to using she/her pronouns, and Butcher themself is referred to using they/them pronouns throughout this chapter; Rhea Butcher, Twitter post, March 2018, 1:47 p.m., twitter.com/RheaButcher/status/979792359096553477.

13 Amanda D. Lotz, "Linking Industrial and Creative Change in 21st-Century U.S. Television," *Media International Australia* 164, no. 1 (May 2017): 11–16.

14 Michael Curtin, "On Edge: Culture Industries in the Neo-Network Era," in *Making and Selling Culture*, ed. Richard Ohman, Sage Averill, Michael Curtin, David Shumway, and Elizabeth Traube (Middletown, CT: Wesleyan University Press, 1996), 197.

15 Sarah Banet-Weiser, *Empowered: Popular Feminism and Popular Misogyny* (Durham, NC: Duke University Press, 2018), 16–17.

16 Joanna Robinson, "The #MeToo Movement Has a Place in Comedy: Just Ask Cameron Esposito," *Vanity Fair*, May 23, 2018, www.vanityfair.com/hollywood/2018/05/cameron-esposito-me-too-rape-jokes-comedy-take-my-wife#~o.

17 Melissa Kravitz, "How Cameron Esposito Plans to Revolutionize Comedy in 2018," Broadly, December 22, 2017, https://www.vice.com/en/article/ev5z5e/how-cameron-esposito-plans-to-revolutionize-comedy-in-2018.

18 Neil Landau, *TV Outside the Box: Trailblazing in the Digital Television Revolution* (New York: New Focal, 2016), 48.

19 Alexander Doty, "*Modern Family*, *Glee*, and the Limits of Television Liberalism," *Flow Journal* 12, no. 9 (September 24, 2010): www.flowjournal.org/2010/09/modern-family-glee-and-limits-of-tv-liberalism/.

20 Alfred L. Martin, Jr., "It's (Not) in His Kiss: Gay Kisses, Narrative Strategies, and Camera Angles in Post-Network Television Comedy," *Flow Journal* 25 (September 25, 2012): www.flowjournal.org/2012/09/it%E2%80%99s-not-in-his-kiss-gay/.

21 Gael Sweeney, "Beyond Golden Gardenias: Versions of Same-Sex Marriage in *Queer as Folk*," in *Queer TV in the 21st Century: Essays on Broadcasting from Taboo to Acceptance*, ed. Kylo-Patrick R. Hart (Jefferson, NC: McFarland, 2016), 41–61.

22 Anna Ciamparella, "From Good to Bad Stories: Examining the Narrative of Pregnancy in *The L Word* as a Means to Teach and Destabilize Queerness," in Hart, *Queer TV*, 77–92.
23 Rachel Hall, "The Real Reel: Not Just For Lesbians—Tig Notaro's *One Mississippi* Is One of the Most Relatable Shows on TV," Popdust, February 13, 2018, www.popdust.com/one-mississippi-is-one-of-the-most-relatable-shows-on-tv-2534165389.html.
24 Yohana Desta, "Amazon Axes Niche *I Love Dick*, *One Mississippi* in Favor of Mainstream Shows," *Vanity Fair*, January 18, 2018, www.vanityfair.com/hollywood/2018/01/amazon-i-love-dick-one-mississippi-jean-claude-van-johnson.
25 Leger Grindon, *The Hollywood Romantic Comedy: Conventions, History, and Controversies* (Malden, MA: Wiley-Blackwell, 2011), 58–61.
26 Tamar Jeffers McDonald, *Romantic Comedy: Boy Meets Girl Meets Genre* (London: Wallflower, 2007), 85–105.
27 Kyle Stevens, "What a Difference a Gay Makes: Marriage in the 1990s Romantic Comedy," in *Falling in Love Again: Romantic Comedy in Contemporary Cinema*, ed. Stacey Abbott and Deborah Jermyn (London: I. B. Tauris, 2009), 145.
28 Celestino Deleyto, "They Lived Happily Ever After: Ending Contemporary Romantic Comedy," *Miscelánea: A Journal of English and American Studies* 19 (1998): 42–54.
29 Celestino Deleyto, *The Secret Life of Romantic Comedy* (Manchester: Manchester University Press, 2009), 18.
30 Betty Kaklamanidou, *Genre, Gender, and the Effects of Neoliberalism: The New Millennium Hollywood Rom Com* (London: Routledge, 2013), 12–14.
31 For example, Liz Meriwether, "Sex Is Funny. Love Is Funny. So Where Are All Our Great Romantic Comedies?" The Cut, September 8, 2016, www.thecut.com/2016/09/where-are-all-the-great-new-romantic-comedies.html.
32 James J. Dowd and Nicole R. Pallotta, "The End of Romance: The Demystification of Love in the Postmodern Age," *Sociological Perspectives* 43, no. 4 (Winter 2000): 553.
33 Melissa Maerz, "On *A to Z*, *Manhattan Love Story*, and the State of the Rom-Sitcom," *Entertainment Weekly*, October 2, 2014, ew.com/article/2014/10/02/this-falls-rom-sitcoms-feel-like-throwbacks-and-not-in-a-good-way/.

34 Sonia Saraiya, "The Rise of the Rom-Sitcom," AV Club, September 11, 2014, tv.avclub.com/the-rise-of-the-rom-sitcom-1798271986.

35 Lauren Le Vine, "Sorry, Movies, We're Just Not That into You—TV Is Now the Place to Go for Great Romcoms," Refinery29, April 7, 2016, www.refinery29.com/en-us/2016/04/107558/romantic-comedies-tv-shows-movies.

36 Neil Genzlinger, "In *Take My Wife*, Two Comics Seek the Punch Lines in Life," *New York Times*, August 10, 2016, www.nytimes.com/2016/08/11/arts/television/review-take-my-wife-on-seeso.html.

37 Molly Booth, "All the Reasons to Get Excited for *Take My Wife* Season 2," The Mary Sue, June 19, 2017, www.themarysue.com/take-my-wife-season-2/.

38 Robinson, "#MeToo Movement."

39 For example, Patricia Mellencamp, "Situation Comedy, Feminism, and Freud: Discourses of Gracie and Lucy," in *Studies in Entertainment: Critical Approaches to Mass Culture, Volume 7*, ed. Tania Modleski (Bloomington: Indiana University Press, 1986), 90–94.

40 Joanna Robinson, "It's Not Too Late to Save One of TV's Most Urgently Important Shows: Season 2 of *Take My Wife* is in Need of a New Home," *Vanity Fair*, August 16, 2017, www.vanityfair.com/hollywood/2017/08/take-my-wife-season-2-new-home.

41 Ann M. Ciasullo, "Making Her (In)Visible: Cultural Representations of Lesbianism and the Lesbian Body in the 1990s," *Feminist Studies* 27, no. 3 (Fall 2001): 577–608.

42 Adrienne C. Rich, "Compulsory Heterosexuality and Lesbian Existence," in *Feminism and Sexuality: A Reader*, ed. Stevi Jackson and Sue Scott (New York: Columbia University Press, 1996), 136.

43 Lisa Duggan, *The New Homonormativity: The Sexual Politics of Neoliberalism* (Durham, NC: Duke University Press, 2002), 179.

44 Doty, "Modern Family."

45 For example, Esposito tweeted that the series had an all-women writers' room and nearly half of the writers were women of color in the second season. Women were represented in every aspect of production from cinematography to the soundtrack. Also, in the second season, 83 percent of the cast were women, 25 percent women of color, and 54 percent LGBTQ+; Cameron Esposito, Twitter post, August 2017, 4:33 p.m., twitter.com/cameronesposito/status/895397595517829120.

46 Ash Kinney d'Harcourt, "From Assimilation Narratives to 'Regular Stories': Celebrity Image, Production Culture, and On-Screen Visibility in *The Mindy Project* and *Insecure*," *Genre en Séries: Cinéma, Télévision, Médias*, no. 13 (Spring 2021).

47 Cameron Esposito, Twitter post, August 2018, 12:18 p.m., twitter.com/cameronesposito/status/1027242599004794882.

48 Cameron Esposito, "New Hope, New Pain, Same Old Divorce," *New York Times*, September 13, 2019, www.nytimes.com/2019/09/13/style/modern-love-cameron-esposito-divorce.html.

49 Erika Harwood, "Comedians Cameron Esposito and Rhea Butcher Announce Their Split," *Vanity Fair*, August 8, 2018, www.vanityfair.com/style/2018/08/comedians-cameron-esposito-and-rhea-butcher-announce-their-split.

50 Cameron Esposito, Twitter post, November 2019, 1:51 p.m., twitter.com/cameronesposito/status/1199415293992488965.

Act 2

Love in a Time of Precarity
Romcom Realism

6

In Love and Up in Smoke

HAROLD & KUMAR AND THE ROMANTIC TURN OF THE POST-9/11 STONER COMEDY

Maya Montañez Smukler

The *Harold & Kumar* films of the early 2010s—*Harold & Kumar Go to White Castle* (2004), and especially *Harold & Kumar Escape from Guantanamo Bay* (2008)—bring together two seemingly incongruent genres, the stoner comedy and the romantic comedy, within the framework of post-9/11 satire.[1] For the cinematic stoner protagonist, drugs are the primary object of desire, acting as the central narrative device that creates character motivation and plot chaos, while the romcom focuses on a core couple's incompatibility until enough hijinks bring them together in harmony. At their heart, however, these comedies share key genre conventions: a screwball humor dictated by confusion and mayhem; often-mistaken identities, false truths, and mistrust; frequent disregard for law and order, usually resulting in a chase; and an unlikely hero—or heroes—who suffer various scenarios of humiliation to finally, in the end, triumph.

John Cho's Harold Lee and Kal Penn's Kumar Patel, Korean American and Indian American actors/protagonists, are rare examples within romantic comedy of Asian American leads, both of whom "get the girl" in the end. Beyond contributing to the romcom genre some much-needed inclusive casting, in *Harold & Kumar* story elements predicated on race and ethnicity shape the way the quest for the joint coincides with the quest for love and, in the process, enacts a collision with the kind of xenophobia and racism that was emblematic of the early post-9/11 years. In particular, *Harold & Kumar Escape from Guantanamo Bay* combines the familiar romcom tropes of the wedding crasher and runaway bride with political satire of the early 2000s' national security policies. Early in the film, the Office of Homeland

Security racially profiles Harold and Kumar, an act of discrimination that propels the plot by creating continuous problems for the two to solve. By the end of the movie, the buddies outsmart several racist nemeses, leading to victories that clear their names from the terrorist no-fly list, which in turn allows the friends to travel freely to reunite with their respective love interests. For Harold and Kumar, racism is an ongoing battle that they fight with equal parts comedy and conviction, while weed emboldens their sense of adventure at the expense of any good judgment, and romantic love makes them better friends.

A Four-Way: Buddy Film, Romcom, Stoner Flick, Screwball

The male buddy film—more commonly known, in the last fifteen years, as the "bromance"—is an offshoot of the romantic comedy genre: at the center of each is the core couple who are opposites in every way, but in the former (male) friendship takes the place of romance as the final harmonizing resolution.[2] In both genres, the couple's differences create the conflict that drives the narrative into constant chaos, while keeping the pair close so as to incrementally reveal how their polarity attracts them to one another. Ultimately, their ability to reconcile by film's end endears them to the audience and to each other, by amending all bad behavior and uniting them as friends and/or lovers.

Like the romcom and buddy genres, the stoner film frequently revolves around a pair or sometimes a group of friends' adventures, this time, in weed—involving some combination of the trouble they get themselves into in the pursuit of obtaining marijuana, the influence of the drug itself, and the mischief that results from their being high, which frequently takes the form of a confrontation with authority (i.e., parents, the police, the government, powerful drug dealers). So too do opposites attract in the stoner genre: bonded by their shared love of intoxication, the friends must have opposing personality traits—the otherwise law abiding vs. socially deviant, the romantically shy vs. brazen, the super-stoned vs. just stoned—in order to create narrative tension and chaos.

Key to the stoner film are genre conventions that originated in the screwball comedy. In the mid-1930s, the genre became popular in Hollywood, with the release of films such as *It Happened One Night* (1934), *My Man Godfrey* (1936), and *The Awful Truth* (1937), that paired slapstick comedy with romantic comedy in a web of mistaken identities, miscommunications, flat-out lying, revenge, and love triangles. With stoners in a constant mental fog, a screwball-like state of confusion is the norm, and misunderstandings plague their every move, causing bedlam. Whether disposing of the lit joint when the cop pulls them over or struggling to outsmart the competing drug dealer, the stoner protagonists' interactions with figures of authority and power—and their struggle to conceal their drug habit—is the leading source of mayhem.

Opposites Attract: Stoner Buddies and the Quest for Love

The *Harold & Kumar* stoner-buddy franchise has always had its roots in romantic comedy. The series centers on two best friends and roommates, Harold and Kumar, who are in their twenties, have known each other since college, and are polar opposites. Harold Lee, outside of his recreational pot smoking, follows closely the rules of social conduct. He is gainfully employed at an investment banking firm, but, while Harold is an excellent employee, he lacks professional confidence and is an easy target for his conniving coworkers, who bully him into doing their work. Kumar Patel, in contrast, is a brilliant underachiever who mocks his father's wishes that he follow the family tradition and become a doctor, choosing, instead, the pursuit of weed. Where Harold is reserved, Kumar is bold; where Kumar is impetuous, Harold is pragmatic.

In *Harold & Kumar Go to White Castle*, romance provides a secondary plotline behind the buddies' late-night quest for pot and White Castle hamburgers. The film's narrative follows the misadventures of Harold and Kumar as they stumble through New Jersey looking for, in this story, the elusive fast food chain White Castle. Early in the film, Harold, finding himself waiting for the elevator alongside neighbor Maria (Paula Garcés), with whom he is secretly in love, fantasizes a confident version of himself initiating charming elevator talk and the two laughing easily. Still dreaming, their sexual tension builds until they fall into each other's arms and kiss passionately. Back in reality, Harold fidgets silently next to Maria, barely able to squeak out a weak "goodbye" when the two exit the elevator.

Harold's shyness hinders his ability to make a love connection; Kumar, who is bold, also tends to fumble his way through romance. Kumar is as enthusiastic as he is crass when it comes to women. In *White Castle* he wears a t-shirt that reads "I Love Bush: the pussy, not the president" and another shirt featuring a cartoon (pussy)cat with a magnet hanging from its mouth. While evidenced by his taking any chance he gets to flirt and proposition women who for the most part are responsive, whether it's a bout of diarrhea (afflicting the women involved) or an emotional breakdown (suffered by Kumar), circumstance, usually related to his drug use, gets in the way of consumption. As dictated by the conventions of the buddy picture, what is incongruent about the friends—their polar opposite personalities—draws them together, and, in the case of romance, their blunders with women create rifts between the two guys that they will ultimately resolve, making them even closer friends.

White Castle's romantic subplot sets up what will be a main narrative in its sequel, *Escape from Guantanamo Bay*. In the first film, Kumar, the more confident and irreverent of the two, teases and badgers Harold, affectionately, to pursue his love interest. In the midst of their weed and burger quest, the men randomly—as is the norm in stoner films—drive past a movie theater playing a John Hughes double feature of *Curly Sue* (the title of a real kids' film that also doubles for various slang terms befitting *Harold & Kumar*'s gross-out humor) and *Sixteen Candles*. When neighbor Maria emerges from the theater, Kumar urges Harold to say hello. "You said you two have nothing in common, but you two have the same lame taste in movies," laughs Kumar, while Harold freezes with anxiety. "Dude . . . it's 1 a.m. in the morning and who do we see but your dream girl," Kumar entices as he recasts the romcom meet cute to star Harold and Maria: "Just pretend that you are a nerdy Asian version of Tom Hanks and she's a hot Latina Meg Ryan, with bigger tits." When Kumar shouts to Maria from the driver's seat, Harold panics and jams the accelerator, and the buddy film slapstick takes over as the two men careen, out of control, down the street until they drive off the embankment and crash, into their next misadventure.

By the end of *White Castle*, after a night of buying weed, then losing the weed, fighting a group of white racists, being racially profiled by the police, put in jail (where they find more weed), meeting Neil Patrick Harris (who is "trippin' balls" on Ecstasy), riding a wild cheetah, and crashing and stealing cars, the friends arrive at their final destination. Harold, by film's end, has grown some balls of his own. After eating thirty sliders and drinking four large sodas, he confronts his coworkers with a newfound bravado and then, home again, in the elevator, shares his real feelings for Maria. "I had the craziest night of my life tonight and I guess I learned that if you want something or someone, you have to go for it," Harold gushes, breathless and on the verge of euphoria, before exclaiming, "Fuck it," and embracing and kissing Maria. When Harold tells Kumar that Maria is on her way to Amsterdam, and he will have to wait until she returns to pick up where they left off, the love of weed and the love of romance become the perfect match. In a 2004 pre-widespread decriminalized marijuana United States, Kumar is ecstatic at the opportunity to follow Harold's heart to the sacred stoner city.

Escape from Guantanamo Bay picks up where *White Castle* left off, opening with Harold in the shower, lost in the reverie of his elevator kiss with Maria, as the title credits appear in elegant cursive script, and Louis Armstrong sings "What a Wonderful World." The romantic facade is broken violently by Kumar on the toilet. "I'm taking the most incredible dump of all time. May I remind you that we both just ate thirty burgers and four large orders of fries," Kumar brags to a disgusted Harold, who pulls the shower curtain back in horror. "What the fuck dude. . . . You couldn't wait until I was out of the shower?" No. Absolutely not. In *Escape from Guantanamo Bay*, the tender romance of falling in love collides head on with the rambunctious vulgarity of the stoner buddy lifestyle, and the romance plus comedy begins.

The ideal romantic comedy coupling is predicated on extreme opposites, making Harold and Kumar the perfect couple. Harold is prim, proper, highly organized, and clean. The subsequent opening credits sequence sets up what a complementary pair the friends are in illustrating how they are diametrically opposed, revealed in the way each packs for their trip to Amsterdam. Harold's closet, filled with neatly stacked boxes and color-coordinated ties hanging carefully on a rack, looks like an ad for the Container Store. Meanwhile, Kumar's closet is like the commercial for Febreze air freshener in which the doting mother cautiously enters her teenage son's room and, stepping over piles of dirty laundry, sprays air freshener into dirty sneakers. Harold reads *Forbes* magazine while Kumar reads (fictional porn magazine) *Vagina*; Harold irons while Kumar masturbates.

In both films, Harold begins each adventure as the hesitant and reserved one, taking the entirety of the film's running time to find his sense of self and courage. Even though *White Castle* ends with him and Maria confessing their attraction to one another, at the start of *Escape from Guantanamo Bay* Harold has regressed to feeling hamstrung by his familiar insecurities, confessing to Kumar as they arrive at the airport, "I just realized something.

Maria's going to think I'm a stalker—I'm following her to Amsterdam." In contrast, Kumar finds confidence in any opportunity to confront authority, especially when offered the chance to challenge racism, xenophobia, patriotism, and the medical establishment. In *Escape from Guantanamo Bay*, Harold rediscovers his daring through the pursuit of romance, and Kumar, who will never give up his swagger as slacker extraordinaire, by the film's finale has focused his bravado on winning back his lost love.

"Why does everything have to be a big argument with you?" So Harold asks after Kumar confronts the TSA agent who racially profiles them at the airport en route to Amsterdam. "Because this is America, dude, and as long as I have my freedom of speech no one's going to shut me up." At this instant of expressing his righteous indignation, the film slows, and a gentle musical score lights up as Vanessa (Danneel Harris), Kumar's girlfriend from college, is spotted across the airport. In a rare moment, matched only by him and Harold meeting Neil Patrick Harris high on hallucinogens, Kumar is speechless. Vanessa, no longer the punk rock pothead he dated in college, is glammed up in business casual attire and engaged to the preppy Republican Colton (Eric Winter), an "Abercrombie-wearing douchebag," according to Kumar, who flashes a bright, deceiving smile their way. Colton brags about their wedding to take place in a week, his father's ties to George W. Bush, and his own job in the State Department, telling an impressed Harold, whose own job was secured through Colton's connections, "The president was supposed to be at the wedding, but you know how busy he is." During this exchange, Kumar bites his tongue and grimaces, giving a questioning yet knowing eye roll to Vanessa, who looks back with signs of panic already registering. Colton, shaking a worshipful Harold's hand, flaunts his connection to the Bush Administration and says the prescient line: "If you ever need anything, I'm your man." As the couples go their separate ways, the scene employs slow motion again as a visual cue for romantic longing and regret. Kumar looks after Vanessa in bewilderment at what he has lost, and Vanessa, being marched off by Colton, looks backs with an unspoken plea to be rescued. The romantic comedy threesome of the love interest triangulated between two prospective suitors, one good and one bad, has formed.

As its timely title signals, in *Escape from Guantanamo Bay* politics and romance are intertwined. When Kumar gets caught with a homemade *bong* on the plane to Amsterdam, he and Harold are falsely accused of bringing a *bomb* onboard and of being terrorists and are sent to Guantanamo Bay detention camp. The odd couple then start their journey of escape—from the prison made infamous after September 11, 2001, from a KKK meeting in the Deep South, from a villainous Homeland Security agent, and from a drug-addled Neil Patrick Harris. Harold is furious at Kumar for being so reckless. "You couldn't fucking wait," he barks as they prepare to be interrogated by Homeland Security after being taken off the flight. "We were about to have all the legal weed we wanted—in Amsterdam!" Later, after the two have escaped from prison and are making their way to Texas to take Colton up on his (disingenuous) offer of help, Harold snaps at Kumar as he mourns the derailed trip to meet Maria, "This was not supposed to be a trip to the South. This was supposed to be the most romantic trip of my life . . . not like you would understand . . ." Kumar, who is sarcastic and playful about romance, is forced to face his own feelings. Through this journey of political persecution he comes to realize that he must be a better friend to Harold, and that he loves Vanessa and must stop her marriage to Colton. *Escape from Guantanamo Bay* follows the tradition of screwball romantic comedies in that all character relationships are riddled with duplicity and deceit: Colton is not only Kumar's archrival for Vanessa, but instrumental in the guys' false imprisonment under the Bush administration's domestic terrorism watch.

Cheech & Chong: Looking for a Joint

The *Harold & Kumar* films build on the legacy of comedy team Cheech & Chong (Richard "Cheech" Marin and Tommy Chong) and their definitive stoner film *Up in Smoke* (1978), the first of the pair's seven buddy pictures. In *Up in Smoke* the quest for weed, as would become the narrative device defining the genre in subsequent films, is intertwined with the conventions of the road film to devise a narrative and literal path for the heroes' slapstick journey. Or, as Marin described the plot of the film: "Two guys meet and decide to form a band, but first they need to find a joint."[3] Cheech, as "Pedro," and Chong, as "Man," meander through their noncommittal 1970s lifestyle choices: Pedro is in a rock band, and Man, who travels with a set of drums, is disowned by his wealthy parents for lack of direction. The two buddies' meet cute happens on the side of the road when Chong's shabby Volkswagen Bug breaks down and Cheech picks him up hitchhiking. Pedro and Man take to the road, first in Pedro's classic low-rider "Love Machine" and then in a delivery van literally made of marijuana in which they transport weed between the United States and Mexico, eluding border patrol and stateside police. The guys arrive in Los Angeles just in time for the film's finale at a battle of the bands at the Roxy Theatre on Hollywood's Sunset Strip. In the stoner film often the most mundane task, such as getting up in the morning and getting to band practice, is the characters' biggest challenge, while the conflict with authority—in *Up in Smoke*, an undercover police operation led by Sergeant Stedenko (Stacy Keach)—comprises a major event that only the most spaced-out goofball can derail with accidental acts of sabotage.

The comedy team of Cheech & Chong began performing live, initially as a rock band that quickly included improvised comedy sketches, in a nightclub owed by Chong's family in Vancouver in the late 1960s. In 1971, concert promoter and band manager Lou Adler signed the pair and produced their first album, *Cheech & Chong*, which sold one hundred thousand copies in its first four months. The guys' humor reflected the counterculture/hippie zeitgeist of the late 1960s and 1970s and was rooted in the cultural politics of the era: the generation gap, identity politics, immigration policy debates, sexual liberation, and pervasive recreational drug use. Throughout the 1970s, the duo released several albums, five of which received Grammy nominations, with their LP *Los Cochinos* winning for Best Comedy Recording in 1972. *Up in Smoke*'s narrative was loosely constructed from many of the pairs' jokes and the characterizations popularized in their live shows and on their albums, which by 1978 had sold as many as ten million copies.[4] Unsurprisingly, *Up in Smoke* the movie was a hit: made for $1.7 million at Paramount Pictures, the film grossed $65 million within its first year.[5] In

Tommy Chong and Richard "Cheech" Marin, *Up in Smoke*.

1978, an enthusiastic stoner audience wasn't a shock. As *Variety* observed, without much astonishment, "Here is a possibly first major studio release of a comedy based on marijuana. Since several millions of Americans are by estimate addicted to the weed, there's presumably a large potential audience. Fire marshals may have trouble with 'no smoking regulations' when this pic unreels."[6]

Cheech & Chong's comedy during the 1970s established the stoner genre, one that borrowed conventions from the buddy film. Creating oppositional characters, as was expected in buddy films, out of a couple of hippie stoners seemed close to impossible when their being high blurred many noticeable personality traits. As the first "doper" comedy, Cheech & Chong introduced protagonists who lived outside of expected social codes and found opposition in those around them. Pedro and Man's ongoing quest for the joint and subsequent altered states created constant conflict with the police and the government, with the men unable to follow the most obvious traffic laws or even conduct basic human functions such as urinating on point in the urinal. An "us vs. them" comedic rapport takes hold between the unlikely heroes and the establishment, its humor enhanced by the enduring imbalance between the characters: when one is more stoned, more paranoid, more sober than the other, the pratfalls, clowning, and narrow escapes increase.

Up in Smoke brings an examination of race and ethnicity to the buddy-stoner formula: Marin, born and raised in Los Angeles, is Chicano, and Chong, born and raised in Canada, is half Chinese and half Scottish-Irish. The pair were the only Chicano-Chinese comedy team in Hollywood at the time, and their humor actively played on this combination. Taglines for their early albums began "From one Chicano and one Chinese...," with "Cheech" and "Chong" printed in exaggerated "low-rider" and "Chinese" block letters. A common feature in Cheech & Chong's comedy is what Christine List identifies as the "self-directed" or "in-group-created" stereotype, in which the comedians reframe derogatory images in a way that allows them to control the joke and in the process expose the images' inherent social prejudice.[7] In Cheech & Chong's stoner world, clashes with authority—frequently represented by white, male-dominated law enforcement—are the pair's leading source of conflict. Cheech is clearly identified as Chicano through costume, language, and the car he drives. It is through these identifiers that he upsets negative Chicano stereotypes of gangsters, banditos, and greasers: Cheech's

Pedro is far too playful to be dangerous, far too stoned to be threatening, and too much of a hippie to be a gangster. Chong's race/ethnicity, in *Up in Smoke*, is never identified beyond his last name and the color of his skin. His eclectic look is perhaps best described by Marin upon meeting his future comedy partner for the first time in the late 1960s: "[Chong] had long, wild black hair parted in the middle . . . he had a scraggly and sparse Fu Manchu moustache and goatee . . . and he was brown, which I took to be a good sign. The overall effect was of a hippie-biker-Mongolian-weight lifter. And he had gold-framed eyeglasses and a big gap in his front teeth. You know, your typical topless, improvisational-theater look."[8] Chong's mix of so many cultural identifiers, some of them incongruent with one another (hippie/weightlifter, biker/improvisational theater performer), clearly marks him as an outsider, and his ambiguous race/ethnicity, never named but clearly different, not only challenges the Anglo status quo, but also destabilizes neat categories of race and ethnicity in which stereotypes are prone to develop.

Together, the comedy team brings trickster elements to their characters, qualities that are rooted in the 1960s counterculture, antiestablishment, "Question Authority" mindset.[9] As two brown men on the run from a group of white policemen, their stoner hippie antics give them outlaw status and a cunning that is almost always accidental. Pedro encounters Sergeant Stedenko in the bathroom and accidentally urinates on the officer, which distracts Stedenko from arresting the burnout for possession of narcotics. When the van made of marijuana begins to self-ignite, the traffic cop who pulls the guys over acquires a contact high so becomes more worried about satisfying his munchies than busting them. The buddies are too high to be conniving and clever and outsmart the authorities, and it is their inability to plot and plan, while still getting away nonetheless, that humiliates and disempowers their pursuers even more. It might be a badge of honor to be duped by a master thief, but to be outwitted by a couple of sloppy, unemployed, ragamuffin counterculture types clowning around is just embarrassing.

Melvin Donalson finds that the interracial buddy film served historically as Hollywood's romanticized version of race relations in America. This genre is dependent on harmony and reconciliation between the races, in a heteropatriarchal cinematic world where capitalism is humane and democracy for all has been achieved, thus "proposing to audiences that by consuming racial egalitarianism on the screen, they have participated sufficiently in responding to the complex racial issues prevalent in society."[10] As an outcome of the civil rights movement of the 1960s and the change the movement enacted for racial justice within the social and political systems of the United States, by the 1970s interracial buddy comedies pairing African American and Anglo heterosexual male actors/characters became popular. During this time, some of the most successful comedy teams were Gene Wilder's collaboration with Cleavon Little in *Blazing Saddles* (1974) and Wilder's work with Richard Pryor in several films (including *Blazing Saddles*, for which Pryor was one of the film's screenwriters), a partnership that lasted into the 1990s. The interracial, Black-and-white buddy film maintained its popularity into the Reaganite 1980s with movies like *48 Hrs.* (1982, Eddie Murphy and Nick Nolte) and what would become the *Lethal Weapon* franchise (1987, Mel Gibson and Danny Glover), although, notably, in this era, the characters became law enforcement agents, to defuse their previous threat as countercultural outlaws. Presumably, a white costar would appeal to the status quo/white audience and a Black partner would provide crossover appeal to audiences of color. An interracial pair that both exceeds the Black/white paradigm and comprises two men of color confuses the cinematic ideal of racial reconciliation for real-world, white America and in doing so confirms that the country's ethnic/racial demographic is larger than Black/white, expanding the range of conflict and resolution to a multicultural/multiethnic scope. Even more detrimental to the fantasies of the interracial buddy film—and comprised of two buddies who are not white—is that when combined with the stoner genre the result is the ultimate outsider narrative.

"When we started writing screenplays the characters were always representative of us and our friends, and a lot of our friends are Asian dudes and Indian dudes," explain *Harold & Kumar* cowriters Jon Hurwitz and Hayden Schlossberg, who are both white. "I think the fact that Cheech and Chong existed gave us the confidence to take Harold and Kumar and put them front and center in a movie."[11] In the *Harold & Kumar* films, the pairing of Korean American and Indian American buddies spurs an intentional confrontation with racism, xenophobia, and global political paranoia. In *Escape from Guantanamo Bay*, Harold and Kumar are hunted by Office of Homeland Security Secretary Ron Fox (Rob Corddry), whose capacity for evil is matched only by his capacity for buffoonery. When the pair are taken into federal custody, and Fox sees for the first time who in reality are two regular, dazed and confused American guys, he exclaims with glee, "North Korea and Al Qaeda working together; this is bigger than I thought." Fox's stupidity and prejudice are so overwhelming that even his staff grimace at the depths of his ignorance.

In the tradition of stoner slapstick, *Escape from Guantanamo Bay*'s social satire is obvious, over the top, and bawdy. Based on real historical associations, events, and people, the punch lines of the jokes take aim at the profiling and prejudice that was rampant in post-9/11 American politics. Kumar, while on the plane to Amsterdam, is seen through a white passenger's nightmarish hallucination with a beard and turban, mimicking an Al Qaeda terrorist. Harold is called "Hello Kitty," and Kumar's parents are misidentified as "Arab" and then (Native American Indian) "Chief" by Secretary Fox, who brings in an interpreter to translate their unaccented perfect English. The film employs racial and ethnic stereotypes from all directions, including self-directed stereotypes, similar to the strategies used by Cheech & Chong, mining them for comedy and in the process harnessing negative images into weapons of cultural critique.[12] Preconceptions about Asians as overachievers who are good in math and science are also enlisted, but in an effort, through humor, to give depth to the protagonists' arcs. Harold excels at his investment banking job, but struggles to find courage in his personal life, which he eventually does. And Kumar, who is (owing to the improbable universe of the stoner film) a brilliant surgeon even before medical school, must wrestle with his slacker disposition.[13]

Wedding Crashing as Political Protest

Harold and Kumar's outsider status—in terms of race, ethnicity, and sobriety—position them as the ideal romantic comedy male heroes. The romcom resolution relies on the underdog making a show of strength in the final scenes. In stoner films the protagonists are rebels; drugs keep them on the outside of the law and social norms. For Kumar, pot's mellowing effects help him to maintain a life as an underachiever, a goal he has happily set for himself. In the case of Harold, though he opts for a conventional, law-abiding path of hard work, his aspirations to be professionally successful and upwardly mobile are constantly derailed by his drug use, which land him in impossible situations that force him to be brave and, in turn, the accidental rebel.

Initially, Harold is horrified when Kumar lets out that he is desperate to find Colton, not just because of his government connections, but because they are going to break up his wedding to Vanessa. "Colton is the only one who can help us out at this point," Harold exclaims. "I cannot believe you are willing to fuck that up!" Colton is not only an obstacle between Kumar and Vanessa, but the self-important, rich Ivy Leaguer is a decisive wedge between the two friends. "I just hate that fucking asshole, OK," Kumar says adamantly. But Harold has had it with his pal, whose poor judgment and pleasure-seeking priorities have turned them into fugitives. "I like him better than I like you right now," taunts Harold. "You know what he got me? A job. You know what you got me? Thrown into Guantanamo Bay." When it is revealed that Colton is not an ally to the guys and turns them into the authorities, Harold and Kumar unite in fury. "You *are* a douchebag, you fucking douchebag," screams Kumar, finally right about something. "Yeah, the last thing I was going to do was let you guys ruin my wedding," Colton smirks. Harold, stunned that his professional idol has betrayed them, is furious. "When we get out of here, I'm going to fucking kill you!" Colton laughs as the guys are handcuffed and carted off by the FBI. "You're not one of those kung-fu Asians, you're a pussy banker!" Emboldened by rage, Harold screams back, "I'm going to fuck you up, bitch!" before being shoved into a security van. Like the romcom hero who suffers humiliation and loss before discovering what it is he loves most and must fight for, Harold, toward the end of this long strange trip, transforms degradation into rage and asserts himself.

Crashing the wedding is a key narrative trope in romantic comedies: the hero/heroine declares his/her love in a power play at another couple's altar by stealing away the soon-to-be spouse and, as a result, reinstating harmony in a misaligned relationship universe. In classical Hollywood the genre of romantic screwball comedies flourished, popularizing themes of commitment, in which a couple is brought together, and reaffirmation, in which an estranged couple is reunited. Kristine Brunovska Karnick argues that during this classical studio era the myth of the American Dream, defined by hard work and conventional heterosexual love and marriage, drives these narratives of commitment and reaffirmation.[14] In *It Happened One Night* (1934), newspaper man Peter Warne (Clark Gable), in love with bratty socialite Ellie Andrews (Claudette Colbert), waits in a getaway car as her father derails her wedding to the wrong man while walking her down the aisle. In *The*

Philadelphia Story (1940), Tracy Lord (Katharine Hepburn) spends the night before her wedding to fiancé George Kittredge (John Howard) with wedding crasher Macaulay Connor (Jimmy Stewart) before realizing, in the morning, that she must remarry her ex-husband C. K. Dexter Haven (Cary Grant). In *The Lady Eve* (1944), Jean Harrington (Barbara Stanwyck) creates a false identity in order to marry and then divorce Charles "Hopsie" Pike (Henry Fonda) so that she can fall in love with him again—and him with her—as her real self. According to this genre's worldview, holy matrimony is ready-made for chaos and controversy. Having misaligned lovers reunite in the nick of time within the sacred space of marriage, especially one that isn't their own, momentarily upends social order before reinstating traditional values with the formation of a new couple.

In *Escape from Guantanamo Bay*, Harold and Kumar spend the entire film crashing things. They crash the canary yellow convertible their friend Raza (Amir Talai) lends them as a getaway car; they crash as dinner guests at the house of an incestuous brother-sister/husband-wife couple in the backwoods of Alabama; they crash a KKK bonfire, as unexpected witnesses and then targets; and, on their way to crashing Vanessa and Colton's wedding, they crash through the roof of President Bush's house. The guys' chance meeting with the president brings them face to face with their tormentor—the film's chief satirical target being the second Bush administration's policies implemented post-9/11—and, in true screwball fashion and with utmost stoner improbability, the hawkish Republican leader of the free world becomes the hero of this lefty stoner romcom. *Escape from Guantanamo Bay* is explicit in its left-leaning political message, but Harold and Kumar find a way to ridicule everyone, including themselves, which protects the film from becoming didactic—or, at least, not funny. The movie parodies President Bush's reputation as a slacker with a daddy complex, who is controlled by vice president Dick Cheney. The three guys smoke pot and bond over meddling fathers and joke about the perils of Guantanamo Bay, before the president clears Harold and Kumar's record and they seal the deal with a bunch of high-fives.

Full of presidential bravado, Harold and Kumar make an executive entrance and storm the wedding just as Vanessa starts down the aisle. The men are out of place in every way: they are dressed for a formal gathering in borrowed hunting gear; they are Korean and Indian, liberal-leaning, and from the Tri-State area in an all-white, conservative, suburban Texan crowd;

and they are still stoned from partying with the president, at an otherwise sober ceremony. The pair's difference, which throughout the film has had them on the run, is now their mark of power. "I loved you, man," shouts Harold with remorseful anger before punching Colton out cold. When Kumar recites a corny poem he wrote in college about the number pi, braving embarrassment to pay tribute to the past that he and Vanessa share, true love has been restored, between the lovers and the best friends. These two men of color, disheveled and road weary, traipsing through the white tulle of the wedding party, confront the longstanding institutionalized racism that has informed the casting of Hollywood's romantic leading man as nearly always white. Criminal(ized) drug use and bad-mannered busting up of a wedding aside, the hero dude duo and the interracial couplings—Indian-Caucasian and Korean-Latina—they form play with the utopian notion of the American melting pot in the face of an ostensibly irony-free, unjust, and xenophobic post-9/11 world.

Gender Trouble

The romantic comedy has traditionally aimed at a heteronormative female audience, as the genre plays into assumptions about women and their proclivity for romance. The female half of the romcom couple battles the wrong

Kumar (Kal Penn), Vanessa (Danneel Harris), Harold (John Cho), and Maria (Paula Garcés) in *Harold & Kumar Escape from Guantanamo Bay*.

guy to eventually find out he is the right "one." As a counterpart, stoner comedies have traditionally been geared toward an imagined male audience populated (as are stoner comedies themselves) by sloppy underachievers sprawled on sagging sofas, bonded in a fog of junk food cravings, centerfold fantasies, and sexual inexperience. The appeal of the unruly guy character is that his drug use makes him an outlaw, while the goofiness of pot keeps him endearing. In a 2007 *New Yorker* think piece, critic David Denby identified what he called the "striver-slacker romance" emerging in romantic comedies during the early 2000s, in which a likeable yet immature man is paired with a highly capable and attractive woman, providing Hollywood with the chance to "[pull] jokes and romance out of the struggle between male infantilism and female ambition."[15] Apparent here is how the slacker male love interest and the stoner male protagonist are cut from the same cloth, especially with regard to the male privilege the two enjoy, resulting in an easy hybrid of the genres. The slacker habits resulting from chronic pot smoking are culturally more acceptable when played out by men—a notable exception is Anna Faris in *Smiley Face* (2007)—as it is understood that the higher he ranks as a social outcast or troublemaking "bad boy," the more desirable he becomes as a romantic fixer-upper on his way to becoming the "one."

Typically the interchange between romcoms and stoner films plays into retrograde heteronormative gender expectations. The stoner guy's love interest tends to be a sober gal; thus, the romantic comedy's friction of opposites attracting rests in his flaw of being perpetually high and hers in being disapproving. In *Half Baked* (1998), Dave Chappelle's stoner protagonist at first hides his drug habit and his stoner pals and their low-grade dealing operation from love interest Mary Jane Potman (Rachel True), who is staunchly antidrugs because her father is in prison for possession. In *Knocked Up* (2007), Katherine Heigl plays Alison, an aspiring adult with beauty queen looks who has a drunken one-night stand with Seth Rogan's frumpy Ben, who lives with a bunch of fellow stoner slackers. The two must adjust their striver-slacker lifestyles when they find out that she is pregnant. In both films, after a series of comical mishaps and introspective revelations, the men choose romantic love over life as a single stoner dude, and the female love interest accepts him as a work in progress.

Harold & Kumar, with *Escape from Guantanamo* as the (three-film) franchise's more consummately romantic comedy entry, upholds this gender

Kumar, Vanessa, and Harold rejoice as they flee her wedding to Colton in *Harold & Kumar Escape from Guantanamo Bay*.

dynamic of the hybrid stoner-romcom by celebrating the disobedient man paired with the beautiful and poised woman. Kumar, forever the disheveled troublemaker, arrives on the bridal path dressed in camouflage cargo pants and wearing a t-shirt with an illustration of a woman on her hands and knees whose outlined figure is filled in with the Confederate flag, with "Southern Style" written underneath, standing in stark contrast to Vanessa's glamorous traditional white wedding gown. "I can't promise you the kind of lifestyle Colton could, and I can't promise you that I can mature overnight," Kumar pledges to Vanessa before drawing a blank. "Sorry, I smoked weed with the president and I totally forgot what I was going to say . . . I can promise you that I will always love you and will never try and make you into something you are not." He wins her over with his honesty and respect for her personal freedom, and she accepts his offer to love her and, in the process, sacrifices any expectation of having an adult relationship.

This is the guys' story, and, while romance intertwined with political satire drives the plot and shapes the narrative themes, the men experience romantic love with women only through, and secondary to, their platonic friendship with each other; the primary relationship is between the buddies. Not much is known about Vanessa's character except that she was once a party girl responsible for introducing Kumar to pot back in college, when he was a corruptible nerdy student. But questions about why she became involved with the status-seeking, corrupt Colton, or the nature of her own career aspirations—in a film in which all the characters are identified in some way by their (non)professional status—remain unaddressed. Even less is revealed about Maria, except that she is Harold's "angel" and is beautiful and a model for *High Times* magazine. These female characters function essentially as objects of desire, the hard-won achievements for these messy men. In genre terms it is necessary for the men to stay messy, even after declaring their love and coupling up by film's end. As cleaned-up and functioning adults, there is no friction between the two friends and thus no fun, for what is most interesting and funny about the stoner romcom are the lengths to which the buddies must go to *get the girl*, not the actual *getting her* in the end.

Harold and Kumar as outsiders are elevated to hero status through male bonding organized around drug use. Toward the end of the film, the two are splayed out in a stereotypical masculine setting—W's rumpus playroom with pinball machines, a game of darts with an Osama bin Laden target, and hunting trophies mounted on the wall—when Harold confesses, through a thick haze of smoke, to the commander in chief that after everything he and Kumar have been through he's not sure he can trust the government anymore. "Trust the government?" replies President Bush, as he looks thoughtfully at his joint. "Heck, I'm in the government and I don't even trust it." As a melodramatic score swells in the background, he gives some sage advice to the two young men: "You don't have to believe in your government to be a good American, you just have to believe in your country." Harold and Kumar, slack-jawed from the effects of the Alabama Kush they have been smoking, pause for a stoner beat before rejoicing in the nonsensical. "Exactly, exactly . . . ," Kumar amens before the men turn back to their joint. In this scene, the humor is manifested in a satirical critique of President Bush derived from his known past drug use and his perceived ineptitude in handling issues of national security; thus the male camaraderie that typically informs the stoner buddy film reconciles the political discord that has driven the plot. Emboldened by this patriotic pep talk among men, and high on the president's pot, which is laced with cocaine, the guys head off to bust up Vanessa and Colton's wedding.

Stoner love in the Trump era, so far, has not found any kind of political reconciliation. At the time of this writing, it is too soon to even consider how the most far-fetched parody can recast the current U.S. president, Donald

Trump, with any ounce of ironic affection. In fact, the current state of political dystopia finds the stoner romantic comedy in peril and in a despair that is distinctly female. Stoner comedies have been male territory since their start, until recently: Ilana Glazer and Abbi Jacobson, costars and cocreators of *Broad City* (2014–2019), a scripted series from Comedy Central, introduce a joyous, female-centric, sex-positive, feminist intervention into this testosterone-laden terrain. Glazer and Jacobson have received criticism from some scholars who cite a tendency of the white, middle-class characters toward "racial impersonation" and a casual approach to economic disparity.[16] Where the show and its creators do work hard is in grabbing the conventions of the male-dominated stoner film and turning them on their head by resituating the genre in a narrative universe that is less about witnessing the journey of the outsider-to-hero and instead predicated on the belief that being different is an assumed asset from the start.

In *Broad City* best friends Ilana Wexler and Abbi Glazer romp around New York City, which serves as their endless playground. The series, at its core, is a coming-of-age story, or at least an attempt by these characters to come of age while continuously falling and tripping over their lists of goals and aspirations. The series begins with Abbi at age 26 and Ilana at age 23. Each are precariously underemployed, Ilana as a temp with no work ethic and Abbi as an aspiring illustrator and a fitness trainer who for many episodes flounders at her day job on the cleaning crew of a fashionable Manhattan sports club.

Broad City fits within the stoner-buddy genre in obvious ways: the series' main characters are two best friends, and their adventures with each other, which are often uninhibited due to intoxication, drive the narrative. However, *Broad City* veers somewhat from these formulas in that the buddies, while different in some ways, are almost never at odds. For example, Ilana is famously more sexually open than Abbi, who in comparison is shy and less verbose in acting on and expressing her desires. But, where these kinds of differences create conflict and havoc between Harold and Kumar that must be resolved over the course of the film, for Abbi and Ilana the distinctions inspire celebration in and appreciation of one another, boosting each other's confidence and self-worth, episode after episode.

In many ways, *Broad City* operates within a postfeminist framework in how consumerism functions as a means to individual female empowerment.[17] Abbi and Ilana exist in a constant state of economic instability. A lack of funds keeps the gals motivated to save or scheme and meet short-term goals of shared personal achievement in the form of concert tickets, air conditioners, birthday dresses, and special dates to celebrate their friendship. (A middle-class upbringing with parents who still offer financial support and friends who are more fiscally responsible also help make these purchases feasible.) The besties maintain a laissez-faire attitude about financial security influenced by their privilege, the carelessness of their youth, and the lack of judgment caused by smoking so much weed. In spite of this casualness and the show's emphasis on the pairs' own pleasure and entertainment, the women's attention to the need for and urgency of feminism, as a political platform and ideology and cultural belief system, does not waver. From volunteering at an abortion clinic, to the enormous portrait of Oprah above Abbi's bed (and the tattoo of the media icon she has on her back), or the time Ilana volunteered for one day at Hillary Rodham Clinton's New York City 2016 campaign headquarters where the friends got to meet the presidential candidate (3.5, "2016"), feminism remains a steady focus throughout the series.

In the "Witches" episode (4.6) of *Broad City* that aired in October 2017, a mere eight months into the Trump presidency, Ilana discovers that she is suffering from "dead pussy," a posttraumatic reaction to the election. "Basically I have had more sex than, like, anybody in the entire world," she confides to her therapist Betty (Marcella Lowery) upon introducing her problem. "I haven't come since the election. And I'm a come queen." Distraught and on the verge of a nervous breakdown, Ilana is reassured by her counselor that she is not suffering alone; this "pussy constipation" is looking like a national epidemic. "Orgasms have been down 140 percent since Trump has been elected," Betty tells her patient. It is then through mindful rage masturbation that Ilana finally breaks the curse, as Betty coaches her, spread-eagled and armed with a vibrator, to climax. First, Ilana must work through a frenetic montage of news clips featuring President Trump surrounded by supporters holding bright pink "Women for Trump" signs while an audio loop of his infamous claim of "grabbing [women] by the pussy" reverberates. When she finally does orgasm it is to an avalanche of female idols: Michelle Obama, Hillary Rodham Clinton, Rosa Parks, Sally Ride, Beyoncé, Rihanna, Lily Tomlin, Gloria Steinem . . . there is no end to the women who fuel Ilana's sexual desires. Emboldened by her vulva therapy, Ilana, her body still vibrating with pleasure, heads off to meet Abbi at a celebratory witches' ceremony deep in Central Park. If the bumper stickers and t-shirts are true, and the future is in fact female, then it seems that stoner comedies and their ability to be romantic *and* funny in a Trump and post-Trump world will be determined, not so much by reconciliation over a shared joint, but by the genre's ability to share that joint with those not in the boys' club.

Notes

1. The third film in this franchise, *A Very Harold & Kumar 3D Christmas* (2011), fits within the conventions of the stoner film and draws on some conventions of the romantic comedy, but with less attention paid to political satire.
2. For a discussion of contemporary bromance films, see Maria San Filippo, *The B Word: Bisexuality in Contemporary Film and Television* (Bloomington: Indiana University Press, 2013), 156–201. See also *Reading the Bromance: Homosocial Relationships in Film and Television*, ed. Michael DeAngelis (Detroit: Wayne State University Press, 2014).
3. Cheech Marin and John Hassan, *Cheech Is Not My Real Name: But Don't Call Me Chong!* (New York: Grand Central, 2017), 163.
4. Lonnie Burr, "Diplomats of Dope Comedy," *Los Angeles Times*, October 1, 1978, search.proquest.com/docview/158680559/CE6CF9C79435455FPQ/41?accountid=14512.
5. Charles Schreger, "Cheech, Chong: Joint Success," *Los Angeles Times*, July 11, 1979, search.proquest.com/docview/158963001/113210B20D864998PQ/303?accountid=14512.
6. "Film Review: *Up in Smoke*," *Variety*, September 13, 1978, search.proquest.com/docview/1401336388/113210B20D864998PQ/19?accountid=14512.
7. Christine List, "Self-Directed Stereotyping in the Films of Cheech Marin," in *Chicanos and Film: Representation and Resistance*, ed. Chon A. Noriega (Minneapolis: University of Minnesota Press, 1992), 183–94.
8. Marin and Hassan, *Cheech Is Not My Real Name*, 77.
9. List, "Self-Directed Stereotyping," 188.
10. Melvin Donalson, *Masculinity in the Interracial Buddy Film* (Jefferson, NC: McFarland, 2006), 11.
11. Jon Hurwitz and Hayden Schlossberg, "Moments That Changed the Movies: *Up in Smoke*," *Academy Originals*, June 1, 2015, www.youtube.com/watch?reload=9&v=QLNKahFyOXg.

12 Here I draw on List's discussion of "negative stereotypes as cultural weapons," in "Self-Directed Stereotyping," 184.
13 For a discussion of how the *Harold & Kumar* films engage with Asian American and ethnic stereotypes, see David Gillota, *Ethnic Humor in Multiethnic America* (New Brunswick, NJ: Rutgers University Press, 2013), 139–46.
14 Kristine Brunovska Karnick, "Commitment and Reaffirmation in Hollywood Romantic Comedy," in *Classical Hollywood Comedy*, ed. Kristine Brunovska Karnick and Henry Jenkins (New York: Routledge, 1995), 131–32.
15 David Denby, "A Fine Romance," *New Yorker*, July 16, 2007, www.newyorker.com/magazine/2007/07/23/a-fine-romance.
16 Rebecca Wanzo and Kyla Wazana Tompkins, "Brown Broads, White TV," *Los Angeles Review of Books*, March 16, 2015, lareviewofbooks.org/article/brown-broads-white-tv/.
17 Yvonne Tasker and Diane Negra, "Introduction: Feminist Politics and Postfeminist Culture," in *Interrogating Postfeminism*, ed. Yvonne Tasker and Diane Negra (Durham, NC: Duke University Press, 2007), 1–16.

7
Romance as Business in the Capitalist Metropolis

JOHNNIE TO'S *DON'T GO BREAKING MY HEART 1* AND *2*

Tom Cunliffe

Johnnie To's romantic comedies *Don't Go Breaking My Heart* (hereafter *DGBMH*) *1* (2011) and *2* (2014), the first of which is set around the time of the 2008 financial crisis, use volatile stock exchanges as the backgrounds for their triangular and pentagonal love stories, respectively.[1] This setting links the dynamics of romance to the ultracapitalistic environment of Hong Kong, in which the logic of financialization extends to all aspects of life, including love and coupling. This chapter analyses the two *DGBMH* films to rethink the romantic comedy as a genre that interrogates the ethics of capitalism by considering the way the diptych's film style and narrative choices explicate the entanglement between the overwhelmingly consumerist and market-driven mindset of the characters with their approaches to romance and love. While on the surface both films appear to celebrate the capitalist status quo, their inflection of the romantic comedy genre implies a potentially irresolvable conflict between romantic coupling and the capitalist ethos of acquisition and production of an economic surplus.

The ideological underpinnings of the romantic comedy continually change in response to transformations in the social, cultural, and economic contexts of love and intimacy. Robin Wood describes the key to the success of the Fred Astaire and Ginger Rogers romantic musical comedies, mostly made in the 1930s, as follows: "What we love about Astaire and Rogers is that they convince us momentarily that the ideal romantic love our culture programs us to believe in can, against all common sense, be realized."[2] This essentially maps out the contours of the romantic comedy genre as a whole—the desire of two people to fall in love and form a lasting relationship will be fulfilled. The comedic interludes that keep two lovers apart until the final moments of a film serve as a way to interrupt such dreams, throwing a wrench into the works to question such breezy conceptions of romantic love. So, as James MacDowell points out, while the romantic comedy, especially in its more modern iterations, queries the dominant ideologies of love and romance, it is also a genre that "is unlikely to offer a full-out dismissal of the concept of romantic love."[3] Putting MacDowell's precept to the test, in the *DGBMY* films the ideal of romantic love appears to be submerged and struggling for its life within the ultracapitalist world of investment banking in the Hong Kong metropolis.

Johnnie To's romantic comedies have been marginalized in favor of his gangster/crime thrillers, both in critical studies of his work and in terms of film distribution in the West. Of course, this neglect of the romantic comedy is not unique to Hong Kong cinema. Romantic comedy generally travels poorly outside the boundaries of national cinemas; the Bollywood variation, which plays to large diasporic audiences, is a rare exception. Adrian Martin argues that contemporary film criticism generally neglects the romantic comedy genre, often in favor of violent action films, owing to a bias that "physical action is somehow more cinematic than actors delivering sparkling dialogue . . . [that replays that] old, auteurist fixation on the visual."[4] Johnnie To himself has lent his support to the idea that his romantic comedies, which generally perform well at the local box office, are essentially made to pay the bills for his more personal crime thrillers, which have made him famous globally as an "action auteur," but generally founder at the local box office.[5] To's romantic comedies are typically seen as mere commodities, while his more personal films are treated as artistic statements.[6] Yet this view negates the formal and narrative invention of his romantic comedies, which are often made with his creative partner, codirector and scriptwriter Wai Ka-fai.[7] It also neglects the linkages of sociopolitical and economic critique between To's more personal works and the "commodities." Whatever the genre, To's films reflect cultural and sociopolitical trends locally in Hong Kong, nationally in China, and globally.

For instance, the *DGBMH* films share themes with more widely screened To films that critique the capitalist system, such as *Life Without Principle* (2011), which explores the ethically bankrupt world of stock market speculation. This film frequently, and quite bluntly, likens investment to gambling, or to fraud. An extended sequence, filmed with a disquieting coldness, in which a bank clerk, in order to meet her monthly targets, persuades an elderly lady to put her savings into a "high-risk" investment, reveals the ruthless nature of the financial world. Consumer culture too is critiqued in a blackly humorous scene in which, after a failed robbery attempt, a cop asks the robber's girlfriend accomplice about her motive. She replies: "New phone, new bag, and new cosmetics! Everything needs money!" The film also questions to what extent global market forces further marginalize the already marginalized in society. It would be reductive to directly apply the attitudes displayed by *Life Without Principle* to similar issues in *DGBMH 1* and *2*, but the fact remains that Johnnie To made the first *DGBMH* and *Life Without Principle* in the same year. Both take place against the backdrop of global financial crashes, but operate in vastly different registers, due to the way the characters in *DGBMH 1* and *2* negotiate the flows of romance and love alongside their obsession with the stock market and consumer culture. Their fixation on the stock market, which reflects their internalization of the values of consumerism, parallels their ambivalent attitudes toward love. Both market speculation and love become games of choice and addictions to adrenaline rushes without deeper meaning or connection. As John Berger has remarked, once capitalism became speculative it "ceased to be first and foremost productive."[8] These two films take place in a setting dominated by market speculation and consumerism to highlight the ways love and romance are influenced by this constantly fluctuating milieu.

Don't Go Breaking My Heart

The world of the *DGBMH* films—gleaming skyscrapers, high-risk investment banking, high-class restaurants and stores, phone and tablet screens—shape the characters' approaches to love. This influence is realized by the way visual and dramatic aspects of the films are fused together. Take the way in *DGBMH* the initial flirtation between Shenran (Louis Koo) and Zixin (Gao Yuanyuan) is shot. After breaking up with her boyfriend, financial analyst Zixin starts spending time with the down-and-out alcoholic architect Qihong (Daniel Wu). Qihong's inspiration is revived after meeting, and falling for, Zixin. He quickly begins to design a building based on the contours of her shadow that he sees illuminated on a wall by a car light. Meanwhile, Shenran, high-flying CEO of a brokerage firm who works in the skyscraper opposite Zixin's, initiates a cute exchange with her from his office window. Shenran's creative use of Post-it notes, a colorful paper flower stuck to his window, and his later performance of magic tricks, which we see from Zixin's point of view, encourages her to respond in kind, by creating a giant flower and sun out of colored paper that she holds up for Shenran to see. Ignatiy Vishnevetsky points out that the film never tries to explain why these characters are attracted to each other; proximity and boredom appear to be the defining factors. Zixin's attraction to Shenran, Vishnevetsky argues, appears to derive from nothing more than his being "the handsome guy across the street"; romance here becomes, literally, "window-shopping."[9] As Anne Friedberg illustrates, shopping is often determined more by desire than need, and "to shop," as a verb, suggests choice and "empowerment in the relation between looking and having."[10] The shop window is the stage for "visual intoxication [and] the site of seduction for consumer desire."[11] In the *DGBMY* diptych, window-shopping describes both how these characters approach their objects of affection and how the glass windows enclose each character, placing them in a (window) frame within a frame, like an object in a department store window. This framing device visualizes the connection being made between romance and consumerism. Virtuoso cinematic technique captures the breezy and graceful delight of these inter–office building exchanges, even as we remain aware that these towering skyscrapers symbolize, and house, corrupted economic institutions.[12]

After this first round of "window-shopping," Zixin discovers Shenran's name and looks him up on her laptop as she sits by a fountain. Shenran's face pops up on his company's website, which lists him as company CEO and rock climbing champion. This idea of "window-shopping" continues here, with Zixin looking him up in a way that recalls online shopping. She closes her laptop looking pleased at what she has discovered. Meanwhile, Qihong is sitting on the other side of the fountain; each is unaware of the other's presence. Both get up and walk away in separate directions. Near misses between two potential romantic partners abound in romantic comedies, but here the lack of physical communication is linked to Zixin's proclivity for window-shopping—both through the glass windows of her office building and through the images on her computer screen. The mise-en-scène at this early stage of the film is one in which screens and glass dominate, separating and compartmentalizing people from each other. This visual motif communicates a recurring theme in the film: the difficulties in establishing a relationship within this transitory, superficial milieu.

The theme of consumerism as courting embodied in the film's window-shopping sequences comes to the forefront when Zixin returns to her desk. She and Shenran carry on their silent, comic, and flirtatious play-acting, each viewing the other through their office windows. As they engage in this flirtation, Shenran notices the voluptuous Angelina (Larisa Bakurova) dancing in her office on the floor below Zixin's, each woman enclosed by a square window frame. Shenran becomes visibly distracted as he gazes at Angelina, but neither Zixin nor Angelina is aware of the other's presence. Shenran arranges a date by miming the act of eating. From Shenran's perspective, the camera pans down from Zixin's office window to Angelina's, to show both their positive replies. He returns to his desk with a bemused expression, clearly struggling with the choice he must make.

In the next sequence Qihong is working passionately on the architectural design inspired by his meeting, and instantly falling in love with, Zixin. Loyal and steadfast in his pursuit of her, Qihong studiously ignores any other romantic opportunities that present themselves. Throughout the film Qihong is depicted as the perfect gentleman, while Shenran is a charismatic womanizer. Forgetting her promise to meet Qihong for a date that falls at the same time as her date with Shenran, so Zixin too is implicated in the way the multitude of choice on offer puts in question the fulfillment of romantic love. This is visualized through the actual locations used in the film: the gleaming skyscrapers provide a panoply of romantic possibilities through their compartmentalized glass windows. The city of Hong Kong itself, in the

Visualizing the comparison between romance and consumerism in *Don't Go Breaking My Heart*.

shiny, ultracommercial version of it that the *DGBMH* films depict, powerfully shapes the characters' relationships with each other.

This critique of consumerism is continued in a different register in the subsequent sequence. Shenran stands up Zixin after he picks Angelina. After Zixin discovers this, she goes to a high-class restaurant and gorges herself on several dishes. Her taking refuge in consumption suggests the way these characters rely on money and luxury to cover up some kind of lack or emptiness in their lives. Shortly after this she suddenly remembers her planned date with Qihong and rushes to the meeting spot. Qihong, however, has already left in disappointment. Zixin looks around dejectedly, before a cut to a shot of the famous Hong Kong skyline at night, lined with the neon names of banks and companies of the type Zixin works for. This again suggests the impact that the financial district and its values have on the characters and their inner worlds. To's aforementioned *Life Without Principle* uses similar inserted shots of the Hong Kong skyline, to much more devastating critical effect. Zixin and Qihong's romantic disappointments, and Shenran's remorse at picking Angelina over Zixin, are further linked to stock market fluctuations when the first act of the film draws to a close with the onset of the 2008 financial crisis. As chaos erupts in the financial offices, the camera careens around these gleaming skyscrapers, showing Zixin and Shenran looking at each other in dejection. One shot that slowly zooms toward Zixin at her desk, framed by a window with thick grey borders, makes it seem more as if she is trapped in a prison cell than an office. She looks across at Shenran's empty office and sees the silly Post-it note creation stuck to his window; a reverse shot shows a close-up of a mournful-looking Zixin. The romantic possibilities this milieu appears to offer seem destined to fail, like the financial crash that ends this first movement.

The film then jumps to three years later, with Qihong, still pining for Zixin, (coincidentally) setting up his business in Shenran's old office and Shenran becoming CEO of the bank Zixin works for. A scene shortly after the "three years later" title elucidates how the film's style draws out the conundrum of choice that seems unable to satisfy the characters. After Zixin discovers Shenran is her new boss, she announces plans to quit due to his past transgressions with Angelina. Shenran, eager to get closer to her, persuades her to stay on for at least three months and asks her to write a report. He later calls her and tells her to meet him at an auto showroom with the report, and he asks her to test-drive a car while he checks the report. A rapid-fire sequence of quick camera pans, flurries of motion, and cuts follow during the test drive, before they return to the showroom. After Zixin meekly expresses approval of Shenran's choice, he decides to buy the car. Zixin starts in surprise, asking why Shenran has not even stopped to think about it. This dialogue is spoken as they are rapidly striding through the dealership, the salesperson literally running to keep up, and the camera rapidly following their movements. An abrupt cut, timed to perfection, features Zixin to the left of the frame, Shenran in the center, and the salesperson to the right. The sudden stillness of the camera here when Shenran halts his march breaks the gliding rhythm of the sequence, emphasizing the rapidity with which a decision must be made. Shenran asks, "Hold on, is that a 'No'?" Zixin replies, "What do I care? Buy it if you want," to which Shenran reiterates to the salesperson that he will buy the car. What does this decision mean? As Shenran strides out of the shop, the salesperson asks him what color car he would like, and Shenran tells him to ask Zixin. As Shenran drives off Zixin shouts out after him, "I'll just close my eyes and pick whatever." This sequence underscores a key theme of the film: these characters have no inherent interest or investment in what they are choosing. Shenran appears to stage this drama of choice as a ploy to get closer to Zixin; it is never mentioned whom the car is for, and no further reference is made to it. But this does not negate Shenran's attitude that decisions must always be made rapidly, and the speed at which this sequence takes place—conveyed through the characters' movements, the (visual and aural) zooming of the car, the rapid cuts, and the almost constant movement of the camera—provokes an adrenaline rush much in the same way consumerism and stock market speculation do. Neither Shenran nor Zixin cares what they are buying. By logical extension the money they make from investment and market speculation is also an empty endeavor, a desire burned out almost before it even ignites, just as their romantic desires seem at once intense and fleeting.

Zixin continually flip-flops between her attraction to Shenran's alpha male magnetism, ably captured in Louis Koo's portrayal, and the warmth and loyalty of Qihong, encapsulated by Daniel Wu's purposefully understated performance. Shenran's waywardness usually precipitates the swing of Zixin's affections from him to Qihong. This unresolvable emotional conflict maintains the classic structure of romantic comedy—keeping partners apart for as long as possible—and it is genuinely unclear whom Zixin will choose at the end. Tom Gunning writes that the relationship in *I Know Where I'm*

Going! (1945) "possesses the secret of every love affair; forging a relation to a universal, if not cosmic experience that, at the same time, seems fundamentally unique and individual."[13] The relationships in *DGBMY*, however, struggle to be unique and individual, due at least in part to the influence that the financial and hyperconsumerist world they inhabit appears to have on Zixin and Shenran, effects which rub off on Qihong too.

For example, in a scene that follows the "three years later" title card, Zixin returns to Hong Kong from a research trip in China to investigate new restaurant investment possibilities. She outlines the pros and cons of two different restaurants to her colleagues and considers whether their shares will go higher or lower. Her indecisiveness begins to sound strangely like her indecision toward her two suitors, and the ebbs and flows of the stocks she describes mirror her fluctuating affections. The universe we are in here is one in which the stock exchange and love present similar problems: lots of choices but little certainty. The mise-en-scène also highlights the performativity of Zixin's actions, since this scene is intercut with shots of Shenran watching at a distance with obvious pleasure at discovering he is Zixin's new boss and thus can reacquaint himself with her. Establishing shots present Zixin and her colleagues in the foreground with Shenran watching in the background; there follows individual shots of Zixin's "performance" and cuts to individual shots of Shenran looking on. Toward the end of Zixin's speech on the pros and cons of each investment possibility, a behind-the-shoulder shot shows Shenran's perspective. This point-of-view shot of him watching Zixin's "performance" visually delineates his assessment of the pros and cons of Zixin herself. It is as if he is deciding whether to "invest" his attention and time on her, in a manner analogous to Zixin's weighing up investment possibilities.

Performance becomes an increasingly important factor in the topsy-turvy plot in which Shenran and Qihong rise and fall repeatedly in Zixin's estimation, culminating with each male suitor trying to outperform the other through increasingly extreme actions. Gunning describes love stories as spending "less time on the outcome than on the dalliance, the lingering, during which love builds and becomes inevitable."[14] In *DGBMH*, however, dalliance is replaced by eccentric actions, as exemplified by the magic tricks Shenran uses to woo the ladies in adjacent buildings. Qihong, in his new office opposite Zixin's, also starts to perform for Zixin, using magic tricks similar to those Shenran performed earlier, which she watches in amusement through her neighboring office window. Qihong, we gather, performs these tricks a little desperately, knowing Zixin missed their date three years previously due to Shenran's magic display. But these actions are purely performance, rather than genuine expressions of affection, with Qihong's imitation of Shenran's tricks reinforcing this; they fail to conjure up genuine feelings of intimacy and communication. Qihong performs his tricks at night under a spotlight as if on a stage, heightening the already theatrical effect. The framing of these performances through glass windows again recalls Friedberg's description of "window shopping" as eliciting consumer contemplation by means of arranging window displays to draw the gaze and desires of passing window-shoppers.[15] Shenran, from a window horizontally across from Zixin's, watches Qihong's performance in dismay as he sees Zixin's attention moving from him toward Qihong. In this ultracapitalist milieu, looking either becomes enmeshed with ownership or evokes bitterness in not having. In another scene, Qihong cooks for Zixin in his office, while Shenran invites another woman to eat in his office, so that each dining pair can see the other through their office windows. Shenran, becoming increasingly jealous, tells the woman he is with to feed him, all the while looking through the window to see Zixin's reaction, his performance masking his displeasure at being displaced. In a comically lackadaisical way he also feeds the woman while anxiously looking to see what Zixin and Qihong are doing. When Zixin pulls down the blinds of the office window to block Shenran's view, he jumps up and shouts out, "What's going on?," as if the curtains had fallen in the middle of a scene in a play. The womanizing Shenran balks at

The office becomes a stage for a performance of fighting in *Don't Go Breaking My Heart*.

the idea of Zixin claiming the right to see men other than him. Later, Shenran angrily confronts Qihong about Zixin. Zixin's colleagues watch them fight from the vantage point of their office window opposite Qihong's. The stage metaphor is underscored by wide-angle shots of Qihong's office that take up the whole image; the space visually morphs into a stage on which this fight is taking place.

DGBMH by no means condemns its characters; it places them, rather, in a landscape full of romantic possibilities, hopes, and desires. But the film's narrative and visual strategies make clear that these desires have no chance of being fulfilled, because they are intrinsically linked to the values of capitalism: money, status, and competition, values that thwart or undermine individual fulfillment. These characters' desires are ultimately constituted by the system they inhabit. The materialist world these characters live and work in necessarily conflicts with their need for intimacy and connection, but none of the characters undergoes any sort of transformation or attempt to struggle against this system and so has no hope of addressing the issues that block romantic fulfillment.

The motifs of romance as window-shopping and performance culminate in a wildly over-the-top finale, in which the competition between Shenran and Qihong reaches literally absurd heights. After Shenran proves incapable of being a "martian" in love—that is, to have eyes only for Zixin—Zixin chooses Qihong. But, even after this choice, Zixin clearly still has feelings for Shenran. This is visualized when Shenran goes to Zixin's hometown of Suzhou in search of her, and an image of Shenran staring out of a taxi window is immediately followed by a rhyming image of Zixin looking out a car window, a rhyme accentuated when their vehicles pass each other. Both are clearly thinking of the other, despite Zixin being on her way to meet Qihong's parents. During this meeting Shenran arranges for a wedding ring to be placed in a menu and given to Zixin, while a giant banner reading "Marry Me" is unraveled on the rooftop of the building opposite. On the phone with Zixin, as they again look at each other through glass windows, Shenran tells her she is the only one for him, but Zixin cannot believe him. Qihong then upstages Shenran's actions when the same words appear in huge electronically illuminated letters on the giant skyscraper opposite the hotel. He bends down on one knee, and Zixin finally accepts Qihong's proposal. Shenran graciously accepts defeat as he puts his thumb up in the air from the rooftop of the building opposite, and Qihong, now hugging

Zixin, reciprocates. They all wave at each other, and the film abruptly ends. Both men's desperate attempts to win Zixin come off as lacking sincerity and intimacy, since they essentially do the same thing. The conventions of romantic comedy demand that Zixin eventually must choose one of her suitors. But, in the film's marketized, consumerist milieu, the romantic escapades increasingly fail to produce anything more than empty gestures and instability. Zixin's choice at the end seems arbitrary, as if either suitor could have worked. This doubt over Zixin and Qihong's "happily ever after" ending is precisely what the sequel plays on.

Don't Go Breaking My Heart 2

The sequel, in fact, casts a somber shadow over the lighter, warmer first film. The narrative satisfaction of most romantic comedies hinges on the romantic couple walking into the sunset happily ever after. This often happens at the expense of an excluded partner who loses at love, with the jilted party easily dismissed because true love transpired to bring the romantic narrative to a satisfying close.[16] While *DGBMH* complicated this framework, *DGBMH 2* seems intent on demolishing it. The sequel opens innocently enough, with a series of chance encounters that link together old and new characters. Yang (Miriam Yeung), referred to by Zixin as the "Goddess of Stocks," is having trouble fitting her Ferrari into a tight parking space and wishes for a handsome guy to help her. Who should oblige but Shenran, who offers assistance as he passes by. Meanwhile, at a boutique down the street, Zixin tries on a wedding dress in preparation for her marriage to Qihong. On his way there, Zixin's brother Paul (Vic Chou), a designer who just happens to own a luxurious yacht, notices Yang and is instantly besotted with her. With this character set-up accomplished and the elite world these characters occupy established, a manic series of romantic encounters ensues: coincidences, misunderstandings, and passions that switch from high to low faster than the stock market crashes that punctuate the film. Qihong is busy on a building project in Suzhou, which delays the wedding; apart from several curiously subdued Skype conversations with Zixin, he barely appears in the film until the end. This plot device means Zixin is alone in Hong Kong, with Shenran still prowling around the central business district. Zixin, who has remained unsure about the romantic choice she made in the first film, becomes even more conflicted as Shenran enters again into her sights.

Several plot flourishes convey the difficulty of establishing a relationship within this financial-urban milieu. When, at film's start, Zixin asks her idol Yang if she can work for her, Yang asks her if the market will go up or down in a month. Zixin replies, "Up . . . since a weak stock market leads to speculating in QE [quantitative easing]." Yang replies that if she is wrong, she will get the job. She is wrong and gets her reward. Why this would get her the job is not specified, but it appears to be a comment on the speculative, unproductive, inequality-exacerbating nature of the financial markets, which connects to the characters working in this milieu consistently making the *wrong* choices in their love lives. In one of the film's wackier plot points, Yang and Paul steal a psychic octopus that can predict losers (but not winners), which they use to predict sporting contests and the financial markets, a further instance of choices leading to loss or disappointment.

The stock market itself plays a bigger role in this film than in the first. For instance, during a meeting, Yang takes her colleagues to look through the window at the office windows in the opposite building to see how Shenran is reacting after the stock market plunges. *DGBMH 1*'s use of office windows relates almost exclusively to the romantic plot, but here the stifling processes of financialization shatter even this potential window of romantic possibility. In another scene, Paul invites Yang to his luxurious yacht for dinner. Settings of luxury are often used in romantic comedies to explain how the potential pair has the leisure to focus so single-mindedly on love. Stanley Cavell points out that these luxurious settings "require central characters whose work can be postponed without fear of its loss," to allow games to be played and fun to be had between the pair.[17] Yet, in another marker of the way the working milieu of finance short-circuits romantic fulfillment, when Yang is onboard Paul's yacht eating dinner, she pulls out a tablet to check on the stock market. She is more interested in playing stocks than playing games with her potential partner.

Daniel Kasman observes that the "market-and-consumerism focus of all the characters [in *DGBMH 2*] is part and parcel with *how they love* and *how they treat their love lives*. The women and men are objects to aspire to owning, to capture and consume; once gotten the magic is gone and they move on either to something new or to the object they now no longer have" (emphasis in original).[18] The film consistently presents paired scenes to elucidate this consumerist ethos. Shenran meets Yang by helping get her car into a tight parking spot. After they start dating, Shenran meets another woman and takes her out. Yang sees them together and once again is stuck in a tight parking space; this time Paul comes to the rescue. Thus begins a love triangle between these three similar to the one in *DGBMH*. Shenran's juggling act between romancing Yang, pursuing various other women, and his pining for Zixin reaches screwball levels of madcap comedy when he and the camera race from room to room trying to keep apart five women including Yang, who all visit his office to celebrate his birthday, while Zixin watches this farce from her office opposite. After Yang discovers Shenran's multiple transgressions, she goes off with Paul. Creating another paired scene, the next day Shenran asks Yang to dinner at the same restaurant where he lost Zixin in the first film. These paired scenes suggest that the characters are less fully individualized personalities, at least as romantic possibilities, than interchangeable commodities. Here, Shenran tells Yang he felt the same breathlessness when he saw her with Paul as he did when he saw Zixin go off with Qihong; he asks Yang to marry him, and she says yes. These repeated pairing scenes remind us of the multiple choices on offer and that nothing has changed in Shenran's approach: he makes grand declarations only when he worries he is about to lose something.

While Shenran carries on these fast-paced shenanigans, he also spends some of his nights in Zixin's old apartment, which he now rents, going to sleep watching a video filmed on his phone in *DGBMH* of Zixin dancing and singing in her office. Later in the film, Yang walks into Shenran's rented apartment and sees Shenran asleep beneath the image of Zixin dancing in her office projected on his wall. At this moment, from Yang's perspective, Zixin is literally the woman of Shenran's dreams. But, for Shenran, it seems that it is not Zixin herself but this image of her that is the dream woman, an idealized projection that Zixin herself cannot possibly live up to. In *DGBMH*, Shenran told Zixin that this filmed image of her dancing kept him going through the "hard times" when he moved to America after the financial crash. Yet, even when he has a chance to meet her again three years later, he makes a genuine effort to pursue her—or, perhaps, the image of her on his phone—only when he is in danger of losing her.

The narrative fluctuations continue as it becomes clear that neither Shenran nor Zixin know what they really want. The morning after Yang witnesses Shenran's "night" with Zixin, Shenran puts the wedding rings that he gave to Zixin in the first film and Yang in the second into the psychic octopus's tank for help, mirroring the way Yang uses the octopus to predict

Yang (Miriam Yeung) watches Shenran (Louis Koo) sleeping beneath images projected onto his wall of Zixin (Gao Yuanyuan) singing and dancing, in *Don't Go Breaking My Heart 2*.

stock market performance. Shortly after, Shenran hesitatingly tells Yang that what she witnessed the night before was his farewell to Zixin, yet minutes later he chases after Zixin, having spotting her through the windows of the offices opposite. Despite Zixin's attempts to escape from Shenran, eventually fleeing to Suzhou for her wedding with Qihong, we see her in her wedding dress looking despondently out of the car window on her way to the ceremony. The image and tone of this shot mirrors a similar shot discussed above from the end of the first film, as Zixin seems uncertain and ambivalent about her final destination. In seeming reply, Shenran performs his most outrageous gesture yet and begins to climb up the skyscraper in which Zixin and Qihong will marry, with all five of the films' main characters glimpsing Shenran through windows at various levels of his climb.

The film saves its most vicious skewering of the conventions of the romantic comedy for the finale, after Shenran is rescued from the skyscraper's roof. All five characters converge in the wedding ceremony lounge as Shenran tells Zixin he wants to give their love one last shot, while Qihong tells a distraught Zixin that she can choose again if she wishes. This conclusion echoes the choice Zixin had to make in the first film, only this time she chooses Shenran. Meanwhile, Paul professes his love to Yang, only to be rejected, although as Yang leaves in the elevator Paul rushes after her and kneels down to put on her shoes. This is the most intimate gesture of the entire film, but, since Yang has already declined Paul's marriage proposal, and their relationship resembles Zixin and Qihong's, their future happiness is not assured. Shenran and Zixin rush to an elevator, and, on the way down, three busty women get on, causing Shenran to have a nosebleed, a recurring comic gag throughout both films that here portends, despite Zixin's apparent amusement, that Shenran is incapable of change. The film ends on a cateogorically tragic note that sums up the undermining of romantic comedy conventions in this ultracapitalist context. After Qihong has been abandoned, he stands alone in the deserted marriage suite drinking whiskey, ironically surrounded by the vast arrangements of pink and white flowers intended for his wedding. He hoarsely sings, "I would do anything for you," from a famous Chinese pop song by Faye Wong. This also references *DGBMH*'s ending, since violins played the melody of this song in the restaurant where Zixin accepted his proposal. He wryly smiles, and the film ends with him taking a long swig of whiskey. This final image of *DGBMH 2* severely challenges the ideal of romantic love constructed in pop songs and romantic comedies by lingering on the broken-hearted character. No happily ever after seems possible for any of the couples within this consumerist, speculative, urban milieu.

Conclusion

When scrutinized to a closer degree than their glossy look and lighthearted tone appear to warrant, the *DGBMH* films ask the intensely relevant question of where human priorities lie within the system of capitalism. The romantic comedy's foundations shake when this world of financialization and unquenchable consumerist desire appears to lock down its characters and delimit their possibilities for growth. Would these characters be any happier and would their futures be more optimistic if they could escape from their consumerist, speculative, high-stakes lifestyles? Who knows, but these two films reveal the trials and tribulations of love shaped by—and as precarious as—the system that encourages fluctuating stock markets and permits the crashes that punctuate each film. Once a love story ends there is no assurance that the happy couple will remain happy; the way a narrative continues living after it has finished within a constructed work of art is part of the transience and permanence of the logic of both art and the human emotion of love.[19] The circular narratives in the *DGBMH* films, in which the characters seem doomed to repeat the same mistakes, fails to proffer the traditional happy couple at either film's end, and it seems that none of the characters will be fulfilled in their relationships. Through visual and narrative means, the two films posit that the intrinsic nature of late capitalism in its most extreme forms pierces the bubble of romantic love, revealing the flimsy ideological foundations of romantic comedy.

Notes

1. The Chinese titles are 單身男女 *1* and *2*, which literally translate as "Single men and women."
2. Robin Wood, "Never Never Change, Always Gonna Dance," *Film Comment* 15, no. 5 (September–October 1979): 31.
3. James MacDowell, "Romantic Comedy: Love, Nervousness & Intertextuality," Alternate Takes, February 15, 2009, www.alternatetakes.co.uk/?2009%2C2%2C222.
4. Adrian Martin, *Mysteries of Cinema: Reflections on Film Theory, History, and Culture, 1982–2016* (Amsterdam: Amsterdam University Press, 2018), 304–5.
5. In a 2001 interview, Johnnie To acknowledges the market conditions his production company Milkyway Image (set up in 1996) must consider by clearly delineating between the goals of their commercial genre movies (aimed at achieving box office success, such as that of romantic comedy *Needing You* [2000]) and their less profitable personal movies (the crime thrillers). See Shelly Kraicer, "Interview: Johnnie To and Wai Ka-fai," *Senses of Cinema* 18, December 2001, www.sensesofcinema.com/2001/feature-articles/to_and_ka-fai/.
6. Since the formation of Milkyway Image in 1996, roughly one-third of Johnnie To's output as director has been in the "commercial movies" category, including romantic comedies, romances, and comedies.
7. Wai Ka-fai is credited as one of several coscriptwriters on both *DGBMH* films. Wai is also credited as codirector with To on *DGBMH*, while To takes sole directing credit for *DGBMH 2*.
8. Kate Kellaway, "John Berger: 'If I'm a storyteller, it's because I listen,'" *Guardian*, October 30, 2016, www.theguardian.com/books/2016/oct/30/john-berger-at-90-interview-storyteller.
9. Ignatiy Vishnevetsky, "Laissez-faire Love Triangle," Mubi Notebook, August 28, 2011, mubi.com/notebook/posts/laissez-faire-love-triangle.

10 Anne Friedberg, *Window Shopping: Cinema and the Postmodern* (Berkeley: University of California Press, 1993), 57.
11 Friedberg, *Window Shopping*, 65.
12 Towering skyscrapers are often employed as symbols of corrupted economic and social institutions, particularly in science fiction and film noir films, but I see no reason that the same cannot apply to romantic comedies, especially when put into context with To's aforementioned *Life Without Principle*.
13 Tom Gunning, "On Knowing and Not Knowing on Going and Not Going, Loving and Not Loving: *I Know Where I Am Going!* and Falling in Love Again," in *The Cinema of Michael Powell*, ed. Ian Christie and Andrew Moor (London: BFI, 2005), 95.
14 Gunning, "On Knowing and Not Knowing," 96.
15 Friedberg, *Window Shopping*, 66.
16 Meg Shields, "The Romantic Comedy Ideology," Film School Rejects, July 17, 2018, filmschoolrejects.com/romantic-comedy-ideology/.
17 Stanley Cavell, *Pursuits of Happiness: The Hollywood Comedy of Remarriage* (Cambridge, MA: Harvard University Press, 1981), 88.
18 Adam Cook, "TIFF 2014. Dialogues: Johnnie To's *Don't Go Breaking My Heart 2*," Mubi Notebook, September 13, 2014, mubi.com/notebook/posts/tiff-2014-dialogues-johnnie-tos-dont-go-breaking-my-heart-2.
19 Cavell, *Pursuits of Happiness*, 108.

8

Obvious Child, Bookshops, and Postcrisis Romcom Urbanism

Martha Shearer

In *When Harry Met Sally* . . . (1989), Harry (Billy Crystal) and Sally (Meg Ryan)'s friendship begins, after a series of less amenable encounters, in a bookshop. In the wake of that film's success, romantic comedies, especially when set in New York, often replicated the film's vision of urban life, emphasizing urban iconicity but also urban culture, with romantic comedy protagonists typically working in creative professions as architects, writers, magazine editors, and the like. Bookshops would reappear too, notably in *You've Got Mail* (1998) and *Notting Hill* (1999), while in romcoms such as *Serendipity* (2001) and *Definitely, Maybe* (2008) books have a critical narrative function: both examples incorporate quests for one specific secondhand book of great personal value. The genre's preoccupation with books and bookshops is such that it is skewered in romcom parody *They Came Together* (2014) as its protagonists bond, in a bookshop, over their mutual love of "fiction books."

The recurrence of books and bookshops in the genre connects romance with a romanticization of literary culture that often equates to a focus on upper-middle-class cultural capital. But bookshops also came to prominence in the romcom at a time when independent bookshops were coming under pressures from competition with chain stores. Laura Miller notes that, while independent booksellers first started collaborating and forming a collective identity when faced with major competition from chains in the 1970s, it was the emergence of superstores in the 1990s that saw independent bookshops "engaged in rhetoric and action they recognized as explicitly political and oriented toward exposing the conflicts of interests within their industry."[1] This activism drew on the kind of antichain rhetoric also directed at, for example, Starbucks.[2] Books, however, were special: "In the valorization of the independent bookseller, one hears distaste for a number of tendencies associated with capitalism and the process of rationalization, as well as a sense that books are exceptionally moral objects deserving of protection from these forces."[3]

The specialness of bookshops grants them the possibility of generating resistance to those "tendencies associated with capitalism," or at least to the expression of cultural anxieties about the relationship between capitalism, culture, and the built environment. Miller notes, however, that while "one can occasionally hear the wistful suggestion that it would be nice if books and bookstores were not private property, that the world would be a better place if books and the means to distribute them were available to everyone," independent booksellers instead tended to stress "bigness."[4] Tara Brabazon similarly notes that bookshops, specifically San Francisco's City Lights, and their surrounding neighborhoods tend to possess an "enclave consciousness," such that a bookshop, rather than actually generating any meaningful political opposition, is a "fount of critique, criticism, distinctiveness and opportunity."[5] In that context, bookshops often have come to be nostalgically romanticized. Jim Collins argues that the struggling bookshop owners of *You've Got Mail* and *Notting Hill* "replaced the starving young artist as the epitome of romantic cultural chic, embodying a sweet, but nonetheless, comical earnestness in their disdain of the marketplace for the pursuit of higher cultural ideals."[6]

The bookshop's special position has resulted in films that highlight and mourn its unstable position in contemporary New York, generating narratives from threats to the continued survival of independent bookshops. An early example, *Crossing Delancey* (1988), opens with a party at the bookshop where Isabelle (Amy Irving) works, celebrating it being recently saved from closure. Most prominently preoccupied with the urban bookstore's changing fortunes, *You've Got Mail* stages a conflict between Kathleen's (Meg Ryan) quirky independent children's bookshop and the latest branch of Fox Books, a chain that Joe (Tom Hanks) manages. Kathleen's store, which has supposedly "been there forever" (somewhat eliding the history of the Upper West Side's gentrification) is ultimately forced to close, clearly inspired by the closure of the same Shakespeare & Co. that had appeared in the Nora Ephron–penned *When Harry Met Sally*... due to competition with a nearby branch of Barnes & Noble.[7] *You've Got Mail* is notable for its deviation from what Diane Negra has argued was a hallmark of romantic comedy of the

1990s and early 2000s: an "intensely romanticized city" that posited a relationship between couple and city whereby "the union of one is somehow bound up with the unity of the other."⁸ *You've Got Mail*'s Upper West Side *is* intensely romanticized, but also under threat, and the union of the couple occurs only after the loss of the most intensely romanticized site in that city, Kathleen's Shop Around the Corner. Negra does identify another cluster of films that foreground urban conditions in ways that deviate from generic norms. She argues that *Kate & Leopold* (2001), *Two Weeks' Notice* (2002), and *How to Lose a Guy in Ten Days* (2003) "conjoin fantasies of romantic transcendence with direct or oblique invocations of the integrity of the Manhattan infrastructure," responding to post-9/11 anxieties about the built environment with a reassertion of ideological gender boundaries. The anxieties of the bookshop romcom are not produced by terrorist atrocities, however, but by capitalism.⁹

If the bookshop's status was precarious before the 2008 financial crisis, it seems unsurprising that after the crisis it would reemerge as a purposeful setting. In *Obvious Child* (2014), as in *You've Got Mail*, an independent bookshop is forced to close. But, far from the upper-middle-class milieu of the Ephron films, Donna (Jenny Slate) lives in hipster Williamsburg and works at a radical bookshop (named Unoppressive Non-Imperialist Bargain Books—a real West Village bookshop). The film is a prime example of the shifts the romantic comedy has undergone in recent years: not only in its swing from peak popularity to apparent death, but also in its move from the glossy urban affluence of studio romcoms to the grittier recessionary anxiety of indie romcoms.¹⁰ Over the last decade, a wealth of scholarship has sought to understand how the crisis has reshaped culture and modes of representation.¹¹ With particular pertinence for the romantic comedy, Diane Negra and Yvonne Tasker have argued that the crisis has revealed how "postfeminist culture's key tropes—a preoccupation with self-fashioning and the makeover; women's seeming 'choice' not to occupy high-status public roles; the celebration of sexual expression and affluent femininities—[were] enabled by the optimism and opportunity of prosperity (or the perception of it)."¹² They suggest that in recessionary culture "female centered genres are undergoing an affective transformation that leads away from (plausible) romantic comedy toward other kinds of texts such as moody vampire dramas."¹³ But we can also identify a shift in the romantic comedy itself toward indie romcoms privileging young women engaged in precarious creative labor in gentrifying bohemian neighborhoods—for example, in *Celeste & Jesse Forever* (2012), *A Case of You* (2013), and *Appropriate Behavior* (2014).[14]

Stanley Corkin argues that the revival of the New York romantic comedy in the late 1970s was reliant on the city's incipient gentrification at that time.[15] The romcom's depiction of independent bookshops points to gentrification as a simultaneously cultural and material process, both romanticizing a particular model of urban culture and identifying pressures of both competition from big business and the workings of the real estate market. In the wake of the 2008 crisis, when the romcom's vision of urban prosperity has become untenable, those anxieties are especially acute. *Obvious Child* is a striking example of the indie romcom's concerns with precarity, urban instability, and crisis, connecting the bookshop's closure to a series of crises Donna experiences at once. In this chapter, I situate *Obvious Child* as a bookshop romcom within that postcrisis urban context. Its use of the genre's bookshop tropes reworks its literary romanticization to a recessionary context in ways that sidestep addressing the urban fractures it reveals.

Taking Back the Romcom

Books and bookshops are fundamental to *Obvious Child*'s romantic narrative. When Max (Jake Lacy) and Donna first meet, she is in a tailspin after being recently dumped and told that she will lose her bookshop job due to its imminent closure. A few weeks after their one-night stand (and after Donna has discovered that she is pregnant), Max walks into the bookshop as it's being packed up to find Donna sitting in a box, looking forlorn. When he proposes a date, she uses the shop closing as an excuse not to accept (thus avoiding informing him of her pregnancy). They are later again reunited via books, when he returns a book to his business studies professor's apartment, only to reencounter Donna, who is, unbeknownst to him, his professor's daughter. The film reasserts the romcom's identification of books with romance, but also the instability of the bookshop itself, with its bookshop closure subplot.

The bookshop closure is in this case, however, just one facet of a larger crisis Donna experiences in the film. Early scenes proceed as an accumulation of Donna's own personal crises: a breakup, a job loss, an unwanted pregnancy, and a subsequent abortion. Those crises also shape the film's aesthetic. Immediately after her breakup, she returns home and drinks heavily

Packing up the bookshop in *Obvious Child*.

straight from a wine bottle while leaving her ex a series of erratic voicemails, edited together using jump cuts. The editing here becomes a representation of her fractured state of mind, using temporal discontinuity as a visual expression of her internal disarray. These editing patterns are replicated in Max and Donna's later one-night stand, visually situating it as a symptom of Donna's crisis. That disarray is also conveyed through the film's set pieces. Donna is a stand-up comedian, and we see her perform at several critical junctures. The warmly received opening set—before her boyfriend dumps her in the comedy club's bathroom—is later followed by a disastrous one in which she launches into a drunken, largely joke-free tirade about her relationship breakdown as audience members heckle her and walk out.[16] By associating the bookshop closure with a more general experience of crisis on Donna's part, *Obvious Child* might be read as a reframing of the bookshop romcom in the context of crisis, one of the effects of which is to foreground the bookshop's material instability.

But *Obvious Child* also differs significantly from, say, *You've Got Mail* in its lack of specificity about, or even interest in, the causes of that closure. Donna's manager simply tells her "the landlord's kicking us out in six weeks." This very lack of specificity is more suggestive of the rent hikes and gentrification that have caused many of the city's small businesses to close—and a presumption of the audience's knowledge of the prevalence of such closures—than of direct competition with either chains or e-commerce, the core features of independent bookstore activism in the 1990s and 2000s. Moreover, in New York in particular, one of the key ways in which gentrification has been controversial and contested in the last decade has been its impact on small businesses. Jeremiah Moss, founder of the grassroots activist project #SaveNYC, which campaigns to protect small businesses, identifies a shift around 2005 whereby small shops, bars, and restaurants "seemed to be going faster than ever, replaced by national chains and upscale businesses ... all looking the same."[17] *Obvious Child*'s director Gillian Robespierre's account of the store's inclusion in the film is very much in line with such rhetoric:

> The narrative in the movie of the store shutting down was very much a deliberate comment on the struggles that independent businesses face, especially in New York City with rents being astronomical, as well as the general decline in actual books being sold and the advancement into the digital age.... I grew up in New York City in the '80s and '90s when the city was only mom-and-pop stores. Starbucks didn't rule the streets and banks were not on every corner. We always wanted Donna to work in a small bookshop where the environment felt very familial (that's very much the vibe of Jim [Drougas]'s shop [Unoppressive Non-Imperialist Bargain Books]).[18]

This kind of antigentrification activism relies on a contrast between the distinct local character of small businesses as opposed to bland, corporate standardization, a contrast common to antichain independent bookseller activism. Miller argues that bookstore chains "contribute to a world where commercial districts look increasingly alike," so that "the demise of the independent bookseller is a reminder of how large, impersonal, powerful institutions are controlling more and more aspects of our lives."[19] Contemporary small business activism points to the powerful larger force of gentrification, as well as of chains, but does so in similar terms, seeing institutions like independent bookshops as vital to the city's character and therefore to efforts to resist gentrification.

By drawing on this context in the crisis it stages for the bookshop itself, I would suggest that *Obvious Child* exposes gentrification-induced urban fractures that become more visible in the film's treatment of its other key setting: Williamsburg, where Donna lives and where most of the film takes place. Williamsburg is also where she meets Max, who has come to the comedy club—and indeed to Brooklyn in general— because one of his clients' wives had heard about it. His presence is therefore an act of tourism that frames his and Donna's subsequent faltering romance in terms of a corporate-bohemian encounter that corresponds to contemporary local conflicts. Williamsburg was one of a number of U.S. neighborhoods that became distinctive in the 1990s for their arts scenes after ethnic, working-class residents had been displaced by higher rents.[20] In that respect, Williamsburg has much in common with Chicago's Wicker Park, the subject of Richard Lloyd's landmark study *Neo-Bohemia* (2006). Wicker Park's 1990s transformation "from a relatively obscure and depopulated barrio into a celebrated center of hip urban culture" shaped the culture produced there.[21] The "gritty aesthetic of the local scene," he argues, is "imprinted on the aesthetic representations produced by cultural creators, representations that evoke the glamour of urban instability, available to be consumed at a safe distance." An identification with the neighborhood's "grit" allowed those cultural creators to "reassure themselves of their legitimate claim to edginess, though the neighborhood itself also teeters uneasily on the verge."[22] Sharon Zukin contrasts that aestheticization of grit in consumer culture with "the bland homogeneity of corporate offices and suburban homes," with clear parallels to the reaction against rationalization that Miller sees in contemporary bookseller activism.[23]

More recently, however, Brooklyn has seen the impact of what Loretta Lees calls "super-gentrification": "the transformation of already gentrified, prosperous and solidly upper-middle-class neighborhoods into much more exclusive and expensive enclaves."[24] That acceleration of gentrification as a process threatens not only Brooklyn's older, working-class communities but also upper-middle-class neighborhoods and the earlier, bohemian gentrifiers. Zukin describes this as a crisis of "authenticity"—defined as "a continuous process of living and working, a gradual buildup of everyday experience, the expectation that neighbors and buildings that are here today will be here tomorrow"—and identifies the loss of local small businesses as symptoms of this loss of the city's "soul."[25] Especially since the financial crisis, "grit" has become ever more loaded, understood always in relation to the perceived threat of supergentrification and corporate homogeneity. Cultural claims to edginess based on affiliation with gritty neighborhoods are now themselves sites of gentrification panic, focused especially on young white creative women. *Girls* (HBO, 2012–2017), for example, generated considerable concern and hostility at its apparent white, middle-class representational displacement, and a similarly hostile reaction greeted both Taylor

Swift's 2014 track "Welcome to New York," widely received as a "gentrification anthem," and her subsequent appointment as New York City's "official welcome ambassador."[26]

Rebecca Wanzo argues that 21st-century comedy has seen the emergence of a new, abject millennial female subject: "Abjection is often a principal sign of these characters' precarity: they inhabit spaces where they often recoil from others and vice versa, and their constant association with that which is considered gross (like dirt, vomit, and feces) is habitually a sign of what emotional and economic insecurity has wrought."[27] Donna shares that emotional and economic insecurity, and both the film and her character are preoccupied with not only her bodily crisis, as in her unwanted pregnancy and abortion, but also her bodily functions: there are numerous bathroom scenes, she pees in the street, in her stand-up routines she talks about "what a vagina does to underpants" and holding in farts in the early stages of dating her boyfriend. Her mother characterizes Donna's romantic type as "smelly," referring to a previous boyfriend who did not use deodorant for environmental reasons. In postcrisis cinema and television, the urban grit of alternative culture manifests in the abject. Max, by contrast, is consistently presented as neat, ordered, and square: a business student, coming from a small town with a school in a barn, taken aback by Donna peeing in the street. Max and Donna's first shared screen time occurs when, drinking, she walks into the comedy club's gender-neutral bathroom, its walls covered with graffiti, and then puts her glass down next to him; he, meanwhile, is meticulously washing his hands and wearing a neatly ironed shirt tucked into belted pants. Donna articulates the difference between her and Max both as a cultural one and as one between chaos and order; whereas Max is "like a Christmas tree," she is "the menorah on top that burns it down." In her final stand-up sequence toward the end of the film, she begins by contrasting herself with an idea of an adult woman with a "schedule" who does not worry about "why the bathroom smells in a weird way," both reinforcing the connection between Donna and the abject and implying a contrast between Donna and the kinds of professional woman who were romcom leads in precrisis studio romcoms; see the emphasis on stressed, uptight professional women in *Kate & Leopold* (2001), *Just Like Heaven* (2005), and *Fever Pitch* (2005), for example.

John Limon argues that stand-up comedy is rooted in a "tense intimacy" between performer and audience rooted in an avowal and disavowal of abjection, a tendency of which Lenny Bruce telling his audience, "I am going to piss on you," to 17 seconds of laughter is exemplary. Limon situates the emergence of stand-up in what he calls "the suburban moment of modern American culture."[28] Its popularity in the 1960s relied on a desire for the sex and aggression repressed by suburbanization's flight to civility, where what is most abject in comedy is "the city and its commercial filth, the body and its excrement."[29] *Obvious Child* reframes that urban/suburban tension as one between bohemian grit and the gentrification that threatens to sanitize it, a desire rendered not repulsive by being filtered through a conventionalized relationship between performer and audience and managed by the romantic comedy's conventionalized structuring oppositions. The contrast between Max and Donna is explicitly connected to place: when she mocks his slip-on loafers, he says, "Welcome to Brooklyn, where they judge you by your shoes." The film delights in messing up Max's controlled neatness in his encounters in Brooklyn, where he farts in Donna's face as she pees in the street and later steps in dog shit, whereas Donna displays herself as a mess when on-stage. Melissa Hair argues that *Obvious Child* reworks generic convention by positing the genre's "comic collision" (borrowing a term from Claire Mortimer) not between the central couple but between conventional romcom femininity and Donna's "own, apparently 'masculine,' actions and behavior."[30] I would suggest that the film does both, but that both of these collisions serve to contrast chaos, grit, and the abject with order, neatness, and the corporate.

The film narrativizes a conflict between an old and new Brooklyn (this "old" Brooklyn, of course, displaces other "old" Brooklyns; the film's cast is

Max (Jake Lacy) and Donna's (Jenny Slate) first encounter in *Obvious Child*.

notably white). Lauren Berlant claims that "to the degree that a love story pits lyrical feelings about intimacy against the narrative traumas engendered in ordinary or public life, it participates in the genre of romance: the love plot provides a seemingly non-ideological resolution to the fractures and contradictions of history."[31] The specifically urban fractures that the bookshop's closure makes apparent are drawn out in the conflict between different waves of gentrification in Brooklyn that Max and Donna represent. Yet, by the end of the film, even Donna's financial instability is something the film has effectively forgotten, reframing around her bodily crisis and the film's romantic resolution. Although in the moment in which she sees a doctor and requests an abortion she is stunned by the cost, which is more than her rent, it is never revealed how she comes to pay for it; as for her job loss, we are simply told that weeks later she has found work as a "back-up receptionist." Julia Kristeva's theorization of the abject reads it as drawing us to "the place where meaning collapses."[32] While Donna's disastrous set might lead that way, *Obvious Child* proceeds from that moment to situate Donna's crisis-induced identification with the abject in binaries of order and disorder, the corporate and the bohemian: not disturbing systems and order, but granting secure, unthreatening meaning.

Despite its more "alternative" stylings, *Obvious Child* is even more politically toothless than *You've Got Mail*. When the Shop Around the Corner is forced to close, Kathleen is able to find an alternative career, yet the loss of the shop looms uncomfortably over the film's conclusion. When love interest/business rival Joe tries to reassure her that it "wasn't personal," she replies, "But it was personal to me," due to the shop's overwhelming identification with the memory of her mother. Moreover, when the shop was threatened with closure, her leftist newspaper columnist boyfriend (Greg Kinnear) had written supportive op-eds, and both she and he had been involved in protests. While *You've Got Mail* draws on the kind of independent bookseller activism that Miller analyzes, *Obvious Child* simply presents its characters' immediate acceptance of its shop's fate, even though that shop is clearly depicted as a radical bookshop and despite the occurrence in reality of antigentrification activism around threats to independent bookshops, including at the real Unoppressive Non-Imperialist Bargain Books.[33] This passivity is evident from the outset; when telling her that the store must close, Donna's boss follows up with "Sometimes we just have to let go of the things that we love," and "Listen, change is good, Donna." Despite the radicalism suggested by the bookshop's name (or, indeed, its real-life counterpart's engagement in antigentrification activism), it stands instead for a passive hippie acceptance of urban development's steamrolling effect.

The film ultimately demonstrates adherence to "resilience" as a contemporary ideal: the need to be a resilient subject, the need for cities to be resilient. Robin James defines resilience as a distinctively neoliberal means of recycling "damage" into more resources: damage is "incited and made manifest" only to be "spectacularly overcome," an overcoming that is "broadcast and/or shared," bringing the person who has overcome the reward of "increased human capital, status, and other forms of recognition and recompense, because: finally, and most importantly, this individual's resilience boosts society's resilience."[34] Much of *Obvious Child* is devoted to displaying Donna's "damage," to the incitement of her various crises, to making her pain and struggles "manifest," and she herself broadcasts overcoming that damage in her stand-up. Crucially, what makes Donna's arc fit this trajectory is how she uses her damage for her most triumphant moment creatively. Her final stand-up set focuses on her abortion, which will take place on the following day, and is punctuated with shots of her audience lovingly gazing and smiling at her, signaling that this set is something special, different, important. Even though we also see Max walk out (this is how he learns of her pregnancy and abortion), he returns the next day to accompany her to the procedure. Amelie Hastie argues that this final set is notable for the visible intimacy of the relationship built between Donna and her audience, part of a pattern running through the film in which Donna in her most vulnerable state greets audiences both on-screen and off through "entreaties to be seen: to be recognized and to be known in both weakened and resilient states."[35] This is also the moment when Donna can be seen, by an audience, to have not only mastered her challenges, but to have mastered presenting herself as having done so, such that her invocations of the abject are not repulsive to her audience; instead, they indicate her own mastery over stand-up as a form. James's argument that the work of resilience leads to reward and recompense is implicit not only in how Donna has become closer to her mother and Max, both of whom have been framed as representing the orderly and the corporate, but also in that her triumphant set is a professional act, increasing her cachet as a comedian. When Donna has dinner with her father early in the film, he tells her, "Creative energy sometimes comes from the lowest moment in your life." Change is not only good, but productive.

Hair argues that, through its inclusion of an abortion, *Obvious Child* "actively rejects" the dominant heteronormative values of Hollywood cinema and so "radicalizes romcom convention."[36] This, I would suggest, is a generous reading of a film that concludes with the union of a heterosexual couple who have made clear that their individual desires are to procreate (including a sequence in which Max envies the relationship of an older couple in a restaurant and speaks of his desire to be a grandfather), but in the future. It is, however, a reading that the film itself promotes. The film concludes with Max and Donna, as she's recovering after the abortion, choosing a movie to watch; when Max observes, "It is nothing but romantic comedies," Donna replies, "Oh, boo, I just hate that type of film." This moment, and Lacy and Slate's knowing delivery, positions *Obvious Child* as overtly revisionist. That interpretation was reinforced by the film's marketing, which produced an image of Slate as Rosie the Riveter with the words "Take back the romcom": not just revisionism, but feminist revisionism.

But, if we return to the urban fractures raised by the bookshop and to how the film engages with gentrification and the impact of financial crisis on the urban landscape, Donna's life crisis in all its facets allows the film to address that impact in ways that would have been inaccessible to precrisis studio romcoms. Doing so enables the genre of the romantic comedy to be "taken back"—not in the sense of being appropriated for feminist ends, but of being successfully adapted to an altered cultural, socioeconomic, and urban context. While the film disrupts spatiotemporal continuity early on, it also demonstrates an urge toward a restoration of romcom aesthetic order, repeatedly using unmotivated shots of the skyline to mark the passage of time, establishing a sense of coherence via its iconicity, despite the street-level emphasis on disordered grungy bohemia. Another shot frames Donna in front of a bookcase that includes a copy of James Sanders's *Celluloid Skyline: New York and the Movies*, subtly situating the film in a history of New York's cinematic representation, emphasizing continuity rather than disruption.[37] If we read the film's conclusion, its union of the film's heterosexual couple and the reconciliation that suggests between what they represent in urban terms—gentrification and its class conflicts—*Obvious Child* ultimately posits the *necessity* of such a reconciliation. In order to become resilient, Donna needs not to protest but to accept the inevitability of change, to herself and to her romantic choices, but also to her city.

Obvious Child effectively sacrifices the bookshop and all it stands for—the romcom's tradition of nostalgic literary romanticization, the cultural assumption that books themselves are special objects that ought to be protected from the ravages of capitalism, the bookshop as a fount of critique—in order to construct its romantic narrative. It retains a sense of the bookshop's distinction, its expression of an alternative culture, but as one half of a romcom romantic binary. This is the resilience of genre at the bookshop's expense. A useful counterpoint here is *You* (Lifetime/Netflix, 2018–), in which bookshop romanticism is turned malevolent by making its obsessive, romantic bookseller hero a serial killer. In that case, and especially in its second season, gentrification is assumed but in ways that do little to threaten the bookshop's existence; Joe (Penn Badgley) instead both desires and despises his new hipster clientele. In sharply different ways, these examples adapt the bookshop's identification with romantic narratives into altered forms of generic text, *You* becoming a thriller and *Obvious Child* reworking the romcom for a rapidly gentrifying urban landscape. Yet *Obvious Child*'s refusal to use the bookshop as a site of resistance even as its shop faces closure indicates the film's primary concern: how to claw a fundamentally conservative romantic comedy out of conditions in which the genre's urban and material representational foundations are threatened. In this light, the film seems less like a radical, revisionist break with romcom tradition than a generic dead end.

Notes

1 Laura J. Miller, *Reluctant Capitalists: Bookselling and the Culture of Consumption* (Chicago: University of Chicago Press, 2006), 161.
2 Miller, *Reluctant Capitalists*, 213.
3 Miller, 216.
4 Miller, 193.
5 Tara Brabazon, "When Bohemia Becomes a Business: City Lights, Columbus Avenue, and a Future for San Francisco," *Human Geographies: Journal of Studies and Research in Human Geography* 5, no. 1 (May 2011): 48.

6 Jim Collins, *Bring on the Books for Everybody: How Literary Culture Became Popular Culture* (Durham, NC: Duke University Press, 2010), 40–41.
7 Collins, *Bring on the Books*, 61.
8 Diane Negra, "Structural Integrity, Historical Reversion, and the Post-9/11 Chick Flick," *Feminist Media Studies* 8, no. 1 (March 2008): 52.
9 Negra, "Structural Integrity, Historical Reversion," 51.
10 On the "death" of the romcom, see Shelley Cobb and Diane Negra, "'I Hate to Be the Feminist Here . . .': Reading the Post-Epitaph Chick Flick," *Continuum* 31, no. 6 (2017): 757–66.
11 See, for example, Manuel Castells, Joao Caraca, and Gustavo Cardoso, eds., *Aftermath: The Cultures of the Economic Crisis* (Oxford: Oxford University Press, 2012); Kirk Boyle and Daniel Mrozowski, eds., *The Great Recession in Fiction, Film, and Television: Twenty-First-Century Bust Culture* (Lanham, MD: Lexington, 2013); Diane Negra and Yvonne Tasker, eds., *Gendering the Recession: Media and Culture in an Age of Austerity* (Durham, NC: Duke University Press, 2014); and Alberto Toscano and Jeff Kinkle, *Cartographies of the Absolute* (Winchester, UK: Zero, 2015), 157–83.
12 Diane Negra and Yvonne Tasker, "Gender and Recessionary Culture," in *Gendering the Recession: Media and Culture in an Age of Austerity*, ed. Diane Negra and Yvonne Tasker (Durham, NC: Duke University Press, 2014), 1.
13 Negra and Tasker, "Gender and Recessionary Culture," 18.
14 On the indie romcom and the creative city, see Martha Shearer, "Frances Doesn't Live Here Anymore: Gender, Crisis, and the Creative City in *Frances Ha* and *The Giant Mechanical Man*," in *The City in American Cinema: Film and Postindustrial Culture*, ed. Johan Andersson and Lawrence Webb (London: Bloomsbury, 2019), 351–73.
15 Stanley Corkin, *Starring New York: Filming the Grime and the Glamour of the Long 1970s* (Oxford: Oxford University Press, 2011).
16 This sequence stands as an interesting contrast to another text about a recently dumped female stand-up, *The Marvelous Mrs. Maisel* (Amazon Prime, 2017–), where Midge's (Rachel Brosnahan) very recent breakup prompts her not to bomb but to wander onstage and produce a hilarious stream-of-consciousness set that launches her comedy career. She also has a disastrous set later in the series, but it comes at the point where

her life is most "together," built around her experiences starting a job at a department store. While both rely on their "damage" to enable creative expression, only Donna risks that damage's becoming self-destructive.

17 Jeremiah Moss, *Vanishing New York: How a Great City Lost Its Soul* (New York: Dey Street, 2017), 179.
18 Quoted in Karen Loew, "The Unconventional, Extra-Ordinary Village Bookstore That Movie Directors Can't Resist," Off the Grid: The Blog of the Greenwich Village Society for Historic Preservation, August 7, 2014, gvshp.org/blog/2014/08/07/the-unconventional-extra-ordinary-village-bookstore-that-movie-directors-cant-resist/.
19 Miller, *Reluctant Capitalists*, 216.
20 Sharon Zukin, *Naked City: The Death and Life of Authentic Urban Places* (Oxford: Oxford University Press, 2010), 43.
21 Richard Lloyd, *Neo-Bohemia: Art and Commerce in the Postindustrial City*, 2nd ed. (New York: Routledge, 2010), 8.
22 Lloyd, *Neo-Bohemia*, 100.
23 Zukin, *Naked City*, 37.
24 Loretta Lees, "Super-Gentrification: The Case of Brooklyn Heights, New York City," *Urban Studies* 40, no. 12 (November 2003): 2487.
25 Zukin, *Naked City*, 6.
26 On the reception of *Girls*, see Faye Woods, "*Girls* Talk: Authorship and Authenticity in the Reception of Lena Dunham's *Girls*," *Critical Studies in Television* 10, no. 2 (Summer 2015): 37–54. On Swift, see Julianne Escobedo Shepherd, "Taylor Swift's New Song Is the Gentrification Anthem NYC Didn't Need," Jezebel, October 20, 2014, jezebel.com/taylor-swifts-new-song-is-the-gentrification-anthem-nyc-1648607040; Anna North, "Taylor Swift's Unwelcome P.R. Campaign," Op-Talk, October 28, 2014, op-talk.blogs.nytimes.com/2014/10/28/taylor-swifts-unwelcome-p-r-campaign/; Kyle Kramer, "Let Taylor Swift Teach You How to Be a New Yorker," Noisey, October 27, 2014, https://www.vice.com/en/article/64kd9r/taylor-swift-welcome-to-new-york-tourism-global-welcome-ambassador; and Laura Rosenfeld, "A Boutique Blames Taylor Swift for Killing New York City in a New Mural," Tech Times, October 31, 2014, www.techtimes.com/articles/19206/20141031/taylor-swift-new-york-boutique-mural.htm.
27 Rebecca Wanzo, "Precarious-Girl Comedy: Issa Rae, Lena Dunham, and Abjection Aesthetics," *Camera Obscura* 31, no. 2 (2016): 29.

28 John Limon, *Stand-Up Comedy in Theory, or, Abjection in America* (Durham, NC: Duke University Press, 2000), 2.
29 Limon, *Stand-Up Comedy in Theory*, 27.
30 Melissa Hair, "'I'd Like an Abortion Please': Rethinking Unplanned Pregnancy Narratives in Contemporary American Cinema," *Feminist Media Studies* 19, no. 3 (2019): 8; Claire Mortimer, *Romantic Comedy* (New York: Routledge, 2010), 6.
31 Lauren Berlant, *Desire/Love* (Brooklyn, NY: Punctum, 2012), 92.
32 Julia Kristeva, *Powers of Horror: An Essay on Abjection*, trans. Leon S. Roudiez (New York: Columbia University Press, 1982), 2.
33 Jeremiah Moss, "Help Unoppressive, Non-Imperialist Books," Jeremiah's Vanishing New York, October 18, 2012, vanishingnewyork.blogspot.com/2012/10/help-unoppressive-non-imperialist-books.html.
34 Robin James, *Resilience & Melancholy: Pop Music, Feminism, Neoliberalism* (Winchester, UK: Zero, 2015), 12–13. Emphasis in original.
35 Amelie Hastie, "On the Contagion of Vulnerability," *Film Quarterly* 68, no. 4 (Summer 2015): 63.
36 Hair, "I'd Like an Abortion Please," 7.
37 James Sanders, *Celluloid Skyline: New York and the Movies* (New York: Alfred A. Knopf, 2003).

9

Connecting with Strangers

Cosmopolitanism, Romance, and Hospitality in Transnational Romantic Comedy

Manuela Ruiz

A Cosmopolitan Approach to Contemporary Romantic Comedy

In an era defined by unprecedented connectedness and mobility in which identities, ideas, cultures, and politics are embedded in the global and the transnational, contemporary cinema represents cosmopolitanism not as an abstract philosophical perspective, but rather as a complex reality entrenched in people's everyday interactions, practices, and routines. Recent critical work has begun to theorize cosmopolitanism as performative. From a sociological perspective, Zlatko Skrbiš and Ian Woodward suggest that it would be particularly relevant to explore "how cosmopolitanism is performatively accomplished and cultivated by the fusion of action and disposition within particular environments and settings," a project that could extend to encompass the study of the performative nature of cosmopolitanism in the visual arts.[1] By paying attention to the methodological dimension of cosmopolitanism, these authors conclude, it may be possible to understand the dynamics of the forces of globality, and also, I would add, contemporary cinema's engagement with those forces.

Like individuals, movies may be understood as "performers of cosmopolitanism." As Celestino Deleyto argues, a cosmopolitan approach to film studies should focus on "how everyday cosmopolitanism is turned into discourse—how visual texts may evolve a specific set of formal strategies to insert themselves within a global society in which cosmopolitanism has become a prestigious cultural asset."[2] Identifying the formal strategies through which film narratives engage with cosmopolitan concerns would be the first step in the direction of a cosmopolitan perspective on cinema.

Borders and cosmopolitan spaces demand particular scrutiny in an exploration of how films create meaning in a globalized world. The border, as Deleyto has put it, "becomes a vantage point from which to look at films as well as one from which films look at the world under globalization."[3] In the cinematic space of transnational romantic comedies, I will argue, cosmopolitanism is performed not only through cross-cultural plotlines and cinematic constructions of borders, but also through the mapping of a new hybrid generic territory at the intersection of romantic comedy and melodrama. Prominent markers of cosmopolitanism articulate the films' emphasis on the performance of openness to the Other and the specific transformations brought about by that openness.

As is the case with other film genres like melodrama or science fiction, representations of identity and human relations within recent romantic comedy manifest a significant cosmopolitan turn. Encompassing Hollywood productions and European films, an emerging trend that I have labeled "overseas romances" offers cosmopolitan visions of personal life and self-transformation in the global age.[4] *Under the Tuscan Sun* (2003), *A Good Year* (2006), *The Holiday* (2006), *Vicky Cristina Barcelona* (2008), *Eat Pray Love* (2011), and *Chinese Puzzle* (2013) are examples of this ongoing cycle, which includes other titles such as the *Before Sunrise, Before Sunset, Before Midnight* trilogy (1995, 2004, 2013), *Notting Hill* (1999), *P.S. I Love You* (2007), *My Life in Ruins* (2009), *10,000 Kms* (2014), and *Leap Year* (2020), among others. Overseas romances explore transnational landscapes of intimacy, love, family life, parenthood, and divorce by exploring how everyday practices in the sphere of private life result in ethical choices, emotional experiences, affective bonds, and interpersonal negotiations in the vast, challenging space of a globalized world. In these narratives, processes of cosmopolitan self-transformation, manifested through unexpected international quests for identity and happiness, come to the foreground and shape the development of romantic and comic plotlines. The utopian, transformative space of romantic comedy is defined as a cosmopolitan territory in which gender identities, family structures, and romantic expectations must be questioned and validated. *Samba* (2014), directed by Olivier Nakache and Eric Toledano, belongs to a new expanding subcycle of overseas romances, including *The Visitor* (2007), *El Dios de Madera* (2010), *The Hundred-Foot Journey* (2014), and *Exit Marrakech* (2015), films that differ from the group of transnational romantic comedies previously listed in that they are centrally concerned with dramatizing a paradoxical view of cosmopolitan encounters and global connections as utopian and transformative but also repressive and alienating—or, in generic terms, as simultaneously romantic and melodramatic, thus pushing romantic comedy in new directions.

Loosely adapted from Delphine Coulin's novel *Samba pour la France*, Toledano and Nakache's film places a cross-cultural unconventional romance at the center of a cosmopolitan plotline, in contrast to the film's literary source, in which the character of the film's female protagonist, Alice, does not appear. *Samba* narrates the story of a young Senegalese citizen, Samba Cissé, forced to move from Senegal to France in order to provide financial support for his family after his father's death. Samba (Omar Sy) has been living with his uncle in Paris for ten years as an illegal resident, making ends meet as a dishwasher in the hope of one day becoming a chef. After inquiring about his residence permit to determine eligibility to apply for permanent residency, he is informed that his case has been denied, then is arrested and sent to a detention center for undocumented immigrants. For Alice (Charlotte Gainsbourg), there providing pro bono legal assistance, Samba is her first case, and their relationship will soon move beyond the boundaries of her volunteer social work. Perceived pejoratively as a failing hybrid generic text amounting to "a more-serious-than-not cross cultural romance"[5] and as "a social dramedy-cum-romantic comedy," *Samba* was dismissed by a number of film critics as being neither solid enough as a drama nor funny enough or even categorizable as a romantic comedy.[6] In my view, however, *Samba*'s generic hybridity should be understood not as an example of a flawed narrative structure or tonal register, but rather as an effective strategy for articulating the film's ambivalent ideological discourse on cosmopolitanism. The space of romantic comedy in the film is on the one hand identified with an alluring cosmopolitan landscape where men and women can discover promising opportunities for self-fulfillment in unfamiliar settings and cultures, but on the other reveals how intimate cosmopolitan encounters may result in moments of intolerance, prejudice, anxiety, and frustration. By crossing into melodramatic terrain, *Samba*, like other contemporary transnational romantic comedies, ultimately highlights the fragility and fluidity of a far-reaching phenomenon that Ulrich Beck and Elisabeth Beck-Gernsheim have theorized as the "globalization of love."[7]

This interplay between romantic comedy and melodrama makes visible the complexity of the challenges confronting the contemporary notion of romantic love.

Romantic comedy and melodrama diverge most significantly in their characteristic narrative resolutions, with comedy always open to reconciliation and happiness while melodrama invariably evokes misery and frustration. However, it must be noted that romantic comedy and melodrama do not simply exist as separate formal categories but in relation to one another, which has resulted in a rich generic interplay. The interaction between these genres moves in two directions, as Kathleen Rowe [Karlyn] observes, for "romantic comedy usually contains a potential melodrama and melodrama a potential romantic comedy." Melodrama, Rowe [Karlyn] argues, "depends on a belief in the possibility of romantic comedy's happy ending, a belief that heightens the pathos of its loss." Similarly, romantic comedy "depends on the melodramatic threat that the lovers will not get together."[8] The connection between melodrama and comedy has also been conceptualized by Deborah Thomas as a fluid duality of spaces: the world of melodrama appears threatening and oppressive, whereas comedy represents a more welcoming and benevolent place.[9] The most sophisticated comedies, Thomas suggests, are precisely those that "acknowledge the presence and threat of the melodramatic world and succeed at defusing it or keeping it at bay"—a definition that, in my view, accurately describes the film under discussion in this chapter.[10] Melodrama is mostly about power and escape, while comedy ultimately concentrates on potential transformation, issues of paramount importance in the context of social and interpersonal cosmopolitan relations. Thomas's mapping of generic categories thus implies that the boundaries between the comedic and the melodramatic are by no means fixed; the distinction sometimes simply depends on point of view.

Oscillating between the utopian optimism of romantic comedy and the anxiety and skepticism typical of melodrama, *Samba* contributes to the redefinition of a generic territory, in which central narrative elements within the genre of romantic comedy such as the "learning process" or the popular "happy ending" are intertwined with contemporary concerns about the impact of cosmopolitanism on romantic relations. The convention of the learning process,[11] which focuses on how the members of a couple redraw the boundaries of their own space in order to create a common ground congenial to romance and love, is specifically codified in the narrative as a process of "cosmopolitan learning," which leads the characters into self-reflexive engagement with difference more pronounced than that offered by the genre's typical narrative of interpersonal negotiation.[12] Through the tension encapsulated in an evolving host/guest characterization—initially focusing on Alice as a fragile member of a seemingly unwelcoming hosting society for undocumented migrants, and on Samba as a forced, unwilling guest in the culture Alice represents—the film relies on generic hybridity to build its own dual discourse on romantic entanglements in a cosmopolitan context. The conventional romantic comedy learning process intersects with stories of deep emotional crisis typical of melodrama in order to visualize human relations in which care, affection, and intimacy are grounded on the transformative potential of connecting with strangers. The distribution of power between the protagonists is eventually renegotiated under the pressure of not only romantic protocols but also the intercultural borders separating these characters. In this way, as a result of the emotional intensity and dramatic implications of the cosmopolitan encounters it depicts, a transnational romantic comedy like *Samba* envisions experiences of transformation that go beyond romantic comedy's traditional goal of couple formation, just as it also offers the final utopian possibility of a better future that melodrama conventionally denies.

An interplay between closeness and distance, trust and risk, inclusion and exclusion, emotional intimacy and limited connections, lies at the core of the Janus-faced perception of cosmopolitanism articulated by *Samba*, a film in which the gloomiest shade of cross-cultural encounters lurks side by side with visions of a romantic "ethics of sharing."[13] The vicissitudes of Alice and Samba's intimate relationship exemplify the kind of openness individuals may perform to connect with one another within a cosmopolitan framework, in which the centrality of romantic love is downplayed in favor of notions of openness, hospitality, and empathy. Thus, transnational romantic comedy expands on the genre's existing repertoire of narrative motifs so as to encompass the cosmopolitan potential of encounters with diversity as a promising source of self-fulfillment different from the ideals of coupledom associated with traditional models of romantic love. *Samba*, as a representative of the contemporary subcycle of overseas romances, encapsulates a transitional moment in which the concept of romantic love may be supplemented by other patterns of intimate relations primarily grounded on the desire to be open to the Other. The terms under which desire, affect, and

Downplaying the centrality of romantic love in favor of notions of openness, hospitality, and empathy in *Samba*.

emotion are negotiated within cosmopolitan encounters, and their congruent romantic commitments and pursuits of happiness represented cinematically, are essential constituents of a new aesthetic and ideological territory that romantic comedy has just started to explore.

Through my analysis of the embodied cosmopolitanisms represented in *Samba*, I intend to illustrate not only the fluidity of generic boundaries in contemporary romantic comedy but also the potential of cosmopolitan theory to explain the engagement of filmic texts with new forms of caring, loving, and belonging within a multicultural world. In this context, the richness and variety of romantic comedy can be fully acknowledged only when we consider "the secret life of romantic comedy"—in other words, when we look at the genre from a more flexible and less deterministic approach, one that moves beyond compulsory heterosexuality and monogamy and the happy ending.[14]

Connecting with Strangers: Hospitality and Openness in Romantic Comedy

In a world in which borders are intensely contested, cosmopolitanism can turn out to be inescapable rather than subject to choice.[15] While opening up new paths toward self-fulfillment, cosmopolitan experiences do not always involve promising opportunities and connectedness for mobile subjects. In the context of exile and expatriation, rootlessness, alienation, and isolation may also become constituent elements of transnational life.[16] Regardless of the status or cause of their migration, migrants are confronted with questions of acceptance and belonging, exclusion, exploitation, security, and survival—issues tackled by a growing number of contemporary romantic comedies and dramas. *Samba* capitalizes on the tensions and dilemmas inextricably linked to the unwilling cosmopolitanism that is nowadays experienced by large numbers of individuals in transit, who have to overcome many kinds of barriers to integrate within their host cultures. As a cultural text, the film locates its discourse about migrant transnationalism and cosmopolitanism at the level of individual pursuits of happiness, romantic expectations, and intimate relations rather than of political and economic agendas, even though these dimensions are also present in the narrative.

In *Samba*, the daily struggles that Samba, Walid (Tahar Rahim), and the film's many other unnamed characters face as undocumented immigrants—including their difficulties in making a living, their need to use fake identities, and their constant fear of being arrested and deported to their home countries—exemplify the most dramatic dimension of cosmopolitanism as a source of rootlessness, exclusion, poverty, and despair. "Abject cosmopolitanism," which focuses particularly on subaltern mobilities and immobilities, is introduced at film's start when a long-take opening scene leads audiences from a high-class wedding party directly into the hotel kitchen dishwashing unit, where we first meet Samba, the eponymous male protagonist.[17] Later in the narrative, the focus on abject cosmopolitanism is also reinforced through the double identity embodied by Walid, who pretends to be called "Wilson" and to come from Brazil when his real name is, in fact, Walid, and his home country is Algeria. As he explains to Samba, he decided to use a false identity on the grounds that Brazilian people receive a more welcoming response from the French host culture than citizens of Algerian origin, making it easier for him to make a living in Paris.

Located at the center of *Samba*'s multiprotagonist plotlines, abject cosmopolitanism becomes the raw material for some of the most comic and melodramatic moments in the film and thus plays a key role in the definition of generic boundaries in the text. For instance, on the comic side, *Samba* contains amusing "lost in translation" moments at the detention center, with linguistic barriers leading to comic misunderstandings between elderly NGO volunteers who cannot hear properly and immigrants unfamiliar with the French language. Similarly, the slapstick police chase that has Samba and Walid fleeing over the roof tops of Paris provides a touch of humor, especially when Walid/Wilson, drawing on his false identity as a citizen from Brazil, performs a pretend Brazilian version of a popular Diet Coke advertising campaign featuring a male striptease for an audience of female office workers. Contrasting melodramatic episodes associated with Samba's forced friendship with Jonas (Issaka Sawadogo), an asylum seeker he meets at the detention center in Paris, constitute an underlying dramatic subplot running parallel to and in tension with the romantic comedy main story line. One of the most striking moments in this melodramatic subplot shows Samba's struggle for his life during a vicious fight between the two men that ends with Jonas's death upon falling into the Seine. An erroneous police report leads both Alice and Lamouna (Younger Fall), Samba's uncle, to believe that the dead man found in the river is Samba and not Jonas, a dark plot twist that, paradoxically, happily grants Samba a way to become a legal French citizen at film's end.

"Cosmopolitanism-from-below" constitutes the narrative foundation for the romantic and emotional attachments established between the film's characters, Alice and Samba particularly.[18] After his arrest and detention, Samba becomes Alice's first case as a volunteer legal aide, her prescribed therapy after having suffered at some point in the recent past a violent episode of professional burnout that resulted in a devastating nervous breakdown. Against the advice of a colleague, Alice becomes personally invested in Samba's case, as she feels that getting to know and help Samba awakens positive feelings in her, including romantic attraction. Being hospitable to Samba soon means much more to Alice than just allowing somebody to feel safe and welcome in a foreign cultural landscape.

Drawing on Jacques Derrida's account of ethics *as* hospitality, Gideon Baker argues that thinking cosmopolitanism through hospitality remains a necessary exercise in cosmopolitan thought. Hospitality, in spite of its long history of identification with the host, must also be identified, in our global world, with the Other. In Baker's terms, far from being mutually exclusive, "identity (host) and difference (guest) are mutually constitutive in hospitality," and self-definition is consequently subordinated to the dynamics of a cosmopolitan ethics of hospitality, an idea that remains central to the unfolding of the main romantic plotline in *Samba*.[19] Alice, the film's protagonist, redefines her identity precisely through her responsibility to the Other and through her empathy and openness to difference. The central dilemma Alice confronts is that of deciding how to translate an unconditional hospitality into intimacy and romantic commitment, a decision that will eventually constitute a major turning point in her life.

The boundaries between self and Other, host and guest, become significant in *Samba* as the threshold of cosmopolitan hospitality and the dividing line between sexes in a romantic and emotional self-transformation process. Alice can succeed in her own quest for self-renewal only once she decides to engage truly in a cosmopolitan ethics of hospitality with Samba by paying attention to the singularity of the Other; she comes to see him not just as an unwilling guest she has to protect but as a friend and, at some point, also as a desirable romantic partner. Going back to Baker's notion of cosmopolitanism as hospitality, it can be argued that *Samba*, just like an increasing number of contemporary films, presents subjectivity as defined by openness and vulnerability—in other words, by hospitality. Alice reshapes her life prospects in terms of her connection with the Other with whom she has decided to engage. Being herself more fragile than Samba, Alice finds a new kind of empowerment in her emotional commitment to the "normalisation of difference": her own lived experience of cosmopolitanism as hospitality both within her domestic space and in the more inhospitable official settings of detention centers and court.[20] Alice's decision to go beyond the recommended limits concerning emotional closeness with the immigrants she helps as an NGO volunteer catalyzes a remarkable self-transformation. Thanks to Samba's encouragement and empathy, Alice finds someone to lean on. Their relationship goes beyond romantic commitment into a sphere of cosmopolitan affection and mutual support. This is made evident by the end of the film, when, wearing Samba's football t-shirt as a token of good luck, Alice eventually faces her insecurity and returns to work after a long period of depression, with the aim of recovering her managerial position in the corporate world, and, most important, a new sense of control over her own life.

The dynamics of the host/guest relationships depicted in *Samba* articulate a discourse on cosmopolitanism and romance in which identity and difference must be read together rather than in isolation. In a reformulation of the conventional learning process of romantic comedy, which demands a flexible, open-minded attitude from the members of the potential future romantic couple as they negotiate the terms of their relationship, *Samba* identifies the protagonists' newly acquired disposition to connect with other cultural realities by means of what Fazal Rizvi calls "cosmopolitan learning." As Rizvi argues, "A global imagination now plays a crucial role in how people engage in their everyday activities, consider their options and make their decisions within the new configurations of social relations," thus widening the scope of human ethics to encompass not only local but also global concerns.[21] In the process of their cosmopolitan learning experiences, Alice and Samba seem to realize that cosmopolitanism is no longer just a philosophical and ethical behavioral code but a "structure of feeling" and an "empathetic and inclusive set of identifications" that Mica Nava has labeled "visceral cosmopolitanism."[22] It is by developing interdependent relationships as hosts and guests that the film's protagonists bring about the necessary conditions for this type of cosmopolitanism to emerge.

During their first conversation at the detention center, Alice experiences immediate empathy with Samba's needs, just as Samba becomes interested in her apparent vulnerability when he expresses curiosity about why Alice needs to take a variety of pills on a regular basis. Similarly, Alice's genuine interest in details of Samba's life not recorded in official immigration legal proceedings, as when she decides to keep a picture of Samba as a child that she finds in his case file and gazes at with intense tenderness, draws attention to an explicitly emotional dimension of cosmopolitanism and to the centrality of the notion of openness in cosmopolitan encounters. For Alice, being cosmopolitan entails getting involved in a learning process of self-transformation through her openness to the Other, which eventually allows both her and Samba to recover their emotional balance and reshape their romantic expectations. As a performative and strategic practice, cosmopolitan openness is by no means a universal phenomenon, and the paths to becoming open are, therefore, multiple and diverse. For Manu (Izïa Igelin), Alice's co-counselor and friend, a university law student for whom providing free legal services for immigrants represents an individual commitment to fighting against global inequality, cosmopolitanism involves taking a political stance that exceeds the sphere of emotional attachments. Leaving aside her mistaken motivation for a romantic affair with Walid/Wilson, which she comically attributes to her interest in "men from South America," so too does Manu's transnational romance amount to an act of political activism grounded on notions of hospitality and openness typical of cosmopolitanism.[23]

Through different learning processes or aspects of biography and personal experience, individuals may become more open to cultural difference, or, on the contrary, more prejudiced. In *Samba*, Alice, as a cosmopolitan host, discovers the potential of openness to transform the self in moments of deep emotional unbalance and alienation. Legally sentenced to perform community service following her violent outburst at work, Alice embarks on an experience of cosmopolitanism that calls for a dialogue with the Other, what Kwame Appiah has termed "ethics in a world of strangers"—an interaction that for her opens up new opportunities for self-knowledge, as well as unexpected avenues for romance.[24] By supporting Samba in his attempt to avoid deportation and assuaging his distress after being legally ordered to leave France, Alice progressively emerges from her pathological isolation and emotional coldness. Openness and cosmopolitanism, as Skrbiš and Woodward have put it, "both engender something positive and enabling, evoking acceptance and engagement rather than rejection and distance."[25] Samba's attitude toward Alice's issues of self-esteem and alienation in the social and professional world provide clear illustration of the extent to which this positive impulse is identified not only in social theories, but also in films as the "driving force" of a cosmopolitan disposition.

On being officially informed that he must wait a year before he can apply again for French citizenship, Samba directs his anger toward Alice, who confirms that he will need to accept this transitional period if he really wants to settle in France. However, he immediately apologizes and attempts to find out why a woman like Alice who, as Samba himself remarks, does not match the typical profile of NGO members helping undocumented migrants (namely, law students and retired citizens), would take any interest in him. Samba starts to realize that Alice feels a deep emotional connection with and an emerging romantic attraction to him when she misunderstands him during a conversation concerning Samba's current interest in a certain woman, thinking that he is referring to Alice as his love interest. At this point, Samba confesses to Alice that he cares about her but only sees her as a special person in his life and not as a potential romantic partner. As the narrative progresses, Samba will eventually discover that Alice's interest in him had started when they first met; during their first sexual encounter, which takes place in Alice's apartment, Samba discovers the purloined picture of him as a child and intuits what Alice's having taken it reveals. Samba learns more about the reasons for Alice's crisis and begins to identify with her when he realizes that both are facing oppression, albeit of different kinds, as a result of neoliberal, capitalist pressures. Samba's learning process reaches a climactic point when he accompanies Alice to another of her therapy pursuits, in which she grooms horses to relieve stress and anxiety. As Samba aids Alice's recovery by paying attention to her needs and feelings, he seems to play the romantic comedy role of "right partner," even if he does not fully share Alice's desire to start a romantic relationship.

As the plot unfolds, characters began to discover the transformative potential of their cosmopolitan openness in memorable moments of empathy and affection for the Other. The naïve romantic and sexual desire for Samba that Alice displays during a late-night encounter, when she tells him about her problems of emotional coldness, reinforces the affective dimension of cosmopolitan learning validated by the film. The proximity of cosmopolitan openness to romantic compatibility between Samba and Alice is further highlighted when Samba jokingly hesitates between kissing Alice in a "traditional" or "not traditional" style, a private joke between them that means kissing her either romantically or platonically. In the end, Samba's hesitation to embrace Alice in desire and Alice's initial disappointment at Samba's friendly kiss on her cheek overturns the romantic kissing scene that positions the couple within the field of romantic comedy's visual and narrative rhetoric. Determined to pursue their individual dreams of freedom and self-fulfillment, Alice and Samba's cosmopolitan learning is not explicitly located within the conventional boundaries of romance typical of the romantic comedy genre, as they are not visualized as a couple at the time of narrative closure. Nevertheless, the parallel shots of Samba caressing horses, just as Alice did as therapy, and the image of a smiling, self-confident Alice wearing Samba's football t-shirt under her formal business suit, together with the lyrics of the soundtrack repeating that "to know you is to love you," turn these final individual shots into sketches of a promising new beginning for both characters and for their likely future, maybe intimate, encounters.

In other words, in the absence of a more conventional image of romantic couple, the final scenes still constitute a plausible happy ending.

Cosmopolitan Encounters in Romantic Comedy: Happy Endings beyond Romantic Love

Samba, like a growing number of contemporary films, brings to the foreground the dilemmas associated with an uneasy cosmopolitanism that refuses to ignore prejudice and aversion as potential constituent elements of cosmopolitan thought.[26] By focusing on undocumented migrants as they struggle to integrate into their host cultures, *Samba* presents cosmopolitanism as always "vulnerable to the seeds of anti-cosmopolitanism," a paradoxical duality that recent transnational romantic comedies like *Samba* codify through generic hybridity and, more specifically, through unconventional formulations of the traditional happy ending.[27] While focusing on intimate relations and the pursuit of romantic satisfaction and happiness, *Samba* does not end with a final couple and yet still assuredly offers a happy ending in

Empathy and intimacy across borders: desire in cosmopolitan encounters in *Samba*.

which the utopian optimism that characterizes narrative closure in romantic comedy is explicitly at work.

Samba's positioning as an unwilling guest in Alice's life dramatizes moments of loneliness, sacrifice, and family dislocation, memories of misery endured at home followed by an array of legal and financial difficulties in exile, in dramatic subplots of struggle and survival typical of the melodramatic mode. On the other hand, the narrative is centrally structured around notions of hospitality, openness, affection, and self-transformation, elements unequivocally congenial to the artistic realm of romantic comedy. Samba's uneasy cosmopolitanism, maintained through the dramatic tension between moments of hope and despair, slapstick humor and violence, romance and tragedy, eventually privileges the utopian possibilities fostered by the kind of self-transformation typical of romantic comedy over the pessimistic expectations congenial to melodrama. Generic hybridity thus helps audiences to interpret filmic representations of cosmopolitan encounters as a variable mixture or reshaping of romantic and melodramatic conventions consonant with the ambivalent nature of cosmopolitanism as simultaneously transformative and pessimistic. This is particularly true at the moment of narrative closure, when the future of cosmopolitan encounters is hinted at.

Ending in an unconventionally nonromantic but light-hearted, fairy-tale mood, with both protagonists, Samba and Alice, determined to pursue happiness beyond the limits of social pressure, *Samba* still seems uneasy about the potential of cosmopolitanism to guarantee human rights and to enhance affective bonds between hosts and guests in a multicultural context. Through its slightly contrived, deus ex machina ending, shaped by a mistaken-identity plot twist, the film acknowledges in a purely melodramatic fashion that contemporary cosmopolitan identities are still defined for some, depending on your home country, on the grounds of sacrifice and self-denial rather than of freedom. Yet the film resorts to the romantic comedy generic repertoire to convey a simultaneous final sense of hope and trust, connected to the ethic of hospitality dramatized through Alice and Samba's relationship.

Samba's final legal status as a French citizen, made possible by his adopting the identity of the now-dead Jonas, implies a certain kind of self-denial that downplays any sense that his dreams for a better life, including the possibility to love and be loved, have finally come true. By the end of the film, Samba is able to live freely in Paris, pursue his goal of working as a chef, and have the chance to make a decent living, but only under another person's name. Attempting to persuade Samba to look at the bright side of his difficult experience of forced cosmopolitanism, Alice assures him that she will never forget his real name and suggests he can always use his name as if he were talking about the famous Brazilian rhythm it refers to so that he never becomes disconnected from his real identity. In the end, Alice ends up exchanging roles with Samba as she becomes a privileged guest in a world of abject cosmopolitans she had previously ignored, where receiving both empathy and practical help from your host community is by no means easy or even possible. Looking at the world from the other side of the border redefines her sense of reality and identity; the engagement with difference is no longer outside her immediate social concerns and her intimate sphere of affection and romantic expectations. This cross-border perspective is precisely one of the important lessons that Alice and Samba learn from their potentially romantic cosmopolitan encounters.

"Border crossing," understood as a geographical, cultural, and emotional transition, emerges as a challenging but rewarding task for the characters in *Samba*. The film's open ending ultimately leaves it to us to decide

Openness and the ethics of sharing: new romantic ideals in globalized societies in *Samba*.

whether we consider cosmopolitanism an antidote to global inequalities, thanks to the humanizing power of hospitality, or a limited framework for intercultural encounters that may frequently turn into a social and cultural battlefield in which intolerance and violence establish new barriers between individuals and between potential romantic partners. By exploring an uneven generic territory at the intersection of romantic comedy and melodrama, *Samba*, like many other recent intercultural romantic comedies, invites audiences to catch a glimpse of the transformative/romantic and alienating/melodramatic dimensions of transnational quests for identity by focusing on how individuals might turn uncertain opportunities into satisfying cosmopolitan realities and experiences of intimacy.

Any consideration of hospitality is invariably limited by the realities and structures of life and society, but cosmopolitan ethics nevertheless continue to offer the potential for rewarding interpersonal relations and emotional balance. Reflecting critically on the side effects and implications of a whole new set of social, economic, and cultural practices affecting not just financial and geopolitical organization but also human ethics and the intimate sphere of private lives and romantic attachments, these transnational romantic comedies aim to articulate a specific emotional, artistic, and ideological look at a world that can no longer be understood outside the parameters of global realities. *Samba*, like a number of other narratives in the overseas romances cycle, visualizes fluid cosmopolitan patterns of romantic relations in which care, affection, and intimacy are founded on the power of hospitality beyond borders and on the transformative potential of connecting with strangers in a global world.

Notes

1 Zlatko Skrbiš and Ian Woodward, *Cosmopolitanism: Uses of the Idea* (Newbury Park, CA: Sage, 2013), 24.
2 Celestino Deleyto, "Looking from the Border: A Cosmopolitan Approach to Contemporary Cinema," *Transnational Cinemas* 8, no. 2 (2017): 97.
3 Deleyto, "Looking from the Border," 100.
4 Manuela Ruiz, "Cosmopolitan Spaces and Generic Boundaries in Hollywood Overseas Romances," in *Culture, Space and Power: Blurred Lines* (Lanham, MD: Lexington, 2016), 139–50.

5 Peter Debruge, "Film Review: *Samba*," *Variety*, September 17, 2014, variety.com/2014/film/festivals/film-review-samba-1201308117/.
6 Jordan Mintzer, "*Samba*: Toronto Review," *Hollywood Reporter*, May 9, 2014, www.hollywoodreporter.com/review/samba-toronto-review-730569.
7 Ulrich Beck and Elisabeth Beck-Gernsheim, *Distant Love: Personal Life in the Global Age* (Cambridge: Polity, 2014).
8 Kathleen Rowe [Karlyn], *The Unruly Woman: Gender and the Genres of Laughter* (Austin: University of Texas Press, 1995), 49, 110.
9 Deborah Thomas, *Beyond Genre: Melodrama, Comedy and Romance in Hollywood Films* (Dumfries, SCT: Cameron & Hollis, 2000), 9.
10 Thomas, *Beyond Genre*, 92.
11 See Steve Neale, "The Big Romance or Something Wild? Romantic Comedy Today," *Screen* 33, no. 3 (Autumn 1992): 284–99.
12 See Fazal Rizvi, "Toward Cosmopolitan Learning," *Discourse: Studies in the Cultural Politics of Education* 30, no. 3 (2009): 253–68.
13 Stephanie Plage, Indigo Willing, Ian Woodward, and Zlatko Skrbiš, "Cosmopolitan Encounters: Reflexive Engagements and the Ethics of Sharing," *Ethnic and Racial Studies* 40, no. 1 (2017): 4–23.
14 Celestino Deleyto, *The Secret Life of Romantic Comedy* (Manchester: Manchester University Press, 2009), 175.
15 See Ulrich Beck, "Global Inequality and Human Rights: A Cosmopolitan Perspective," in *Routledge Handbook of Cosmopolitan Studies*, ed. Gerard Delanty (London: Routledge, 2012), 302315.
16 See Steven Vertovec, *Transnationalism* (London: Routledge, 2009).
17 See Peter Nyers, "Abject Cosmopolitanism: The Politics of Protection in the Anti-deportation Movement," *Third World Quarterly* 24, no. 6 (December 2003): 1069–93.
18 See Kobena Mercer, ed., *Cosmopolitan Modernisms* (Cambridge, MA: MIT Press, 2005).
19 Gideon Baker, "Cosmopolitanism as Hospitality: Revisiting Identity and Difference in Cosmopolitanism," *Alternatives: Global, Local, Political* 34, no. 2 (2009): 110. See also Jacques Derrida, *Of Hospitality* (Stanford, CA: Stanford University Press, 2000).
20 See Mica Nava, *Visceral Cosmopolitanism: Gender, Culture, and the Normalisation of Difference* (London: Bloomsbury, 2007).
21 Rizvi, "Toward Cosmopolitan Learning," 257.

22 See Nava, *Visceral Cosmopolitanism*.
23 See Gerard Delanty, "The Cosmopolitan Imagination: Critical Cosmopolitanism and Social Theory," *British Journal of Sociology* 57, no. 1 (March 2006): 25–47.
24 Kwame Anthony Appiah, *Cosmopolitanism: Ethics in a World of Strangers* (New York: W. W. Norton, 2008).
25 Skrbiš and Woodward, *Cosmopolitanism*, 53.
26 Jackie Stacey, "The Uneasy Cosmopolitans of *Code Unknown*," in *Whose Cosmopolitanism? Critical Perspectives, Relationalities, and Discontents*, ed. Nina Glick Schiller and Andrew Irving (New York: Berghahn, 2014), 171.
27 Skrbiš and Woodward, *Cosmopolitanism*, 52.

10

"Money Can't Buy Me Love"

RADICAL RIGHT-WING POPULISM IN FRENCH
ROMANTIC COMEDIES OF THE 2010S

Mary Harrod

It is often forgotten that the French word for homeland, *la patrie*, symbolized the French Revolution, upon which the modern nation-state was founded, as a woman giving birth. This superimposition of maternity onto a word whose roots are in the Latin for "father" (*pater*) is a neat figure for the union of genders, ultimately in the service of procreation, central to both nationalist ideologies and the economy of the romantic comedy genre. Because of such overlapping interests—most basically, in progeniture, but also in units of social organization from the dyadic couple to the "family" of nation—romcoms are predisposed to speak to issues of nationhood. This chapter will focus on themes of nationhood, and especially right-wing populism, in French romcoms of the 2010s. Although right-wing populism has different histories internationally, I refer with this idea to its common definitions in the West and especially Europe, which closely associate the radical right with nationalism, as well as with "antielitism." My analysis will demonstrate how recurring tropes of the recent French romcom address and promote such ideological positions. In the process, I will shine light on the specificities of, firstly, nationalism, and, secondly, strains of antielitism in the local generic context, arguing that the second typically proves to be an offshoot of the first within the films under scrutiny.

Examining French romcoms of the 2010s extends my earlier analysis of the emergence and consolidation of this popular genre in the 1990s and post-2000.[1] As such, this chapter surveys the key directions taken by the genre in this period, picking up on trends retrospectively identified up to 2013 and considering how they have evolved as the decade matures.

While I do not claim that all French romcoms are informed by radical right-wing ideologies—nor indeed that any film articulates, intratextually, any one meaning—I will argue that certain conservative or retrograde strands have become pronounced and pervasive in the genre during this period. After briefly considering the contemporary French romcom's importance as a (trans)national genre, I will focus first on three recurrent tendencies of recent films: explicit celebrations of French culture conceived in traditional and nostalgic terms; obsessive interrogations and validations of heterosexual family structures; and a marked accentuation of homophobic, bromantic, and patriarchal elements in the genre. I will then consider romcoms displaying a parodic attitude toward generic and cultural values coded as North American—albeit one typically embedded in layers of "self-reflexive" postmodern irony. I will finally argue that geocultural and generic self-awareness, constituting one of the complexities of the hybrid French genre *à l'américaine*, is useful for interrogating the concept of radical ideology as well as its antithesis, conformity, for their different meanings in diverse contexts.

Boy Meets Girl Meets Nation

While it may not be possible to describe the contemporary French romcom as populist in any blanket way, claiming it as overwhelmingly popular seems straightforward. While I understand genre as unfixed, a descriptive category that might be applied as productively to niche auteur fare as to the mainstream, nonetheless French films hewing closely to the recognizable format of romantic comedy have to date certainly retained if not increased the enormous popularity that they enjoyed at the end of the 2000s. In my analysis of the French romcom from around 1990 to 2010, with an addendum surveying the years 2010–2013, I noted that "popularity is the salient feature, with many romcoms . . . featuring in the top ten (in fact almost always five) French films at the domestic box office every year since 2005."[2] This holds true for subsequent years up to 2017, the last one for which records are available.[3] In that year, the top three French comedies—three of the top five French films—at the national box office were *all* variants of romcoms: in descending order of popularity, the high-concept *Alibi.com* (2017); the wedding-set comedy of manners *Le Sens de la fête/C'est la vie* (2017); and the interracial bromance *Épouse-moi mon pote* (2017). Such success is significant because,

Table 10.1: French Romcoms in the Overall Top 50 at the French Box Office 2014–2017

Since the genre cannot be exhaustively defined, this is an indicative list, including comedies with strong romcom elements. I have not included broadly family-focused comedies involving little romance *Adopte un veuf* (2016, 1.09 million entries) or *Demain tout commence* (2017, 1.13 million entries).

2014

Title	Overall position	Position within French (co)produced films	Admissions (in millions)
Qu'est-ce qu'on a fait au Bon Dieu?/Serial (Bad) Weddings	1	1	12.34
Supercondriaque/Superchondriac	2	2	5.27
Samba	9	4	3.15
Fiston	24	11	1.93
Barbecue	31	14	1.61
Sous les jupes des filles/French Women	41	16	1.36

2015

Title	Overall position	Position within French (co)produced films	Admissions (in millions)
La Famille Bélier/The Bélier Family	3	1	5.35
Papa ou Maman/Daddy or Mommy	14	4	2.89

2016

Title	Overall position	Position within French (co)produced films	Admissions (in millions)
Retour chez ma mère	22	4	2.20
Papa ou Maman 2/Divorce French Style	47	14	1.19

2017

Title	Overall position	Position within French (co)produced films	Admissions (in millions)
Alibi.com	8	3	3.60
Le Sens de la fête/C'est la vie	14	4	3.02
Épouse-moi mon pote	19	5	2.47
Il a déjà tex yeux/He Even Has Your Eyes	37	9	1.39

Figures sourced from CNC France.

if film and other narratives help establish cultural codes, the more widely they are consumed, the greater their power to shape mass perceptions.

On the other hand, while in 2013 there was clear evidence of "the global profile of a handful of French films," that situation has not been sustained.[4] Exemplary films receiving sufficient distribution and exposure abroad to guarantee significant visibility up to that moment included *Le Fabuleux destin d'Amélie Poulain* (*Amelie*, 2001), *Décalage horaire* (*Jet Lag*, 2002), *Prête-moi ta main* (*I Do*, 2006), *Hors de prix* (*Priceless*, 2006), *De vrais mensonges* (*Beautiful Lies*, 2010), *L'Arnacœur* (*Heartbreaker*, 2010), and *Populaire* (2012). Since then, even moderate export successes have proved elusive, with those distributed in multiple foreign territories consigned to limited exhibition (*Barbecue*, 2014) and/or mainly the festival circuit (*Les Combattants* [*Love at First Fight*, 2014]). The international success of blockbuster *Le Fabuleux destin d'Amélie Poulain* or, to a lesser extent, *L'Arnacœur*, has not been repeated, and nor has the "sleeper" arc of lower-budget auteur romcom *Le Goût des autres* (*The Taste of Others*, 2000), which grossed over $600,000 in the United States. Even the $20-million *Samba* (2014), starring Anglo-French international icon Charlotte Gainsbourg alongside Omar Sy, fresh from his *Intouchables* (*Untouchable*, 2011) success, grossed only $149,805 at the U.S. box office. Only the exhibition opportunities afforded by Netflix somewhat ameliorate the very recent picture, with among a few others the Netflix Original romcom *Blockbuster* (2018) as well as the family comedy-romcom hybrid *Il a déjà tes yeux* (*He Even Has Your Eyes*, 2016) both available in the Anglosphere.

Notwithstanding such possible exceptions, as well as the poor performance of romcoms generally at the global box office since 2013, the new circumscription of the French romcom's orbit is partly a function of the renewed nationalism that characterizes today's genre.[5] To illustrate this point, one film proves exemplary: the 2014 breakout success *La Famille Bélier* (*The Bélier Family*). French romcoms often blend with family narratives, and this is the case here, with a rites-of-passage narrative thrown in. The story focuses on a family of deaf dairy farmers who rely on their able-bodied daughter Paula to mediate between them and the world, until the situation is threatened by a teacher's suggestion that she should audition for Radio France in Paris. Meanwhile, she falls for a boy from the French capital. In marketing terms, the film was able to capitalize on the fame of its young female star, Louane Emera, as a runner-up on *The Voice: la plus belle voix*. This televisual parentage reflects the production's genesis within domestic culture, as does the identity of its principal, first-time screenwriter Victoria Bedos, the daughter of veteran actor Guy Bedos: an example of the phenomenon of dynastic nepotism that is exceptionally widespread within French cinema. However, according to Stéphane Célérier from coproducer and distributor Mars Films, so extraordinarily well-received was the film at preview screenings in France that before its official release it was presold in multiple foreign territories including the United States, where it was also to be remade. Indeed, experts were predicting not only a César Award (which would later go to Emera for Most Promising Actress), but success on the scale of global hit *Intouchables*.[6]

Yet the film totally failed to reproduce its domestic success abroad, never even penetrating the lucrative U.S. market. Phil Powrie and I have argued elsewhere that *La Famille Bélier*'s themes, like its stars, appeal to the French market and perhaps even a nationalistic sensibility.[7] Notably, the deaf family is portrayed as markedly conservative, as well as being highly idealized. For instance, the father (François Damiens) runs for town mayor in order to promote local interests and community while being openly scornful of modernizing changes, such as the need for broadband. Their "salt of the earth" existence appears entirely fulfilling to them (no mention is made of the real-world problems besetting French farmers), as they exude health and vitality, crystallized in a high sex drive, and their family is portrayed as a proudly self-sufficient social unit. The parallels with a certain idea of the French nation are not hard to see, given the centrality of both familial metaphors and rural communities in the "retraditionaliz[ing]" impetus of nationalism.[8] Moreover, the narrative prominence of a pubescent daughter chimes with such interests, when we recall that the female body is one of the clearest historical focal points for anxieties about the protection of national identity (and other bloodlines)—as reflected by the revolution-era image of *la mère patrie* (motherland). This connotation is underscored when Paula starts her period, making her available for courting by *le Parisien*, the boy who unwittingly fuels her interest in the singing career that will uproot her from her community. That the film ends on an upbeat note but with Paula leaving for Paris suggests its availability for varying ideological interpretations. However, there is no doubt that this is a narrative working through issues of identity connected to tensions between tradition and progress and "unifying" viewers around a nostalgic celebration of rural French life.[9]

Further, many of the drives *La Famille Bélier* reveals and appeals to are not merely nationalistic but inherently populist. The film is set in the Pays de la Loire-Brittany-Lower Normandy border region, historically associated with the right wing (although socialist influence has taken hold in Brittany since the 1970s, and indeed the far right may be less entrenched there than elsewhere in France, notably in the north). Nostalgia is expressed by the diegetic centrality of the songs of Michel Sardou, adored by Paula's singing coach (Éric Elmosisno). This is particularly remarkable since his character is portrayed as having been forced to take a job in what he sees as a rural backwater, after the glories of Paris. His musical taste heralds a trajectory that will see him finding his work in a provincial high school fulfilling after all, a fate mirrored, too, by that of *le Parisien*, who also appears adapted to country life at the end of the film, reversing and to an extent counterbalancing Paula's outward movement toward the modernizing metropolis. For Sardou's music is associated not only with the working classes, but, more specifically, the political right. Indeed, the critic in center-right magazine *Le Figaro* dubs detractors of Sardou's music "caricaturally left-wing" and those of the film excessively intellectualist ("the thinking press").[10]

Lest this appear an isolated or extreme example, Brittany also provides a counterpoint to urban cultures in a contemporaneous romcom equally nakedly caught up in the negotiation of issues of progress versus tradition that again exploits Elmosisno's persona: *Chic!* (2015). Like *La Famille Bélier*, this may have been produced with an eye on the export market, as it draws heavily on *The Devil Wears Prada* (2006) and stars international veteran actress Fanny Ardant as a wrong partner for Elmosisno. On the other hand, its inspiration is nothing less anachronistic than a La Fontaine fable, "Le Rat de la ville et le rat des champs" ("The Town Rat and the Country Rat"), and the resulting narrative proves reactionary almost to the point of caricature.[11] The plot focuses on a prima donna international fashion designer, Alicia (Ardant), and her director of communications, Hélène (Marina Hands). When Alicia is jilted by a lover and threatens to refuse to design her next collection, Hélène hires a gigolo to woo her. However, Alicia takes an improbable liking to plain (-speaking, -living, and -looking) Breton landscape gardener Julien (Elmosisno), hired—and just fired by "hard-nosed bitch" Hélène—to beautify the corporation's grounds. Equally implausibly, he allows himself to be bribed into courting Alicia and moving into Hélène's Parisian home for the duration of the charade. Instead, Hélène and Julien

The Breton coast cannot conceal the inward-looking ending of *Chic!*

fall in love, prompting her to quit her job, soften her businesslike appearance, and relocate to northwestern France, whose stunning coastline captured in sweeping pans provides a spectacular backdrop to their union. In opposing this life to a vision of international business depicted as vapid and dehumanizing, including through cross-cutting in the final sequence, *Chic!* joins hit lottery-win comedy franchise *Les Tuche* (*The Tuche Family*, 2011, with further installments in 2016 and 2018) and a raft of money-oriented smaller and/or auteur comedies of the 2000s in responding to the threatening encroachment of global capitalism by offering narratives that defensively shore up patriarchal nationalist values.[12]

The Family of the French

Many of the films described above evoke the topos of the family. In *Chic!*, Julien assumes Hélène's ex left her because she wanted children, when it was the other way around. While this may to some degree counter the cliché of women's reproductive "destiny," the move is largely undermined by Hélène's evident pathology (for instance, she cruelly has Julien thrown out of her offices for demanding pay she does not deny he is owed) and her storyline's contribution to a growing French romcom trend for women's work to be entirely swept aside by love.[13] Julien, in contrast, is a single father, while his business partner buddy's exceptionally close relationship with his mother figures the local community in familial terms. *La Famille Bélier* is among a slew of post-2013 romcoms whose titles explicitly evoke the family's status as a site of cultural interrogation. These include *Retour chez ma mère*

(*Back to Mom's*, 2016), *Papa ou Maman 1* and *2* (*Daddy or Mommy* and *Divorce French Style*, 2015 and 2016), *C'est quoi cette famille?* (*We Are a Family*, 2016), the Juliette Binoche vehicle *Telle mère, telle fille* (*Baby Bump*, 2017), and *Les Dents, pipi et au lit* (*The Full House*, 2018)—alongside the broader comedy *Adopte un veuf* (*Roommates Wanted*, 2016), literally meaning "adopt a widow." By way of comparison, similar cases from the previous two decades number over half a dozen, such that a dogged and ostentatious focus on the family in recent romcoms represents an intensification of an existing tendency.

Papa ou Maman and its sequel speak to the importance of film titles and easily seizable high concepts in potentially symptomatizing and shaping cultural ideas. This franchise's arresting conceit is that the central couple (Laurent Lafitte and Marina Foïs), parents of three, have decided to divorce; however, unlike in more dramatic treatments ranging from the Omar Sy vehicle "dramedy" *Demain tout commence* (*Two Is a Family*, 2016) to the harrowing, internationally distributed *Jusqu'à la garde* (*Custody*, 2017), neither parent wants the children! Such an irreverent move for the subgenre of comic films about divorcing families is unexpected against a backdrop of repeated narratives of anxiety around child welfare—including also *Happy Few* (*Four Lovers*, 2010), invoked by Foïs's starring role in both—and the films' success is striking. As both parents are motivated by career opportunities to travel with international organizations, the legacy of advanced capitalism is apparent, and further visible in their spacious and open-plan detached family home outfitted with huge windows and a view of countryside, more evocative of moneyed neighborhoods in the United States than in France. However, because the parents' work opportunities concern, for him, a humanitarian mission in Haiti and, for her, a Scandinavian placement through an engineering company, women's incorporation into the neoliberal workplace is initially more closely aligned with rampant individualism than men's in this film.

The narrative milks comedy from the callousness toward dependents posited by its setup, as each parent tries to be as useless as possible to encourage the children to live with the other. The mother's "lapses" are particularly extreme—wringing humor from the incongruousness between naked self-interest and the ethics of care superimposed onto idealized concepts of motherhood—as she behaves in sexually inappropriate ways at her children's social events and poisons them by feeding them pasta cooked in a detergent-streaked pan. All the same, it is "Mommy" who ends up taking the kids, mirroring the global sociological tendency—although they accompany her to Denmark. The film ends ambiguously with her, in an epilogue, returning to France months later, pregnant thanks to a one-off liaison with her husband during the film's resolution. By the second installment, Mommy and Daddy are set up in two different houses on the same street, Daddy with his live-in lover. All four children are ferried back and forth with dizzying regularity; the film constructs their potential emotional destabilization as banal and a source of physical comedy. Things start to go awry when Mommy, too, produces a serious boyfriend, prompting patriarchal jealousy—again, with obvious implications about gendered double standards and their wide recognizability-cum-acceptability for French audiences. The series ends by moving from the second film's envisioning of an extreme example of *la famille recomposée* (literally "reconstituted" or "reorganized"), which is both a sociological reality and a cultural trope for clinging to some version of the family at all costs, to resurrecting the nuclear family ... although the cycle was revisited via a spin-off TV show broadcast in 2018 on French TV channel M6.

Papa ou Mama 2's ending clearly acts as a palliative to fears about the impact of individualistic cultures, and the ever-increasing demands of modern work, on social bonding and the family. The significance of this issue, arguably underlined by the popularity of the franchise, stems from the fact that family ties, especially parent-child relationships, have often been seen as potentially outside capitalist economies, yet today child-rearing may also be being increasingly constructed as a site for individualistic

The spacious and open-plan house in *Papa ou maman*.

"self-actualization" or achievement. The problems with such an ideological move are underlined in the ensemble buddy romcom *Barbecue*, when a middle-aged mother, Olivia (Florence Foresti), comments on the "swindle" of parenthood, complaining that nobody is forewarned what a one-sided exchange parenting constitutes. *Papa ou Maman 2* banishes the uncomfortable suggestion of parenthood as an off-putting "nonprofit" endeavor from its resolution; however, this potential truth is surely a key selling point for a nation whose traditionally very high birth rate has begun since 2015 to drop off sharply.[14] This change was foreseen by feminist Élisabeth Badinter, in a discussion of the increasingly impossible pressures on French women to fulfill multiple roles. Badinter rightly constellates this partly within the increasing penetration of U.S.-associated discourses about gender equality.[15] It is easy to see the arc of the protagonists of *Papa ou Maman*—who go from globe-trotting to cultivating their own garden, from experimenting with new influences and partners to returning to a familial unit underpinned by blood ties—as promulgating a nationalistic fantasy, even as the film's ambivalences about corporate global values are undermined by the privileged lifestyle of its protagonists.

Heterosexual Masculinity and the (B)romance of Gallic Patriarchy

A more backward-looking manifestation of anxiety about the fate of the heterosexual family, alongside a celebration of primitive forms of masculinity, is discernible in overtly homophobic strains within recent French romcoms. Once again, these developments have earlier roots; however, the obsessive recuperation of heterosexuality reaches new heights in the 2015 film *Toute première fois* (*I Kissed a Girl*).[16] This film, which sold a solid 337,387 tickets domestically, contributes to the emergence of the meme of "coming in"—a gay person "going straight"—also referenced en passant, demonstrating its cultural incorporation, in *Épouse-moi mon pote*.[17] Thus, *Toute première fois* focuses on Jérémy's (Pio Marmaï) realization during his engagement to his long-term partner Antoine (Lannick Gautry) that he has fallen in love with a Swedish woman, Adna, played by Franco-Polish model Adrianna Gradziel. In this way it blends romcom with a man-child rites-of-passage narrative, doubling up the fatalistic generic momentum of its protagonist's progress toward fulfillment in heterosexual love.

Much humor derives from comic reversals, notably the fact that Jérémy's family are supportive of his gay identity to the point of extreme deprecation of heterosexuality, with his father comparing the conformity of "bourgeois marriage" unfavorably to "the brave act of gay marriage." This appears (perhaps unintentionally) ironic in view of the extreme middle-class homonormativity of magazine editor Jérémy and doctor Antoine's metropolitan Parisian lifestyle, including a luxurious apartment. Yet what is striking is that the (pro)queer characters, with the exception of Antoine, are constructed as dislikeable. These include a camp, self-involved artist friend of the main couple's who paints vaginas in extreme close-up. More startlingly, Jérémy's parents appropriate their son's gay identity as a badge of cool for their own pseudobohemian allegiances and treat their more conventional daughter disdainfully. Incredibly, when she has a baby, they pronounce childbirth "disgusting." Meanwhile, "coming in" and coupling up with a beautiful, sexually liberated blonde, who also becomes Jérémy's employee, is reimagined as a transgressive act.

Queerness in *Toute première fois* intersects with discourses of not only class but also (trans)national identity. The way in which the public face of queer has moved from a strong association with mass popular cultures to appropriation by the bourgeoisie is reflected by Jérémy's parents' stance. However, this evolution has been inseparable from queer culture's growing cosmopolitanism, making it a signifier of the transnational middlebrow.[18] Fascinatingly, Jérémy rejects the identitarian, U.S.-originated face of queer

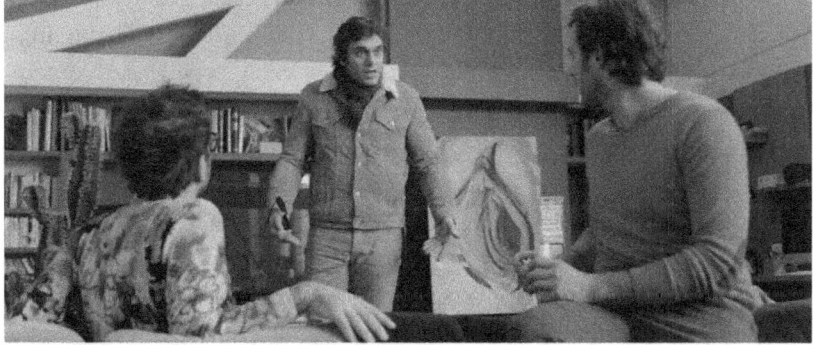

The othering of women through a painting of female genitalia is the backdrop to gay masculinity in *Toute première fois*.

when he articulates his distaste for gay pride. His union with Adna is consolidated in a different transnational space, as he is forced to follow her to Sweden when she discovers his engagement to Antoine. Consequently, Jérémy and his unreconstructed friend Charles fly to and trek across the frozen North, where he finds Adna in a hot tub with her family and proves his love by performing a local rite of plunging into freezing water. Scandinavia can be seen here to represent a hazily delineated core of Old European values. The liberal attitudes evoked by images of Adna's family relaxing seminaked together provide a patina of modernity. However, just as bathing in hot springs forms part of ancient Nordic tradition, the superficially "liberal European" overlay conceals reactionary if not mythological social structures based on the handing over of women from their fathers to suitably "virile" suitors. Arguably, this film carves out a more insidiously retrograde and antiglobal/anti-American ideological position than does, for instance, *La Famille Bélier*, precisely because it distances itself from open populism or bombastic nationalism. This is thanks to its pro-Europeanism and only subtle recuperation of the national, in the final sequence, on French soil. Here again, the setting—the interracial gay wedding of old friends of Jérémy and Antoine's—smacks of hip modernity while also functioning as a stand-in for Jérémy and Adna's generically anticipated straight wedding. Moreover, the queerness of any principal characters is pushed out of the spotlight, and gay masculinity characterized by impotent enmity toward heterosexual couples and women specifically, as Antoine secretly spits in Adna's drink.

The logic of homophobia as the handmaiden of patriarchy reverberates through John Alberti's analyses of masculinity in recent U.S. romcoms, in which he reads male characters' investment in straightness as a leitmotif of bromantic narratives that seek to negotiate men's changed place in contemporary society—even when dealing with apparently on-trend, contemporary, metropolitan masculine identities.[19] I have hinted at the importance of bromantic elements in *Toute première fois* through Jérémy's friendship with inveterate womanizer Charles —Franck Gastambide, drawing on the persona known to French viewers from the buddy comedy *Les Kaïra* (*Porn in the Hood*, 2012)—through which the narrative is also able to position the less openly immoral protagonist at one remove from patriarchy's most brazenly misogynistic face. More generally, while bromance was already an important feature of French romcoms by 2010, dovetailing with the longstanding French buddy comedy tradition, the centrality of male-male bonding to the genre has only become more entrenched since then. Salient examples include *Barbecue* (2014), *Fiston* (2014), and the domestic megahit *Qu'est-ce qu'on a fait au Bon Dieu? (Serial [Bad] Weddings*, 2014). Furthermore, the sending up of homoerotic subtexts within such relationships in the critically lauded romcom-drama *Les Deux amis* (*Two Friends*, 2015) and lately also the hit *Épouse-moi mon pote*—whose title (*Marry Me, Buddy*) evokes *I Love You, Man* (2009)—affirms the ready cultural intelligibility of the phenomenon of women's replacement by male friends in narratives otherwise coded as romantic.[20]

The reinforced patriarchal masculinism of French romcoms underscores alignments with nationalist ideologies, when we recall that "nationalism has typically sprung from masculinized memory, masculinized humiliation and masculinized hope."[21] Moving beyond nationalism and into potentially more specifically populist ideological territory, a comparable masculinist as well as broadly antielitist trend that echoes U.S. tendencies, while adding a local nuance, concerns the emergence of the "lout" or his close cousin the "beta male."[22] This figure has been birthed from the Judd Apatow stable, to complement his still-populous French predecessor the "melodramatized male."[23] The appearance of French louts has not even been couched in the same neuroticism as in Hollywood films, lacking the dysfunctional or even protopathological associations Alberti identifies in Seth Rogen's Ben (*Knocked Up* [2007]) or Steve Carell's Andy (*The 40-Year-Old Virgin* [2005]), respectively. The persona of well-known comic actor Manu Payet is paradigmatic here, in a glut of very recent comedies including *Tout pour être heureux* (*Dad in Training*, 2015), which marries a family focus with the trope of educating the adult man, and especially his own directorial debut, *Situation amoureuse: c'est compliquée* (*Relationship Status: It's Complicated*, 2014). In this film, diminutive in stature and unremarkable-looking, if not without boyish charm, Payet's protagonist, Ben, is unapologetic as to his beta or even ceta status. We open with a (nostalgic) *Annie Hall*-esque flashback, voiced over by the hero, to his schooldays as a "C student" who fell in love with a girl physically and socially out of his league. His loutish and bromantic connotations emerge when he asks his attractive present-day fiancée, Juliette (Anaïs Demoustier), if he can use his "feebleness card" to be excused from an evening planning their wedding to go out with his male friends. Here, regressive masculinity is signaled by Ben's superhero T-shirt (echoing the presence of this culture in Apatow films, as well as in the 2005 romcom *Ma vie en l'air* [*Where Is the Love?*]), and soon after by his insistence on retaining his messy habits in "my own flat" that he shares with Juliette. The narrative's plot motor is the return to France from the United States of Ben's childhood crush Vanessa (Emanuelle Chriqui), a gorgeous restauranteur who inexplicably falls for him—as did his successful businesswoman fiancée—despite his modest career as an events photographer-filmmaker. That this happens precisely because of his lack of overbearing alpha traits is implied by a scene in which Vanessa is unimpressed by the "romantic" gestures of a pickup artist who approaches her in an art gallery with pretentious lines, pronouncing herself much more taken with Ben's habit of adopting silly poses in front of paintings to make her laugh. This film presents the infantile male as so much a stock figure as to be ripe for (affectionate, self-knowing) parody later on when Ben, dumped by Juliette, descends into a depression that reduces him to the explicit status of a baby whose food needs to be mashed up by his bromance buddy Sylvain (Jean-François Cayrey). Still, one quick video promising an overhaul of his approach to personal hygiene and tidiness, and Juliette is won back over to the film's once more insouciant protagonist.

Such beta masculinity in contemporary French romcoms recalls 2010's *L'Arnacœur*, where markers of seductive con artist Alex's (Romain Duris) earthy Gallicized identity, including breath smelling of Roquefort cheese, were compared favorably to "sterile" Anglo-Saxon worldly success.[24] This echo throws into relief the hybridization of the different ancestries of "French" carnality and "American" loutishness in the contemporary French stereotype of desirable masculinity. Joanne Nagel's historical analysis of masculinity and nationalism implicitly foregrounds Frenchness when she argues that in the late 19th and 20th centuries "US and European male codes of honour" have "reflected masculine ideals such as liberty, equality and fraternity."[25] In the 21st century, in any case, a cultural obsession with asserting expanded norms of "ordinary" legitimate French masculinity demands to be read in the same context as the nationalist and/or populist sentiment bubbling up in the remarkable French support for the far-right Rassemblement National in the 2017 elections and other areas of both local and global contemporary French politics and life.[26]

Reflexivity and Radicalism

Like *L'Arnacœur*, masculinist romcoms of the 2010s often embrace the same pseudoironic approach they take to promoting backward visions of French masculinity when it comes to their schizophrenic evocations of global—especially U.S.—culture as both inspiration and menace. Such fears are perhaps most obvious in the continued presence in the genre of wrong partners inflected with globalized values, including bilingual Vanessa of *Situation amoureuse*. This film's mediation of conflicted sentiments about the United States is apparent from the fact that the turning point in Vanessa's friendship with Ben occurs when she calls him "amazing" in English, prompting a music and dance fantasy sequence that suggests the influence of Americanized "clip culture."[27] Yet Ben's reconciliation with Juliette is set up, by contrast, as a return from narcissistic masculine fantasies of worldliness to French realism and authenticity.

A similarly retreatist dynamic underpins *Blockbuster*, where Lola (rising romcom star Charlotte Gabris) has a dalliance with a romantic international NGO worker during a split from immature protagonist Jérémy (Syrus Shahidi). This self-referentially named film reflects the influence of today's interpenetrating multimediascape at the level of its form, which includes multiple ostentatiously digital and other interfaces, animations and other hyperartificial in-camera effects, and hybrid genre aesthetics from sociorealist-accented cinematography and locations to a love story enacted partially in superhero costumes. Saturated in comic book and film culture because of Lola's job in the equally archly named Comic Books Shop and the main couple's fetishizing of superheroes (again), *Blockbuster* begins as an extensive embedded home video about their relationship, being made by Jérémy to cheer up his dying father. Thus fakery, always the sparring partner of romance, is the fiber of their relationship. Related to such thematizing of issues of authenticity, *Blockbuster* is also compulsively aware of its transatlantic positioning. Although "American" superhero culture is strongly associated with performative artifice in the narrative, its inextricable embedding in French culture is evident through its aesthetically retro and narratively cult status. As for film culture, the central duo peppers their (French) dialogue with cinematic phrases in English, often misquoted, evoking the changed status of cultural tropes once they cross national borders. Similarly, when Jérémy exhorts himself to perform his role in the home video with the words

"Do it for America!," this phrase's original jingoistic overtones are mockingly undercut through contextual displacement. Hence, generic citationality in French films can be a cover for nationalistically inflected distancing from and jibing at the United States. Further, it is significant that Jérémy and Lola's performances in fact serve the interest of Jérémy's ailing father. This vulnerable patriarch embodies French patriarchy in crisis, as underscored by the absence of any women in the family to visit the sickbed alongside Jérémy and his older brother. *Blockbuster*'s mise-en-scène of filmmaking can therefore be read as a mise en abyme of French genre film production's appropriation of global models and platforms, for French (economic) benefit but also, paradoxically, for insular and nationalistic self-narrativization. Since down-to-earth Lola's eventual fatigue at Jérémy's constant performing of both love and superhero antics nearly destroys their relationship, authenticity is enshrined as outside the realm of (paradigmatically U.S.) genre representation. Her plea to him to give her "nothing but the truth" again evokes the French realist tradition—but it is made by video, and they are reconciled while dressed as Spiderman and Wonder Woman! It is as though, faced with the impossibility of exact emulation, *Blockbuster* in the end defiantly but nonsensically positions itself in opposition to the popular U.S. culture that nonetheless permeates it to the last. Such a move is symptomatic of the increasingly acute contradictions of the ever more inward-looking French romcom *à l'américaine*, whose apparently dwindling export potential also contrasts with the international saleability of realist (and other high art) cinema traditions.

The odd nexus of values presented by recent romcoms which are self-aware enough about the unpalatability of their ideological frameworks for many audiences, and so color articulations of reactionary ideologies with more culturally current elements through theme (*Toute première fois*) and/or postmodern ironies and aesthetics (*Situation amoureuse, Blockbuster*), foregrounds the different meanings of radicalism in disparate cultural contexts. Radicalism is often conceptualized as synonymous with progressive positions; however, radical right-wing movements prescribe a break with recent innovations in favor of a return to earlier values. Thus, the "coming-in" film is anticonformist by virtue of being radically—boldly—regressive. Similar nuances need applying to any so-called elites being critiqued. Notably, given anglophone romcom criticism's frequent censure of the genre's aspirational capitalist values, French ambivalence about neoliberal commerce (including, in *Blockbuster*, franchise and mass films themselves) might appear a "democratizing" breath of fresh air. However, I hope to have shown the extent to which this "radical" ideology derives from populist and particularly anti-American sentiments that the same groups would be unlikely to applaud.

Exceptions (or Exceptionalism?)

Before concluding, mention should be made of ethnicity in these films, where—seemingly against the populist argument—diversity has always been more visible than in U.S. equivalents and is now so normalized as to have become a generic trope. Ethnic minorities are not only ubiquitous, but, increasingly, they play ethnically unmarked roles, as with Manu Payet, who is from La Réunion, or *Blockbuster*'s Syrus Shahidi, of Iranian origin. Female examples, though less numerous, include the Franco-Algerian Camélia Jordana and Franco-Iranian Golshifteh Farahani. However, as elsewhere in French cinema, "color-blindness" excludes Black identities, a fact underlined by the story line of *Il a déjà tes yeux*, whose comic plot arises when a Black French couple adopt a white baby.[28] It might also be argued that characters' very lack of ethnic markers, celebrating a secular culture that is as embattled as any aspect of contemporary republican life, promotes nationalistic fantasies about ethnic minorities' incorporation as French citizens. Such an ideology perpetuates the ideals of a republicanism that constructs Frenchness as, although special, individually achievable rather than a "blood and soil" essence. Interestingly, given the (paternalistic) familial configurations of much colonial rhetoric, the trace of universalist-exceptionalist ideology in romantic comedy can be seen here to offer a racialized image of the *famille recomposée* of the nation.

Nonetheless, some recent mass-popular French romcoms resist categorization as populist. The hit film *Épouse-moi mon pote* indicates how my arguments about the way in which even interracial romances appear to promote Frenchness may be complicated by considering questions of (in this case *beur*) authorship, since this narrative's mixed-race couple finally emigrates to Morocco. It also shows a somewhat more tolerant attitude toward queer identities than does *Toute première fois*, even if these are caricatured (since star performer Lacheau's character discovers he's gay by performing camp gayness to marry a friend in need of a visa). In opposition to the bromance trend, meanwhile, some films—including multistar vehicle *Sous les jupes des filles* (*French Women*, 2014), and two romcoms focused on working single mothers, *Lolo* (2015) and *Victoria* (2016)—look back to the French romcom's 1990s feminist roots, in giving center stage to the challenges faced by women today, conceived along broadly Western and middle-class lines. All the same, in seeking to apprehend the most striking developments within the genre, I have been confronted with a body of films characterized by retrenchment if not outright panic—albeit one multifarious and ambivalent enough to remind us of the political and geocultural situatedness on which binaries of tradition and progress, and therefore radicalism, repose.

Notes

1. Mary Harrod, *From France with Love: Gender and Identity in French Romantic Comedy* (London: I. B. Tauris, 2015).
2. Harrod, *From France with Love*, 21.
3. The strong performance of romantic comedies has been a significant factor in the overall rise to a position of extreme market dominance of film comedies at the French box office since 2008. See Mary Harrod and Phil Powrie, "New Directions in Contemporary French Comedies: From Nation, Sex and Class to Ethnicity, Community and the Vagaries of the Postmodern," *Studies in French Cinema* 18, no. 1 (2018): 2–3.
4. Harrod, *From France with Love*, 21.
5. Strikingly, not a single film made after 2012 features in Box Office Mojo's top 100 highest grossing romcoms, for reasons surely partly connected to the rise of streaming platforms well suited to "domestic," rather than spectacular, genres: www.listchallenges.com/top-100-grossing-romantic-comedy-films/checklist/3 (accessed September 9, 2020).
6. Nathalie Simon, "*La famille Bélier*: le silence est d'or," *Le Figaro*, December 15, 2014, www.lefigaro.fr/cinema/2014/12/15/03002-20141215ARTFIG00273--la-famille-belier-le-silence-est-d-or.php.
7. Harrod and Powrie, "New Directions," 8.
8. Joanne Nagel, *American Indian Ethnic Renewal: Red Power and the Resurgence of Identity and Culture* (New York: Oxford University Press, 1996), 193.
9. Jean-Christophe Buisson, "*La famille Bélier*: Il suffira d'un signe," *Le Figaro*, December 19, 2014, www.lefigaro.fr/cinema/2014/12/19/03002-20141219ARTFIG00232--la-famille-belier-il-suffira-d-un-signe.php.
10. Buisson, "Il suffira d'un signe."

11 "La belle et le jardinier," *Journal du Dimanche*, January 4, 2015, www.lejdd.fr/Culture/Cinema/Chic-la-belle-et-le-jardinier-avec-Fanny-Ardant-710234.

12 See Thomas Pillard, "Les 'comédies d'argent' dans le cinéma français des années 2000: rapports de genre et échanges économico-sexuels," *Studies in French Cinema* 18, no. 1 (2018): 52–70.

13 Harrod, *From France with Love*, 103–6, 210.

14 Institut national d'études démographiques (INED), "Changes in Fertility," February 2020, www.ined.fr/en/everything_about_population/data/france/births-fertility/changes-fertility (accessed September 14, 2020).

15 Élisabeth Badinter, *Le Conflit: la femme et la mère* (Paris: Flammarion, 2010).

16 My thanks to Mélanie Boissonneau for pointing out this film and highlighting the prominence in France of Manu Payet, discussed later, as well as to her colleagues Raphaëlle Moine and Thomas Pillard for the invaluable opportunity to present this research at Paris III: Sorbonne.

17 See "Toute Première Fois," AlloCiné, www.allocine.fr/film/fichefilm_gen_cfilm=228720.html (accessed September 9, 2020). The blockbuster comedy *Les Garçons et Guillaume, à table!* (*Me, Myself, and Mum*, 2013) is comparable in tracing the protagonist's arc from presumed gayness to heterosexuality.

18 Rosalind Galt and Karl Schoonover, "Hypotheses on the Queer Middlebrow," in *Middlebrow Cinema*, ed. Sally Faulkner (London: Routledge, 2016), 201–3.

19 John Alberti, *Masculinity in the Contemporary Romantic Comedy: Gender as Genre* (London: Routledge, 2013), 62–5.

20 See Harrod and Powrie, *New Directions*, 13.

21 Cynthia Enloe, *Bananas, Beaches, and Bases: Making Feminist Sense of International Politics* (Berkeley: University of California Press, 1990), 45.

22 Alberti, *Masculinity*, 27.

23 Alberti in the same passage also identifies this figure in U.S. films. See Harrod, *From France with Love*, 108–13.

24 Harrod, 206–7.

25 Joane Nagel, "Masculinity and Nationalism: Gender and Sexuality in the Making of Nations," *Ethnic and Racial Studies* 21, no. 2 (1998): 245.

26 For instance, appearing on BBC Radio 4's "The World This Weekend," on May 13, 2018, Célia Belin of the Brookings Institution, Agathe Démarais

from the *Economist* Intelligence Unit, Malcolm Chalmers from the Royal United Services Institute, and historian Jonathan Fenby commented on the nationalism underlying President Macron's steps toward consolidating and projecting French military power globally, obfuscated by his pseudopositioning in the European Parliament as an international democrat standing for liberal values. A contrario, the ongoing and increasingly globally imitated *anti*governmental *Gilets jaunes* populist movement includes both right- and left-wing elements.

27 Charlie Michael, paper delivered at roundtable "Contemporary French Film Comedy: Industry, Identity, Ideology," University of Warwick, March 2, 2018.

28 See also Régis Dubois, *Les Noirs dans le cinéma français* (La Madeleine: Leitmotif, 2016).

Act 3

Reimagining "Happily Ever After"

11

The Radical Middle

Jane the Virgin, *Crazy Ex-Girlfriend*, and the Subversive Potential of the Television Post-Romcom

Elizabeth Alsop

Contemporary scholars of romantic comedy tend to treat the genre in its late 20th- and 21st-century iterations as more or less moribund—a perspective either stated explicitly or implied by the authors' focus on the cinematic products of an earlier, more golden era.[1] Even as recent work by Tamar Jeffers McDonald, Kathrina Glitre, and Celestino Deleyto makes the case for cinematic romantic comedy as an overlooked site of ideological richness and narrative complexity, it also suggests that the genre, after reaching an apex in the 1930s and 1940s and undergoing a radical revival in the 1970s, is now all but dead on arrival.[2] Jeffers McDonald concludes her 2007 study by noting that "there seems to be a crisis of faith observable in the current stale products of the genre," and expressing her hope that "romantic comedy will continue to evolve" in the more sex-positive, formally experimental, and political directions of the 1970s films that she positions as a promising alternative to the "neo-traditional" romcoms that emerged at the end of the last century and have subsequently come to dominate the field.[3]

This chapter identifies grounds for hope regarding the romcom's continued "evolution," but locates that potential less squarely in cinema than in the historically related but narratively and culturally distinct medium of serial television—a form that, at the time Jeffers McDonald was writing, had yet to achieve the critical adulation it enjoys today. Television—and, perhaps more surprisingly, network television especially—provides a space for more progressive and formally ambitious romantic comedy, as exemplified by my primary case studies: *Jane the Virgin* (2014–2019) and *Crazy Ex-Girlfriend*

(2015–2019), series created by Jennie Snyder Urman and the team of Aline Brosh McKenna and Rachel Bloom, respectively, for the CW Network, which have since become available to stream on Netflix. I suggest that we understand the series' radical energy as the product of not only (or not simply) their showrunners, instrumental as they are to the style and sensibility of the shows, or to the cultivation of female-driven and ethnically diverse writers' rooms.[4] Rather, this chapter links the genre revisionism of the series to the unique structures, narrative affordances, and cultural positioning of serialized TV drama, which enable modes of generic experimentation that would be more difficult to achieve within the confines of feature-length film.

Of particular significance is the way seriality allows for more diachronic as well as synchronic forms of subversion, yielding possibilities for genre conventions to be complicated both within and over the course of episodes and seasons. In particular, the serial TV drama makes possible an exponentially expanded middle: an increased space for digression, reversal, and continual movement both toward and away from the traditional telos of the romantic comedy—namely, the "happy ending" marked by the union of the (typically heterosexual) couple. By maximizing the time of storytelling, I suggest, the TV romcom also maximizes the space of ideological possibility, thus highlighting the more broadly revisionist and specifically feminist affordances of seriality for deferring or disrupting what theorists of the genre have often treated as a near-inevitable trajectory toward coupledom. Recent examples of female-created and -driven television reveal a particular interest in mobilizing serialized comedy (and dramedy) for the purposes of feminist critique, as illustrated by shows including *Catastrophe* (Amazon, 2015–2019), *Girls* (HBO, 2012–2017), *I Love Dick* (Amazon, 2016–2017), and *Insecure* (HBO, 2016–), in which sexual and romantic relationships tend *not* to culminate with the requisite "happily ever after."[5]

In the case of these two CW series, such critique is often concentrated in the paradiegetic spaces distinct to each show: *Crazy Ex-Girlfriend*'s musical numbers, and *Jane the Virgin*'s voice-over narration. The second season of *Crazy Ex-Girlfriend*, for instance, includes a show-stopping performance titled "The Math of Love Triangles" (2.3, "All Signs Point to Josh . . . Or Is It Josh's Friend?"), in which heroine Rebecca Bunch—played by cocreator Bloom, styled as Marilyn Monroe in *Gentlemen Prefer Blondes* (1953)—sends up one of the romcom's most overused tropes: the heroine's choice between two romantic partners, a scenario the show itself both dramatizes and problematizes. In *Jane the Virgin*, meanwhile, the narrator frequently affects disbelief at the series' goings-on ("OMG friends, we left Jane dating Rafael in secret..." "If it sounds straight out of a telenovela, it *is*...") (4.11, "Chapter Seventy-Five"; 1.4, "Chapter 4"). In addition to these more contained instances of metacommentary, there are also the inherently subversive aspects of the series' diegeses, including the willingness of both shows to question their heroines' romantic ambitions and forestall the connubial bliss regarded as the romcom's generic birthright.

In this sense, both the series' explicitly parodic moments (expressed in musical spectacle or self-reflexive narration) and the experimentation catalyzed by their open-ended structure contribute to the sense of the programs' generic "post-ness," their critical distance from some of romantic comedy's defining conventions. "Post-" in this context doesn't signify "postmodern," however, since in neither instance does irony militate against the sincere sentiment that is also and equally part of both shows' DNA. Thus it is not entirely accurate to suggest, as one critic recently has of *Crazy Ex-Girlfriend*, that its "focus on spoofing romcom clichés has always made it seem like an anti-romantic comedy."[6] Rather, both series take seriously the tradition of romantic comedy and its generic others—the telenovela, in the case of *Jane the Virgin*, and the Hollywood and Broadway musical in *Crazy Ex-Girlfriend*—while suggesting that such fandom also necessitates reckoning with the various functions those genres have been made to serve. In this light, it is especially significant that *Jane the Virgin* makes its heroine a romance author, since it positions affection for cultural forms as a prerequisite to, or even a *mode of*, rigorous critique of them. (That *Crazy Ex-Girlfriend* will reveal, in its finale, that Rebecca has embarked on a career writing and performing original songs sends a similar message.)

What these shows are "post-," then, is not romance, but the conventions that have so often constrained its presentation in popular culture and circumscribed the range of desires and outcomes permitted the female protagonist. *Crazy Ex-Girlfriend* regularly thematizes this distinction, as when Rebecca's neighbor-turned-friend Heather (Vella Lovell) counsels her to share her feelings with potential romantic partner Greg: "Say, 'Dude, I dig you, I got the feels.' I mean, angels don't have to be singing and some crap" (1.18, "Paula Needs to Get Over Josh!"). Heather's objection is not to romantic sentiment per se, so much as the sensationalized, prescribed expression of it. These two series offer a model of TV romantic comedy that is at once radical *and* respectful, ambitious for the genre's continued transformation in a medium that, at least in the 21st century, is less restricted—by time, by box office demands, by preexisting formulae—and perhaps less burdened by expectation.[7] In so doing, they resist default conceptions of female-oriented serialized drama as a conveyor of only the most formulaic pleasures.

The Tyranny of the End, the Possibilities of the Middle

The happy ending is often invoked as the defining characteristic of the romcom. Glitre begins her study noting that "it is extremely rare for a romantic comedy to end without the union of a couple," while Deleyto concurs, "There can be little doubt that the happy ending is a recurrent convention of the genre."[8] Both nevertheless agree that "excessive concentration on this feature" has distorted critical understandings of the genre, encouraging (false) impressions of romantic comedy as inevitably conservative.[9] Glitre sees this outsized attention to endings as a byproduct of David Bordwell's "neoformalist" model, which, by emphasizing causality as the organizing principle of classical Hollywood cinema, has led to the "excessive privileging of the teleological project" and reduction of "narrative complexity to the constant linear structure of beginning-middle-end as representing stability-disruption-stability."[10] Deleyto further observes that this excessive focus on endings has minimized the role of *comedy* within romantic comedy, leading to the "relegation, often the virtual disappearance, of the rest of the comic narrative from critical discussion, especially of the middle section."[11]

Deleyto's observation is especially relevant for the analysis of serialized romantic comedy, in which the "middle section" necessarily makes up a far greater proportion of the narrative than in a feature-length film. Indeed, where cinematic narrative typically adheres to the norms Peter Brooks outlines for literary narrative, whereby the "anticipation of retrospection"—of a definitive *end*—constitutes "our chief tool in making sense of narrative," serial television necessitates a different interpretive approach.[12] The protracted and variable duration of the TV series, in comparison to the more finite and self-contained medium of the novel or feature-length film, challenge Brooks's conception of plot dynamics, which "structures ends . . . against beginnings . . . in a manner that necessitates the middle as detour."[13] However inescapably the audience's understanding of a TV series may be shaped by its eventual end, the significant expansion of the middle precludes regarding it as mere preamble or "detour."

Indeed, the economics and industrial norms of TV production complicate the model of proleptic reading outlined by Brooks, given that, as Jason Mittell argues, "while every television series begins... not all of them end—or at least not all series conclude."[14] Here Mittell references television's "spectrum of closure," which ranges from the "fully arbitrary" to the "completely planned": from "stoppage," to more deliberate "wrap-up," to the still-more-intentional "conclusion," and, finally, the true finale, a "conclusion with a going away party."[15] While every series eventually *ends*, then, many, if not most, lack genuine finales, a concluding installment motivated by other than "extratextual" factors.[16] Thus, while Mittell concedes that "conclusions offer a sense of finality and resolution, following the centuries-old assumption that well-crafted stories need to end," he also notes that the American TV industry challenges that assumption by "equat[ing] success with an infinite middle and relegat[ing] endings to failures."[17] Michael Z. Newman and Elana Levine do note that prime-time dramas attempt to differentiate themselves from the "lack of closure" associated with the soap opera—and ensure their own "aesthetic legitimacy"—by placing "immense importance" on endings, a phenomenon illustrated by the discourse surrounding the finales of acclaimed series such as *The Sopranos* (HBO, 1999–2007), *Lost* (ABC, 2004–2010), and *Breaking Bad* (AMC, 2008–2013).[18] But, on balance, serialized programming has placed less emphasis on ends, relative to other narrative media. The rise of streaming content and corresponding changes in TV distribution and consumption further complicate the rhetorical functionality of endings. Casey McCormick, for one, argues that platforms like Netflix (which carries both series discussed in this chapter) effectively "subver[t] the power of endings," noting that "on-demand contexts... divorce endings from the paratextual hype and social buzz that accompanies most season and series finales. Sometimes, as a result of auto-play functions, we may not even realize that we've reached a finale."

These two structural features of serialized television—its amplification and elevation of the middle, and relative depreciation of the end—are central affordances of the TV romcom, which may indefinitely defer the normative climax of romantic coupling. This is not to say that cinema might not similarly redistribute its narrative attention, maximizing the "disruptive" potential of the middle and downplaying the importance of the "stable" end, to use Glitre's language.[19] Intriguingly, there are recent examples of Hollywood romantic comedy in which the *beginning* expresses the most radical sense of possibility. Amy Schumer's *Trainwreck* (2015), for example, initially presents a heroine with unabashed appetites for sex and alcohol, before gradually domesticating her, so that by the final act she is successfully and monogamously coupled. Even more revealing is *27 Dresses* (2008), the hit romantic comedy written and directed by *Crazy Ex-Girlfriend* cocreator Brosh McKenna. In the film's opening set piece, the protagonist Jane (Katherine Heigl) takes part in two weddings simultaneously. Screwball hijinks ensue, as Jane's high-speed commutes and back-seat costume changes lead to predictable confusions (forgetting to remove her bindi, for instance, while dashing between an Indian ceremony and an American one) and the requisite meet cute (with an undercover wedding columnist). Although the film leaves overt expressions of cynicism to Jane's best friend, Casey (Judy Greer), who complains that weddings are nothing more than "forced merriment, horrible music, [and] bad food," the sequence itself tacitly endorses that perspective, implying through strategic cross-cutting that weddings are little more than a checklist of nuptial events (toast-giving, cake-cutting, bouquet-throwing), interchangeable but for slight cultural variations. Although the sequence ostensibly demonstrates Jane's devotion to the ideal of matrimony, her self-conscious performance of these supposedly sacred rituals constitutes a subtle critique of them. As in *Trainwreck*, the film's skeptical orientation to its subject matter dissipates over the course of the film, suggesting that such mutinous sentiments may be expressed only in the film's opening acts, ensuring sufficient time to neutralize any disruptions to the status quo.

These two Hollywood examples suggest the benefits of redirecting critical attention to the romcom's introductory and intermediary stretches as a means of counteracting the teleological bias that, Deleyto and Glitre argue, obscures the more variable developments within this flexible narrative stretch. In short, a middle-oriented methodology disrupts the tyranny of the ending, the idea that "'The End' is the meaning."[20] This idea is particularly problematic in the context of classical Hollywood cinema, given that, as Glitre observes, endings were often "determined by generic convention, rather than narrative logic" and further constrained by the Production Code.[21] In this light, it's logical to suggest that the concluding sequences of a studio-era romantic comedy may be the *least* revealing of their sensibility. One could think, here, of noir-ish women's films like *Mildred Pierce* (1945) and *Gilda* (1946), whose overdetermined conclusions, in which alienated characters find themselves suddenly and improbably reconstituted as couples, serve to underscore the compulsory nature of the "happiness" on display. By contrast—and as feminist media scholars such as Tania Modleski have long recognized—serialized narratives have an increased potential to defer such forced resolutions and to render even their apparent achievement provisional, at least so long as the show is on the air.[22] *Crazy Ex-Girlfriend*, for instance, ends its first season with what would appear to be a concession to generic formula. In a whirlwind sequence, Rebecca and high-school paramour Josh Chan (Vincent Rodriguez III) declare their love at another couple's wedding, then consummate it with a moonlit lovemaking session on top of a convertible. In the postcoital conversation that follows, however, Rebecca's habit of overdisclosure unnerves Josh, such that the couple's "love story," as Rebecca calls it, is derailed as soon as it begins.

Whether we attribute this reversal to a radical authorial sensibility or an industry imperative to create narrative complications sufficient to justify subsequent seasons, the result is the same: a season finale that, in its narrative contours, looks less like *Bringing Up Baby* (1938) or *Clueless* (1995) than *The Graduate* (1967)—that is, one that ends with the desultory aftermath, rather

"I'm so excited our love story can finally begin!" (*Crazy Ex-Girlfriend*).

than the ecstatic union, thereby questioning the possibility of the couple, rather than celebrating them. Similarly, *Jane the Virgin* followed the long-deferred marriage of star-crossed couple Jane (Gina Rodriguez) and Michael (Brett Dier) with an even more radical reversal: not just the climactic scene of Michael's shooting (a turn of events that, however shocking, conforms to the narrative tradition of the telenovela), but another, more mundane, crisis—the newlyweds' struggle to achieve sexual compatibility, something popular romantic comedy has seldom (if ever?) sought to narrativize.

Now that both series have concluded, it is possible to confirm that neither abandoned its radical ambitions. *Jane the Virgin* delivered the more traditional happy ending, by concluding with the wedding of star-crossed lovers Jane and Rafael, while *Crazy Ex-Girlfriend* ends with Rebecca contentedly uncoupled. Yet even *Jane the Virgin*'s outwardly conventional outcome is offset by the accumulated complications of the preceding five seasons. Both *Jane the Virgin* and *Crazy Ex-Girlfriend* were series that over their runs saw minor characters and romantic alternatives proliferate, subplots amplify, and the heroines' professional lives gain in complexity and narrative prominence. In short, even now that the finales have aired, the show's conclusions—discussed in more detail below—are in many ways rendered subordinate to their expansive and frequently wayward middles. In place of the happy ending, then, I propose that we prioritize the "uncertain middle," the space of greatest ambiguity and ideological possibility, a span that may be radical in its imagination of either unhappiness or forms of happiness and personal fulfillment that romcoms have not traditionally put on display.

"Straight out of a Telenovela, Right?!": Irony and Affection in *Jane the Virgin*

In *Jane the Virgin*'s pilot, the heroine, Jane Villanueva, joins her mother, Xiomara (Andrea Navedo), and grandmother Alba (Ivonne Coll) on the couch to watch an episode of their favorite telenovela, *The Passions of Santos*. Although all three characters clearly cherish this multigenerational ritual, Jane's devotion to the genre doesn't stop her from critiquing its excesses. "Of course I'm going to watch, you guys got me hooked on these things," Jane explains. "But you really have to know, telenovelas have ruined romance for me" (1.1, "Chapter One"). The line reflects the twinned impulses animating creator Urman's show: genuine admiration for the telenovela tradition from which it springs, and playful skepticism about its conceits. Indeed, a foundational premise of the show is that Jane is both a romantic and a realist: a romance writer, whose own love-and-marriage plot is continuously thwarted in ways far more quotidian, troubling, and painful than anything dramatized by her "stories." By the fourth season, viewers could be forgiven for finding the show perverse in its refusal to resolve the central love triangle—a pattern of forestallment that represents one of the show's most radical commitments.

In its simultaneous appreciation and revision of a popular genre, *Jane the Virgin* recalls a number of now-canonical series on the CW (formerly the WB) Network, including *Buffy the Vampire Slayer* (1996–2003) and *Gilmore Girls* (2000–2007), which paid homage to horror and screwball comedy, respectively, even as they revised their dominant tropes.[23] *Jane the Virgin*—and, to a different extent, *Crazy Ex-Girlfriend*—integrate these two attitudes toward generic convention, modeling a *post*postmodern approach in which affection prevails, and genre is never only a set of signifiers to be mined. Indeed, in its unabashed enthusiasm for the soap opera, *Jane the Virgin* seems intent on valorizing a mode of feminized entertainment whose pleasures continue to be reflexively denigrated as "guilty." As critic

The Villanueva women enjoying *The Passions of Santos* (*Jane the Virgin*).

Kathryn von Arendonk notes, "On *Jane*, silliness can be a demonstration of intelligence rather than a negation of it, and the proud ownership of telenovela tropes is a way to claim the importance of women's stories." In other words, the generic appreciation practiced on *Jane the Virgin* constitutes a *politics* that corrects for a long history of condescension toward traditionally feminized media like daytime soap operas.[24] The show's main characters are accordingly unapologetic in their fandoms, whether for telenovelas, grilled cheese, God, or sex. (As Xiomara quips in the pilot, "Don't judge . . . the best way to get over a man is to get under a new man, trust.") Significantly, one of the principal sources of the show's admixture of sincerity and irony is the male narrator, whose recaps and signature refrain "I know, straight out of a telenovela, right?!" reflect a deep familiarity with the genre. This intimate, self-reflexive appeal to the audience invites us to share his enjoyment of even the genre's most outlandish conventions. (That Netflix encourages viewers to "skip the intro" is especially troubling in this context, since *Jane the Virgin*'s introductory recaps are less paratext than primary text, a crucial part of the show's structure.)

In foregrounding the recap, *Jane the Virgin* amplifies one of the most recognizable and readily mocked features of soap opera storytelling: its bias toward exposition and narrative redundancy.[25] By making *Jane the Virgin*'s explicitly expository elements—voice-over, supplemented by playful use of on-screen text and title cards—its most visually and narratively experimental, Urman does not simply reclaim but actively celebrates those aspects of the soap opera that have come in for most regular disdain.[26] This agenda is explicitly endorsed in the fourth season, when Jane's telenovela-star father, Rogelio (Jaime Camil), explains his desire to adapt *The Passions of Santos* for a U.S. audience by noting, "It's about bringing telenovelas to America and giving the genre the respect it deserves" (4.13, "Chapter Seventy-Seven").

The issue of time is particularly salient in enabling such metacommentary. As the narrator remarks at one episode's conclusion, "Telenovelas of course have twists and turns . . . they have ups and downs . . . and they have gut punches that come out of nowhere" (4.12, "Chapter Seventy-Six"). This seemingly unremarkable assessment of the genre's structure conceals a crucial insight: that all these moments of digression and deflation are made possible by the nonlinear progression of serial television temporality. What licenses *Jane the Virgin*'s unorthodoxy, then, is not only its self-reflexive engagement with telenovela tradition, but its willingness to make a virtue of the serialization often regarded as one of the genre's (and the medium's) liabilities, a source of "feminized excess" that threatens to "overrun the narrative."[27] By the season 4 finale, which ends with what was widely perceived by fans to be a shocking disclosure, the "stable" outcome expected in romantic comedy was once again in jeopardy. The show has broadened its focus beyond the romantic conflicts that organized its initial season to include other, often more pressing plots involving familial relationships, terminal illness, immigration status, career success, financial security, and the challenges of coparenting. Even as other serial dramas have leaned away from these kinds of conventionally "soapy" themes, *Jane the Virgin* has consistently, thoughtfully reclaimed them.

It is worth noting that, even at the moment of maximum alignment with romantic norms, *Jane the Virgin* finds ways to sustain its self-reflexivity. For instance, the show's emotionally buoyant finale—in which Jane marries Raphael and the entire cast gets an unambiguously happy ending—is subject to heightened scrutiny within the episode itself, with both the narrator and the characters participating in an intensified metacommentary on the nature of "endings," and the extent to which they arrive overburdened by expectation. A flashback early in the finale, for example, reveals a young Jane protesting the imminent conclusion of *The Passions of Santos* ("But Lina watches *Days of Our Lives* with her family, and they're on season 34!"). But, as Alma reminds her, in contrast to open-ended American soaps, telenovelas "always have an ending. But it's a happy one. The good people get what they deserve. And there's usually a wedding!" (5.19, "Chapter One Hundred"). Indeed, the show follows this edict, along with the expectation that any lingering "big secret[s]" be resolved. In this way, by proleptically laying out the script the finale will then self-consciously follow, *Jane the Virgin*, as it has always done, playfully comments on its adherence to the telenovela's generic norms—and, in so doing, exceeds them.

Romance Is Irrelevant: *Crazy Ex-Girlfriend*'s Friendship Plots

A successor and avowed imitator of *Jane the Virgin*, *Crazy Ex-Girlfriend* initially appears to share *Jane the Virgin*'s simultaneous affection for and subversion of both the romcom and an adjacent genre—not the telenovela, in this case, but the musical. If anything, cocreators Brosh McKenna and Bloom make even more playful use of romantic comedy's principal texts and tropes, with Rebecca's BFF Paula (Donna Lynne Champlin) aghast at her friend's ignorance of *Twilight* (2008), which she calls "only the single greatest love story since Shakespeare... in Love" (1.7, "I'm So Happy That Josh Is So Happy!"). Rebecca displays an even more intense fascination with popular media-derived discourses of heterosexual love; a recurring motif, for instance, is her lifelong fascination with the pseudo-Disney film *Slumbered*, whose signature ballad—sung multiple times in the first season and reprised in the fourth—is clearly designed to encapsulate Rebecca's romantic ideals: "In one indescribable instant the whole world falls awayyyy...." (1.18).[28]

At the same time, of course, the series displays a pervasive and increasingly open distrust of such discourse. The pilot, for instance, takes aim at one of the romcom's most familiar set pieces: the makeover montage, in which the heroine readies herself for a romantic encounter. Rebecca's preparations take place, however, to the tune of the "Sexy Getting Ready Song," a musical number in which she performs the masochistic labor—plucking, tweezing, waxing, squeezing into Spanx—that the female beautification regime actually requires.[29] To underscore the point, the number introduces an extradiegetic character, the rapper Nipsey Hussle, who accompanies Rebecca but then breaks off, disgusted by what he's witnessed: "This is some patriarchal bullshit!" (1.1, "Josh Just Happens to Live Here!"). A similar theme animates "Put Yourself First," the putatively go-girl anthem whose lyrics ("make yourself sexy / just for yourself") lampoon pop culture's repackaging of "patriarchal bullshit" using the postfeminist argot of female empowerment (1.10, "I'm Back at Camp with Josh!"). By the fourth season, in which Rebecca has "come to terms with the full scope of the damage these narratives can do," Brosh McKenna and Bloom are devoting not just discrete songs but entire episodes (e.g. 4.11, "I'm Almost Over You") to the deconstruction of the romcom genre.[30]

While *Jane the Virgin* takes a comparably benign view of pop culture–derived notions of romantic love, *Crazy Ex-Girlfriend*, then, conveys a far more jaundiced perspective. As Heather informs Rebecca, "The moment you're craving isn't anchored in real emotion—it's a script, dictated to you by your society's patriarchal love narratives" (an insight, paradoxically, she confesses to having gleaned "from this month's *Glamour*"; 1.18). Even Rebecca, in thrall to those "love narratives," displays at least a periodic awareness of their perniciousness. "That's why I don't read this drivel,"

"Put Yourself First in a Sexy Way" (*Crazy Ex-Girlfriend*).

she comments about Paula's *Us Weekly*, "because it perpetuates the very misogynist myth that women can't get along. . . . Look at this cover: femme fight, girl feud, who wore it better—it's like, who wore it *equally*?" (1.3, "I Hope Josh Comes to My Party!"). Popular media (including the romantic comedies penned by Brosh McKenna) are clearly identified as a catalyst and contributor to Rebecca's Bovarysme, her self-destructive pursuit of a culturally derived vision of romantic love.[31] It's telling that when, in the season 1 finale, she finally confesses her feelings to Josh using the language of popular romance ("I'm so excited that our love story can finally begin!"), the result does not consolidate their union but jeopardizes it. Indeed, the increasingly calamitous stakes of Rebecca's obsession with Josh—she sacrifices a job, loses multiple friends, endangers her health, and nearly takes her own life—make it clear that the series, however farcical in spirit, questions the real, lived consequences of received ideas about romance on the women who absorb them. If, as Brosh McKenna has commented, "romcoms and princess narratives are a huge part of normalizing irrational behavior in pursuit of love," *Crazy Ex-Girlfriend* deliberately *un*normalizes it.[32] Thus, the stalking often presented in Hollywood romcoms under the guise of comedy (as in *27 Dresses*, whose male lead tracks the heroine's movements using her stolen calendar) manifests here in a plot involving Trent (Paul Welsh), an *actual* stalker who physically endangers Rebecca and a number of her friends.

In this sense, the series offers a definitive critique of what essayist Francine du Plessix Gray calls the "sexual-industrial complex," which has "bullied and propagandized" women into submission to a "cult of romantic love."³³ Even more consequential than its "exploitation of female sexuality," Gray argues, has been its tendency to "dichotomize human affection along lines of deviance and normalcy, genitality and platonic love, instead of leaving it as a graduated spectrum of emotion in which love, friendship, sensuality, sexuality can flow into each other as they did in the past."³⁴ Shows like *Crazy Ex-Girlfriend* seek to restore that spectrum, by attending to interstitial or nonbinary modes of affiliation that, as Gray and others have argued, have historically gotten short shrift in Western narrative traditions—such as Paula and Rebecca's "passionate friendship"; the homosocial camaraderie among Josh's group of high-school buddies; and the bond that links Heather and Rebecca, as surrogate and egg donor, respectively, for the bisexual Daryl and his gay partner, White Josh.³⁵ Indeed, while the show's tongue-in-cheek title signals its focus on romantic obsession, its more enduring preoccupation may be friendship. As Heather confides to the abnormal psychology class for which she's been ostensibly "profiling" Rebecca, "I don't want to label her, I just want to be her friend" (1.4, "I'm Going on a Date with Josh's Friend!").

Seen in this light, the romance plot that provides the ostensible impetus for the show's action emerges as something of a MacGuffin or a Trojan horse, used to smuggle into the series a host of other concerns.³⁶ That possibility emerges most forcefully in the third season, in an episode entitled "Josh Is Irrelevant" (3.6), which focuses on Rebecca's negative reaction to a new psychiatric diagnosis following her suicide attempt. A subordinate plot concerns Josh's attempt to make amends to Rebecca so as to assuage his guilt about his presumed role in her collapse. In the final scene, Josh arrives at Rebecca's apartment, poised to apologize, until he overhears her telling friends, "This is not Josh's fault. I mean, it feels weird to even say Josh's name. . . . I haven't even thought about him in days. Truly. It's almost like Josh is irrelevant. It's not even about Josh. *Maybe it never was*" (my emphasis). Here Rebecca makes explicit what had hitherto remained at the level of subtext: that her romantic fixation has been a red herring, distracting her (and the audience) from the more pressing problem of her mental health.

Josh's own deflation at having been downgraded in narrative importance might mirror that of viewers, who have, perhaps—much like Paula, in the show's early seasons—come to share Rebecca's outsized emotional investment in their romance.³⁷ From the start, the series portrays Paula's behavior, particularly her vicarious participation in her friend's courtship, as at least as "crazy" as Rebecca's. As Paula confesses to Rebecca, midway through the first season, "You need to be with Josh . . . if not for you, then for me. My marriage is like *The Walking Dead*—we're all just trying to get out alive. You and Josh, your love story. . . . It gives me hope" (1.7). The finale communicates Josh's similar attachment to this "story," and especially, to his status as its romantic hero:

> JOSH: Rebecca has been obsessed with me since she was sixteen. I ruined her! This is on me, man, I gotta do something, see Rebecca, make things right.
> HECTOR: Or, you don't.
> JOSH: Or, I do.
> HECTOR: Or, you really, really don't.

The debate, in which Josh's friend Hector (Erick Lopez) emerges as the feminist voice, highlights the self-aggrandizing logic of chivalry, which has characterized Western representations of romance since the Middle Ages. Not surprisingly, the episode sidelines the show's male characters, centering the action almost exclusively around Rebecca's female friends, her "hashtag girlgroup forever" (3.6).

In a profound and arguably more radical way than *Jane the Virgin*, then, *Crazy Ex-Girlfriend* disrupts the generic standards and practices of romantic comedy, by suggesting that the pursuit of romance might be both pathological and, ultimately, peripheral. Episodes like "Josh Is Irrelevant" and, later, "Nathaniel Is Irrelevant" (3.13) represent the most pointed articulation of a thesis latent throughout the show: that, despite pervasive messaging to the contrary, the search for romantic fulfillment should be an optional rather than a compulsory plot in women's lives. Jeffers McDonald's working definition of the romcom—a genre that "has as its central narrative motor a quest for love" and "portrays this quest in a light-hearted way and almost always to a successful conclusion"—is profoundly destabilized by Brosh McKenna's and Bloom's series, which continually challenges the exceptional status of romantic love as narrative impetus and triumphant force.[38] Instead, care and affection in the show more consistently arrive from nonromantic sources—friends, doctors, neighbors, coworkers, exes, even former frenemies—and take a surprisingly diverse array of forms. In this sense, the series, jujitsu-like, turns the romcom's promise of happiness against itself, making the initial *pursuit* of that happy ending, though not achieved in its desired form, a catalyst of other, demonstrably more meaningful, forms of self-actualization.

It's a theme that finds fullest expression in that finale. As Rebecca puts it—in an open-mic speech delivered to a roomful of friends, colleagues, and former lovers—"I came to this town to find love, and I did. I love every person in this room. Each and every one of you" (4.17, "I'm in Love"). But, as becomes clear in the episode, Rebecca has also found something beyond love in its platonic form; she has discovered a vocation, writing and performing the kinds of songs for which the show's viewers, to this point, have been the only audience. Though she is less accomplished in her creative endeavors than Jane, Rebecca's similar turn toward art-making underscores a central message to emerge from both shows: namely, the importance of women *creating* narrative as well as consuming it. While *Jane the Virgin* has always presented its heroine's creative life as compatible with and even inextricable from her romantic one, *Crazy Ex-Girlfriend* suggests that for Rebecca creativity was not initially commensurate with coupledom—leading to what we learn, in flashback, was her rejection of all three potential suitors, and a year-long hiatus from romance. Declaring that she might be "finally ready" for romantic love, she nonetheless ends by decisively downgrading its importance—noting that she won't "'en[d] up' with someone, because romantic love isn't an ending. Not for me or for anyone else here. It's just part of your story. A part of who you are." In so doing, Rebecca articulates the philosophy and critical sensibility that guided both series over their multiseason runs. Leveraging the temporal scope and narrative extensibility of the serial form, *Crazy Ex-Girlfriend* and *Jane the Virgin* gradually, almost surreptitiously, reframe the romcom, positioning it as a genre in which romance is only "part of [the] story"—and the marriage plot, just one among many.

Toward Post–Romantic Comedy

A central contention of this chapter has been that the serial format opens up space to revise and complicate some of romantic comedy's most entrenched conventions, including its default correlation of the heroine's "happiness" with her achievement of (hetero)sexual monogamy, domestic stability, and successful coupledom. By contrast, seriality—with its at least theoretically open-ended temporality—offers expanded narrative terrain, creating opportunities for ideological intervention precluded by the stricter temporal and structural mandates of feature-length film. In practice, these two 21st-century instantiations of serialized romantic comedy demonstrate the power of TV storytelling to simultaneously celebrate *and* recalibrate what critics like Adrian Martin tout as one of the most plastic and chameleonic of genres.[39] Considered together, *Jane the Virgin* and *Crazy Ex-Girlfriend* encourage theorizing the romcom as *neither* incurably conservative *nor* militantly progressive, but, rather, as a genre equipped to both reflect and actively comment upon the ways in which desire has been mediated for and marketed to women. In so doing, these two series advance the case of feminist media historians like Elana Levine and Linda Williams, who situate the melodramatic mode in general, and the soap operatic form in particular, as central influences on American culture. Through relentless innovation and interrogation of narrative cliché, Urman, Bloom, and Brosh McKenna's work serves to consolidate the romcom's status as a cultural force, rather than mere "guilty pleasure."

Notes

1. Adrian Martin is among the critics to problematize this narrative—both the "usual Hollywood diagnoses" that contemporary romantic comedy "is in the doldrums," and the critical overreliance on a "so-called classic era of the 1930s and 40s" substantiated by a "shallow pool of high-quality examples": "In the Mood for (Something Like) Love: The Situation of the Romcom Today," *Cinéaste* 39, no. 1 (Winter 2013): 16, 17.
2. A characterization complicated not only by the recent success of mainstream romcoms like *To All the Boys I've Loved Before* (2018) and especially *Crazy Rich Asians* (2018), which as of late 2018 became the highest-grossing romantic comedy of the last decade, but also by prominent examples of LGBTQ+ romance on-screen, including in *Call Me by Your Name* (2017) and *Happiest Season* (2020).
3. Tamar Jeffers McDonald, *Romantic Comedy: Boy Meets Girl Meets Genre* (New York: Wallflower, 2007), 112.
4. Urman, for instance, has been frank about the importance of diversity in her writers' room. As Kathryn von Arendonk's recent profile reports, "*Jane*'s writing staff is now made up of ten women and three men; four

of them are Latinx, and one of Urman's first hires was Carolina Rivera, who's also written for Spanish-language telenovelas like *Amor Cautivo*" ("The Anti-Prestige Showrunner," *Vulture*, September 30, 2018, www.vulture.com/2018/09/jane-the-virgin-jennie-snyder-urman-profile.html).

5 Indeed, considering such shows in relation to the romcom would advance the project of writing "a complete history of romantic comedy," which Adrian Martin, for one, suggests would need not only to encompass more non-canonical films but also to factor in "as much television as cinema, especially in the era of *Sex and the City* and beyond" ("In the Mood," 19).

6 Bernstein, "How *Crazy Ex-Girlfriend* Became TV's Most Surprising Feminist Comedy," *Guardian*, November 13, 2018, www.theguardian.com/tv-and-radio/2018/nov/13/crazy-ex-girlfriend-rachel-bloom-feminist-comedy.

7 Further licensing experimentation may be the more general critical neglect of romantic comedy, with Martin noting, as recently as 2014, that the genre "does not receive much serious critical attention" ("In the Mood," 18).

8 Kathrina Glitre, *Hollywood Romantic Comedy: States of the Union, 1934–1965* (Manchester: Manchester University Press, 2006), 1; Celestino Deleyto, *The Secret Life of Romantic Comedy* (Manchester: Manchester University Press, 2011), 24. Along similar lines, Frank Krutnik and Steve Neale argue that the presence of a happy ending is constitutive of comedy more generally, noting that it "can be the primary—occasionally, even, the only—convention involved." Krutnik and Neale, *Popular Film and Television Comedy* (London: Routledge, 1990), 13.

9 Deleyto, *Secret Life of Romantic Comedy*, 24.

10 Glitre, *Hollywood Romantic Comedy*, 14.

11 Deleyto, *Secret Life of Romantic Comedy*, 24.

12 Peter Brooks, *Reading for the Plot* (Cambridge, MA: Harvard University Press, 1984), 23.

13 Brooks, *Reading for the Plot*, 107.

14 Jason Mittell, *Complex TV: The Poetics of Contemporary Television Storytelling* (New York: New York University Press, 2015), 319.

15 Mittell, *Complex TV*, 319–22.

16 Mittell, 319.

17 Mittell, 321.
18 Michael Z. Newman and Elana Levine, *Legitimating Television: Media Convergence and Cultural Status* (New York: Routledge, 2012), 90, 82.
19 Glitre, *Hollywood Romantic Comedy*.
20 Glitre, *Hollywood Romantic Comedy*, 15.
21 Glitre, 16.
22 For more on the feminist potential of seriality, see Tania Modleski's early and important work on the soap opera, including her 1979 article "The Search for Tomorrow in Today's Soap Operas: Notes on a Feminine Narrative Form," *Film Quarterly* 33, no. 1 (Autumn 1979): 12–21.
23 Put another way, Urman's show—like its network forerunners—is not simply metafictional, in the manner McCormick attributes to a more recent wave of Netflix content, but persistently and explicitly metageneric: *about* both the romcom genre and the soap opera. Casey McCormick, "TV Finales: On Demand Endings," *Flow* 23, no. 5 (2017): www.flowjournal.org/2017/03/on-demand-endings/ (accessed September 9, 2020).
24 See Newman and Levine's chapter "Not a Soap Opera" (80–99) in *Legitimating Television* for a historical overview of this phenomenon.
25 For a more complete examination of soap opera form, and the role of exposition and repetition within it, see Jennifer Hayward's *Consuming Pleasures: Active Audiences and Serial Fictions from Dickens to Soap Opera* (Lexington: University of Kentucky Press, 1997), especially chapter 3 (135–96). Interestingly, Hayward hypothesizes that viewing practices enabled by more recent technologies like the DVR (fast-forwarding, recording) have led to "less explicit repetition in present-day soaps" (140).
26 In so doing, they participate in a long tradition of feminist scholarship that, like Elana Levine's capsule history of the "Melodrama and the Soap Opera," *Feminist Media Histories* 4, no. 2 (Spring 2018): 117–22, argues for the cultural, aesthetic, and industrial centrality of these two "long denigrated, feminized forms" (120). See also Levine's *Her Stories: Daytime Soap Opera and U.S. Television History* (Durham, NC: Duke University Press, 2020).
27 Newman and Levine, *Legitimating Television*, 92. See also Amanda D. Lotz, who notes that historically U.S. television favored episodic as opposed to serialized programs, since "they could be aired out of order

and didn't require that audiences see every episode for them to make sense" and thus proved "more valuable in syndication." Lotz, *We Now Disrupt This Broadcast: How Cable Transformed Television and the Internet Revolutionized It All* (Cambridge, MA: MIT Press, 2018), 93.

28 The fictional film and song reemerge as an important plot point in season 4, where it's revealed that Rebecca's young half-brother, Tucker, may have been similarly warped by his love of musicals, including *Slumbered* (4.4, "I'm Making Up for Lost Time").

29 In this regard, its closest analogue may be a film like *Bridget Jones's Diary* (2001), in which Bridget's (Renée Zellweger) pre-date preparation includes unflattering close-ups and doubts about her "granny panties"—yet this lightly comic interlude is brief, and far less pointed in its critique.

30 Katy Waldman, "The Final Season of *Crazy Ex-Girlfriend* Should Be a Novel," *New Yorker*, December 28, 2018, www.newyorker.com/culture/culture-desk/the-final-season-of-crazy-ex-girlfriend-should-be-a-novel.

31 See Brosh McKenna's interview with Vulture, in which she cites "romantic comedies and Disney-princess musicals" among the show's influences, noting "the similarities between the two genres is the idea of being sold some happily-ever-after that's going to fix your life, particularly marketed to women. . . . The theme here is the behaviors that are treated as normal in society but are actually quite crazy." Stacey Wilson Hunt, "*Breaking Bad*, Lena Dunham, and 13 Other Influences on *Crazy Ex-Girlfriend*," Vulture, April 19, 2016, www.vulture.com/2016/04/crazy-ex-girlfriend-influences-breaking-bad-lena-dunham.html.

32 Brosh McKenna quoted in Hunt, "*Breaking Bad*."

33 Francine Du Plessix Gray, "On Friendship," in *Adam & Eve and the City: Selected Nonfiction*, (New York: Simon & Schuster, 1987), 284.

34 Du Plessix Gray, "On Friendship," 283.

35 See Sharon Marcus's *Between Women: Friendship, Desire, and Marriage in Victorian England* (Princeton, NJ: Princeton University Press, 2007) for an account of the ways representations of female friendship, in particular, remain overlooked in accounts of the novel, a theme often hiding in plain sight.

36 Thanks to Angus Fletcher for suggesting this conceit's relevance to understanding television storytelling. *Orange Is the New Black* (Netflix, 2013–2019) creator Jenji Kohan has also used the phrase to describe her approach to the series, noting in a radio interview that, "in a lot of

ways, [character] Piper [Chapman] was my Trojan Horse." Terry Gross, "*Orange* Creator Jenji Kohan: 'Piper Was My Trojan Horse,'" *Fresh Air*, NPR, August 13, 2018, www.npr.org/2013/08/13/211639989/orange-creator-jenji-kohan-piper-was-my-trojan-horse.

37 Paula's knowledge of romcom tradition is most fully illustrated in an episode during the fourth season, in which she provides Nathanial with an exhaustive taxonomy of the genre (4.11).

38 Jeffers McDonald, *Romantic Comedy*, 9.

39 See Martin, who suggests that "more than other genres (such as action or horror), romcoms are especially wedded to the fickleness of fashions and the speed of the mass-media zeitgeist" ("In the Mood," 16).

12

The Awkward Truth

FRACTURED ROMANCE AND THE ART OF
DECOUPLING IN THE FILMS OF HONG SANG-SOO

Sueyoung Park-Primiano

Since his 1996 debut as director of *The Day a Pig Fell Into a Well* (*Tweji ka umul e ppajin nal*), Hong Sang-soo has constructed his auteur persona around an unrelenting commitment to interrogating and explicating failed romantic connections between (heterosexual) men and women in contemporary South Korea.[1] His idiosyncratic obsession with baring the truth about emotional relations between men and women has often led to comparisons with Eric Rohmer and Woody Allen for their shared persistence in returning to this theme.[2] While the worlds created by these filmmakers are populated by characters with romantic entanglements solely motivated by self-interest and caprice, Hong's characters lack the usual charm and innocence found among Rohmer's, in such films as *Pauline at the Beach* (*Pauline à la plage*, 1983) or *Boyfriends and Girlfriends* (*L'Ami de mon amie*, 1987). Moreover, their mating rituals rarely involve extensive wooing or courtship to evolve into long-term—albeit terminal—relationships worthy of nostalgic reflection, as found in Allen's films, such as *Annie Hall* (1977) or *Manhattan* (1979). To the contrary, Hong's characters' brief encounters, while not always as fatal as in his more serious debut feature, which involves double murders and a suicide, are unscrupulously abrupt and aggressive and produce the sort of cringey affect that tend to leave an acrid taste in one's mouth.

In *Tale of Cinema* (*Kŭkchangjŏn*, 2005), for example, an underachieving filmmaker, Dong-soo (Kim Sang-kyung), relentlessly pursues an actress, Young-shil (Uhm Ji-won), whom he encounters exiting a movie theater, and begs her to relent to have sex with him. After much drinking and a declaration of love by Dong-soo, they have intercourse. There is no foreplay, no romance, and no music to hide the fact that this encounter serves as a distraction for both characters. For Young-shil, the sex is an act of grief, having just visited in the hospital the gravely ill filmmaker to whom she is indebted for launching her acting career. For Dong-soo, it is an act of jealousy and open hostility against the very same director, who has found greater fame and success than he. It is befitting, then, that, after the forgettable and regrettable sex, the woman finally succeeds in frustrating the man's ongoing demand for her attention and affection by uttering the same emphatic, onomatopoeic command "Ttuk!," often expressed by Korean mothers to sternly discipline young children who will not stop crying or whining.

In *On the Occasion of Remembering the Turning Gate* (*Saenghwal ŭi palgyŏn*, 2002), Kyung-su (Kim Sang-kyung), a moderately successful actor who has just lost a role following the box office failure of his last film, travels to Ch'unch'on, a city north of Seoul, to visit with a writer friend, Sung-wu (Chu Sang-mi). When he arrives, Sung-wu introduces Kyung-su to a female acquaintance, an attractive dancer named Myung-sook (Ye Ji-won), hoping to impress her. Despite being aware (or because) of his friend's romantic feelings for the dancer, Kyung-su shamelessly pursues and sleeps with her and, the morning after, attempts to flee and return to Seoul to avoid confrontation.

Therefore, it is not surprising to find film critic Tony Rayns decrying the "lazy" comparison with Rohmer and offer up Alain Resnais instead as

Tale of Cinema: Dong-soo (Kim Sang-kyung) pursues Young-shil (Uhm Ji-won).

a closer analogue for Hong's "relish of social embarrassments."[3] As such, Hong's characters' unsettling experiences are more likely to trigger repression than fond remembrance, and, frustratingly, the characters rarely overcome their narcissism in order to be capable of change or growth, despite moments of exposure and flashes of self-awareness. Moreover, these awkward moments are intensified by Hong's customary immobile framing and sudden zooms that tend to fix his victims of circumstance (both on-screen and in the audience) for greater scrutiny. In this way, Hong's characters disrupt audience identification and fail to elicit any deep-felt compassion from viewers, who are unceremoniously abandoned to pick up the pieces of the fractured narratives on their own and vicariously learn from the characters' misadventures.

Given Hong's propensity to demand more from his audience than most filmmakers, one might regard his films to be the ultimate anti-date movies, for they rarely, if ever, leave viewers "in the mood for love." Yet his consistent and persistent focus on exploring the explosive and less-than-ideal nature of romantic entanglements between men and women compels comparison with the cloying meet-cute encounters and teleologically driven couplings that are the hallmarks of romantic comedy. Hong's disavowal of traditional filmmaking and romcom clichés, of sentimentality and idealized love—made most explicit by his fractured and fragmented narratives and minimalist cinematographic style—demonstrates his films' clear dialogic relationship with the popular genre. Indeed, Hong himself has made the comparison (albeit ironically and paradoxically) when he declared, "I deny clichés and pursue cute things."[4] With this demurral, a suggestive and playful provocation, Hong appears to both reject familiar conventions and embrace the popular genre. Adopting this lede, my chapter adds another dimension to explorations of Hong's work that examine the structure of his signature narrative and its ties to South Korean culture and history. Specifically, my attention will focus on the extradiegetic influence of the familiar genre of romantic comedy on the reception of Hong's films. I will argue that awareness of and familiarity with the conventions and tradition of the romantic comedy can sharpen our understanding and heighten our experience and appreciation of his work. Hong's "relish of social embarrassments" is one of the many motifs in his films that reflect common and natural phenomena in the art, or artlessness, of courtship among contemporary South Koreans. These motifs support the argument that Hong's films serve as a cultural critique and an intervention to expose the entrenchment of traditional narrative: as a salve for or an antidote to the artifice of the romantic comedy, however temporary, that Hong himself seems unable or reluctant to wholly abandon.

Unsurprisingly, Hong's stubborn refusal to cater to the general audience, his withholding of sentimentality and wish fulfillment in his narratives, combined with his distinctly (and increasingly) minimalist shooting and editing style, have not yielded the kind of popular success Rohmer and Allen enjoyed, however much Hong has succeeded in enamoring critics at major film festivals and securing a niche audience among cinephiles at home and abroad. Hong also stands in stark contrast to some of his contemporaries in South Korea, such as Bong Joon-ho (*The Host* [*Gwoemul*, 2006] and *Parasite* [*Gisaengchung*, 2019]) and Park Chan-wook (*Oldboy*, [2003] and *The Handmaiden* [*Agassi*, 2016]), whose films have both been recognized at international film festivals and broken domestic box office records. By the select dedicated fans who find pleasure and humor in Hong's antagonistic characters and narratives, he has been celebrated as a structuralist filmmaker with recurring themes and variations within individual films and across his oeuvre. In fact, Hong's "forking-path narratives"—a label coined by David Bordwell in *Film Futures* to describe nonlinear or multilinear narrative films that experiment with alternative plotlines with flashbacks, such as in *Sliding Doors* (1998) and *Run Lola Run* (1999)—have provoked the most intense interest among film scholars who examine his work.[5] The film's elliptical editing, parallelisms, narrative ambiguity and complexities, and rejection of objectivity have been relished as an alternative to classical Hollywood style and as a neoliberal answer to South Korea's national identity.[6] To some, Hong's narrative is a riddle or puzzle to disassemble and reassemble.[7] To another, his films are a work of "subline," a variation of the sublime, in the way each character "faces an obstacle, is turned away, and continues to fall, even when the tangible goal . . . is achieved," encountering with increasing frustration at every turn a "sublime blockage."[8] Hong is acutely aware of the general public's lackluster response to his work, which has not dissuaded him from his commitment to his personal vision. Instead, he has self-deprecatingly acknowledged this explicitly in many of his works, in which his filmmaker protagonists alternately enjoy fan adulation from cinephiles—which Hong's surrogates consistently exploit to their advantage—or endure visceral anger and vilification by audiences at their film screenings. In *Like You Know It All* (*Chal aljido mothamyŏnsŏ*, 2009), for example, an art-house filmmaker, Kyung-nam (Kim Tae-woo), travels to Chechŏn province to judge a local film festival, where he is greeted by festival programmers and fellow judges with profuse praise by festival programmers ("You are a famous director, everyone says so"; "You are a true artist"; "Your films gave me insight into human psychology. I wouldn't have understood some people without your films"). The flattery is not enough to fuel Kyung-nam's oversized ego, however, for he diminishes in size when, at a festival reception, the crowd's attention shifts to a younger director who has enjoyed major box office success. That night, while brushing his teeth, Kyung-nam mutters to himself, "My next film will draw two million. A film for two million." Ultimately (and characteristically for Hong's male protagonists), Kyung-nam leaves the festival with a tarnished reputation, for drinking and sleeping through the entire trip and succeeding only in offending everyone, including his close friend, whom he betrays by seducing his wife. In the film's second half, Kyung-nam travels to Chejudo, an island on the Korea Strait, to guest lecture at a friend's film class. During the postscreening Q&A, much to his chagrin, an intrepid female student demands to know why he persists in making films that no one understands or enjoys. Again, unchanged from lessons he should have learned from the first half of the film, Kyung-nam leaves more chaos in his wake, further destroying his relationships by sleeping with his former mentor's wife and betraying everyone he knows.

On one occasion, after a press screening of *Right Now, Wrong Then* (*Chigŭm ŭn matko kŭ ttae nŭn tŭlida*, 2017), Hong was asked by a reporter why the scene in which the protagonist's film is being shown has only one person in attendance at the theater. Hong's blunt and unequivocal response was "Because it is true!" With this ready reply he confirmed and exposed the way his personal experience provides inspiration for his films, for once verifying a comparison Hong has fruitlessly attempted to dodge, in spite of many of his characters being tied to the film industry and the leading male characters frequently resembling him in appearance and profession. Any attempt at such deflection has since been squashed after Hong confessed, at the 2017 Seoul press screening for *On the Beach at Night Alone* (*Pam ŭi haebyŏn esŏ honja*, 2017), to having an extramarital affair with the film's female lead, Kim Min-hee. Kim's collaboration with Hong began with *Right Now, Wrong Then*, and she has since become his muse, leading

Like You Know It All: Kyung-nam (Kim Tae-woo) confronts a hostile audience.

the cast in all of Hong's subsequent films. Despite the scandal, this case of life-imitating-art-imitating-life was hardly surprising to the Korean public or to anyone remotely familiar with his work. In keeping with his irreverent on-screen humor, Hong defiantly addressed his transgression in his 2017 film *Claire's Camera* (*K'ŭlaeyŏ ŭi k'amera*) by naming the male protagonist, a fifty-year-old filmmaker attending the Cannes Film Festival, "So Wansoo," and the young female protagonist and his love interest, who is portrayed by none other than Kim Min-hee, "Man-hee."[9]

Undeterred by his films' lackluster performance at the box office, Hong is one of the few filmmakers who enjoy the freedom to make his idiosyncratic films without too much concern about box office returns, buoyed in part by his continued critical success at international film festivals. He has also shielded himself from the career repercussions of modest box office returns by having established his own production company, Jeonwonsa, and by working efficiently and economically with minimal crews on shoestring budgets. The prolific filmmaker has averaged about one film a year, and, more recently, two. It took him three weeks to produce the aforementioned *Right Now, Wrong Then*, and only two weeks to produce *Claire's Camera*, which was shot on location in Cannes to coincide with his attendance at the Cannes Film Festival.

Romantic Comedy in Situ

In *Consuming the Romantic Utopia: Love and the Cultural Contradictions of Capitalism*, Eva Illouz asserts that romantic love in America became the "center stage of culture" and the "focus of a collective utopia" at the beginning of the 20th century, transforming marriage from "a businesslike, functional, advantageous and dynastic institution" into a "grail of perpetual personal fulfillment, an unfailing wellspring of happiness that, in thousands of films, magazines and novels, came to seem a basic human right."[10] Indeed, as the theme of romance became incorporated within the emerging mass market and associated with consumption, the romantic comedy genre enjoyed its most sophisticated cultivation in the 1930s and early 1940s in the U.S., from screwball comedy to the "comedy of remarriage" (to be discussed further below), during the height of classical Hollywood.[11] In South Korea, the treatment of romantic love in comedic form has its origins in the post-Korean War (1950–1953) reconstruction era, when a handful of romantic comedies appeared in the war-torn nation. Fantasies such as *Hyperbola of Youth* (*Chŏngch'un ssanggoksŏn*, 1956), *Holiday in Seoul* (*Sŏul ŭi hyuil*, 1956), *The Love Marriage* (*Chayu kyŏrhon*, 1958), and *The Female Boss* (*Yŏsajang*, 1959) offered escape from spiritually and materially depressed conditions. This was also seemingly a reflection of and reaction to Hollywood's greater influence and the impact of American culture on the southern peninsula since the U.S. military's occupation of South Korea in the aftermath of the Pacific War (1941–1945). With the arrival of the U.S. military came the deluge of American mass culture, promoting a "'visual utopia' that combined elements of the 'American dream' (of affluence and self-reliance) with romantic fantasy."[12]

Hyperbola of Youth, a modern-day prince-and-the-pauper story, features two male friends, one rich and one poor, who exchange places in order to cure their respective ailments of gluttony and malnutrition, then fall in love with each others' sisters and combine households to overcome class difference and eliminate poverty. In *Holiday in Seoul*, a misunderstanding between a female obstetrician and her newspaper-reporter husband during their trip to the metropolis is overcome by their solving a crime together that also functions to preserve their marriage. In *The Love Marriage*, a loose adaptation of Shakespeare's *King Lear*, the travails of love and marriage unfold among the three daughters of a wealthy doctor: the eldest daughter, whose confession while on her honeymoon of an illicit romance leads to her husband's flight to America and a three-year separation; the second daughter, who, to her father's disapproval, falls in love with her penniless tutor and is forced to leave home; and the third daughter, who rejects an arranged marriage to a wealthy businessman in favor of her father's headstrong assistant. Aptly for a genre film predetermined to avoid tragedy, each daughter's love and marriage leads to an implausible happy ending. More outrageously, in *The Female Boss*, a successful executive and publisher of a popular magazine, *Modern Woman*, falls in love with and marries the one man who refuses to kowtow to her professional demands and to whom she relinquishes her position as head of the company; happily submitting to the confinement of the domestic sphere, she becomes a full-time housewife. In this way, while dangling free love as desirable and glamorous as well as a panacea for poverty and established social hierarchy, the fulfillment of this love is ultimately deemed too risky and its rebellious potential crushed; in these films, any sign of individualism and challenge to patriarchy and tradition enacted by these new women are ultimately repressed and punished.

According to Stanley Cavell, in his landmark work *Pursuits of Happiness: The Hollywood Comedy of Remarriage*, the romantic comedies of the classical era that he collectively categorizes as the "comedy of remarriage," beginning with *It Happened One Night* (1934), are about more than the commodification of love, escapism amid the Depression, or even the emergence of the "new woman." Instead, they should be read as "parables of a phase of the development of consciousness at which the struggle is for the reciprocity or equality of consciousness between a woman and a man" who "harbor a vision which they know cannot fully be domesticated, inhabited, in the world we know," and thus constitute fantasies that "express the inner agenda of a nation that conceives Utopian longings and commitments for itself."[13] Likewise, albeit responding to different historical circumstances, with the landscape utterly destroyed and country bifurcated into North and South, and attempting with modest degrees of success to bring about gender consciousness and equality, South Korea's classical romantic comedies may be read as parables of a nation struggling with extreme social and political upheaval. Despite the impending recovery and improvements to its economy, South Korea would face more suppression of freedom of expression in the next three decades under the autocratic rule of Park Chung-hee's military junta (1963–1979), succeeded by the comparably repressive regime of Chun Doo-hwan (1980–1988).

Under such oppressive conditions, it is not surprising that the next cycle of romantic comedy does not return until the 1990s, when the genre was rekindled in an attempt to awaken gender consciousness, beginning with *The Marriage Story* (*Kyŏrhon iyagi*, 1992) and followed by *Mr. Mamma* (1992), *That Woman and That Man* (*Kŭ namjawa kŭ yŏja*, 1993), *A Bosom Man* (*Kasŭm dallin namja*, 1993), and *How to Top My Wife* (*Manura chuggigi*, 1994). As astutely summarized by An Jinsoo in his essay "Anxiety and Laughter in Korean Comedy Films," these films represent a major departure from early comedies by eschewing class distinction and family unity, altogether:

> The protagonists live in studio apartments, drive their own automobiles and work in highly specialized fields. The films are not concerned with any economic problems, an issue that had previously been an important thematic element of Korean comedy films. Nor are the characters defined in terms of their relation to (extended) family members. Instead, they are figured primarily as competent professionals with refined cosmopolitan tastes, who are overtly concerned with the maintenance of their private space and sexual relationships. The comic moments of these films consist primarily of sexual jokes which also celebrate the joyful conjugal relationship of the newlyweds. However, the subversive possibility of sexual liberation is rigidly contained by the effort to conceal the sexual insecurity of men. While these films poke fun at the insecurity of the male protagonists, sexist humor essentially serves to denigrate and domesticate female protagonists.[14]

Indeed, despite South Korea's move toward democratization, with the election of the first civilian president taking place in 1992, and continuing economic growth, as reflected in the characters' affluent lives and successful careers, these films were primarily star vehicles that represented fantasies of gender equality only to return to preserving patriarchy.[15] Such films set the precedent for the context in which Hong debuted as a director with a fresh take on man-woman relationships in contemporary South Korea.

Hong Sang-soo, the Anti-Traditionalist

Similar to the early 1990s films mentioned above, rarely do we get a glimpse of a family in Hong's films. When we do, it is a fractured and dysfunctional one, as in the aforementioned *Tale of Cinema*, in which Hong offers a film-within-a-film (a mise en abyme, incorporated into the narrative as a film made by the protagonist) to deliver a scathing attack on the controlling, traditional parents whose vehement refusal to allow their son to pursue a career as a painter nearly drives him to suicide. Such a complete portrait of a nuclear family is an aberration in Hong's films, however, and when any family member is represented it is usually the lone mother, who routinely wields an exorbitant amount of influence over her son. This is most explicit in *Hahaha* (2010), in which the mother's emotional detachment and ambivalence toward her son, the protagonist, results in his desperate and possessive attempts to win her affection while also attempting to woo an equally indifferent woman who works as a museum guide. It wasn't until his most recent film, *Hotel by the River* (*Gangbyŏn hot'ael*, 2018), that Hong finally explored the father-son dynamic, although, once again, even in her absence the mother is depicted as emotionally manipulative and controlling. As evidenced by these examples, the majority of Hong's films are arguably male-centered, in a departure from the conventional romantic comedy, which is often female-centered and dismissed as at best "women's pictures" and at worst as "chick flicks," but whose territory has recently been encroached upon by the recent crop of "bromances" best represented by *Pineapple Express* (2008) and *I Love You, Man* (2009). However, unlike these Hollywood releases—which may be extensions of or alternatives to war films and cop-buddy films with their hypermasculine, homosocial bonding rituals—in Hong's films this focus does not bode well for the male characters, who tend to be deeply flawed and without charm (to be discussed in more detail below).

Moreover, unlike in the traditional romantic comedy, Hong's characters are rarely glamorous, even when they are portrayed by stars, although they tend to lead glamorous lives. They are, however, typically cosmopolitan, highly educated, well traveled, and well-to-do. On the surface, this may appear to be a commonality between Hong's films traditional romantic comedy, but it is important to note that the principal characters' occupations are not tied to the *chaebŏl* (large family-owned conglomerates, such as Samsung and Hyundai), or to the law or medical professions. In a departure from these established occupations, traditionally pursued and respected as a measure of individual success, the characters are artists, academics, gallery owners, film festival organizers, poets, musicians, and novelists—unhindered by concerns about finance and in possession of ample and flexible leisure time to get away to a beach resort or retreat to Paris at a moment's notice. While perhaps unintentional, this disavowal of traditional professionalization may be read as a sharp rebuke of the country's financial crisis, which led to the 1997 bailout by the International Monetary Fund. At the same time, in accordance with the romantic comedy, the characters (à la those of Mike Nichols and Woody Allen) are very much of the affluent and educated class. According to Cavell, by its very nature the romantic comedy "privileges the upper classes, those with wealth and leisure time, those who can contemplate and ponder and pursue the good life, those who are educated and well-to-do who can experience life's material excess with flowing drinks and meals."[16] And anyone who has seen Hong's films knows that there are always abundant meals and a steady flow of drinks.

In fact, drinking scenes are Hong's signature flourish. The glaring difference here from traditional romantic comedy is that the unhealthy consumption of alcohol is not a means of smoothing out social ineptitude (i.e., alcohol as a social lubricant) or a plot device to create misunderstandings that push the narrative forward. Quite the opposite: the heavy drinking

Hahaha: the drinking ritual.

disinhibits Hong's already awkward characters to expose, not elide, their pettiness, old grudges, cowardice, selfishness, self-delusion, deception, and ambition. And, more often than not, this exposure through intoxication leads to abject humiliation and further alienation, especially by Hong's male characters, who use drinking to make known their attraction to and desire for the women in their company, who in turn are very much aware that the alcohol-fueled entreaties are far less than promises of eternal love. Time and time again, in a drunken stupor, the male protagonist will profess his undying love for the woman he just met or was reunited with; on one occasion, he even declares his intention to marry her. In *Right Now, Wrong Then*, which unfolds as a diptych, a filmmaker arrives in the town of Suwon to deliver a lecture and launch a retrospective of his own work. Having arrived a day early, he spends the day pursuing and seducing a young painter, at first through flattery and deception and then with brutal honesty. It is during the characteristic drinking sequence that the filmmaker professes his love and proposes. This proposal, obviously without expectation for follow-through, is made all the more extreme when he surprisingly produces a ring from his pocket and, in its absurdity, creates narrative dissonance that amplifies the act's artificiality: here, it is a clear departure from romantic comedies that purport love at first sight as not only to be believed but also to be desired.

In addition, these male protagonists' professions of love are acts of subterfuge, ruses to escape their existential crises. The meet-cute moment that rapidly unfurls into alcohol-induced intimacy generally occurs when Hong's characters are at their most vulnerable, professionally or personally. While this may be true for both male and female characters, it is typically the male protagonists who seem the more unable to let go of their egos or resistant to confronting their imperfections: his manuscript has been rejected by a publisher; his colleague is more successful; he has lost the part in a film he campaigned for; his affair with a student has been exposed; he is wanted by the law for a misdemeanor; he has been eviscerated by moviegoers who attend a screening just to heckle him. All of these moments offer a chance for reflection and growth, but the characters' narcissism leads them to reject introspection, propelling them instead to seek affection from and pursue physical contact with the opposite sex. This isn't to say that Hong's male characters are devoid of genuine feelings or that they are not worthy of redemption, but their inability to sit with discomfort—only a few male characters appear capable of personal insight—suggests that they will not change and are forever doomed to repeat their mistakes; they are compelled to act in ways that trap them in a self-destructive cycle forever. And, frustratingly, women succumb to relentless supplications of these male protagonists, sometimes seduced by the authority or celebrity status of a director, an influential professor, or a publisher. The most extreme example of this dogged, drunken pursuit is in *Oki's Movie* (*Okhŭi ŭi yŏnghwa*, 2010), in which a female college student is eventually worn down by the end of the film and acquiesces to the male protagonist's desire. The most refreshing alternative to this formula can be found in *Woman on the Beach* (*Haebyŏn ŭi yŏin*, 2006), in which the female protagonist, Mun-sŏk (Ko Hyŏn-jŏng), declares that she never repeats things in her life and chooses to escape the cycle after a distasteful affair with a cowardly and deceitful filmmaker.

As mentioned earlier, these drunken encounters and awkward conversations are made all the more tense and painful for the audience by the director's use of long takes—their rhythm sometimes begrudgingly interrupted by slight pans and unexpected sudden zooms, more often than not on an object rather than an actor—that insist on absolute focus and recognition on the part of the viewer that they are watching a film. This rigid, lengthy scrutiny is what allows greater participation from the audience: suddenly, the oft-repeated, mundane scene opens up to allow room for deeper consideration, character study, and narrative fulfillment. With Hong's long takes and ironic eye, his characters' foibles, motives, inhibitions, insecurity, and other flaws are laid bare. Aesthetically, Hong's decisions regarding cinematography serve to strip down the image to its most basic essence. Sometimes this means removing color and shooting in black-and-white, as in *The Day He Arrives* (*Pukch'on panghyang*, 2011) and *Virgin Stripped Bare by Her Bachelors* (*O! Sujŏng*, 2000). And sometimes (as in *Hahaha*) it also means eliminating movement with the use of still black-and-white imagery when he wants the audience to focus closely on the contrasting contents of the film. In this way Hong makes his authorial intentions known, and it requires a tacit agreement between Hong and the viewer for his efforts to be appreciated and rewarded in return. Unlike the glossy shots found in traditional romantic comedy, there is nothing precious about the image in Hong's work, nothing sentimental in the intimate moments. What may also not be as obvious to non-Korean viewers is Hong's use of available or natural light.

In South Korea this means using cold fluorescent lights for interior shots; never flattering, they are intended to illuminate the truth of the shot rather than to deceive.

Finally, Hong's clearest tie to the romantic comedy is through his engagement with the genre's familiar trope of coupling. His compulsion to repeat this trope across his films allows first for easy comparison with the traditional narrative, then exhibits contrast in the unconventional and nonlinear way in which the story unfolds. Occasionally, as noted earlier, the same plot is revisited within the same film, using the same actors and locations (*Right Now, Wrong Then*), but introducing minor variations in the characters' actions to build and comment on the first iteration of the plot. Most often the plot involves a romantic triangle between two men and one woman, as in *Virgin Stripped Bare by Her Bachelors* or *Oki's Movie*. There are variations on this arrangement that feature two women and one man in the mix (as in *Night and Day* [*Pam kwa nat*, 2008], *The Day After* [*Kŭ hu*, 2017], and *Claire's Camera*) or two women and two men in a romantic quadrangle (as in *Woman on the Beach* or *Hahaha*). Yet the characters do meet by chance (and perhaps this is the meaning of Hong's cryptic intention to pursue "cute," as noted earlier), and Hong celebrates cinema's ability to record the aleatory, only to paradoxically refute it, by indulging in multiple perspectives and repetitions of this innocent moment. Through these expressions and aesthetic choices, Hong's films serve as an antidote to the conventional romantic comedy, and thus an alternative, for the sake of its greater truthfulness. His work rejects artifice and questions character motivation and perception. There is plenty of discussion of love, but never an endorsement of eternal love. There are romantic moments, however fleeting, but they ultimately end in failure, usually disastrously and sometimes violently. He offers no traditionally happy endings or easily won pleasures. Unlike romantic comedies, his films are not vehicles for our fantasies, but a collection of parables for us to reflect on our own motivations to connect romantically and succeed in finding true romance.

Notes

1 All Korean names, words, and titles have been romanized according to the McCune-Reischauer system, with the exception of those names and titles (e.g., Hong Sang-soo or Seoul) already in common English usage.

Asian names have been presented in Asian style, with family name first and given name last, unless there is a common or preferred Western form for the individual or authors.

2. See, for example, Nicolas Rapold, "Films of Hong Sang-soo Capture Pleasures and Pratfalls of Attraction," *New York Times*, May 17, 2017, www.nytimes.com/2017/05/17/arts/hong-sang-soo-films-at-cannes.html; and Lee Hyo-won, "Hong Sang-soo Explains His Improvisational Methods for Fast Filmmaking," *Hollywood Reporter*, May 20, 2017, www.hollywoodreporter.com/news/hong-sang-soo-explains-his-improvisational-methods-fast-filmmaking-1005875.
3. Tony Rayns, "Funny Valentines: Mating Rituals and Alternate Realities in the Films of Hong Sangsoo," *Film Comment* 51, no. 3 (May–June 2015): 57.
4. Moonyung Huh, *Hong Sangsoo*, trans. Jin-Young Yook (Seoul: Korean Film Council, 2007), 13.
5. David Bordwell, "Film Futures," *SubStance* 31, no. 1 (2002): 88–104. See also Warren Buckland's anthology *Puzzle Films: Complex Storytelling in Contemporary Cinema* (Malden, MA: Wiley-Blackwell, 2009), which gathers essays on a number of films variously identified as "puzzle films," "mind-game films," "multiple-draft films," "modular-narrative films," or "twisted-narrative films."
6. Kyung Hyun Kim, "Death, Eroticism, and Virtual Nationalism in the Films of Hong Sangsoo," *Azalea: Journal of Korean Literature & Culture* 3 (2010): 135–69.
7. Marshall Deutelbaum, "A Closer Look at the Structure of Hong Sangsoo's *Hahaha*," *Asian Cinema* 23, no. 2 (2012): 157–66; Michael Unger, "Hong Sangsoo's Codes of Parallelism," *Asian Cinema* 23, no. 2 (October 2012): 141–56.
8. Akira Mizuta Lippit, "Hong Sangsoo's Lines of Inquiry, Communication, Defense, and Escape," *Film Quarterly* 57, no. 4 (Summer 2004): 26.
9. This film also boasts Hong's second collaboration with Isabelle Huppert, who was first seen in *In Another Country* (*Tarŭn nara esŏ*, 2012), further tightening his connection to and affection for French cinema beyond Rohmer and Resnais, as is also evidenced by a cameo appearance by Jane Birkin in Hong's 2013 film *Nobody's Daughter Haewon* (*Nugu-ŭi ttal-to anin Haewŏn*).
10. Eva Illouz, *Consuming the Romantic Utopia: Love and the Cultural Contradictions of Capitalism* (Berkeley: University of California Press, 1997), 48.

11 Stanley Cavell, *Pursuits of Happiness: the Hollywood Comedy of Remarriage* (Cambridge, MA: Harvard University Press, 1981).
12 Illouz, *Consuming the Romantic Utopia*, 31.
13 Cavell, *Pursuits of Happiness*, 17–18.
14 Jinsoo An, "Anxiety and Laughter in Korean Comedy Films," in *Post-Colonial Classics of Korean Cinema*, ed. Chungmoo Choi (Irvine: Korean Film Festival Committee at the University of California, 1998), 37.
15 For example, Choi Min-soo, the lead male character in both *The Marriage Story* and *Mr. Momma* and the son of Choi Mu-ryŏng (the most popular male lead of the late 1950s and 1960s during the Golden Age of South Korean cinema), and Shim Hye-jin, the female lead in *The Marriage Story*, were two of the biggest box office draws at the time.
16 Cavell, *Pursuits of Happiness*, 17.

13

Addicted to Love

The Productive Pathology of the Romantic Comedy in the Netflix Series *Love*

John Alberti

The episodic nature of the TV series has long posed a challenge to the romantic comedy, one of the most teleological of cinematic genres. While the classic movie romcom rushes forward to a definitive conclusion at the altar, the TV series aspires to defer narrative conclusion, and cancellation, indefinitely. As a result, sitcoms built on or incorporating a romcom narrative—when will Sam and Diane, Ross and Rachel, Jim and Pam finally get together?—typically face a postconsummation crisis: Now where do we go?

This narrative tension has only increased in the era of over-the-top binge programming, with the emergence of what Aymar Jean Christian calls "indie TV," programs meant for and thriving on niche audiences too small to satisfy the revenue demands of broadcast television.[1] The three-season Netflix serial romcom *Love* (2016–2018), created by Leslie Arfin and Paul Rust (who also costars as Gus) and based loosely on their own relationship, thematizes this teleological conundrum. Produced and with some episodes cowritten by the bromance auteur Judd Apatow, *Love* radically destabilizes the narrative teleology of the romcom, the question of where the relationship between the main characters of Mickey (Gillian Jacobs) and Gus is going, even where we as viewers *want* it to go.

I will discuss *Love* as part of an ongoing, at times ideologically contradictory, but ultimately productive destabilization of the performances of gender, sexuality, and generic expectation in the 21st-century romcom. I am particularly interested in the ways that *Love* pathologizes the romantic comedy and the larger social constructions and expectations that both inform and are defined by the genre. While Arfin has described the motivation for the series as "what happens when the honeymoon is over," the series itself questions whether "what happens" next is even possible, and whether the entire premise of the romcom and of romantic love may not be pathological. These questions center around the character of Mickey, a program manager for a narcissistic satellite-radio self-help therapist, who understands her own life in terms of addictions to drugs, alcohol, and, most pointedly, sex and relationships. Underscoring the connection between romantic love and addiction, *Love* destabilizes both the romcom as genre and our experience as romcom viewers, forcing us to confront the question of our own desires and subject-positions as we struggle with defining just what a happy ending for Gus and Mickey would look like.

The idea of the obsolescence and imminent extinction of the romcom genre goes back at least to Brian Henderson's 1978 essay "Romantic Comedy Today: Semi-Tough or Impossible?," which argued that feminism and the cultural upheavals of the 1960s and 1970s were undermining the heteronormative marriage plot, a thesis updated and elaborated by Frank Krutnik in the 1990 article "The Faint Aroma of Performing Seals: The 'Nervous' Romance and the Comedy of the Sexes."[2] The genre has persisted, in part by thematizing its incorporation of and negotiation between conservative and progressive cultural scripts. As Krutnik put it almost thirty years ago, "Even while acknowledging the contemporary breakdown of marriage, these films manifest a yearning for rules, norms, and boundaries within which The Couple can come, and stay, together."[3] Arguments like Henderson's, Krutnik's, and my own risk overstating the ideological stability of the pre-1970s romcom in making the case for a radical rupture with that tradition.

Odd couple Gus (Paul Rust) and Mickey (Gillian Jacobs) in *Love*.

Consider, for example, the conclusion of *Pillow Talk*, the Doris Day-Rock Hudson sex comedy from 1959 that seems to define the heteronormative romcom formula, with Hudson's scheming, predatory "bachelor" Brad sexually liberating Day's stereotypically repressed Jan, while ultimately capitulating to the law of mandatory marriage. After the words "The End" appear on the screen over two satin pillows representing our two lovers, additional pillows in pink and blue appear, each with "Not Quite" written on them, an acknowledgment that the prospect of marriage represents a phase shift, not an ending, with a subtle comic warning about how sexual fulfillment within marriage equals endless procreation.

Rather than a stable endorsement of 1950s gender norms, the plot of *Pillow Talk* veers between endorsing and subverting gender performance, with the closeted gay actor Rock Hudson playing a straight character who pretends to be gay as part of an elaborate seduction scheme that culminates in an infamous rape scene, with Brad bursting into Jan's bedroom and carrying her against her will across the city to his bachelor pad while bystanders smile or look away—a depiction of romance as violence in a movie that also plays for comedy a sexual assault on Jan by a college student. Immediately before the closing credit sequence, the narrative ends on a subplot involving an obstetrician who comes to believe that father-to-be Brad instead represents the world's first pregnant man: "I'm going to have a baby!" Brad announces as he tries to get away from the doctor's attentions. "Of course you are!" the doctor agrees.

In fact, this comic skepticism about happy heteronormative endings and the stability of marriage conventions defines the history of the American cinematic romcom. Consider the "divorce comedies" of the 1920s written by Jeanie Macpherson and directed by Cecil B. DeMille. Their titles—*Don't Change Your Husband* (1919); *For Better, For Worse* (1919); *Male and Female* (1919); *Why Change Your Wife?* (1920)—reflect social anxiety over marriage, gender, and sexuality connected to rising middle-class divorce rates in the 1920s. One of the most influential meditations on the genre, Stanley Cavell's *Pursuits of Happiness*, argues that many great screwball comedies of the 1930s and 1940s begin with divorce and feature characters negotiating gender and intimacy in order to recouple, a process Cavell links to that earlier historical crisis over the meaning and legitimacy of marriage, and even society itself: "The overarching question of the comedies of remarriage is precisely the question of what constitutes a union, what makes these two into one, what binds, you may say sanctifies in marriage. . . . In thus questioning the legitimacy of marriage, the question of the legitimacy of society is simultaneously raised, even allegorized."[4]

My interest in both the pathology and endurance of the romcom centers on how the 21st-century romantic comedy—and the bromance subgenre in particular—reflect recent cultural destabilizations and reimaginings of the performance of gender. Specifically, I examine how the romcom and gender performance come together in the concept of genre seen, as Stephen Neale puts it, as "systems of orientations, expectations and conventions."[5] Neale goes on to argue that comedy operates in part to foreground an awareness of these systems: "What comedy does, in all its various forms and guises, is to set in motion a narrative process in which various languages, logics, discourses and codes are, at one point or another—at precisely the points of comedy itself—revealed to the audience as fictions."[6] For the romcom, these include the discourses and codes of romance and gender. Or, as Arfin put it in discussing how the series emerged from her own reflection on her relationship with Rust, "I'd said to Paul, 'I know I love you, and it's like, why?' It's not just, '*You're my soul mate.*'"[7]

As Celestino Deleyto argues, following Neale, the romcom is better understood as a system or even a game than as a fixed repository of cultural values: "The genre does not have a specific ideology—a single discourse which upholds the values of marriage and the stable heterosexual couple—but, more broadly, it deals with the themes of love and romance, intimacy and friendship, sexual choice and orientation."[8] From this perspective, the contemporary crisis in the romantic comedy stemming from changing ideas about gender performance and politics and the specific narrative crisis created by episodic storytelling in the age of Netflix are one and the same. Furthermore, the relentless teleology of the cinematic romcom's heteronormative happy ending has always in a sense been an illusion, the actual "happy endings" fewer and more problematic than our stereotypes of the genre. This faith in the conservatism and stability of the conventional romcom, whether as a critique of what is seen as its inherently reactionary politics or as a form of cultural nostalgia, can cause us to underestimate the genre's ability to formulate its own version of social critique: "The apparent universality of the happy ending and its obvious conventionality have led many to defend an homology between the genre's narrative structure and a stern defense of monogamy and heterosexuality, distorting what, in my view, is its main discursive space: the exploration of love and human sexuality and its complex and fluid relationships with the social context."[9]

In the contemporary era, this "exploration of love and human sexuality and its complex and fluid relationships with the social context" finds expression mainly through two overlapping experimental tropes: the one extends "the apparent universality of the happy ending and its obvious conventionality" through the diversification of gender, ethnicity, race, and sexual identity; and the other, following the bromance, radically challenges "conventional" heteronormativity and performances of gender. Each has what seems to be "conservative" and "subversive" modes, but, as Deleyto observes, these modes are fluid and radically indeterminate. The indie romcom *Obvious Child* (2014), for example, normalizes abortion within a traditional meet-cute heteronormative romance, while *Crazy Rich Asians* (2018) positions itself as radical in foregrounding Asian experiences within a consumerist Hollywood-style presentation with all the tropes of a neotraditional 1990s wedding romcom. Both films offer self-aware commentaries on the romcom genre while also foregrounding our investment as viewers in the genre's tropes, including our complex and conflicting desire for and idealization of the happy ending.

For *Love*, the romantic comedy and the idea of romantic love are approached as symptoms and pathologies, working within the contemporary social tropes of self-help and addiction, and especially a "one day at a time" antiteleology that constantly undermines the narrative drive toward "happily ever after" in favor of "what happens when the honeymoon is over." This dual approach to the idea of "addicted to love"—romantic love as addiction, and attachment to the romcom as addiction—defines how in *Love* the "various languages, logics, discourses and codes" of both the cinematic and cultural genres of romantic love are "revealed to the audience as fictions." In this way, the experience of watching *Love* implicates both its characters and viewers in this addiction.

Hence, the title of the series itself points to a strategy, shared with other postmodern romcoms and especially the work of Judd Apatow, of subjecting every trope of the romcom/romance plot to the question "Why?" In my own work on gender performance, the initiating question has been "Why men?" For me, the "problem of the contemporary romantic comedy as a genre . . . is the problem of men as a genre; specifically, what use are men in the contemporary romantic comedy?"[10] This problem provides the foundation for the Apatow bromance, and *Love* is populated with bromantic types: the sweet, unemployed slacker Randy (Mike Mitchell), who becomes the "love" interest for Bertie (Claudia O'Doherty), Mickey's new Australian immigrant roommate; and Chris (Chris Witaske), Gus's cheerful but clueless friend, an aspiring stunt actor, at the Springwood Apartments, a complex populated by lonely male losers of every age. Gus himself is a version of the "nerdy nice guy," or, as Apatow puts it, "a man who appears like he'll be nice, and then he turns out to be more complicated than that."[11] And a man who appears to be—or is trying to perform the role of—a man, a point comically underlined by Gus's pep talk to himself in the mirror in the season 1 episode "Party in the Hills" (1.4), where he tells himself, "You're like, a man." Or, as Mickey characterizes him soon after they meet, "a 40-year-old 12-year-old."

Love simultaneously interrogates and indulges in the tropes of the contemporary romcom—the meet cute; the dating montage; the quirky best friends; the creepy ex—through a combination of single-camera, revisionist realism and the parallel tropes of the showbiz satire, a kind of postmodern comic realism (*Atlanta* [FX, 2016–], *Search Party* [TBS, 2016–], and *High Maintenance* [web, 2012–2015; HBO, 2016–] are its current exemplars) that locates the characters' ideas about love and romance within the larger media culture, making the characters both the subjects and consumers of the romcom genre. This connection is made explicit in "One Long Day" (1.2), a version of the meet cute in which Mickey and Gus more or less aimlessly tool around hipster Los Angeles after meeting at a minimart, getting stoned and carrying out minimal errands, including accidentally stopping at Gus's ex's place, where she gives him a box full of his belongings. In their ride home, Gus fulminates about relationships—"Relationships are fucking bullshit," he says, to which Mickey agrees—and they place the blame on books, movies, and songs, culminating in movie buff Gus hurling his DVDs out the car window.

This establishment of the pathology of heteronormativity is reinforced from the beginning by Mickey's reckless and addictive behavior, including having sex with her boundary-violating boss so that he can't fire her for resisting his advances and then spectacularly breaking sobriety at a friend's party, where she confronts two pathological exes and reveals her own history of impulsive behavior. Her subsequent relationship with Gus coincides with her renewed commitment to sobriety and emotional health, although both

Mickey and the series resist the implication that "nice guy" Gus will save "wild child" Mickey; indeed, as we will see, Gus has issues of his own, and the nice guy exterior masks a streak of selfishness, passive aggressiveness, and anger management issues.

This combination of suspicion regarding the tropes of romance and gender—what Gus refers to as that "old weird gender stuff," after he opens the car door for Mickey on their first (and completely self-conscious) "official" date—is counterbalanced by what we might call Apatow's utopian project. As the title of Amy Nicholson's 2015 profile of Apatow in the *Village Voice* puts it, "Judd Apatow Wants to Make the Real World as Nice as His Movies." In the article, Lena Dunham describes Apatow as "this incredibly sensitive, emotional creature whose comedy is always, at its root, about love and all its complexities. . . . Judd roots for humanity, for romance, for the idea that people can grow and change."[12] In developing *Love*, Rust says he told Apatow "how much it meant to be a part of somebody who's trying to put out in the world that it's OK to be kind to people, and it's OK to be thoughtful and present."[13]

This tension between the pathology of the heteronormative romcom and Mickey and Gus's desire to be a "couple" reflects the tension between the conservative and progressive, the traditional and the revisionary, that informs and complicates the postmodern romcom's exploration of the fictionality of gender performance. In *Love*, as mentioned earlier, Gus and Mickey express their "yearning" for traditional "rules, norms, and boundaries" implied by the idea of the "couple," yet these "rules, norms, and boundaries" also apply to Mickey's battle with addiction and Gus's desire to grow up, to be "like, a man" and not a "forty-year-old twelve-year-old." The teleology of the "couple" remains in doubt, at least through the first two seasons, and the characters and narrative express contradictory attitudes toward marriage and family, themes that become a focal point of the third and final season.

On one hand, *Love* portrays Mickey's married friends from college through common satirical tropes of postmodern comedy: self-absorbed and passive-aggressive, obsessed with status while clinging to the signifiers of bohemian indifference, and endlessly discussing their efforts at "woke" child rearing. At Gus's workplace, the set of a ridiculous CW-like TV melodrama about witches in Kansas brilliantly named *Witchita*, he tutors the tween star Arya (played by Iris Apatow, the younger daughter of Judd Apatow and Leslie Mann), whose self-absorbed stage parents treat Arya as their cash cow.

Yet, in *Love*'s focus on the loneliness of young adults struggling to make it in Los Angeles, underscored by the narrative reliance on text messaging and the characters' desperate attachment to their smart phones, family also exerts a powerful emotional pull, as in Gus's found family of friends who regularly gather to devise hilarious theme songs to movies that lack them, such as *Carlito's Way* (1993) or *While You Were Sleeping* (1995). In the episode "The Long D" (2.11), Gus has followed Arya to Atlanta, where she is filming an overblown action movie while Mickey remains in Los Angeles to recommit to sobriety and to take a more active role in her career. As the separation tests their relationship—and as Gus grows more codependent while Mickey pulls away and reconnects with an ex—Gus finds himself eating alone in a diner. A classic nuclear family in a nearby booth takes pity on him and invites him to join them. Touched by their kindness, Gus happily chats with the family before choking up over realizing just how isolated his life is. At the same time, Mickey finds herself tempted by the bourgeois conventionality of her ex Dustin (Rich Sommer), with whom she has had an earlier explosive argument. They talk about their desire to "have a happy family" to compensate for their own dysfunctional upbringings (to which the episode "Marty Dobbs" [2.8], in which Gus meets Mickey's alcoholic and emotionally abusive father, attests). Mickey, only half kidding, expresses her willingness to "bake cookies" in the role of traditional homemaker, although as viewers we resist this outcome, both for the disappointing conservatism of this imagined heteronormative couple formation, and because the role is so out of keeping with Mickey's fierce independence and the ambition she is just beginning to acknowledge and pursue.

Even more pathologically (if parodically), in the season's final episode, "Back in Town" (2.12), Dustin has a "breakthrough" in therapy and proclaims, "I am entitled to be in a relationship with Mickey." This scene featuring Dustin's obsequious therapist suggests a critical, even cynical, perspective on therapy and self-help; the series' focus on various approaches to "therapy" places *Love* clearly in Krutnik's tradition of the "nervous romance" initiated by *Annie Hall* (1977), which jump-started Henderson's thesis on the obsolescence of the romcom due to men and women's fundamental psychological instability and neurosis in an era of rapid cultural change and transformation. This obsolescence, however, has come to apply to scripts of gender performance and the "old weird gender stuff," as much as to the romcom itself, with the postbromance, postmodern romcom *Love* building on this increasing self-awareness of gender fictionality and performativity.

Dustin's belief in his "entitlement" to Mickey reflects both a parody of a certain kind of flattering therapy and a reactionary cultural script, one Dustin explicitly links to the romcom narrative. In an invocation of both sex farce and the romcom trope of the final chase scene, à la *Pillow Talk*, Mickey definitively breaks with Dustin and reunites with Gus upon his return to Los Angeles in the season 2 finale only to find herself fleeing from Dustin's stalkerish romcom-style pursuit of her, all the while keeping their dalliance a secret. When Dustin confronts her in Gus's apartment, his argument is right out of the DVDs Gus flung from Mickey's car at the beginning of the series: "This is the story we're going tell our kids. Your mom was dating a loser and I came after her, I chased after her. This guy is a wimp, he's not going to fight for you. You want someone who is going to fight for you." Dustin's mansplaining Mickey's desires echoes both the cultural scripts of romcom teleology and patriarchal gender norms.

In fact, the "wimp" Gus is not going to "fight" for her, in part as the result of his having attended in Atlanta an Al-Anon meeting, where he confronts his own aggressive codependence and recognizes that he needs to respect Mickey's autonomy and agency. In keeping with Apatow's belief in the idea that "people can grow and change," the narrative arrives at a pragmatic endorsement of twelve-step programs, even while subjecting various self-help projects to parody and satire. In "Marty Dobbs," the titular father (Daniel Stern) cruelly mocks Mickey's commitment to Alcoholics Anonymous, seeing it as a "cult" for "people who cannot think for themselves." In the pilot "It Begins" (1.1), however, when Mickey winds up at a storefront quasi-religious meeting with cultish overtones, her tentative attraction to the message of love and encouragement she hears suggests that even dubious versions of self-help speak to a positive desire for change.

The show's qualified and ambivalent relationship toward therapy is embodied by Mickey's boss, Dr. Greg Colter (Brett Gelman), a satellite radio therapist who specializes in love and relationships. Spouting self-help bromides and exuding a smarmy air of fake concern and insight, Dr. Greg is insecure, self-absorbed, and hostile. His and Mickey's relationship becomes especially tense after their sexual encounter, and Dr. Greg repeatedly tells her that she is a monster and will inevitably relapse into addiction. At the same time, the glib catchphrases and self-help clichés he spouts manage to produce moments of insight for the characters, as when in "The Work Party" (2.7) Gus and Dr. Greg meet at a corporate party, with Dr. Greg unaware of who Gus is. They hit it off, and Gus finds himself able to open up about his own insecurities: "I don't even know what the point of feelings are from an evolutionary point of view," Gus explains. Dr. Greg counters with "We are here to connect. We exist to coexist." Gus is actually moved by this idea, however facilely deployed by Dr. Greg, and he immediately makes a connection to the restrictions of gender performance, saying how great it is to "talk to a guy in a way that's open, vulnerable, and sincere."

This bond disintegrates as soon as Greg learns that Gus is Mickey's date, when he warns him that "she's a user" who "doesn't even like" Gus. His outburst is comical and bumbling, and yet the episode ends in an ecstatic moment. After Mickey berates Greg, Gus admits to her that Greg "said everything I worry might be true," invoking the idea of the therapist as manipulative monster. After Mickey reassures him, they take to the dance floor to George Michael's "Freedom! '90." But what freedom are the characters pursuing, and what freedoms do we as viewers desire for them? Freedom from heteronormativity? From the stipulations of the romcom, the genre that also supplies the series with its cultural coherence and relevance?

In his 2016 review of *Love*'s first season, Ian Crouch argued that,

> for ten episodes, Mickey and Gus flail toward each other. They are both too good and not good enough for each other. They're modern constructs who know they are constructs. Dating seems like a bad idea. The series has been renewed for a second season, and there's some reason to hope that, notwithstanding a few passionate kisses and some casual sex, these two characters will do the truly bold thing and never fall in love.[14]

I wonder why he didn't put "fall in love" in quotation marks; if Mickey and Gus are "modern constructs who know they are constructs"—which precisely characterizes the narrative and performative self-awareness of *Love*—then part of what marks *Love* as a pathological romcom is the implication that there is no outside of a cultural construct, no appeal to the idea of transcendent "soul mates."

In the final season, the series confronts the romcom's traditional endgame, as Mickey and Gus grapple with the prospect of marriage. Matrimony becomes explicitly foregrounded, with a midseason episode set at a wedding—"Sarah from College" (3.7)—where Gus reunites with Sarah (Vanessa Bayer), to whom it turns out he was once engaged, the first of several revelations that Gus has kept from Mickey. The two most pivotal episodes of the season, "The Cruikshanks" (3.10) and "Anniversary Party" (3.11), find Gus and Mickey attending his parents' wedding anniversary in South Dakota, where Gus's parents Vicki (Kathy Baker) and Mark (Ed Begley Jr.) enact their own Midwestern version of *Scenes from a Marriage* (1974).

As the season opens, Gus and Mickey's relationship seems to have stabilized, in contrast to the slacker/striver mismatch of Gus's friend Randy and Mickey's roommate Bertie. Mickey has recommitted to sobriety and to her career, which is flourishing, again in contrast to the faux therapist Greg, whose career crashes after a sexist on-air tirade and violent episode at work. Mickey urges Gus to film his movie script, which he begins to do with the help of his friends. And, following conventional romcom formula, the season includes the pivotal "I love you" scene, though, as the episode title "I'm Sick" (3.4) suggests, only as a result of literal pathology: Mickey comes down with the stomach flu and gives it to Gus, who cares for her under the impression that she has food poisoning. The declarations of love come in the middle of an argument over Gus's anger at Mickey for infecting him, but, rather than heartfelt expressions of personal feelings, they sound more like accusations: "Because you love me!"; "Yeah, and you love me!"

Most significantly, indicating the potential "progress" of the relationship, Mickey faces a moment of possible alcoholic relapse in a bar, but manages to walk away, an accomplishment she later shares with Gus. Yet every step in the teleology of their union is shadowed by the fear of addiction and codependency signaled by Mickey's temptation. Gus's continued attendance at Al-Anon meetings highlights the continued exploration of his own pathologies, issues that begin to overshadow Mickey's alcohol and drug addiction. "Everything's not supposed to go great at the right time," he tells the group, foreshadowing revelations later about his disastrous first year in Los Angeles. "I do not believe I deserve to be happy." While Mickey successfully resists relapse, Gus's anger management issues escalate with a road rage incident that nearly results in serious injury, and he begins to lash out at the friends volunteering to help him make his film.

This mix of potential growth and enduring dysfunction defines the "Sarah from College" episode, in which Mickey realizes that Gus's ex-girlfriend Sarah still carries a torch for him. In the kind of third-act revelation that leads to the final crisis in the stereotypical romcom, Mickey discovers that Sarah and Gus had lived together and gotten engaged after Gus moved to Los Angeles, an engagement that included an elaborate proposal at Griffith Park fueled by the romcom conventions Gus and Mickey had belittled at the series' start. But the revelation does not end their relationship, even as it suggests a level of secrecy on Gus's part that mirrors Mickey's continued concealment of her tryst with Dustin.

The episode ends on a poignant note, as Gus takes the seriously drunk Sarah to her hotel and hears her depressed account of what she sees as the wreck of her life: moving to Denver, having an affair with a married man that led to a brief marriage, and becoming a stepmother before her husband left her for yet another woman. Sarah is a victim of the ideology of romantic love who feels she has gone off script, too old to play the ingenue but too young to accept a role as lonely loser. Gus acts both sympathetic and a little guilty, but ultimately the episode seems to provide an object lesson for him in the dangers of romantic illusion.

In the end, Gus and Mickey's trip to South Dakota to meet Gus's supposedly stable, intact family undermines any neat dichotomy between the functional and the dysfunctional, revealing a range of familial pathology—passive-aggressive communication, cycles of teasing and subtle humiliation among siblings, the codependent toleration of his mother's drinking problem, the inability to break out of defined family roles—that finally suggests that Gus has more work to do than Mickey, who has owned her addictions and is trying to address them. This episode leads to what turns out to be the key crisis in Gus and Mickey's tenuous relationship, and it hinges on the very idea of tenuousness. This tenuousness stems from the structural uncertainty of the serial TV romcom that disrupts the teleology of the wedding and honeymoon. If successful season renewals mean either constantly deferring the consummation of marriage or substituting family comedy for romantic comedy, the constant prospect of cancellation threatens to demand sudden resolution or the abandonment of the narrative line. In the case of *Love*, Netflix's cancellation came early enough for Arfin, Rust, and Apatow to plan on the third season being their last, but the exigencies of serial narrative mean being prepared for the end to come at any time (a reality parodied on *Love* in the precarious fate of *Witchita*).

After the announcement in "The Cruikshanks" by Gus's brother and his wife that they are expecting a child, his parents ask Gus and Mickey when they might produce a grandchild. "Don't hold your breath," Gus immediately responds. "What's that mean?" asks a clearly surprised Mickey. "No, I just mean, like, I don't even think we could handle that, that's crazy, so crazy," Gus responds, desperately trying to maintain a joking tone and avoid a scene. "I mean, maybe in . . . four years or something." This exchange, with its focus on "readiness," echoes the teleologic conflict of the romcom as well as the anxiety over reproduction that troubles the end of *Pillow Talk*.

Mickey subsequently challenges in private all of the unspoken assumptions behind Gus's reticence to publicly endorse their stability as a couple. In response Gus reveals his persistent fear that Mickey might relapse, his anxiety that Mickey's moment of progress in stepping back from the brink earlier in the season could go in the other direction. "How do you think sobriety works?" Mickey asks him, and her subsequent declaration about her struggles with alcoholism comes to stand as *Love*'s substitute for traditional wedding vows, signifying both romance as pathology and the contingency of any construction of supposed social permanence: Not "In sickness and health until death do us part," but, rather, "There are no guarantees. All I can promise you is right now I am trying as hard as I fucking can."

After exposing the presumption of Gus's attachment to what Mickey calls "this master plan you've concocted for my life"—a neat summation of the romantic comedy as social script—we and Mickey subsequently learn the rest of Gus's back story: his early promise as a writer after moving to Hollywood and his apprenticeship with filmmaker Ridley Scott, followed by a humiliating fiasco stemming from his overconfidence. After Mickey challenges him about his own weakness in "Anniversary Party," Gus faces his family in a moment of honesty that mirrors the declaration of addiction that begins an AA meeting: "I have serious anger control problems. . . . I'm a fuck up." This moment of clarity leads to a reconciliation between Gus and Mickey, who then revisit and revise the romcom script, as Mickey invites Gus to have another go at the "master plan" for "our future." Gus's revision sounds strangely old-fashioned: moving in together, getting a dog, getting married, and having children ("Very popular these days," Mickey comments, a reminder that Gus's plan remains a contingent cultural script). In the middle of this retro vision of teleological utopia, however, comes this contemporary moment of self-help and self-care: "We get couples therapy," says Gus. "Get nice and sharp and strong," Mickey agrees. No happiness without therapy, and no happiness as permanent state. Using the tropes of therapy and twelve-step programs, *Love* equates its eponymous emotion—and the social and cultural structures, including the romcom, that define it—with addiction, in that both require constant management and care. The finality of happily ever after becomes instead a contingency: an attractive, even utopian, ideal that nevertheless must always be seen as a construct, a social fantasy that exists only at the level of myth.

This sense of radical contingency and ambivalence toward the heteronormative script drives the final episode, "Catalina" (3.12), directed by Lynn Shelton, herself an auteur of the postmodern romcom in movies like *Humpday* (2009), *Your Sister's Sister* (2011), and *Laggies* (2014). Their relationship at a seemingly high point, Gus and Mickey celebrate the ways they have been good for each other: both have taken positive attitudes in their careers, and each feels a sense of purpose and meaning that had been lacking: "You really bring out the best in me." Their newfound sense of confidence—"I feel like we cracked the code to our relationship"—leads to declarations that are at once heartfelt, naïve, hubristic, and potentially the basis for a self-help book: "As long as we're open with each other, and we're real with each other, we're going to be okay," Mickey says, and Gus agrees. Convinced that they will always feel this way, they decide to marry, a decision at once impulsive and assertive, but one that underlines the radical contingency of romcom teleology: When is "the right time"? Even more, the decision implicates the show's viewers, many of whom had been vigorously debating online the viability of Gus and Mickey's relationship. This is what we want, isn't it? Or is it what the romcom insists we want?

The episode plays with this ambivalence on the part of both characters and viewers as what starts as an elopement turns into a party/ceremony for most of the series regulars at a Catalina Island hotel. The wedding begins, but the ceremony and apparently the marriage itself are blocked when a nearby beachgoer suffering a heart attack interrupts Gus and Mickey's heartfelt vows. This reminder of risk and uncertainty also offers a sarcastic commentary on these vows, in keeping with a series that is equal parts cynical and sincere. After announcing to their guests the indefinite postponement

Gus and Mickey navigating the rough road of their relationship in *Love*.

of the wedding, Gus and Mickey decide to "elope" after all, marrying with only their New Age officiator present. This time, rather than their vows, we hear Wilco's wistful and ambivalent love song "You and I."

As Deleyto observes,

> The genre of romantic comedy can, therefore, be described as the intersection of three, closely interrelated elements: a narrative that articulates historically and culturally specific views of love, desire, sexuality and gender relationships; a space of transformation and fantasy which influences the narrative articulation of those discourses; and humor as the specific perspective from which the fictional characters, their relationships and the spectator's response to them are constructed as embodiments of those discourses.[15]

In the cultural laboratory of *Love*, these "historically and culturally specific views" embody a radical uncertainty over gender performance, a pervading sense of contingency and precariousness, and, most of all, a linking of genre to pathology. The series both affirms and renders suspect the romcom's traditional endgame. If Mickey and Gus—and, by extension, the series' fans—are addicted to love, we may be in the era of the twelve-step program romcom, one that denies a cure for addiction but holds out the promise of learning to live with it.

Notes

1. Christian persuasively links the rise of OTT indie TV to the open distribution model of web-based series. See Aymar Jean Christian, *Open TV: Innovation Beyond Hollywood and the Rise of Web Television* (New York: New York University Press, 2018). Michael Curtin has coined the term "matrix media" to describe the digital blurring of boundaries of production, transmission, and reception: "It was no longer a broadcast medium or a network medium, or even a multichannel medium; television had become a matrix medium, an increasingly flexible and dynamic mode of communication." Michael Curtin, "Matrix Media," in *Television Studies After TV: Understanding Television in the Post-Broadcast Era*, ed. Graeme Turner and Jinna Tay (London: Routledge, 2009), 10–19, 13.
2. Brian Henderson, "Romantic Comedy Today: Semi-Tough or Impossible?," *Film Quarterly* 31, no. 4 (Summer 1978): 11–23; Frank Krutnik, "The Faint Aroma of Performing Seals: The 'Nervous' Romance and the Comedy of the Sexes," *Velvet Light Trap* 26 (Fall 1990): 57–72.
3. Krutnik, "Faint Aroma of Performing Seals," 69.
4. Stanley Cavell, *Pursuits of Happiness: The Hollywood Comedy of Remarriage* (Cambridge, MA: Harvard University Press, 1981), 53.
5. Stephen Neale, *Genre* (London: BFI, 1980), 19.
6. Neale, *Genre*, 40.
7. Allison P. Davis, "Lesley Arfin on Love, Selfishness, and the Art of Oversharing," The Cut, February 24, 2016, www.thecut.com/2016/02/lesley-arfin-on-love-and-oversharing.html, emphasis in original.
8. Celestino Deleyto, *The Secret Life of Romantic Comedy* (Manchester: Manchester University Press, 2009), 18.
9. Deleyto, *Secret Life of Romantic Comedy*, 28–29.
10. John Alberti, *Masculinity in the Contemporary Romantic Comedy: Gender as Genre* (New York: Routledge, 2013), 3.
11. Fred Topel, "Judd Apatow Talks *Love*, *Freaks and Geeks*, and the Freedom of Working with Netflix," SlashFilm, January 29, 2016, https://www.slashfilm.com/judd-apatow-love-netflix/.
12. Amy Nicholson, "Judd Apatow Wants to Make the Real World as Nice as His Movies," *Village Voice*, May 27, 2015, www.villagevoice.com/2015/05/27/judd-apatow-wants-to-make-the-real-world-as-nice-as-his-movies/.

13 Nicholson, "Judd Apatow."
14 Ian Crouch, "Swipe Left: *Love* and the Unromantic Comedy," *New Yorker*, February 26, 2016, www.newyorker.com/culture/culture-desk/swipe-left-love-and-the-unromantic-comedy.
15 Deleyto, *Secret Life of Romantic Comedy*, 45–46.

14

Breaking Upwards

The Creative Uncoupling of Desiree Akhavan and Ingrid Jungermann

Maria San Filippo

> Failures are where all these stories come from, not through success.
>
> —Ingrid Jungermann

Desiree Akhavan and Ingrid Jungermann's personal and professional partnership, forged in New York University's graduate film program, engendered their pioneering web series *The Slope* (Vimeo, 2011–2012), in which they play exaggerated versions of themselves, the politically incorrect anti-role models promised by its tagline: "Superficial, homophobic lesbians." A career launching pad for the then-couple, *The Slope* also served as a personal jumping-off point for Akhavan. "It's how I came out to most people in my life," she recalls.[1] As fictionally chronicled in the second season, the couple's breakout project coincided with their relationship's breakup—a subject to which both would return in their subsequent first features: Akhavan's *Appropriate Behavior* (2014), about a recently single bisexual not out to her Iranian-American parents, and Jungermann's *Women Who Kill* (2016), about a commitment-phobic lesbian torn between her bisexual ex (with whom she cohosts a podcast) and a new love interest. The two have continued to revisit their relationship's afterlife with their respective forays into TV: Akhavan's Channel 4/Hulu six-episode series *The Bisexual* (2018), in which she stars as an American in London who, after ending a decade-long relationship with her girlfriend/business partner, starts dating men, and Jungermann's (stalled) deal with Showtime to adapt her web series *F to 7th* (2013–2014), in which she played a "homoneurotic" pre-middle-aged lesbian adrift in queerer-than-thou Brooklyn. Similarly expressive of the transformative potential of "queer failure," the retrospective, reparative processes self-examination and relationship-mourning portrayed in Akhavan's and Jungermann's respective works to date model a queer, feminist praxis that converts loss and insolvency into cultural creation and social critique. In each one's serving as the structuring absence in the other's fictional world, the ex-couple transforms their former romantic and erotic attachments into creative investments that defy masculinist and monogamist models of individualist authorship and proprietary coupling.

Conscious Uncoupling

The "conscious uncoupling" philosophy/fad made (in)famous by former spouses Gwyneth Paltrow and Chris Martin upon publicly announcing their amicable separation in 2014 brought the wellness industry's term for mindful breakups into the cultural lexicon, with its coiner-creator, therapist Katherine Woodward Thomas, going on to publish the self-help bestseller *Conscious Uncoupling: 5 Steps to Living Happily Even After* (2015). Other high-profile creative pairs have since taken up the trend: in 2016, queer power couple Eileen Myles and Joey Soloway outed themselves as a thenceforth "post-couple" in a live performance of "public intimacy" aimed at processing their romance and breakup, while in web-turned–HBO series *High Maintenance* (2012–) cocreators and spouses Katja Blichfeld and Ben Sinclair expounded publicly on their own uncoupling while renewing their vows that the show will go on.[2] In the past few years, platonic partnerships have joined the circuit of uncoupling commemorations packaged as final creative collaborations, with indie film maestros Mark and Jay Duplass's coauthored memoir of filial (dis)union *Like Brothers* (2018), and *Girls* (HBO, 2012–2017) coshowrunners Lena Dunham and Jenni Konner's announcing the "no drama" end to their eight-year producing partnership on the eve of releasing their last joint project, the 2018 HBO series *Camping*.

The last 15 years have seen a proliferation of romcom revisionism, particularly in the form of uncoupling narratives, as the genre has migrated away from Hollywood and into indie, international, and online realms. While contemporary Hollywood studio–produced romcom's one noteworthy uncoupling comedy, the Jennifer Aniston–Vince Vaughn vehicle *The Break-Up* (2006), yielded respectable profits but dismal reviews, the edgy sensibility and downbeat outlook of indie and art cinema suits the turn toward antiromantic revisionism, yielding fictionalized treatments of the uncoupling of such real-life partners-collaborators as Zoe Lister-Jones and Daryl Wein (*Breaking Upwards*, 2009), Josephine Decker and Zefrey Throwell (*Flames*, 2017), and Romane Bohringer and Phillippe Rebbot (*L'Amou flou/In the Move for Love*, 2018). While all feature heterosexual couples, their chronicles of postbreakup experiments with alternative sexual practices (polyamory, committed nonmonogamy) and kinship structures (uncoupled cohabitation) take queer sex cultures and relationality as their model, rejecting the dominant coupling paradigm. At the same time, these films' blending of documentary and fiction unshackles romcom from the neotraditional conventions that enforce aesthetic and ideological conservatism.

Given its renewed purchase for indie filmmakers, and its persistently gendered perception as the preserve of women, romcom seems an apt choice for both Akhavan and Jungermann in conceiving their first feature films. Both exemplify recent strategies for rejuvenating romcom: *Appropriate Behavior* with its queer retelling of *Annie Hall* (1977), *Women Who Kill* with its hybridizing of romcom and Gothic horror genres. By exploring same-sex uncoupling, Akhavan's and Jungermann's autobiographically inspired works offer revisionist resistance to the genre's teleological dictates, which typically reinforce homonormativity (with its overdetermined interest in the couple form) and fixed, rather than fluid, notions of sexual identity. Affirmative uncoupling narratives—especially those that resonate for young or otherwise impressionable queer viewers as what Rob Cover calls "first contact" texts—offer a view past "accepted discourses on sexuality that require both the notions of public self-disclosure and of the 'truth' of the hetero/homo binary," as well as a representation of breaking up as a self-actualizing proposition.[3] As sex-positivity advocate Judith Levine notes, "If sex educators and therapists could drop the bias that long-term commitment is the highest goal and the only [acceptable] context for sexual expression, they might be able to help youngsters . . . relish [short-term] relationships, protect themselves while they last, and bounce back when they are over."[4]

To this end, conscious uncoupling has the potential to be both creatively fecund—a doing through undoing—and ethically fortifying. As some moral philosophers posit, we have an obligation to remember those with whom we have shared significant relational bonds—an obligation to ourselves, for the emotional growth that comes from experiences of intimacy and heartache, and to our former loved ones, whose dignity we risk diminishing by denying their onetime importance to us.[5] Whether applied to the real or fictionalized realm of conscious uncoupling, this commemoration of past partnerships aligns with what lesbian feminist philosopher Ladelle McWhorter defines as a queer ethics: "A way of life or style of existence, that values the conditions that make possible continued self-overcoming through experimentation and questioning, that incorporates practices of reflection upon past decisions and actions, that empowers us to fight discourses and regimes that diminish our own and our community's capacity for self-transformation."[6] Akhavan's and Jungermann's respective uncoupling narratives participate in a larger historical turn within queer studies that emphasizes the reparative potential of retrospection.[7] Envisioned as a hopeful, productive mode of queer oppositionality, this praxis urges the (re)claiming of cultural texts and artifacts of queer failure, those that Jack Halberstam finds "refuse triumphalist accounts of gay, lesbian, and transgender history" and so reject a heteronormative and homonormative "logic of achievement, fulfillment, and success(ion)" that reinforces reproductive futurity and neoliberal capitalism.[8]

Akhavan's and Jungermann's compulsive revisiting of their past relationship in all of their originally scripted work to date resists romcom's teleological drive. In following Sara Ahmed's directive that "to recognize loss can mean to be willing to experience an intensification of the sadness that hopefulness postpones," this mode of retrospection also refuses the imperative of happiness that undergirds individualist ideologies and consumerist models of citizenship.[9] Neither content to look back nostalgically nor attempting to salvage a relationship that had ceased to be viable, Akhavan's and Jungermann's representations of uncoupling question the promise of durable intimacy, a key pillar of the societal entanglement that Lauren Berlant characterizes as "cruel optimism": "a binding to fantasies that block the satisfactions they offer."[10] Echoing Heather K. Love's call in *Feeling Backward* against abandoning preliberation narratives of social exclusion, and in the wake of LGBTQ+ media's mainstreaming, the new wave of queer cinema has maintained its vigor by wallowing in the affective pleasures of romantic torment and lost love with films such as *Blue Is the Warmest Color* (*La vie d'Adèle*, 2013), *Call Me by Your Name* (2017), *Eva and Candela* (2018),

Moonlight (2016), and *Portrait of a Lady on Fire* (*Portrait de la jeune fille en feu*, 2019).[11] While similarly focused on unsustainable attachment and breakup blues, Akhavan's and Jungermann's first features' shared irreverent comedic sensibility sets them somewhat apart from those more earnest films, while indicating that, although uncoupled, they remain simpatico.

Circumventing mainstream Hollywood channels to avail themselves of alternative online, independent, and non-U.S. networks as up-and-coming media creators, Akhavan's and Jungermann's focus on their coupled identity's dissolution likewise deliberately embraces vulnerability, uncertainty, and precarity. As Jungermann expresses in the epigraph to this chapter, experiences characterized by, and as, failures may prove more generative than those deemed successes; as such, the definitions of success and failure need reconfiguring. While these accomplishments and the professional status they confer might appear to endorse the neoliberal conversion of personal relationships into monetized commodities, in fact Akhavan's and Jungerman's creative output actively resists neoliberalism's push to turn others into disposable objects for profit and pleasure. They resist a masculinist, heteropatriarchal artistic tradition that has elevated the male "auteur" and relegated women's creative labor to uncredited, uncompensated "muse." Rejecting that paradigm's "anything for art" self-justification and its related axiom (popularized by another boys' club, the New Critics) of "separating art from artist," Akhavan's and Jungermann's tandem fictionalizing of their breakup foregrounds empathy for one's former partner; neither's self-representation is entirely flattering or self-justifying, and petty or vindictive actions are treated as understandable yet firmly condemned. Thus, their creative praxis is self-empowering without being professionally individualist or interpersonally exploitative. And, lest this appropriation of conscious uncoupling sound offputtingly earnest or tinged with cult-y Goop vacuity, Akhavan and Jungermann's confessed self-absorption is mercifully offset by their shared ironic sensibility—most prominently on display in their first, and last, collaboration.

Superficial, Homophobic Lesbians: *The Slope*

Born as an NYU class assignment and eventually released on Vimeo as two seasons with eight episodes apiece, *The Slope* is named for and set among the lesbian bourgeoisie of Park Slope, Brooklyn, and predicated on a premise concocted by the then-couple: "What if we filmed us talking smack about gay people?"¹² With their off-screen relationship unraveling during the hiatus between seasons, *The Slope*'s focus shifted to address head on—if still with tongue in cheek—their struggle to uncouple. *The Slope* found patronage from queer culture website AfterEllen and alt-comedy impresario Michael Showalter (one of their NYU professors and a guest star in season 2), with Akhavan and Jungermann named among *Filmmaker*'s 25 New Faces of 2012 and appearing on *Out*'s annual Out100 list. Emerging contemporaneously with network TV's crossover hits *Glee* (Fox, 2009–2015) and *Modern Family* (ABC, 2009–2020), *The Slope*'s irreverent (self-)satire answered a demand from queer *and* indie viewers whose tastes ran counter to both those broad(-cast) comedies and *The L Word*'s (Showtime, 2004–2009) soapy melodrama. From its debut episode, "Miserable Animals," in which Desiree and Ingrid (as their characters are named) dispute whether Desiree, as a bisexual, can rightfully reappropriate terms like "dyke," *The Slope* oscillates between barbs directed at an LGBTQ+ community whose self-seriousness they cannot resist mocking, and at the couple's self-professedly "superficial, homophobic" comportment—such as when a canvassing activist asks them, "Do you have a moment for gay rights?," to which they respond, automatically and in unison, "No!" (1.2, "Pretty People"). While their shared misanthropy acts as the magnet that overcomes, for a time, the repelling forces of this odd couple, their ultimate uncoupling disrupts romcom conventions of opposites attracting. And, even as their on-/off-screen relationship founders, *The Slope* established a tone and sensibility that informed their subsequent solo projects.

The Slope's second-season opener, "Talking Space," features Desiree and Ingrid, in separate conversations with friends, revisiting questions of (in)appropriate language with which the series began. To a friend's disparaging of Desiree as "just a cunt," Ingrid responds despondently, "Don't say that word. It reminds me too much of her." Language that previously provoked Ingrid's ire becomes a poignant reminder of her irreverent ex, just as Desiree's exchange with a straight pal recalls the (half-learned) lessons in cultural sensitivity that Ingrid had imparted:

> FRIEND: Dykes don't have that sense of aesthetic.
> DESIREE: I know you don't mean that offensively, but it's actually really messed up to say the word "dyke" if you're not gay. I know it's retarded, but I'm really sensitive about that kind of thing.

As revealed in a sight gag at episode's end, these conversations are happening concurrently in adjoining rooms of their still-shared apartment. The challenge of disentangling lives provides further fodder for knowing lesbian self-satire throughout season 2; as Desiree explains, "It's not like straight couples; we have a life together. We still have a month on our CSA share." Nonetheless, an intertitle introducing a subsequent episode reads, "After much painful deliberation, endless conflict and an ill-advised mushroom trip, Ingrid and Desiree have decided to put an end to their relationship once and for all." What follows depicts Desiree enacting each of the eponymous "5 Stages of Grief" in the space of one party, while another episode finds her dwelling in the anger and denial stages, informing a friend, "I recently was abandoned coldheartedly by my former partner Ingrid... but I love being single. I have all this free time. The time I spent having sex, I now spend watching *Felicity*" (2.6, "Conversion Therapy"). Save for this type of clearly ironic fictional accusation, the humor works precisely because both ex-partners elsewhere describe (off-screen) and represent (on-screen) their breakup as mutually determined. Another episode portrays their futile attempts to forget one another by going on dates—Ingrid with a vapid romcom fanatic, Desiree with a self-professed "polyamorous pansexual"—that drive them back into bed *and* denial.

> DESIREE: Promise me that we'll never break up again and that you'll love me forever and that you'll be the mother of my children.
> INGRID: Desiree, I can't promise that, c'mon.
> DESIREE: You're ruining the mood.
> INGRID: Alright, alright, I promise. (2.2, "Revolving Door")

Though (and perhaps through) parodying on-screen their own ambivalent inertia and self-delusion, the real-life couple moved past the difficult early stages of breaking up, with the series finale (2.8, "Miserable Best Friends Who Used to Be Together") returning them to the site of their first-episode fight, ostensibly to determine custody of their dog—a stray who, having wandered up in that opening episode, initiated their squabbling over what Desiree viewed as Ingrid's "super dykey" instinct to nurture.

> INGRID: This has nothing to do with the dog. This has to do with your not being able to sever ties with me.

DESIREE: I'm having a really hard time.
INGRID: I'm having a hard time too.
DESIREE: Okay, I'll be there for you. Let's help each other through this.
INGRID: We can't hold each other's hands through our own breakup. That's not how it works.
DESIREE: Then why did I bother becoming a lesbian? Aren't you supposed to be best friends forever? That's what the girls in Sleater Kinney did!
INGRID: Well, Ellen and Anne Heche didn't.
DESIREE: Did you just compare me to Anne Heche? Because that is literally the meanest thing that anyone has ever said to me. . . . You just think I'm a fickle bisexual, and that I'm going to go after some douchebag from Bushwick who has an ironic t-shirt startup, and we're never going to be best friends that used to be together.
INGRID: Desiree, you wanted this to end too. We were fighting all the time, and then we started fighting about fighting.
DESIREE: I don't think we fought that much. [*Brief round of fighting about fighting*]
INGRID: Desiree, just because we're both superficial and homophobic doesn't mean that we're meant to be.
DESIREE: A shared disregard for social norms and common human decency is a terrible thing to waste.
INGRID: We had a good run, Desiree.
DESIREE: We did.

Though managing to achieve a degree of closure, this parting scene retains their signature ridicule aimed at gay pop culture, Brooklyn hipsterdom, and their own self-absorption (indeed, when they walk away in separate directions at episode's end, the dog remains behind, tied up and forgotten). With Ingrid's allusion to the series' tagline ("superficial, homophobic lesbians") breaking the fourth wall to recall their real-life uncoupling, their final exchange and the subsequent on-screen title reading "Ingrid & Desiree 2011–2012" is simultaneously ironic and moving.

Even as we mourn that their mutual misanthropy—and the irreverent comedy it yielded over two seasons—is a "terrible thing to waste," their uncoupling proves still more generative, both for deepening *The Slope*'s

Desiree, Ingrid, and dog in *The Slope*'s pilot (*left*) and finale (*right*).

dramatic pathos and for propelling the couple into solo creative ventures once it became apparent that, as Jungermann recalls, "it was impossible, really. . . . All of that stuff was sort of intertwined, the work and the relationship, and there was no way we could work together with not being together."[13] While that solemn recognition was echoed by Desiree's on-screen lament that "We're never going to be best friends who used to be together," the end of *The Slope* marks the starting point of their still abundantly creative uncoupling. Not surprisingly given its "superficial, homophobic" stance, *The Slope*, unlike contemporaneous breakout web series *Broad City* (web, 2010–2011; Comedy Central, 2014–2019), *High Maintenance*, and *The Misadventures of Awkward Black Girl* (web, 2011; retitled *Insecure*, HBO, 2016–), failed to achieve legacy TV adaptation, a first glimpse of how the defiantly imperfect (queer) womanhood that Akhavan and Jungermann flaunt resists modulation for mainstream consumption. Yet it paved the way for Akhavan's and Jungermann's respective first features alongside a veritable cottage industry of similarly irreverent, independently produced comedic web series, including Jungermann's sophomore effort.

Misanthropic, Middle-Aged Lesbian: *F to 7th*

After her split from Akhavan, Jungermann went on to create the 16-episode web series *F to 7th*, also set in "the Slope" (its title refers to the neighborhood's subway stop) and succinctly summed up by its tagline: "Homo-neurotic." Again playing a "misanthropic, middle-aged lesbian" version of herself,[14] the now-single Ingrid confronts her alienation from both extremes of her ostensible community: the "disturbingly happy . . . gaggle of white Park Slope moms" and the "just so goddamned diverse" affectations of queer millennials trampling the "good old-fashioned lesbianism" she holds dear, as

Jungermann put it in an *F to 7th* mission statement published on (and since taken down from) HuffPost.[15] In a season 1 episode (1.3, "Interchangeable"), Ingrid, startled to find the femme she's invited over for sex also sporting a strap-on, protests, "You have long hair!" Indignant, the femme responds, "Just because I don't look like a man means I can't wear a strap-on? I thought you were evolved." Ingrid's comeback—"Just because I'm a lesbian doesn't mean I'm evolved"—announces her disidentification from progressive sexual politics; over the series' run, Ingrid badmouths everything from gender confirmation surgery to bisexuality to other breaches of butch/femme protocol. As in *The Slope*, Ingrid's disenchantment with homonormativity and her derision for Brooklynite queerer-than-thou posturing hit their comic mark because the ultimate target is always the failings, as Jungermann perceives them, of "lesbians like me: lesbians who don't like lesbians."[16] Even as she foregrounds self-deprecation, Jungermann distances her more incendiary sentiments by voicing them through Ingrid and the show's other objectionable (but not unlikeable) anti–role models; as she admits, "I use the characters to be able to say things I've heard, but also things I think and am afraid to say."[17] In her ambivalence toward and occasional defiance of queer discourse policing, Jungermann-as-Ingrid embodies the "dyke anger" that Jack Halberstam claims is needed "in order to embrace a truly political negativity" founded on queer failure rather than success.[18] Halberstam argues that this contrarian stance challenges homonormativity's attempt to commodify queerness and contain its disruptive potential: "In this work, a queer aesthetic is activated through the function of negation rather than in the mode of positivity; in other words, the works strive to establish queerness as a mode of critique rather than as a new investment in normativity or life or respectability or wholeness or legitimacy."[19]

Alongside Jungermann's refusal of what Sara Ahmed calls the false "promise of happiness" offered by homonormative assimilation into the "good life," her alter ego Ingrid, with her willfully regressive rejection of her own longtime lesbianism in reaction to her newfound single status, resists queer self-imagining as "evolved," as well as the "it gets better" teleology of coming out *and* of breaking up.[20] "I'm not your example gay," Ingrid insists to a straight friend who designates her a role model to the elementary school-aged daughter who has already proclaimed herself a lesbian (2.2, "Going In"). Ingrid makes good on her warning when her bitterness about lesbian relationship dynamics finds her proselytizing on behalf of heterosexuality, attempting to impart to the youngster the wisdom acquired from dating women:

> INGRID: Once you get to know women you find that they're really ... difficult and they can be really emotional and passive-aggressive. And if you're a boyish lesbian, they'll make you do things like carry heavy stuff and shovel snow. When you're in a relationship and you're seen as the man even though you're *clearly* a woman, you end up giving and giving and giving, and they just take and take and take. (2.5, "Deny Deny Deny")

In *F to 7th*'s most absurdist episode, "Intersex" (1.8), Jungermann plays two roles, masculine and feminine versions of herself conversing postcoitally. "Do you have a type?" asks the femme Ingrid. "Me but a little softer," the butch Ingrid replies. A riff on the homosexuality-as-narcissism trope, the episode also mocks the exclusivity of assortative mating and the solipsism of singledom—even if the latter is suggested to be a reasonable response to the futility of coupled communion. "We were just different people," one of the Ingrids remarks about why her last relationship ended. "Really different." That failure to connect extends to sex, here imagined as never living up to the onanistic. "You were really good," says one Ingrid. "I feel like I didn't have to tell you anything." "I felt the same way, like you knew exactly what to do," responds the other. The episode concludes with the newly single Ingrid encouraged by her near-mirror image, "I think you should find someone just like you." "That's harder than it seems," replies the other, rupturing the episode's wish fulfillment in a way that reveals the romcom fantasy of finding one's "other half" to be fundamentally egocentric.

Informed as much by her relationship with Akhavan as by her experience being raised a Jehovah's Witness in a conservative small town in Florida, *F to 7th* semifictionally indulges Jungermann's postbreakup bitterness while playfully contesting damaging cultural understandings of gayness as narcissistic, as stemming from childhood sexual abuse (2.4, "Oh Daddy") or religious zealotry (2.1, "Nurture"), and as a choice—the premise of season 2, which chronicles Ingrid's (doomed) experiments with heterosexuality as a remedy for her heartache and alienation from the Park Slope lesbian lifestyle. A considerably higher-profile project than *The Slope*, *F to 7th* features guest appearances (Olympia Dukakis, Janeane Garofalo, Gaby Hoffmann,

Ingrid's butch and femme halves flirting in *F to 7th*.

Amy Sedaris, and, in an encore performance, Michael Showalter); its second season was nominated for a WGA Award. With the report in 2016 that Jungermann would develop a third season for Showtime, *F to 7th* seemed poised to be the latest web series to make the jump to legacy television. The deal came on the heels of Jungermann's releasing her debut feature, *Women Who Kill*, which was awarded Best Screenplay for a U.S. Narrative Feature at the Tribeca Film Festival. Yet Showtime has since dropped the option to develop *F to 7th* and let another Jungermann web series languish, making for a stalled foray into legacy television stateside that Akhavan would also experience, as I discuss below.

A Gay *Annie Hall*: *Appropriate Behavior*

It was Akhavan herself who conceived and termed her debut feature, in which she stars as Shirin, a Brooklyn bisexual emotionally adrift after breaking up with her girlfriend, "a gay *Annie Hall*."[21] Whereas Woody Allen cast former girlfriend Diane Keaton (née Hall) as his eponymous co-lead, Shirin's ex-girlfriend Maxine is played by actor Rebecca Henderson, making for less transparent slippage between Jungermann and her fictionalized character. Yet the ex-couple's shared sensibility is evident, starting with their alter egos' meet cute, a *Slope*-like squabble over Shirin's "incredibly offensive" (according to Maxine) use of the word "dyke" that gives way to shared contempt for "Brooklyn parties and everyone talking about their Kickstarter campaigns." As in *The Slope*, Shirin and Maxine's shared negativity targets politically correct queer folx and Brooklyn hipsters, but also parodies Akhavan and Jungermann themselves, whose own Kickstarter campaign funded *The Slope*'s second season. Though Shirin's entwined personal struggles to move on from the relationship and to come out to her conservative immigrant parents are the film's focus, the supporting storyline following Shirin's job teaching filmmaking to Brooklyn preschoolers (based on Akhavan's former gig) thematizes Akhavan's emerging self-definition as a filmmaker and the precarious labor it involves. In weaving together the fictional and nonfictional, the personal and the professional, *Appropriate Behavior* becomes the vehicle through which Akhavan seeks, and attains, autobiographical agency in the form of creative control. As she recalls of her breakup with Jungermann, "I felt out of control when events were happening and I didn't get to call the shots and this is what I do to be in control. If my heart's broken then I can gain control of that narrative."[22] As in *Annie Hall*, *Appropriate Behavior*'s references to art-making and the creative possibilities of romantic "failure" are at once self-deprecating and self-aggrandizing. But, whereas Allen-as-Alvy's attempt (in the play within the film) to turn his life into art comes off as self-indulgent and humorless, both *Annie Hall* and *Appropriate Behavior* refuse the temptation of wish fulfillment endemic to romantic comedy.

Though Allen's autobiographically inspired narrative remains too focused on—and too indulgent of—Alvy to endorse fully Annie's leaving him, Annie's nascent feminist awareness registers in her increasing resistance to Alvy's attempts to "educate" her. *Appropriate Behavior* revisits this dynamic, most explicitly in a bookstore scene in which Maxine plies Shirin with lesbian texts to "broaden [her] horizons." Taking in the cover of *Stone Butch Blues*, Leslie Feinberg's memoir of pre-Stonewall working-class lesbian life, Shirin echoes Annie's line: "This is some pretty serious stuff here." Though downplayed by Maxine's sarcastic response ("I'm asking you to read some books. You don't need to get your septum pierced—yet"), the scene signals her expectation that Shirin become "more gay." Ultimately, Shirin's prolonged reluctance to come out to her family significantly undermines her relationship with Maxine, who condemns Shirin's evasions as "Don't ask, don't tell." Shirin's defense ("They know, and I know they know. You think I'm a bad person because I'm not coming out on your terms") may well be a self-serving attempt at avoidance, but it also simultaneously signals Shirin's resistance to Maxine's attempts to reshape her.

Appropriate Behavior adapts *Annie Hall's* flashback structure to mount a more pointedly queer, nonteleological trajectory that resists reproductive futurity's pull. With its compulsive lapse into flashbacks comprising the heartbroken Shirin's memories, the film subsumes us within her subjectivity, offering a heightened mode of identification with a rarely represented bisexual Middle Eastern woman that also manifests a resistance to the lure of hope that recalls Sara Ahmed's formulation: "To recognize loss can mean to be willing to experience an intensification of the sadness that hopefulness postpones."[23] The coming-out process is also treated antiteleologically—as ongoing, always incomplete, not necessarily resulting in some decisive moment of rejection or acceptance, and resisting the monosexist imperative of "choosing a side." Whereas Akhavan's insistence on self-identifying as bisexual (despite her much-mentioned distaste for the term) has been steadfast, Shirin and Maxine's relationship will not survive the latter's stinging

Annie Hall's bookstore sequence recreated in *Appropriate Behavior*.

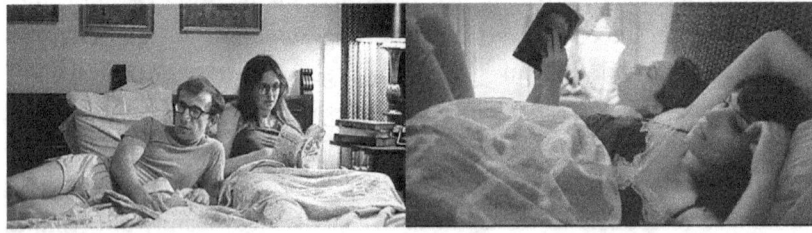

Annie (Diane Keaton) reading up on feminism; Shirin (Desiree Akhavan) resisting *Stone Butch Blues*.

dismissal of it as "just a phase." Yet *Appropriate Behavior* validates Shirin's bisexuality in a way that Maxine and Shirin's family refuse to do.

In *Appropriate Behavior*'s final scene, Shirin and pal Crystal (Halley Feiffer) voice disbelief at the "appropriate" timeline dictated by (neo)traditional romcom, which mandates that women remain sexually chaste until they "put a ring on it"—or at least until after a few dates. Eagerly contemplating a threesome with Shirin's roommates, a Goth couple, Crystal muses, "There are people in this world who go on dates that are perfectly great, and then they wait awhile before they engage in sexual contact." "That's disgusting," Shirin responds, deadpan. "I'm pretty sure it happens outside New York," Crystal agrees. As the film's final words of dialogue, their ironic mockery of the sexually conservative logic that condemns "promiscuity" as practiced by "urban elites" receives particular emphasis. Rejecting the desexualized quality of so many gay romances and the homonormative culture that produces them, *Appropriate Behavior* presents as the film's final coupling (platonic) girlfriends who identify as bisexual and heteroflexible, respectively, but whose mutual logic of desire is decidedly queer.

One further revisionist twist on romcom's conventional couple formation follows, as the camera moves in to isolate Shirin in the frame. An uncoupled woman becomes *Appropriate Behavior*'s final image, invoking other "radical romantic comedies" of the women's liberation era such as *Girlfriends* (1978) and *An Unmarried Woman* (1978), yet by virtue of its framing and duration alluding even more directly and knowingly to the iconic final shot of *The Graduate* (1967), in which the runaway couple ride off into an indeterminate sunset to the strains of Simon & Garfunkel. The musical track chosen for *Appropriate Behavior*'s final scene, Electrelane's "To the East," is equally evocative, not only for being the work of a queer women's act but in undermining with its lyrics any confidence that narrative resolution has been reached: "I want to be with you. I'm just waiting until you say these words: Come back, come back, come back to me." Just as the expected romcom (re)coupling is thwarted, the pat ending of so much conventional gay romance is rejected; Shirin's coming out remains a work in progress and her heartbreak, though muted, is far from fully exorcised. Alongside its queer rewriting of another canonical (and straight cis man-authored) romcom, to conclude with Shirin traveling alone to her own uncertain future circles back to the film's start, when she was also riding the subway rails but crying and not nearly out of the tunnel, so to speak. A fitting ending for a film

The famous final shot of *The Graduate*, reenvisioned for *Appropriate Behavior*.

that has resisted chrononormative teleologies, *Appropriate Behavior*'s open-endedness suits its conception of sexual identities (and the relationships that shape them) as constantly in flux, as becoming rather than being.

Love Isn't Romance. It's Survival: *Women Who Kill*

Further revealing her and Akhavan's shared sensibility, Jungermann's debut feature *Women Who Kill* also was conceived as both an homage to and a queer feminist reenvisioning of a Woody Allen work—in this case, *Manhattan Murder Mystery* (1993), which famously began as an early draft of *Annie Hall* and was to have starred Mia Farrow but was recast with Keaton following Allen and Farrow's breakup.[24] Allen and Keaton's reteaming inevitably invites our viewing them as the middle-aged couple Alvy and Annie might have become had Annie not outgrown the relationship. Keaton's character Carol, career-less and confronting the empty nest with a husband she sees as "stodgy" and "rigid," finds liberation as an amateur detective: "I'm dizzy with freedom!" she exclaims, having started snooping into the suspicious death of their next-door neighbor, a doting wife whose husband seems strangely indifferent to losing his spouse. Though Carol's husband, Larry (Allen), initially regards her as a paranoid fantasist, the black comedy ultimately confirms Carol's hunch that the wife was murdered by a husband intent on, as they say, trading her in for a younger model.

In *Women Who Kill*, Morgan (Jungermann) and ex-girlfriend Jean (Ann Carr) get caught up in an investigation that enlivens their routine existence, in which they cohost a podcast about women serial killers while platonically sharing their Park Slope apartment. Combining seemingly incongruous genres (romcom and Gothic horror) with a deadly dry wit, *Women Who Kill* was inspired, Jungermann reports, by "a mix of my unhealthy obsession with [investigative journalism podcast] *Serial*, my history of failed relationships and a desire to deconstruct romantic comedy structure."[25] Whereas *Manhattan Murder Mystery* reads as an escape from the turmoil of legal wrangling and public condemnation in Allen's personal life, for Jungermann *Women Who Kill* stages a self-confrontation more akin to the psychoanalytically inspired retrospective structure of *Annie Hall* (and *Appropriate Behavior*).[26] And, in comparison to *Manhattan Murder Mystery*, in which the threat posed by Carol's wifely insubordination is ultimately contained and the couple reconstituted, *Women Who Kill*'s "happily ever after" (which has Morgan and Jean still podcasting and seemingly reunited as girlfriends) is thornier for making Morgan a killer, albeit in self-defense. Read as a morbid metaphor for Jungermann's presumed penchant, as Morgan confesses at film's end, for having "hurt some people," Jungermann shares her alter ego's defense: fear of commitment.

The film's tagline, "Love isn't romance. It's survival," is uttered by Morgan's pal Alex (Shannon Patricia O'Neill), who reminds Morgan that it's "the enemy within—self-sabotage" that's keeping Morgan from accepting that ex-girlfriend Jean is "good for you, and you're good for her." For Morgan, imagining love as survival—safe and ongoing—is so, as she puts it, "depressing" that she focuses her desire on Simone, a woman so suspect that she may be the daughter of a serial killer. New to town, of mysterious origins, with exotic looks that contrast noticeably with blonde, wholesome Jean, Simone's vampiric markers are enhanced further through the casting of Sheila Vand, who played the vampire in *A Girl Walks Home Alone at Night* (2014). In one scene, Jean attempts to warn Morgan of the dangers of nonassortative dating:

JEAN: Have you noticed anything strange about her, besides her personality?
MORGAN: No, not really. She's private, she's not like you. . . . You like to talk and share and pick apart things until they don't exist . . . that's why we didn't work out. We shared too much. . . . It's different this time.
JEAN: Yeah, like maybe you're falling for the daughter of a serial killer, at best.
MORGAN: Well, I'd rather be with someone who scares me to death than someone who bores me to death.

JEAN: Fine, move in with her and get married and have a family that she can stab in the middle of the night. . . . I am worried that your life is in danger.

MORGAN: I'm not in danger, okay? I'm just in love.

Convinced that she "shares too much" with Jean, Morgan is drawn to Simone's unknowability and the fear it provokes. Seduced into taking a nighttime walk in the park despite her fear that "there will be rapists or gays in the woods," Morgan's first date with Simone is associated with gay cruising, antithetical to the homonormative ideal of domesticated monogamy. Most menacing of all is Simone's collection of nail clippings labeled with women's names, which doubles as evidence of her mother the serial killer's keepsakes and of this lady-killer's promiscuous sexual history. The link between nail-cutting and lesbian sexual intimacy references a memorable scene of foreplay in the landmark lesbian romcom *Go Fish* (1994), refigured here when Morgan is repelled at Simone's ritual of cutting her nails in bed. The scene resignifies nail-cutting as (at best) personal grooming and (at worst) self-harm, but firmly reorients the act as prelude to emotional rather than sexual intimacy. Preferring to believe that "mystery keeps relationships alive" over her friend Alex's insistence that "we're all disgusting people," Morgan sees here that Simone is all too human, a discovery that drives her to the conviction that Simone herself is a serial killer. Reporting back to Jean, Morgan relays, "Tonight I saw a different side of her and I've been feeling sick ever since." Jean responds knowingly, "Was it a vulnerable side? You get sick to your stomach when people are needy." "I get sick to my stomach when I fear for my life," Morgan shoots back.

Ultimately, Morgan's pathological fear of committed monogamy and its homonormative trappings reveals Morgan herself as the lady-killer, murderous in her refusal of Simone's proposal that they "get fat and boring and argue about nothing, finish each other's sentences, wear each other's clothes, be vulnerable together." Attempting an embrace, Simone instead is impaled on the nail scissors Morgan holds, and the film ends with Morgan as the subject of her own podcast, pleading her case as having acted in self-defense—this metaphorical destruction of the outsider/Other being the necessary sacrifice for Morgan's recoupling with Jean. Marrying romcom and the Gothic, *Women Who Kill* conflates the former's final coupling with the latter's recurrent return of traumatic pasts. That *Women Who Kill* concludes in death, of both the literal and the lesbian bed variety, posits a fatalistic view of (homo)normative coupling. Having eliminated the outsider/Other who, she says, "makes me feel alive and present like the person I want to be, even though I think she might be a murderer," Morgan retreats to the assortative mating partner who "makes me feel like the person I am, and I don't like that person very much."

To read *Women Who Kill* as Jungermann's mea culpa for her breakup with Akhavan—who has discussed her history of self-harm and, like Vand, is Iranian American but who also, like Jean, identifies as bisexual and was Jungermann's creative partner—suggests Akhavan's division into two characters to be another Allen-esque bit of romcom wish fulfillment, one that allows Jungermann to kill her ex and have her too. Yet, like *F to 7th*, *Women Who Kill* also serves as Jungermann's opportunity to rewrite her script, to say (in character) what she failed to express in real life: that, as her alter ego confesses, "I'm not sure I trust myself to make a relationship work—to expose myself." Even as Morgan manages to recommit to Jean, albeit at the cost of killing off the threatening Other (woman), the film registers Jungermann's self-indictment for "beginning or ending relationships . . . based on my need to protect myself. I think if we could all move more into an empathetic state of being rather than a fear-based, self-preservation state, we'd all be a little less lost."[27] Here again, uncoupling is posited as an act of empathy, one that encourages us to recognize and reject our tendency to weaponize love.

An Emotional Intimacy Whore: *The Bisexual*

Like Jungermann, Akhavan struggled to balance professional leverage with creative integrity in the wake of releasing her first feature. Vowing to wait for a worthwhile film project to come along (which she eventually found in the YA adaptation *The Miseducation of Cameron Post*, released in 2018 and awarded the Sundance Grand Jury Prize), Akhavan pitched a television series premised on the question "What if a lesbian did the worst thing in the world a lesbian could do, and became interested in men?"[28] to several major U.S. studios, all of whom passed, offering excuses that they already had a gay series, or a series starring a brown woman, or *Transparent* (Amazon, 2014–2019)—although "nobody had a Middle Eastern show," Akhavan noted wryly.[29] With Sundance (in whose Episodic Lab she developed the project) again offering support, and after impulsively relocating to London, where writer and producing partner Cecilia Frugiuele was living, in 2015, together they landed a production deal for a six-episode series with Channel 4, which released *The Bisexual* in the U.K. during the fall of 2018, with a U.S. release on Hulu shortly thereafter. Inspired by Akhavan's experience of repeatedly being dubbed in the press "the bisexual Lena Dunham" (and variations thereon), and befitting its title, *The Bisexual* constitutes Akhavan's most sustained exploration yet of the complexities of bisexual identity and the misperceptions it provokes. As in *Appropriate Behavior*, the series exceeds the teleological confines of the coming-out narrative, instead parsing the complex intersectional workings of sexual identity. Akhavan's turn to serial television seems particularly well suited to exploring bisexual identity, given seriality's antiteleological open-endedness, the way, as I argue in *The B Word*, it "unfold[s] over time," allowing for "the accumulation of experiences that renders bisexuality representationally *legible*."[30]

Echoing *Appropriate Behavior*, *The Bisexual* begins with uncoupling as Akhavan's character Leila announces a break from her girlfriend of ten years and business partner, Sadie (Maxine Peake), on the cusp of their launching an app and just after Sadie proposes marriage. Terrified by "how [Sadie] could be so sure," Leila feels pulled by the prospect of something, as she explains, "not better. Different." To determine whether the difference she seeks depends on the gender of her object choice(s) or simply novelty, Leila decides to try dating men. Though it shares *F to 7th*'s season-2 premise of a self-professed lesbian experimenting with heterosexuality, that prospect is pitched as absurd and doomed for Ingrid, whereas Leila finds the distinction between genders more or less inconsequential; as she remarks, "I thought sex with a man would be so different, and it's not. Sex is sex." Even if Leila's desire is driven by acceptance of her bisexuality along with a recognition of the monotony of monogamy—having admitted of her decade-long relationship, "At first the sex was really hot, but then we fell into a routine and I didn't want to shake things up—like, if it ain't broke, don't fix it"—the show deliberately contests bisexuality's conflation with promiscuity. To Sadie's accusation that "you will never be fully satisfied," Leila responds, "You can't be with someone ten years and not want other people. . . . No person could give another person all the things they need." As the first season plays out, the *Appropriate Behavior*-style flashback structure of uncoupling romcom will gradually retreat to make way for two TV genre staples, the workplace sitcom and the soap opera, as present-day Leila and Sadie, still coworkers and sharing a (girl) friend group so immersive one character deems it the "lesbian mafia," remain in ongoing contact, permitting the show to frankly confront realities of long-term intimacy, casual sex, and the blurry space between.

Like *Women Who Kill*, *The Bisexual* imagines how Akhavan and Jungermann might have managed had their professional partnership continued after their uncoupling; though where Morgan and Jean languish in codependent denial, friend Deniz (Saskia Chana) greets Leila's insistence that she and Sadie will remain invested in each other's well-being with scornful disbelief.

> LEILA: You can love and support each other and still be on a break.
> DENIZ: Only a lesbian would say that.
> LEILA: Because only a lesbian would be capable of it.
> DENIZ: Sorry, what I meant to say was only a lesbian would be so full of her own shit that she would say that and believe it to be true.

Where Akhavan and Jungermann presumably opted for respectful disengagement while weathering their breakup (and since), Leila and Sadie soon prove Deniz right. Uncoupling initially brings out the worst in them—with repercussions that warn, however comically, against such unbridled antagonism. Belying Leila's assurance to their office staff that, "while we're not feeling so compatible romantically, we're feeling incredibly compatible professionally. Mommy and Daddy love you very much," Sadie's impulsive rebound with their assistant, Hye Me (Cassie Clare), and Leila's juvenile retaliation (spitting gum in Hye Me's hair) lead to a staff uprising in protest of the "super tense and uncomfortable vibe." With Hye Me (echoing Deniz) pronouncing her higher-ups so "full of shit . . . you fill your fancy Aēsop bottles with Imperial Leather," Leila and Sadie first lose their staff's respect, then their staff altogether, as Hye Me and coworker Ruby (Naomi Ackie) land new gigs for a Sheryl Sandberg adherent and Vice, respectively. Though arch as ever in having their would-be protégées selling out to "lean in feminism" and bro culture, this story arc recalls the "impossible" post-breakup dynamic Jungermann described on *The Slope*.

Harkening back to *Appropriate Behavior* while also looking ahead to a hoped-for (but as-yet-unrealized) second season, *The Bisexual* resists the

Sadie (Maxine Peake) and Leila (Desiree Akhavan) called on the carpet for their interoffice drama in *The Bisexual*.

teleological drives of coming out and couple (re)formation; at season's end, Leila remains single, still wrestling with her own prejudice that "when I hear 'bisexual,' I think 'lame slut,'" but at least grappling with the situation that led her to leave Sadie: as she tells her, "I didn't know myself outside of being yours." Alongside her office drama, Leila confronts her new lovers' accusations that she is "self-involved," "an emotional intimacy whore," and—worst of all—in Deniz's scornful assessment, like "a girl from a Judd Apatow movie." "I wasn't aware you were so familiar with his oeuvre," Leila responds, duly chastened. Becoming single forces Leila to evaluate what she wants, from underarm hair to a child, but ultimately in a way that is less selfish for being honest, which is critical, given Sadie's interest in becoming pregnant and the associated temporal constraints: "I gave you my twenties," says Leila. "And I gave you my thirties," replies Sadie, "so who's worse off?" As a lesbian forty-something now-single working woman, Sadie's "choice" to parent is far from guaranteed, and, contra Apatow romcom logic, a (potential) pregnancy is insufficient reason for Leila and Sadie's romantic recoupling, which remains unresolved at season's end. Yet their tentative reconciliation as exes is one of three alternative couplings on display. Leila's flatmate Gabe's (Brian Gleeson) hoped-for "leading lady" Francisca (Michèlle Guillot), a (much younger) foreign exchange student, pronounces

Friends without benefits: *The Bisexual*'s "final couple," Gabe (Brian Gleeson) and Leila (Desiree Akhavan).

their imminent union purely pragmatic. "It's not a real marriage" she says. "It's just for the visa." The third and final (odd) coupling, between platonic pals Leila and Gabe, conjures another couple form long denied by romcom's rejection of "just" friendship between men and women, pointedly refusing the anticipated heterosexual romantic pairing to which a more conventional narrative would have succumbed.

Happily Even After

Though born out of their "superficial, homophobic" partnership, with their screen alter egos continuing to enable Akhavan's performing (as she claims) "the worst aspects of my sexuality,"[31] and Jungermann's working out of her conflicted sense of being one of those "lesbians who don't like lesbians," their output is evidence of the creatively and critically queer potential of uncoupling.[32] Akhavan and Jungermann's enduring mutual dependence is grounded in growth rather than regression, and their work together and apart resignifies their relationship's ostensible "failure" as an impetus for self-reflection and empathy. Though we remain necessarily distant from the actuality of their romance, which has long since ended, the self-description offered up by their most recent fictionalized coupling in *The Bisexual* speaks to its legacy—as announced by the headline gracing a magazine profile of Leila and Sadie's personal and professional partnership that ironically comes out postbreakup: "Our love fuels the work."

Notes

1. Celia Wickham, "Interview with Desiree Akhavan," *Berlin Film Journal*, 2015, berlinfilmjournal.com/2015/05/interview-with-desiree-akhavan/ (accessed September 10, 2020).
2. Hammer Museum, Los Angeles, October 26, 2016.
3. Rob Cover, "First Contact: Queer Theory, Sexual Identity, and 'Mainstream' Film," *International Journal of Sexuality and Gender Studies* 5, no. 1 (January 2000): 71.
4. Judith Levine, *Harmful to Minors: The Perils of Protecting Children from Sex* (Boston: Da Capo, 2003), 167.
5. See, especially, Avishai Margalit, *The Ethics of Memory* (Cambridge, MA: Harvard University Press, 2002).
6. Ladelle McWhorter, *Bodies and Pleasures: Foucault and the Politics of Sexual Normalization* (Bloomington: Indiana University Press, 1999), 198.
7. See, especially, Nishant Shihani, *Queer Retrosexualities: The Politics of Reparative Return* (Bethlehem, PA: Lehigh University Press, 2011).
8. Jack Halberstam, *The Queer Art of Failure* (Durham, NC: Duke University Press, 2011), 23, 94.
9. Sara Ahmed, *The Promise of Happiness* (Durham, NC: Duke University Press, 2010), 75.
10. Lauren Berlant, *Cruel Optimism* (Durham, NC: Duke University Press, 2011), 51.
11. See Heather K. Love, *Feeling Backward: Loss and the Politics of Queer History* (Cambridge, MA: Harvard University Press, 2010).
12. Akhavan quoted in Nick Dawson, "25 New Faces of 2012: Desiree Akhavan and Ingrid Jungermann." *Filmmaker*, 2012, filmmakermagazine.com/people/desiree-akhavan-and-ingrid-jungermann/ (accessed September 10, 2020).
13. Shawn Setaro, "Ingrid Jungermann & *Women Who Kill*," Gum Studios, March 8, 2016, Archived from the original September 21, 2016. Retrieved

December 17, 2020. https://web.archive.org/web/20160921195655/http://www.gumstudios.nyc/gumworks/ingridjungermann.

14 Aymar Jean Christian, "Finding Web TV's *Louie*: Why Views Don't Matter for Indies." IndieWire, June 12, 2014, www.indiewire.com/2014/06/finding-web-tvs-louie-why-views-dont-matter-for-indies-25433/.

15 Ingrid Jungermann, "*F to 7th*: Good Old-Fashioned Lesbianism," HuffPost, October 25, 2012, www.huffingtonpost.com/ingrid-jungermann/f-to-7th-good-old-fashioned-lesbianism_b_2019513.html. This chapter's epigraph quotes Jungermann's transcribed remarks from an interview with the WGAE Digital Caucus, New York, ca. 2016, www.wgaeast.org/onwriting/ingrid-jungermann-f-to-7th-women-who-kill/ (accessed September 10, 2020).

16 Jungermann, "Good Old-Fashioned Lesbianism."

17 Jude Dry, "Tribeca: *Women Who Kill* Director Ingrid Jungermann Has Some Ideas for New Queer Cinema," *IndieWire*, April 15, 2016, www.indiewire.com/2016/04/tribeca-women-who-kill-director-ingrid-jungermann-has-some-ideas-for-new-queer-cinema-289944/.

18 Halberstam, *Queer Art of Failure*, 110.

19 Halberstam, 110–11.

20 See Ahmed, *Promise of Happiness*.

21 Quoted in Dawson, "25 New Faces of 2012."

22 Desiree Akhavan, "Desiree Akhavan's Breakthrough Breakup." *Death, Sex & Money*, WNYC, January 14, 2015.

23 Ahmed, *Promise of Happiness*, 75.

24 Dry, "Tribeca."

25 Diana Martinez, "Tribeca 2016 Women Directors: Meet Ingrid Jungermann—*Women Who Kill*," IndieWire, April 12, 2016, www.indiewire.com/2016/04/tribeca-2016-women-directors-meet-ingrid-jungermann-women-who-kill-202546/.

26 Woody Allen and Stig Björkman, *Woody Allen on Woody Allen*, rev. ed. (New York: Grove, 2005), 255.

27 Martinez, "Tribeca 2016 Women Directors."

28 Aoife Hanna, "Who Is Desiree Akhavan? *The Bisexual* Actress May Well Look Familiar," Bustle, 2018, www.bustle.com/p/who-is-desiree-akhavan-the-bisexual-actress-may-well-look-familiar-12208464 (accessed September 10, 2020).

29 Desiree Akhavan, "*The Bisexual*," Talkback, NewFest, SVA Theatre, New York, New York, October 29, 2018.
30 Maria San Filippo, *The B Word: Bisexuality in Contemporary Film and Television* (Bloomington: Indiana University Press, 2013), 203–4.
31 Akhavan, "What Is Appropriate Behavior?"
32 Jungermann, "Good Old-Fashioned Lesbianism."

15

"I fantasize sometimes about being alone... being in a quiet room, by myself, with no one touching me"

"Wrong-coms" and the End of Marriage in Contemporary Romantic Comedy

Deborah Jermyn

The critical discourse around contemporary romantic comedy has proven persistent in placing it among the most predictable, least innovative of genres. The Hollywood romcom, it is widely argued, is an inherently conservative, didactic vehicle, driven by a desire to promote the heteronormative, bourgeois cultural status quo of Western ideologies. For Alexia L. Bowler, this reactionary impulse has only gained momentum in recent years, so that "what is also apparent, in the typically conservative genre's efforts to cope with shifts in contemporary socio-sexual codes and practices, is the growing intensity of the genre's 'stand-off' with feminism as it ideologically perpetuates reactionary gender regimes that reify hegemonic ideals."[1] Crucially, a common thread in such critiques has been the notion that one of romcom's key aspirations—functions, even—is to endorse marriage. Betty Kaklamanidou, in her work on "the new millennium Hollywood romcom" (and, on one level, in seeming contrast to Bowler's summation), is keen to underline the many nuances in romantic comedy of late.[2] But, while identifying "a kind of revolution" in the genre's recent willingness to cast older women heroines, she suggests that what makes this development stand out as especially remarkable is its coming "in the context of a genre which *usually ends with a wedding and does not question what happens after* the vows have been spoken and the cake has been eaten" (my emphasis).[3] Elsewhere, having warned readers that "it's not a stretch to say that all romantic comedies endorse prescriptive dating/mating practices to some extent," Melissa Ames and Sarah Burcon signal alarm when writing about the Katherine Heigl vehicle *27 Dresses* (2008).[4] With its depiction of "female characters [who] have been dreaming of this day since childhood," the authors caution, such movies "might be said to maintain the status quo that says women should get married because it is simply the expected thing to do."[5] It remains, then, a widely held position that romcom's true grand finale, its ultimate "happy ending," comes in the eventual constitution of a bride and groom, whether the ceremony be explicitly represented, or its inevitability heavily hinted at, before the credits roll.[6]

Of course, over time attitudes toward marriage have changed in romcom, just as in the societies that have produced them. Evidencing this, Claire Mortimer makes a robust case that the imperative of marriage in the 1950s sex comedy, with its reduction of "relationships to their basics: sex and procreation," can be understood in the context of the postwar baby-boom drive.[7] In this chapter, however, I argue that this continuing perception of the genre constitutes an overly crude reading—indeed, even a misrepresentation—of the cultural labor the genre has actually widely undertaken in recent times as it engages with the discomforts and destabilization of contemporary marriage and its meaning. Of significance here, Celestino Deleyto's work on the ideological determinism of genre analysis in romcom and James MacDowell's work on the unthinking acceptance of the omnipresence of the "Hollywood happy ending" have both constituted crucial inquiries into critical assumptions that beleaguer the genre.[8] In the same interventionist spirit, this chapter asks if the existence of an unproblematic endorsement of marriage throughout romcom, and the actual ubiquity of its representations of marriages as unequivocally happy endings, are suppositions that have been subject to overstatement—since, I would contend, this framing works very neatly with seemingly "proving" the (also simplistic) notion that romcoms perform only reactionary cultural work. As MacDowell notes, "the Hollywood 'happy ending' is among the most over-utilised and under-analysed concepts in discussions of popular cinema," it being presumed to be both ubiquitous in Hollywood and by its very nature "inherently ideologically conservative."[9] He undertakes a comprehensive reevaluation of the (mis)use of this concept while—crucially for the purposes of this chapter—his work also underlines the commonplace formulation "that the 'happy ending' requires a 'united romantic couple,'" or at least is its foremost convention.[10]

This rethinking has particularly far-reaching repercussions for (the overwhelmingly pejorative) criticism of romantic comedy, given that it is still widely understood to be driven above all else by the requirement to form a couple at its close. In parallel, then, to MacDowell's findings on the overemphasizing of Hollywood's happy ending, a commonplace presumption has evolved that romcom is riddled with celebratory wedding ceremony finales and an unproblematic veneration of marriage—and, advancing this model of reappraisal still further, this chapter insists that scholarship revisit and challenge this premise.

Conceptually, the intervention made here aligns also with the influential work done by Deleyto, who, arguing for a more nuanced and elastic conception of what constitutes "romantic comedy," contends that the "excessive concentration" on the happy ending in romcom has obscured other features and resulted in "an inexorable circularity in the dominant argument."[11] As he notes, the prevailing critical perspective assumes that

> not only is romantic comedy about love and marriage but it always says the same thing about it, it invariably conveys the same conservative message: if the most important convention of the genre is the happy ending and this happy ending usually consists in the consolidation (or at least the more or less certain promise of consolidation) of a monogamous (and hence patriarchal) heterosexual couple, then it follows that the genre as a whole is conservative because it naturalises, celebrates and reinforces marriage, monogamy and heterosexuality.[12]

The result of the "wholesale capitulation" to such an outlook has been "to homogenise the genre and impoverish individual texts," rather than to recognize and interrogate the many instances at which something more narratively multifaceted and ideologically untidy is happening.[13] What happens, then, when, rather than marriage being the narrative endpoint, the romcom *begins* at this juncture, or some years after it has taken place? How might films in which the convention of the "meet cute" is sidestepped, and that open with an established married couple already in situ, demand that one revisit presumptions about the genre's desire to champion marriage? While reception of the genre has largely homogenized it, generic variation has also been acknowledged of late, capitalizing on the pliability of the appellation as well as recognizing its adaptations, in such designations as the "homme-com," the "zomromcom," and the "prom-com."[14] In line with this practice, I want here to propose the emergence of another significant cycle in recent years, one that chimes with a cultural landscape in which the institution of marriage has come under increasing scrutiny—namely, the "wrong-com," in which the vows, happiness, and inherent "rightness" of the (connubial) couple are laid bare, gauged, and found troublingly deficient. In numerous recent films, the drama is not centered on how or whether the couple will manage to get together by the end, nor is it focused on reconstituting a couple rediscovering one another after (misguidedly) separating, as with the classical Hollywood screwball "comedy of remarriage" tradition. Instead, the married state constitutes the narrative impediment the couple must *overcome*, rather than attain, in order to find desire, harmony, and romance.

In films such as *Mr. & Mrs. Smith* (2005), *Couples Retreat* (2009), *Date Night* (2010), *Crazy, Stupid, Love* (2011), *Hope Springs* (2012), *This Is 40* (2012), *I Give It a Year* (2013), *While We're Young* (2014), and *I Do . . . Until I Don't* (2017), one finds a pattern in which the imagined straightforward ideological veneration of marriage in the genre is difficult to reconcile with the awkward, anxious, and otherwise vexed relationships and narratives that actually unfurl, and in which marriage is figured as deleterious to both men and women in the heteronormative worlds that still predominate here.[15] Hence this chapter more comprehensively delineates and explores what Kaklamanidou briefly touches on as the "'troubled-marriage' cycle," in her discussion of *Couples Retreat*, combining textual analysis of the films noted above with contextual analysis examining the wrong-com as a response to a range of recent political and sociodemographic shifts widely charted by sociologists and other cultural commentators.[16] Drawing on some of the most germane of these studies, including the work of Eric Klinenberg and Rebecca Traister, through this multiply inflected approach I underscore how (again) this frivolously regarded genre has come to proffer a notable site of critical reflection and reevaluation regarding the consequence and desirability of marriage, while recurrently presenting uncomfortable, testing mediations on modern heterosexual relationships. In the process, this chapter embraces Deleyto's call to move on from the crude and "critically tendentious" traditions that have dogged the genre, to instead insist that scholarship examines "what makes the genre rich, varied and, in sum, culturally important."[17]

When "I Do" Becomes "I Did": Identifying the Wrong-Com

The overstating of romcom's investment in marriage is encouraged also by the generic indistinctiveness or hybridity in these films, evident in the intersections between what Jeanine Basinger calls the "marriage movie," and the romantic comedy more broadly. Writing in 2012, she notes that "[the] topic of marriage in the movies . . . has not yet captured the full attention of academia," while also observing Hollywood's longstanding reluctance to explicitly advertise or market films as actually being "about" marriage, despite its prevalence as "a common touchstone" of so many audience members' lives.[18] Both these lacunae, within scholarship and the promotional strategies of the industry, imply unease with probing a somehow humdrum and lowly topic: "The known, not the unknown . . . marriage, in all its boredom and daily responsibilities."[19] Basinger's conception of the marriage movie centers on "how commercial movies told the story of marriage, and how they used it to draw audiences into the theater"—thus, the examples of wrong-coms noted above might just as readily be called marriage movies.[20] Wrong-coms are films, then, that explicitly take explorations of marriage as a central part of their *content* rather than films unimaginatively and perfunctorily appending at their end a reactionary affirmation of marriage as fulfilling and aspirational.[21]

Neither are these films "wedding movies," as Heather Brook terms another body of recent films, though they can certainly be ascribed to the same family tree.[22] The apparent abundance of wedding-focused relationship comedies in recent years, such as the aforementioned *27 Dresses*, *Bride Wars* (2009), or *The Big Wedding* (2013), may again seem to substantiate the idea that romcoms are enduringly built on the expectation of and desire for a marriage. But, as Luke Hockley and Nadi Fadina observe, "wedding movies" actually "*[exist] across a range of genres*" (my emphasis), being only "a subset of romantic comedy," rather than somehow exemplary of it.[23] Indeed, one might legitimately ask if the wrong-coms noted above should even be considered romcoms, if one takes the necessary starting point of romcom to be "boy meets girl," following which genre convention dictates the fated pair must overcome some complication in order finally to form a couple.[24] In wrong-coms, it is rather a case of "boy *met* girl." Protagonist couples are already married and often have children, and it is marriage itself—that aching estrangement wrought by conjugal inertia—that constitutes the obstacle standing in the way of the couple's happiness. However, in contrast to a critical tendency for sweeping statements about romcom's rigidity, Deleyto's work has mapped the vast malleability of the genre as comprised of sprawling nodes that cannot be prescriptively contained.[25] So, while they are wrong-coms, *Mr. & Mrs. Smith* is also an action movie; *Date Night* is also a crime-caper film; *This Is 40* (like others) is a family melodrama. Romcom can be found in many places, then, and certainly within comedies about already married people.

"I don't know, I guess I got lazy. I got boring is what I got": Marriage as Inertia in the Wrong-Com

The contours of this cycle are such that it becomes exigent that criticism and scholarship revisit dominant perspectives on the genre and explore the potential radicalism of this latest iteration. In contradistinction to the long-established paradigm, here one finds the prizes enduringly held up by heteronormative culture—long-term monogamous marriage, and reproduction within matrimony—uncovered, dissected, and found to be destructively dysfunctional. As such, these films suggest a reformist or agitating impulse at work in the genre, even while it still struggles to have any such capacity recognized. Marriage, we learn in wrong-coms—through continued scenes of discontented couples who no longer have anything interesting to talk about, and who climb into bed together at night wearing sweatpants and mouthguards—far from being aspirational is instead experienced as stifling, alienating, and hostile, as sounding the death knell of desire and sex, of spontaneity, joy, and selfhood. The opening restaurant sequence of *Crazy, Stupid, Love*, for example, captures a series of flirtatious couples playing footsie under the table, before the camera settles on a pair of men's scuffed sneakers, which are, by contrast, tellingly distant from the feet of the woman sitting opposite. An excruciatingly banal and stilted monologue commences, in which Cal (Steve Carell) bemoans the fact that "I'm so full. . . . You were right, I shouldn't have eaten all that bread . . . I don't know what I want . . . Shall we split a dessert?" The absence of attraction between the pair is striking next to the erotic displays seen among these other, still desiring, and, it is implied, seemingly *not* long-married couples. Ending his tedious indecision, Cal finally suggests to his wife, Emily (Julianne Moore), that they "both say what we want," at which point she eschews the menu and blurts out, to his horror, "I want a divorce!" The painful, bewildering breakup of their marriage ensues, after Emily admits she was unfaithful with a coworker, and an utterly disoriented Cal finds solace in the friendship of charming but tawdry pick-up artist Jacob (Ryan Gosling). "I made an effort when we were younger, didn't I?" Cal asks Emily in confusion. "I mean, miniature golf, and dancing . . . I don't know, I guess I got lazy. I got boring is what I got." Their unhappiness is all the more arresting given that, together, they constitute one of the most revered cornerstones of romantic fantasy, being "first loves," who fell for each other as high school sweethearts.

In fact, awkward dining scenes form one of the signature set pieces of the wrong-com. A space that elsewhere across culture is cherished as one allowing couples and families to join together, to enjoy quality time, intimacy, and the shared physical satisfactions of good food and company, here becomes a site paying witness to the creeping disintegration of relationships after marriage. In *Mr. & Mrs. Smith*, it is over a weekday pot-roast supper that John (Brad Pitt) and Jane (Angelina Jolie)—secret assassins who discover each other's identity and hence end up trying to eliminate one another—first prepare to slay his and her spouse. The tedious and clearly well-worn routine of small talk and table etiquette that unfolds between them forms a facade of (over)familiarity with which both try to distract their rival from their murderous intentions. In *Date Night*, Phil (Steve Carell) and Claire (Tina Fey) Foster's realization that their weekly "date night" at the local steak house has become drearily predictable and more burdensome than pleasurable sets in

The opening sequence of *Crazy, Stupid, Love*, in which an awkward dining scene bears witness to the disintegration of a relationship after marriage.

motion the comically threatening series of events that follows. Determined to reignite a spark in their relationship and have "one night, one date when we're not just talking about the kids the entire time or what we have to do next week," Phil promises Claire dinner at Claw, an exclusive Manhattan restaurant, then in desperation steals the reservation of another (criminal) couple when they can't get in. And, in *Hope Springs*, dining out with her parsimonious and routine-driven husband, Arnold (Tommy Lee Jones), is ruined for Kay (Meryl Streep) as he habitually complains about prices, speaking to the incompatibility of their desires and the frustrations of her humdrum existence as his wife.

Such scenes are regularly followed by sequences of bad or no sex, since the withering of eroticism that comes with marriage is another recurrent feature of the wrong-com. Phil and Claire, for example, decide to "take a rain check" after Claire temptingly informs him that "those potato skins made me kinda gassy," while Kay and Arnold's meals out are precipitated by her insistence that they travel from their Omaha home to Maine for intensive marriage therapy after years of unacknowledged celibacy and emotional distance. The counseling received there leads to candid and emotive scenes of middle-aged bodies hesitantly and clumsily attempting to rediscover sexual intimacy, encounters that might elicit nervous laughs but which also have a frankness rarely seen in Hollywood (or cinema broadly). In *I Do . . . Until I Don't*, Alice (Lake Bell) is horrified when her husband of seven years summons her for sex, having installed an app on his phone without her knowledge that informs him when she is ovulating. A halfhearted and decidedly unalluring seduction effort follows in the cramped bathroom at his workplace, which she insists they abandon after she sights unflushed feces floating in the toilet. In marked opposition to the rise of "True Love Waits" and other conservative abstinence movements since the 1990s that promote sex within marriage as the only permissible sex, and even promise that sex will be better as a result of abstaining until matrimony, in the wrong-com sex after marriage is at best another household chore that couples undertake indifferently.

"No one wants anything for life": The Fluctuating Social Contexts of Marriage and the Rise of Wrong-Com

The emergence of any cycle of films raises an inevitable question: Why this cycle, at this time? Alongside the invariable industrial need for intermittent generic novelty, in this instance changing social demographics, postfeminism, and marriage equality legislation all offer fruitful contexts for understanding the rise of the wrong-com. First, the experience of and pressures exerted on a marriage entered into today as a lifelong commitment—"till death do us part"—have become significantly different prospects for contemporary couples whose life expectancy now dramatically exceeds that of the last century. In England and Wales, for example, for males, life expectancy at birth increased from 51 years in 1910–1912, to 79 years in 2010–2012, while for females it increased from 55 to 83 years.[26] Hence the opening voice-over in *I Do . . . Until I Don't* from documentarist Vivian Prudeck (Dolly Wells), embarking on her latest film, contends that the traditional terms of marriage should be relegislated to "a seven-year contract with an option to renew." Her project makes clear the archaic and anachronistic status of an institution conceived of at a time when everyone died young by today's standards, when she pronounces "For life. No one wants anything 'for life' . . . Our problem is we live too long. I mean, if we were all dying at 45, then, fine, yeah, 'course, get yourself betrothed. But now we . . . [convict] ourselves to a dreadfully long existence with one partner for half a bloody century."[27]

The extension of life spans has also contributed to the upsurge of single-occupancy households, another social shift with particular salience for the wrong-com. In his 2012 book *Going Solo: The Extraordinary Rise and Surprising Appeal of Living Alone*, Eric Klinenberg notes that, "in 1950, 22 percent of American adults were single. Four million lived alone, and they accounted for 9% of all households. . . . Today, more than 50 percent of American households are single, and 31 million—roughly one out of every seven adults—live alone," while globally in the period 1996–2006, the number of people living alone worldwide increased 33 percent.[28] He attributes this change to a variety of factors including, of course, wealth ("put simply, one reason that more people live alone than ever before is that today more people can afford to do so") and the burgeoning "cult of the individual," such that, according to contemporary wisdom, the search for success and happiness depends less on tying oneself down to another than on opening up the world of possibilities so that one can always pursue the best option. Freedom. Flexibility. Personal Choice. These rank among our most cherished modern virtues.... Not long ago, someone who was dissatisfied with his or her spouse and wanted a divorce had to justify that decision. Today it's the opposite: If you're not fulfilled by your marriage, you have to justify staying in it.[29]

Klinenberg suggests that, within such a cultural climate, "living alone helps us pursue sacred modern values—*individual freedom, personal control and self-realisation*" (my emphasis).[30] Notably, these values accord perfectly with the tenets of neoliberalism. Furthermore, they take on particular resonance for women subjects within postfeminist discourse, becoming aspirations rendered both more anticipated and attainable for certain (educated, professional, economically independent, and otherwise privileged) women who form the ideal subjects of postfeminism. These are women no longer "dependent" on male breadwinner partners as they once were, whose expectations of and opportunities for personal fulfillment outside or alongside the traditional spaces of marriage and children are more manifold, part of a changing culture (for some) that accounts in part for growing numbers of single women. While Rebecca Traister notes in her study of this demographic shift in the U.S. that, importantly, "many single women are poor or struggling," and that many for different reasons feel "ostracized, pressured," still, "statistically across the country, these women are not alone. Their numbers are growing by the year. There were 3.9 million more single adult women in 2014 than there were in 2010."[31] Virtually all the women protagonists in the films noted in this chapter have their own professional lives, and thus the capacity to live independently, and comfortably so, apart from their male partner, and in this respect one must note how a vision of marriage as the terrain of white, middle-class privilege prevails in these films.[32] As dissatisfied wife, mother, and realtor Claire tells her equally jaded husband Phil after their "date night" descends into chaos and he asks her, "Do you ever think about leaving me?," she does not fantasize about being with another man. "No," she says. "If anything, I fantasize sometimes about being alone.... There are times when I've thought about, on my worst day, just . . . going someplace. Like, checking into a hotel . . . being in a quiet room, by myself . . . with no one touching me."

Since the turn of the millennium particularly, years of debate and activism centered on achieving marriage equality seem both to speak to the reverence with which marriage is still regarded, and to suggest that its cultural entrenchment has, if anything, amplified in recent years. But to argue this is to sidestep how the campaign for marriage equality entailed a good deal of questioning the desirability and purpose of marriage in the modern age. Was this institution really something gay rights activists should be focusing their energies on, some asked, given how woven it is with conservative, capitalist, and patriarchal ideologies, as well as in light of the cascades of unhappy stories and countless demoralized subjects it has given rise to among generations of heterosexual spouses?[33] Indeed, Traister argues, "the journey toward legal marriage for gays and lesbians may seem at odds with what looks like a flight from marriage by heterosexuals. But in fact, they are part of the same project: a dismantling of the institution as it once existed."[34] This conversation around marriage equality regularly questioned the appeal of marriage even while seemingly endorsing it, and this renewed scrutiny of the institution's relevance and constraints constitutes another notable context informing the wrong-com's anxious representations of marriage.

The Bitter/Sweet Laughter of Wrong-Com

Still, none of the social contexts, plotlines, and sequences outlined in this chapter, often in somber and perturbing terms, have been highlighted here in order to efface or deny that wrong-coms are still comedies or at least films with comic edges. On the contrary, they offer assorted laughs that are frequently farcical, slapstick, or scatological in form. The wrong-com particularly capitalizes on this latter mode of corporeal comedy, given that discretion around bodily matters often erodes in the course of long-term relationships, particularly after having children, as is evident in renowned gross-out humor specialist Judd Apatow's *This Is 40*. One reason Debbie (Leslie Mann) and Pete's (Paul Rudd) marriage has become especially trying for both parties is evidently the loss of boundaries and privacy within it, and the overfamiliarity this has fostered. Debbie continually walks in on Pete sitting on the toilet playing games on his iPad in the lock-free bathroom, where he has retreated (and failed) to carve out some alone time. He repeatedly and brazenly farts in bed, much to her disgust, and at one point asks her to inspect him for a suspected hemorrhoid. In *Couples Retreat*, which charts the fortunes of four couples visiting a luxury tropical island for couple's therapy, the imposed celibacy or desexualization that marriage brings is blamed particularly on parenting; the tone is set in its comical opening sequence when Dave (Vince Vaughn) thinks he is awakening next to his wife only to discover his toddler son next to him, who unceremoniously announces, "I peed."

Much of this humor is bittersweet indeed, as likely to raise the hackles of a grimacing audience as to raise a smile. Although the couples of wrong-coms are not always parents, children—loud, demanding, frequently anxious, even while unquestionably loved—are reliably framed not just as a source of humor, but as one of the major causes of marital ennui and emotional (not only sexual) detachment within the couple. One of the major motivations for and defenses of marriage—namely, "secure" procreation—is thus configured as inherently *destructive* of marriage. In a particularly visceral family row in *This Is 40*, Debbie's attempt to barter a break from her new mid-life health regime by offering to give Pete a blow job if he turns a blind eye to her having a cigarette descends into screaming carnage among all parties as their two furious daughters pound on their locked door. The film constitutes a quasi-sequel to Apatow's earlier film *Knocked Up* (2007), in which the combative Debbie and Pete are supporting players whose hostile marriage forms a cautionary backdrop to the nascent couple.[35] Here, five years on, they become the protagonists themselves. But the unsettling rawness of this sequence intensifies further still when watched with the knowledge that Apatow cast his own wife and their daughters in the film, with Paul Rudd thus standing in as his avatar of sorts. As Philip French put it in a review, the film can readily be seen as "autobiographical in an emotional rather than literal sense," such that this extratextual insight makes the thread of violent fantasy running through the couple's relationship all the more uncomfortable.[36] Early in the film, Pete asks his buddy whether he has ever imagined his wife's mortality, saying, "This sounds terrible. But . . . do you ever wonder what it would be like . . . if, say, you were separated by something bigger, you know, like death, like *her death*?," and from his friend's response it is apparent this is something he has indeed contemplated quite

"Stop crying!" Another blazing family row bespeaks the tension and rage of life after marriage and children for Debbie (Leslie Mann) and Pete (Paul Rudd) in *This Is 40*.

carefully. Later, Debbie relays to Pete in disturbing detail how if she were to murder him it would be by a process of slow poisoning.

Palimpsests of domestic violence can also be found in other of these films: the moment during therapy in *Mr. & Mrs. Smith* when John too enthusiastically enacts pretending to throttle his wife; the use of the Danger Mouse and Sparklehorse song "Revenge" on the *Crazy, Stupid, Love* soundtrack, which contains the lyrics "In my mind / I have shot you and stabbed you through your heart"; and it surfaces too in Dave's "jokey" throwaway remark, again in therapy, in *Couples Retreat*, that his relationship with his wife is fine because "No one's called 911 in the middle of the night."[37] While such scenes often disavow their violence by framing it as comical in its overt inappropriateness, other scenes do away with comedy altogether, as audiences are confronted with ugly, starkly painful scenes of confrontation and despair. Indeed, they led Richard Brody in the *New Yorker* to describe *This Is 40* as "Bergman-esque" and "Cassavetes-like" (2012), bestowing on the film an art-house gravitas rarely ascribed to this genre.[38] "What are we even doing?" Debbie asks Pete at one of their lowest ebbs. "This is not making me happy. You're not happy. You don't like me. I can feel that. . . . We're like business associates. . . . There's no passion here."

Still, it is important to note in contextualizing the wrong-com that social statistics can invariably be framed in such a way as to serve the desired narrative of the author and can always be met with counterevidence. So, while one might easily turn to today's high divorce rates as proof of the fragility of marriage in modern times, Stephanie Coontz, Klinenberg, and Traister all note, significantly, that people are generally opting to marry *later*, rather than not marry at all, which would suggest the institution's desirability and contours have shape-shifted, rather than been razed.[39] In line with this, David R. Shumway, in his study of the "marriage crisis," finds in film and literary fiction that, even where "marriage is presented as difficult and likely to fail, [happy] marriage remains at least the implicit goal of the characters depicted."[40] Recurrently, the wrong-com's troubled couples *do* eventually find ways to salvage their marriages, or find that they want to try, suggesting that at one level the genre ultimately maintains that marriage remains worth investing in. What makes these wrong-coms part of the broader romcom stable, after all, is that they are comically inclined films that are essentially about the quest to fix a relationship, to somehow find, save, or rediscover love and romance. Therefore, everyone leaves *Couples Retreat* newly committed to their marriage; Kay and Arnold renew their wedding vows on the beach in *Hope Springs*. Despite the hurt he has endured, and, in true romcom fashion, in a heartfelt speech at their son's school in the finale of *Crazy, Stupid, Love*, Cal shares the story of how he met Emily at the age of fifteen, declaring to her and all the assembled crowd, "And I have loved her every minute of every day since I first bought her that chocolate chip mint cone. I have loved her through the birth of our three perfect children. I have loved her even when I have hated her. Only married couples will understand that one . . . I don't know if it's gonna work out . . . I will never stop trying. Because when you find the one, you never give up."

As noted at the start of the chapter, however, a reliance on one-dimensional or otherwise tendentious interpretations of endings conspicuously fails to engage adequately with nuance, with "forgotten middles," as Deleyto puts it, or with the contradictions of Hollywood storytelling and its intricate relationships with the industrial, cultural, and historical contexts it occupies.[41] Thus Cal explicitly voices that which surely forms the undercurrent to the happy ending of every romcom, given the amount of time the genre dedicates to the sheer labor and improbability of achieving a fulfilling, long-term, monogamous union between a man and a woman ("I don't know if it's gonna work out"). In contrast to presumptions about the romcom's inherently conservative pro-marriage flag-waving, these films do not merely raise but relish the uncomfortable specter of the proposition that "the logic of heterosexual marriage," as John Alberti describes it, is broken.[42] In doing so, they form a significant cultural space in which to explore the architecture of marriage and its constraints, even though they do so largely within prescriptively heteronormative, raced, and classed milieux. As such, the intervention I have undertaken underlines how methodologically and intellectually suspect the resistance of certain schools of criticism and academic inquiry into the complexities of this "obvious" genre continue to be, and calls for more scholarship of the kind invigorated by this collection to persist in propounding the sort of provocative inquiry posed here. Talking to a therapist in *Mr. & Mrs. Smith*, Jane struggles to articulate their problem: "There's this huge space between us. And it just keeps filling up with everything that we don't say to each other. What's that called?" "Marriage," replies the therapist, without missing a beat. And, in an analogous spirit, this chapter has counseled that film scholarship must do more to talk about the uncomfortably "huge spaces" in its own work, acknowledging that wrong-coms are often asking the difficult questions we bury elsewhere.

Notes

1 Alexia Bowler, "Towards a New Sexual Conservatism in Postfeminist Romantic Comedy," in *Postfeminism and Contemporary Hollywood Cinema*, ed. Joel Gwynne and Nadine Muller (Basingstoke: Palgrave Macmillan, 2013), 185.
2 Betty Kaklamanidou, *Genre, Gender, and the Effects of Neoliberalism: The New Millennium Hollywood Romcom* (New York: Routledge, 2013).
3 Kaklamanidou, *Genre, Gender*, 84.
4 Melissa Ames and Sarah Burcon, *How Pop Culture Shapes the Stages of a Woman's Life: From Toddlers-in-Tiaras to Cougars-on-the-Prowl* (Basingstoke: Palgrave Macmillan, 2016), 63.
5 Ames and Burcon, *Pop Culture*, 102.
6 It's important to note here that heterosexual, cis-gendered romances (or brides and grooms) still predominate in the genre, even while this chapter examines how aspects of that heternomativity get disrupted within it.
7 Claire Mortimer, *Romantic Comedy* (Abingdon: Routledge, 2010), 16.
8 See Celestino Deleyto, *The Secret Life of Romantic Comedy* (Manchester: Manchester University Press, 2009); and James MacDowell, *Happy*

Endings in Hollywood Cinema: Cliché, Convention, and the Final Couple (Edinburgh: Edinburgh University Press, 2013).
9. MacDowell, *Happy Endings in Hollywood Cinema*, 1, 3.
10. MacDowell, 11.
11. Deleyto, *Secret Life of Romantic Comedy*, 24.
12. Deleyto, 25.
13. Deleyto, 25.
14. Tamar Jeffers McDonald, "Homme-com: Engendering Change in Contemporary Romantic Comedy," in *Falling in Love Again: Romantic Comedy in Contemporary Cinema*, ed. Stacey Abbott and Deborah Jermyn (London: I. B. Tauris, 2009), 146–59; Christopher Tookey, "The World's First Ever 'Zomromcom' Hits Cinemas Just in Time for Valentine's," *Daily Mail*, February 8, 2018, www.dailymail.co.uk/tvshowbiz/reviews/article-2275398/Warm-Bodies-The-worlds-zomromcom-hits-cinemas-just-time-Valentines.html; Stacey Abbott, "Prom-coms: Reliving the Dreams and Nightmares of High-School Romance," in Abbott and Jermyn, eds., *Falling in Love Again*, 52–64.
15. It is particularly important to acknowledge how this cost is felt by both men and women, given that the feminist critique of marriage has for so long held that the institution of marriage is a cornerstone of patriarchy that oppresses women, sanctioning their "exchange value," while advancing and protecting the interests of men.
16. Kaklamanidou, *Genre, Gender*, 92.
17. Deleyto, *Secret Life of Romantic Comedy*, 25.
18. Jeanine Basinger, *I Do and I Don't: A History of Marriage in the Movies* (New York: Alfred A. Knopf, 2012), xiii–xiv, xvii–xix.
19. Basinger, *I Do and I Don't*, xix.
20. Basinger, xiii.
21. See also Basinger, xiii.
22. Heather Brook, "Engaging Marriage: Rom Coms and Fairy Tale Endings," in *The Happiness Illusion: How the Media Sold Us a Fairytale*, ed. Luke Hockley and Nadi Fadina (Abingdon: Routledge: 2015), 145–161.
23. Hockley and Fadina, *Happiness Illusion*, 9–10.
24. See, for example, Mortimer, *Romantic Comedy*, 4.
25. Deleyto, *Secret Life of Romantic Comedy*.
26. "English Life Tables No.17: 2010 to 2012," Office for English Statistics, September 1, 2015, https://www.ons.gov.uk/

peoplepopulationandcommunity/birthsdeathsandmarriages/lifeexpectancies/bulletins/englishlifetablesno17/2015-09-01.

27 The wrong-com has migrated to television too; one fascinating example of a recent series exploring marriage's lifelong commitment "till death do us part" is *Forever* (Amazon, 2018), in which a married couple both die young in quick succession, only to be reunited in an endless suburban afterlife, where the notion of being (quite literally) "together forever" becomes a bleaker and more testing proposition.

28 Eric Klinenberg, *Going Solo: The Extraordinary Rise and Surprising Appeal of Living Alone* (London: Duckworth, 2012), 4–5, 10.

29 Klinenberg, *Going Solo*, 10–13.

30 Klinenberg, 17–18.

31 Rebecca Traister, *All the Single Ladies: Unmarried Women and the Rise of an Independent Nation* (New York: Simon & Schuster, 2016), 7–8.

32 Of the films named above, only *Couples Retreat* features a black married couple, who, significantly, are already separated by the film's opening.

33 See, for example, Peter Robinson, "Gay Rebels: Why Some Older Homosexual Men Don't Support Same-Sex Marriage," The Conversation, November 6, 2017, theconversation.com/gay-rebels-why-some-older-homosexual-men-dont-support-same-sex-marriage-86205.

34 Traister, *All the Single Ladies*, 30.

35 See also John Alberti, *Masculinity in the Contemporary Romantic Comedy: Gender as Genre* (Abingdon: Routledge, 2013), 30.

36 Philip French, "Review of *This Is 40*," *Observer*, February 16, 2013. https://www.theguardian.com/film/2013/feb/17/this-is-40-apatow-review.

37 Space prohibits me from analysis of the multiple intersecting layers of marital frailty in this film that bleed across the text and into "real life," as we watch its stars now understanding that it was both made in the eye of a marriage breakdown (with Pitt and Jolie famously falling in love on set while he was still married to Jennifer Aniston) and prefigures another, future marriage breakdown (given the scandal that surrounded Jolie filing for divorce from Pitt in 2016 after eleven years together, citing "irreconcilable differences").

38 Brody, "*This Is 40* and the Meaning of Life," *New Yorker*, December 21, 2012, www.newyorker.com/culture/richard-brody/this-is-40-and-the-meaning-of-life.

39 Stephanie Coontz, *Marriage, a History: From Obedience to Intimacy or How Love Conquered Marriage* (New York: Viking, 2005); Klinenberg, *Going Solo*; Traister, *All the Single Ladies*.
40 David Shumway, *Modern Love: Romance, Intimacy, and the Marriage Crisis* (New York: New York University Press, 2003), 26.
41 Deleyto, *Secret Life of Romantic Comedy*, 24.
42 Alberti, *Masculinity*, 41.

Acknowledgments

This collection takes as its starting point the so-called "death of romcom" in the late 2000s, and I similarly trace this book's origins to my spring 2008 course titled (a bit too cheekily, in retrospect) *Happy Endings . . . ?: Hollywood Romantic Comedy*. First, then, I have the faculty of UCLA's Cinema and Media Studies Program to thank for making possible one of my first and still most treasured teaching experiences—one that offered the opportunity to screen 35-mm films in the beautiful James Bridges Theater, a gift that seems more exceptional with each passing year. In the intervening decade-plus, I've continued to teach that course in different versions at multiple institutions, and I'm grateful to all the students who shared their enthusiasm for and knowledge of the genre, and who kept aloft my conviction as to the value and necessity of taking romantic comedy seriously.

More recently, the "Radical Romantic Comedy" panel I chaired at the 2018 Society for Cinema and Media Studies Conference was the seed from which first a special issue of *New Review of Film and Television Studies*, then this collection, grew. Gratitude goes out to my copanelists and the issue's contributors for providing early momentum for this project with their trenchant takes and inspiring insights. Kyle Stevens deserves special thanks for serving in both those roles and beyond, first as the journal's editor in welcoming my proposal, then by extending his confidence in handing me the editorial reins—and in the process becoming a good friend (with a shared love for *Moonstruck*).

Thank you to Claire Perkins and Michele Schreiber for including my essay in their "Independent Women: From Film to Television" special issue of *Feminist Media Studies*, and encouraging my developing it as a chapter for this collection. My appreciation to Routledge, Taylor & Francis for granting permission to reprint my chapter and those by Mary Harrod and

Sueyoung Park-Primiano, which originally appeared in the aforementioned special issue.

Tamar Jeffers McDonald generously lent her support to this project early on, and, when administrative commitments prevented her from contributing a chapter, she generously agreed to write a foreword. Thank you as well to Tim Shary for so genially modeling for me the role of editor, and for giving his time and encouragement to this collection.

It was no surprise, given the glowing endorsements that led me to Wayne State University Press, that they proved the perfect match for this project. Acquisitions editor Marie Sweetman has been a ray of light throughout; I'm grateful for her unstinting enthusiasm, warmth, and wise counsel. Thank you to the anonymous reviewer whose feedback appreciably improved our manuscript, and to series editor Barry Grant for his advocacy and advice. Thank you as well to Emily Shelton for her invaluable assistance with copyediting. Project editor Carrie Teefey brought her talents to crafting an object beautiful to behold; my gratitude to her and her team. Thank you as well to Emily Nowak and Kristina Stonehill for their support with marketing and promotion.

Each of my cocontributors has been wonderfully collegial throughout this book's gestation, and so fully devoted to our collective vision that not even a global pandemic proved an obstacle to its on-time completion. Special thanks to Mary Harrod for inviting me to participate in the *Imagining "We" in the Age of "I"* symposium she organized at the University of Warwick in the fall of 2019, where the plenary talk I delivered served as the basis for this book's introduction, and where the connections I made fostered a transatlantic community of colleagues with whom I continue to collaborate, including on this collection.

When a family emergency arose within days of this book's submission deadline, Vernon Shetley rode to the rescue like the proverbial knight in shining armor. I am deeply grateful for his editorial expertise, and for so many spirited romcom viewings and discussions shared over the past twenty years.

When it comes to coupling, I can think of no more shining example than my parents; their fifty-one year partnership is my definitive image of love. I dedicate this book to them.

Selected Bibliography

Abbott, Stacey, and Deborah Jermyn, eds. *Falling in Love Again: Romantic Comedy in Contemporary Cinema*. London: I. B. Tauris, 2008.

Ahmed, Sara. *The Promise of Happiness*. Durham, NC: Duke University Press, 2010.

Alberti, John. "'I Love You, Man': Bromances, the Construction of Masculinity, and the Continuing Evolution of the Romantic Comedy." *Quarterly Review of Film and Video* 30, no. 2 (2013): 159–72.

———. *Masculinity in the Contemporary Romantic Comedy: Gender as Genre*. London: Routledge, 2013.

Alexander, Elizabeth L. "*Jalla! Jalla!* and *Import-Export*: Two Multicultural Romantic Comedies." *Journal of Scandinavian Cinema* 4, no. 3 (September 2014): 281–88.

Allen, Dennis. "Why Things Don't Add up in *The Sum of Us*: Sexuality and Genre Crossing in the Romantic Comedy." *Narrative* 7, no. 1 (January 1999): 71–88.

Allen, Reniqua. "From Love to Melancholy: The Evolution of the Black Bohemian Identity in Black Indie Love Films from Gen-X to Gen-Y." *Journal of Black Studies* 44, no. 5 (2013): 508–28.

Ames, Melissa, and Burcon, Sarah. *How Pop Culture Shapes the Stages of a Woman's Life: From Toddlers-in-Tiaras to Cougars-on-the-Prowl*. Basingstoke: Palgrave Macmillan, 2016.

Angyal, Chloe. "Gender, Sex, and Power in the Postfeminist Romantic Comedy." PhD diss., University of New South Wales, 2014.

Ascheid, Antje. "The Romantic Comedy and Its Other: Representations of Romance in German Cinema Since 1990." In *Generic Histories of German Cinema: Genre and Its Deviations*, edited by Jaimey Fisher, 243–60. Rochester, NY: Camden House, 2013.

Babington, Bruce, and Peter Williams Evans. *Affairs to Remember: Comedy of the Sexes*. Manchester: Manchester University Press, 1989.

Badley, Linda, Claire Perkins, and Michele Schreiber, eds. *Indie Reframed: Women's Filmmaking and Contemporary American Independent Cinema*. Edinburgh: Edinburgh University Press, 2016.

Banet-Weiser, Sarah. *Empowered: Popular Feminism and Popular Misogyny*. Durham, NC: Duke University Press, 2018.

Barreca, Gina. *They Used to Call Me Snow White . . . But I Drifted: Women's Strategic Use of Humor*. Hanover, NH: University Press of New England, 1991.

Basinger, Jeanine. *I Do and I Don't: A History of Marriage in the Movies*. New York: Alfred A. Knopf, 2012.

Beach, Christopher. *Class, Language, and American Film Comedy*. Cambridge: Cambridge University Press, 2002.

———. "'These Are Troublous Times': Social Class in the Comedies of Preston Sturges." In *ReFocus: The Films of Preston Sturges*, edited by Jeff Jaeckle and Sarah Kozloff, 133–44. Edinburgh: Edinburgh University Press, 2016.

Beck, Ulrich, and Elisabeth Beck-Gernsheim. *The Normal Chaos of Love*. Cambridge: Polity, 2004.

Beltrán, Mary C. "The Hollywood Latina Body as Site of Social Struggle: Media Constructions of Stardom and Jennifer Lopez's 'Cross-Over Butt.'" *Quarterly Review of Film and Video* 19, no. 1 (2002): 71–86.

Berlant, Lauren. *Cruel Optimism*. Durham, NC: Duke University Press, 2011.

———. *Desire/Love*. Brooklyn, NY: Punctum, 2012.

Bleach, Anthony C. "Postfeminist Cliques? Class, Postfeminism, and the Molly Ringwald–John Hughes Films." *Cinema Journal* 49, no. 3 (Spring 2010): 24–44.

Bonila, Paul C. "Is There More to Hollywood Lowbrow than Meets the Eye?" *Quarterly Review of Film and Video* 22, no. 1 (2005): 17–24.

Bonos, Lisa. "Netflix Knows We Need an Escape, So It Built a Romcom Factory." *Washington Post*, July 26, 2018. www.washingtonpost.com/news/soloish/wp/2018/07/26/netflix-knows-we-need-an-escape-so-it-built-a-rom-com-factory/.

Bordwell, David. "Happily Ever After, Part Two." *Velvet Light Trap* 19 (1982): 2–7.

de Botton, Alain. "How Fiction Ruined Love." *Financial Times*, April 22, 2016. www.ft.com/content/905bf850-0588-11e6-a70d-4e39ac32c284.

Bozzola, Lucia. "'Studs Have Feelings Too': Warren Beatty and the Question of Star Discourse and Gender." In *Masculinity: Bodies, Movies, Culture*, edited by Peter Lehman, 227–42. London: Routledge, 2001.

Branfman, Jonathan. "Jewy/Screwy Leading Lady: *Crazy Ex-Girlfriend* and the Critique of Rom-Com Femininity." *Journal of Modern Jewish Studies* 19, no. 1 (2020): 71–92.

Brickman, Barbara Jane, Deborah Jermyn, and Theodore Louis Trost, eds. *Love across the Atlantic: US-UK Romance in Popular Culture*. Edinburgh: Edinburgh University Press, 2020.

Britton, Andrew. "Cary Grant: Comedy and Male Desire." *CineAction* 7 (1986): 37–51.

Brodesser-Akner, Claude. "Can the Romantic Comedy Be Saved?" Vulture, December 27, 2012. www.vulture.com/2012/12/can-the-romantic-comedy-be-saved.html.

Brody, Richard. "*This Is 40* and the Meaning of Life." *New Yorker*, December 21, 2012. www.newyorker.com/culture/richard-brody/this-is-40-and-the-meaning-of-life.

Brogaard, Berit. "Love Is Like Cocaine: The Remarkable, Terrifying Neuroscience of Romance." Salon, February 14, 2015. www.salon.com/2015/02/14/love_is_like_cocaine_the_remarkable_terrifying_neuroscience_of_romance/.

Brook, Heather. "Engaging Marriage: Rom Coms and Fairy Tale Endings." In *The Happiness Illusion: How the Media Sold Us a Fairytale*, edited by Luke Hockley and Nadi Fadina, 145–61. London: Routledge, 2015.

Brunsdon, Charlotte. "Post-feminism and Shopping Films." In *The Film Studies Reader*, edited by Joanne Hollows, Mark Jancovich, and Peter Hutchings, 289–99. London: Bloomsbury, 2000.

———. "A Subject for the Seventies: Charlotte Brunsdon Traces the Construction of an 'Independent' Heroine." *Screen* 23, nos. 3–4 (1982): 20–29.

Butler, Judith. *Gender Trouble: Feminism and the Subversion of Identity*. New York: Routledge, 1990.

Canfield, David. "The Romantic Comedy Is Having a Revolution—And It's Happening on TV." IndieWire, July 6, 2015. www.indiewire.com/2015/07/the-romantic-comedy-is-having-a-revolution-and-its-happening-on-tv-60577/.

Carlson, Erin. *I'll Have What She's Having: How Nora Ephron's Three Iconic Films Saved the Romantic Comedy*. New York: Hachette, 2017.

Carson, Diane. "To Be Seen and Not Heard: *The Awful Truth*." In *Multiple Voices in Feminist Film Criticism*, edited by Diane Carson, Linda Dittmar, and Janice R. Welsch, 213–25. Minneapolis: University of Minnesota Press, 1994.

Carver, Terrell. "Sex, Gender and Heteronormativity: Seeing *Some Like It Hot* as a Heterosexual Dystopia." *Contemporary Political Theory* 8 (2009): 125–51.

Casado-Gual, Núria. "Ageing and Romance on the Big Screen: the 'Silvering Romantic Comedy' *Elsa & Fred*." *Ageing & Society* 40, no. 10 (2020): 2257–65.

Cavell, Stanley. *Pursuits of Happiness: The Hollywood Comedy of Remarriage*. Cambridge, MA: Harvard University Press, 1981.

Chaney, Jen. "The Romantic Comedy Is Not Dead—It's Just Not the Same as You Remember." Vulture, January 30, 2017. www.vulture.com/2017/01/romantic-comedy-is-not-dead.html.

Chiasson, Dan. "Design for Long-Term Living." *New York Review of Books*, June 5, 2014. www.nybooks.com/articles/2014/06/05/design-long-term-living/.

Choi, Jinhee. "*My Love, My Bride* (1990): A Comedy of Remarriage?" In *Rediscovering Korean Cinema*, edited by Sangjoon Lee (Ann Arbor, MI: University of Michigan Press, 2019), 260–73.

Ciasullo, Ann M. "Making Her (In)Visible: Cultural Representations of Lesbianism and the Lesbian Body in the 1990s." *Feminist Studies* 27, no. 3 (Fall 2001): 577–608.

Cobb, Shelley, and Diane Negra. "'I Hate to Be the Feminist Here . . .': Reading the Post-Epitaph Chick Flick." *Continuum* 31, no. 6 (2017): 757–66.

Cohan, Steven. "So Functional for Its Purposes: The Bachelor Apartment in *Pillow Talk*." In *Stud: Architectures of Masculinity*, edited by Joel Sanders, 28–41. Princeton, NJ: Princeton University Press, 1996.

Coontz, Stephanie. *Marriage, a History: From Obedience to Intimacy or How Love Conquered Marriage*. New York: Viking, 2005.

Cover, Rob. "First Contact: Queer Theory, Sexual Identity, and 'Mainstream' Film." *International Journal of Sexuality and Gender Studies* 5, no. 1 (2000): 71–89.

Cox, Lara. "Bye-Bye to Betty's Blues and 'La Bonne Meuf': Temporal Drag and Queer Subversions of the Rom-Com in *Bye Bye Blondie* (Virginie Despentes, 2011)." In *International Cinema and the Girl: Local Issues, Transnational Contexts*, ed. Fiona Handyside and Kate Taylor-Jones, 97–108. Basingstoke: Palgrave, 2016.

Critchley, Simon. *On Humour*. London: Routledge, 2002.

Crouch, Ian. "Swipe Left: 'Love' and the Unromantic Comedy." *New Yorker*, February 26, 2016. www.newyorker.com/culture/culture-desk/swipe-left-love-and-the-unromantic-comedy.

DeAngelis, Michael, ed. *Reading the Bromance: Homosocial Relationships in Film and Television*. Detroit: Wayne State University Press, 2014.

Deighan, Samm. "Kneeling on Glass: Elaine May's *A New Leaf* (1971) as Screwball Black Comedy." In *ReFocus: The Films of Elaine May*, edited by Alexandra Heller-Nicholas and Dean Brandum, 85–103. Edinburgh: Edinburgh University Press, 2019.

Deleyto, Celestino. "Between Friends: Love and Friendship in Contemporary Hollywood Romantic Comedy." *Screen* 44, no. 2 (2003): 167–82.

———. "The Comic, the Serious, and the Middle: Desire and Space in Contemporary Film Romantic Comedy." *Journal of Popular Romantic Studies*, October 2011. jprstudies.org/wp-content/uploads/2011/10/JPRS2.1_Deleyto_RomCom.pdf.

———. "Fabulous Illusion: *The Curse of the Jade Scorpion* and the Conventions of Romantic Comedy." *Post Script* 31, no. 2 (Winter 2012): 80–91, 121.

———. "Men in Leather: Kenneth Branagh's *Much Ado about Nothing* and Romantic Comedy." *Cinema Journal* 36, no. 3 (Spring 1997): 91–105.

———. "They Lived Happily Ever After: Ending Contemporary Romantic Comedy." *Miscelánea: A Journal of English and American Studies* 19 (1998): 39–55.

———. *The Secret Life of Romantic Comedy*. Manchester: Manchester University Press, 2009.

Demory, Pamela, and Christopher Pullen, eds. *Queer Love in Film and Television*. Basingstoke: Palgrave Macmillan, 2012.

Denby, David. "A Fine Romance." *New Yorker*, July 16, 2007. www.newyorker.com/magazine/2007/07/23/a-fine-romance.

Dennis, Jeffrey P. *Queering Teen Culture: All-American Boys and Same-Sex Desire in Film and Television*. London: Routledge, 2006.

DiBattista, Maria. *Fast-Talking Dames*. New Haven, CT: Yale University Press, 2001.

Diggins, John Patrick. "*Charlie Wilson's War*: History as Romantic Comedy." *Historically Speaking* 9, no. 3 (January–February 2008): 47–48.

Di Mattia, Joanna. "Thinking about Celine and Jesse: Travelling through Time with the *Before* Trilogy." *Senses of Cinema* 87 (2018): sensesofcinema.com/2018/stardust-memories/thinking-about-celine-and-jesse-travelling-through-time-with-the-before-trilogy (accessed September 11, 2020).

Doherty, Thomas. "The Rom-Com Genre and the Shopping Gene." *OAH Magazine of History*, April 2010, 25–28.

Doty, Alexander. "I Love *Laverne & Shirley*: Lesbian Narratives, Queer Pleasures, and Television Sitcoms." In *Critiquing the Sitcom: A Reader*, edited by Joanne Morreale, 187–208. Syracuse, NY: Syracuse University Press, 2002.

Dowd, James J., and Nicole R. Pallotta. "The End of Romance: The Demystification of Love in the Postmodern Age." *Sociological Perspectives* 43, no. 4 (2000): 549–80.

Dreisinger, Baz. "The Queen in Shining Armor: Safe Eroticism and the Gay Friend." *Journal of Popular Film & Television* 28, no. 1 (Spring 2000): 2–11.

Duggan, Lisa. *The New Homonormativity: The Sexual Politics of Neoliberalism.* Durham, NC: Duke University Press, 2002.

Dyer, Richard. "Monroe and Sexuality." In *Heavenly Bodies: Film Stars and Society*, 19–66. New York: St. Martin's, 1986.

Eagleton, Terry. *Humour.* New Haven, CT: Yale University Press, 2019.

Ehrenreich, Barbara, and Deirdre English. *For Her Own Good: Two Centuries of the Experts' Advice for Women.* 2nd ed. New York: Anchor House, [1979] 2005.

Evans, Peter William, and Celestino Deleyto, eds. *Terms of Endearment: Hollywood Romantic Comedy of the 1980s and 1990s.* Edinburgh: Edinburgh University Press, 1998.

Eyman, Scott. *Ernst Lubitsch: Laughter in Paradise.* Baltimore: John Hopkins University Press, 1993.

Ferriss, Suzanne, and Mallory Young. *Chick Flicks: Contemporary Women at the Movies.* London: Routledge, 2008.

Fincham, Frank D., and Ming Cui. *Romantic Relationships in Emergent Adulthood.* Cambridge: Cambridge University Press, 2011.

Flisfeder, Matthew, and Clint Burnham. "Love and Sex in the Age of Capitalist Realism: On Spike Jonze's *Her*." *Cinema Journal* 57, no. 1 (2017): 25–45.

Frye, Northrop. "The Argument of Comedy." In *English Institute Essays*, edited by Davis Allan Robertson, 58–73. New York: Columbia University Press, 1949.

Fuchs, Cynthia. "Framing and Passing in *Pillow Talk*." In *The Other Fifties: Interrogating Midcentury American Icons*, edited by Joel Foreman, 224–51. Urbana: University of Illinois Press, 1997.

Gaines, Jane Marie, and Charlotte Cornelia Herzog. "Hildy Johnson and the 'Man-Tailored Suit': The Comedy of Inequality." In *Film Reader 5*, 232–46. Evanston: Northwestern University Press, 1982.

Galician, Mary-Lou, and Debra L. Merskin, eds. *Critical Thinking about Sex, Love, and Romance in the Mass Media.* Mahwah, NJ: Lawrence Erlbaum, 2007.

Garlin, Julie C., and Jennifer A. Sandlin. "Happily (N)ever After: The Cruel Optimism of Disney's Romantic Ideal." *Feminist Media Studies* 17, no. 6 (2017): 957–71.

Garrett, Roberta. *Postmodern Chick Flicks: The Return of the Woman's Film*. Basingstoke: Palgrave Macmillan, 2007.

Garwood, Ian. "Must You Remember This?: Orchestrating the 'Standard' Pop Song in *Sleepless in Seattle*." *Screen* 41, no. 3 (Autumn 2000): 282–98.

Gehring, Wes D. *Screwball Comedy: A Genre of Madcap Romance*. New York: Greenwood, 1986.

———. *Romantic vs. Screwball Comedy: Charting the Difference*. New York: Scarecrow, 2002.

Geraghty, Lincoln. "Love's Fantastic Voyage: Crossing between Science Fiction and Romantic Comedy in *Innerspace*." *Extrapolation* 47, no. 1 (2006): 123–33.

Giddens, Anthony. *The Transformation of Intimacy: Sexuality, Love, and Eroticism in Modern Societies*. Stanford, CA: Stanford University Press, 1992.

Gilbert, Joanne. "'My Mom's a Cunt': New Bawds Ride the Fourth Wave." In *Transgressive Humor of American Women Writers*, edited by Sabrina Fuchs Abrams, 203–30. London: Palgrave MacMillan, 2017.

———. *Performing Marginality: Humor, Gender, and Cultural Critique*. Detroit: Wayne State University Press, 1994.

Gilmour, Heather. "Different, Except in a Different Way: Marriage, Divorce, and Gender in the Hollywood Comedy of Remarriage." *Journal of Film and Video* 50, no. 2 (Summer 1998): 26–39.

Glitre, Kathrina. *Hollywood Romantic Comedy: States of the Union, 1934–1965*. Manchester: Manchester University Press, 2006.

———. "Un/true Love: Simulating Authenticity in Contemporary Romantic Comedy." In *Realities and Remediations: The Limits of Representation*, edited by Elizabeth Wells and Tamar Jeffers McDonald, 76–88. Cambridge: Cambridge Scholars, 2007.

Grau, Christopher. "*Eternal Sunshine of the Spotless Mind* and the Morality of Memory." *Journal of Art Aesthetics and Criticism* 64, no. 1 (2006): 119–33.

Greene, Jane M. "Hollywood's Production Code and Thirties Romantic Comedy." *Historical Journal of Film, Radio, and Television* 30, no. 1 (2010): 55–73.

———. "Manners before Morals: Sophisticated Comedy and the Production Code, 1930–1934." *Quarterly Review of Film and Video* 28, no. 3 (2011): 239–56.

———. "A Proper Dash of Spice: Screwball Comedy and the Production Code." *Journal of Film and Video* 63, no. 3 (Fall 2011): 45–63.

———. "The Road to Reno: *The Awful Truth* and the Hollywood Comedy of Remarriage." *Film History* 13, no. 4 (2001): 337–58.

Grindon, Leger. *The Hollywood Romantic Comedy: Conventions, History, and Controversies*. Malden, MA: Wiley-Blackwell, 2011.

———. "Preston Sturges and Screwball Comedy." In *ReFocus: The Films of Preston Sturges*, edited by Jeff Jaeckle and Sarah Kozloff, 25–45. Edinburgh: Edinburgh University Press, 2016.

Guerrasio, Jason. "The Big Hollywood Romantic Comedy is Dead—Here's What Happened to It." Business Insider, August 8, 2017. www.businessinsider.com/why-movie-studios-no-longer-make-romantic-comedies-2017-8?IR=T.

Gwynne, Joel, and Nadine Mueller, eds. *Postfeminism and Contemporary Hollywood Cinema*. Basingstoke: Palgrave Macmillan, 2013.

Haag, Pamela. *Marriage Confidential: Love in the Post-Romantic Age*. New York: Harper Perennial, 2012.

Hachard, Tomas. "When Love Doesn't Last: Richard Linklater's *Before Midnight*." *Los Angeles Review of Books*, May 24, 2013. lareviewofbooks.org/article/when-love-doesnt-last-richard-linklaters-before-midnight/#!.

Harbidge, Leslie. "Redefining Screwball and Reappropriating Liminal Spaces: The Contemporary Bromance and Todd Phillips's *The Hangover* DVD." *Celebrity Studies* 3, no. 1 (2012): 5–16.

Hair, Melissa. "'I'd Like an Abortion Please': Rethinking Unplanned Pregnancy Narratives in Contemporary American Cinema." *Feminist Media Studies* 19, no. 3 (2018): 1–16.

Harrod, Mary. *From France with Love: Gender and Identity in French Romantic Comedy*. London: I. B. Tauris, 2015.

———. "The *Réalisatrice* and the Rom-Com in the 2000s." In "Women's Filmmaking in the 2000s," special issue, *Studies in French Cinema* 12, no. 3 (2012): 227–40.

———. "Sweet Nothings? Imagining the Inexpressible in Contemporary French Romantic Comedy." *Studies in French Cinema* 13, no. 2 (2013): 171–87.

Harrod, Mary, and Katarzyna Paszkiewicz, eds. *Women Do Genre in Film and Television*. London: Routledge, 2017.

Harrod, Mary, Suzanne Leonard, and Diane Negra, eds. *Imagining "We" in the Age of "I": Romance and Social Bonding in Contemporary Culture*. London: Routledge, 2021.

Harvey, James. *Romantic Comedy: In Hollywood from Lubitsch to Sturges*. New York: Alfred A. Knopf, 1987.

Hatch, Kristen. "Girl Meets Boy: Romantic Comedies after Feminism." In *Popping Culture*, edited by Murray Pomerance and John Sakeris, 65–73. 6th ed. New York: Pearson, [2004] 2010.

Hefner, Veronica. "Does Love Conquer All? An Experiment Testing the Association between Types of Romantic Comedy Content and Reports of Romantic Beliefs and Life Satisfaction." *Psychology of Popular Media Culture* 8, no. 4 (October 2019): 376–84.

Hefner, Veronica, and Barbara J. Wilson. "From Love at First Sight to Soul Mate: The Influence of Romantic Ideals in Popular Films on Young People's Beliefs about Relationships." *Communication Monographs* 80, no. 2 (2013): 150–75.

Henderson, Brian. "Romantic Comedy Today: Semi-Tough or Impossible?" *Film Quarterly* 31, no. 4 (Summer 1978): 11–23.

Hersey, Eleanor. "Love and Microphones: Romantic Comedy Heroines as Public Speakers." *Journal of Popular Film and Television* 34, no. 4 (2007): 146–59.

Hettich, Katja. "Re-Orienting Romantic Comedy: Genre Negotiations in Richard Linklater's *Before Sunrise*." In *(Dis)Orienting Media and Narrative Mazes*, edited by Julia Eckel, Bernd Leiendecker, Daniela Olek, and Cristine Piepiorka, 145–64. Bielefeld, GER: transcript Verlag, 2013.

Hobbs, Alex. "Romancing the Crone: Hollywood's Recent Mature Love Stories." *Journal of American Culture* 36, no. 1 (March 2013): 42–51.

Hockley, Luke, and Fadina, Nadi, ed. *The Happiness Illusion: How the Media Sold Us a Fairytale*. London: Routledge, 2015.

Hoerl, Kristen, and Casey Ryan Kelly. "The Post-Nuclear Family and the Depoliticization of Unplanned Pregnancy in *Knocked Up*, *Juno*, and *Waitress*." *Communication and Critical/Cultural Studies* 7, no. 4 (December 2010): 360–80.

Hollinger, Karen. *In the Company of Women: Contemporary Female Friendship Films*. Minneapolis: University of Minnesota Press, 1998.

Holmes, Linda. "Are Romcoms Dead?" National Public Radio, March 4, 2013. www.npr.org/2013/03/04/173424536/are-romantic-comedies-dead?t=1562956633023.

Horn, Katrin. *Women, Camp, and Popular Culture: Serious Excess*. Basingstoke: Palgrave Macmillan, 2017.

Horton, Andrew, and Joanna E. Rapt, eds. *A Companion to Film Comedy*. Malden, MA: Wiley-Blackwell, 2013.

Huls, Alexander. "The Romantic Comedy Is Dying, but Cinematic Romance Is Thriving." *Atlantic*, January 24, 2014. www.theatlantic.com/entertainment/archive/2014/01/the-romantic-comedy-is-dying-but-cinematic-romance-is-thriving/283252.

Illouz, Eva. *Consuming the Romantic Utopia: Love and the Cultural Contradictions of Capitalism*. Berkeley: University of California Press, 1997.

———. *Hard-Core Romance*. Chicago: University of Chicago Press, 2014.
———. *Why Love Hurts: A Sociological Explanation*. London: Polity, 2013.
Jacobs, Diane. *Christmas in July: The Life and Art of Preston Sturges*. Berkeley: University of California Press, 1992.
Jeffers McDonald, Tamar. *Romantic Comedy: Boy Meets Girl Meets Genre*. London: Wallflower, 2007.
———, ed. *Virgin Territory: Representing Sexual Inexperience in Film*. Detroit: Wayne State University Press, 2010.
———. *When Harry Met Sally . . .* London: BFI, 2015.
Jermyn, Deborah. "The Contemptible Realm of the Romcom Queen: Nancy Meyers, Cultural Value, and Romantic Comedy." In *Women Do Genre in Film and Television*, edited by Mary Harrod and Katarzyna Paskiewicz, 57–71. London: Routledge, 2017.
———. "'Glorious, Glamorous, and That Old Standby, Amorous': The Late Blossoming of Diane Keaton's Romantic Comedy Career." *Celebrity Studies* 3, no. 1 (2012): 37–51.
———. "Hollywood's Upper Quadrant Female Audience, *The Intern* (2015), and the Discursive Construction of 'Nancy Meyers.'" *Celebrity Studies* 9, no. 2 (2018): 1–20.
———. *Nancy Meyers*. London: Bloomsbury Academic, 2019.
———. "Unlikely Heroines? 'Women of a Certain Age' and Romantic Comedy." *CineAction* 85 (2011): 26–33.
Jermyn, Deborah, and Janet McCabe. "Sea of Love: Place, Desire, and the Beaches of Romantic Comedy." *Continuum* 27, no. 5 (2013): 603–16.
Johnson, Chandra. "What rom-com failure says about American love lives." *Deseret News*, July 26, 2014. https://www.deseret.com/2014/7/18/20544921/what-rom-com-failure-says-about-american-love-lives.
Johnson, Kimberly R., and Bjarne M. Holmes. "Contradictory Messages: A Content Analysis of Hollywood-Produced Romantic Comedy Feature Films." *Communication Quarterly* 57, no. 3 (2009): 352–73.
Johnson, Merri Lisa, ed. *Third Wave Feminism and Television: Jane Puts It in a Box*. London: I. B. Tauris, 2007.
Julian, Kate. "Why Are Young People Having So Little Sex?" *Atlantic*, December 2018. www.theatlantic.com/magazine/archive/2018/12/the-sex-recession/573949/ (accessed September 11, 2020).
Kaklamanidou, Betty. "Amy Heckerling's Place in Hollywood: Issues of Aging and Sisterhood in *I Could Never Be Your Woman* and *Vamps*." In *ReFocus: The*

Films of Amy Heckerling, edited by Frances Smith and Timothy Shary, 135–54. Edinburgh: Edinburgh University Press, 2016.

———. "'The Bells Are Ringing for Me and My Gal': Marriage and Gender in the Contemporary Greek Romantic Comedy." *Journal of Popular Romance Studies* 2, no. 1 (2011): www.jprstudies.org/2011/10/%e2%80%9c%e2%80%98the-bells-are-ringing-for-me-and-my-gal%e2%80%99-marriage-and-gender-in-the-contemporary-greek-romantic-comedy%e2%80%9d-by-betty-kaklamanidou/.

———. *Genre, Gender, and the Effects of Neoliberalism: The New Millennium Hollywood Rom Com*. London: Routledge, 2015.

———. "Pride and Prejudice: Real vs. Fictional Cougars." In *Female Celebrity and Ageing: Back in the Spotlight*, edited by Deborah Jermyn, 80-91. London: Routledge, 2013.

———. "The Romantico-Sexual Narrative and Intertextuality in *Friends with Benefits* and *No Strings Attached*." In *The Millennials on Film and Television: The Politics of Popular Culture*, edited by Betty Kaklamanidou and Margaret Tally, 155–69. Jefferson, NC: McFarland, 2014.

Kaling, Mindy. "Flick Chicks." *New Yorker*, October 3, 2011. newyorker.com/humor/2011/10/03/111003sh_shouts_kaling.

Karlyn, Kathleen Rowe. *Unruly Girls, Unrepentant Mothers: Redefining Feminism on Screen*. Austin: University of Texas Press, 2011.

———. *The Unruly Woman: Gender and the Genres of Laughter*. Austin: University of Texas Press, 1995.

Karnick, Kristine Brunovska, and Henry Jenkins, eds. *Classical Hollywood Comedy*. London: Routledge, 1995.

Keller, Jessalynn, and Maureen E. Ryan, eds. *Emergent Feminisms: Complicating a Postfeminist Media Culture*. London: Routledge, 2018.

Kendall, Elizabeth. *The Runaway Bride: Hollywood Romantic Comedy of the 1930s*. New York: Doubleday, 1990.

King, Geoff. *Film Comedy*. London: Wallflower, 2002.

Kipnis, Laura. *Against Love: A Polemic*. New York: Pantheon, 2003.

Kirkland, Ewan. "Romantic Comedy and the Construction of Heterosexuality." *Scope: An Online Journal of Film Studies* 9 (October 2007): www.nottingham.ac.uk/scope/documents/2007/october-2007/kirkland.pdf (accessed September 11, 2020).

Klinenberg, Eric. *Going Solo: The Extraordinary Rise and Surprising Appeal of Living Alone*. London: Duckworth Overlook, 2012.

Knadler, Steven. "Blanca from the Block: Whiteness and the Transnational Latina Body." *Genders* 41 (2005): www.colorado.edu/gendersarchive1998-2013/2005/03/01/blanca-block-whiteness-and-transnational-latina-body (accessed September 11, 2020).

Kord, Susanne, and Elisabeth Krimmer. *Hollywood Divas, Indie Queens and TV Heroines: Contemporary Screen Images of Women*. Oxford: Rowman & Littlefield, 2005.

Koresky, Michael. "*Before Sunset*." *Reverse Shot*, January 4, 2005. www.reverseshot.org/reviews/entry/1078/before-sunset.

Kozloff, Sarah. "About a Clueless Boy and Girl: Voice-Over Narration in Contemporary Romantic Comedy." *Cinephile* 8, no. 1 (Spring 2012): 5–13.

Krämer, Peter. "A Powerful Cinema-going Force? Hollywood and Female Audiences Since the 1960s." In *Identifying Hollywood's Audiences: Cultural Identity and the Movies*, edited by Melvyn Stokes and Richard Maltby, 93–108. London: BFI, 1999.

Krefting, Rebecca. *All Joking Aside: American Humor and Its Discontents*. Baltimore: Johns Hopkins University Press, 2014.

Krutnik, Frank. "Conforming Passions? Contemporary Romantic Comedy." In *Genre and Contemporary Hollywood*, edited by Steve Neale, 130–47. London: BFI, 2002.

———. "The Faint Aroma of Performing Seals: The 'Nervous' Romance and the Comedy of the Sexes." *Velvet Light Trap* 26 (Fall 1990): 57–72.

Laine, Tarja. "Not Quite Romantic Comedy." In *Gender: Laughter*, edited by Bettina Papenburg, 55–69. Farmington Hills, MI: Macmillan Reference, 2017.

Landay, Lori. *Madcaps, Screwballs, and Con Women: The Female Trickster in American Culture*. Philadelphia: University of Pennsylvania Press, 1998.

Lang, Robert. *Masculine Interests: Homoerotics in Hollywood Film*. New York: Columbia University Press, 2002.

Lapsley, Robert, and Michael Westlake. "From *Casablanca* to *Pretty Woman*: The Politics of Romance." In *Contemporary Film Theory*, edited by Anthony Easthope, 179–203. London: Longman, 1993.

Leach, Jim. "The Screwball Comedy." In *Film Genre: Theory and Criticism*, edited by Barry Keith Grant, 75–89. Metuchen, NJ: Scarecrow, 1977.

Leadston, Mackenzie. "Happily Never After: The Visual Politics of Contemporary French Interracial Romantic Comedy." *Studies in French Cinema* 19, issue 4 (2019): 335–52.

Lent, Tina Olsen. "Romantic Love and Friendship: The Redefinition of Gender Relations in Screwball Comedy." In *Classical Hollywood Comedy*, edited by Kristine Brunovska Karnick and Henry Jenkins, 314–31. London: Routledge, 1995.

Leonard, Suzanne. *Wife, Inc.: The Business of Marriage in the Twenty-First Century*. New York: New York University Press, 2018.

Lesage, Julia. "The Hegemonic Female Fantasy in *An Unmarried Woman* and *Craig's Wife*." *Film Reader* 5, 83–94. Evanston: Northwestern University Press, 1982.

Le Vine, Lauren. "Sorry, Movies, We're Just Not That into You—TV Is Now the Place to Go for Great Romcoms." Refinery29, April 7, 2016. www.refinery29.com/en-us/2016/04/107558/romantic-comedies-tv-shows-movies.

Levy, Ariel. *Female Chauvinist Pigs: Women and The Rise of Raunch Culture*. New York: Simon & Schuster, 2005.

Lewis, Jon. *The Road to Romance and Ruin: Teen Films and Youth Culture*. London: Routledge, 1992.

Lippman, Julia R. "I Did It Because I Never Stopped Loving You: The Effects of Media Portrayals of Persistent Pursuit on Beliefs about Stalking." *Communication Research* 45, no. 3 (2018): 1–28.

Logan, Elizabeth. "Why Is It So Wrong to Love Romantic Comedies?" *Glamour*, February 14, 2017. www.glamour.com/story/why-is-it-so-wrong-to-love-romantic-comedies.

Lotz, Amanda D. "Linking Industrial and Creative Change in 21st-Century U.S. Television." *Media International Australia* 164, no. 1 (May 2017): 10–20.

MacDowell, James. "Romantic Comedy: Love, Nervousness, and Intertextuality." Alternate Takes, February 15, 2009. www.alternatetakes.co.uk/?2009%2C2%2C222.

———. *Happy Endings in Hollywood Cinema: Cliché, Convention, and the Final Couple*. Edinburgh: Edinburgh University Press, 2013.

Madison, D. Soyini. "*Pretty Woman* through the Triple Lens of Black Feminist Spectatorship." In *From Mouse to Mermaid: The Politics of Film, Gender, and Culture*, edited by Elizabeth Bell, Lynda Haas, and Laura Sells, 224–35. Bloomington: Indiana University Press, 1995.

Maerz, Melissa. "On *A to Z, Manhattan Love Story*, and the State of the Rom-Sitcom." *Entertainment Weekly*, October 2, 2014. ew.com/article/2014/10/02/this-falls-rom-sitcoms-feel-like-throwbacks-and-not-in-a-good-way/.

Maltby, Richard "*It Happened One Night*: The Recreation of the Patriarchy." In *Frank Capra: Authorship and the Studio System*, edited by Robert Sklar and Vita Zagarrio, 130–63. Philadelphia: Temple University Press, 1998.

Manley, Sebastian. "Hal Hartley's Romantic Comedy." In *The Cinema of Hal Hartley: Flirting with Formalism*, edited by Steven Rybin, 77–93. New York: Columbia University Press, 2017.

Marantz Cohen, Paula. "What Have Clothes Got to Do with It? Romantic Comedy and the Female Gaze." *Southwest Review* 85, nos. 1–2 (2010): 78–88.

Marks, Peter. "'Are These Feelings Even Real?' Intimacy and Authenticity in Spike Jonze's *Her*." In *ReFocus: The Films of Spike Jonze*, edited by Kim Wilkins and Wyatt Moss-Wellington, 139–57. Edinburgh: Edinburgh University Press, 2019.

Marshall, Kelli. "*Something's Gotta Give* and the Classic Screwball Comedy." *Journal of Popular Film and Television* 37, no. 1 (2009): 9–15.

Martin, Adrian. "In the Mood for (Something Like) Love: The Situation of the Romcom Today." *Cinéaste* 39, no. 1 (Winter 2013): 16–20.

Martin, Alfred L., Jr. "It's (Not) in His Kiss: Gay Kisses, Narrative Strategies, and Camera Angles in Post-Network Television Comedy." *Flow Journal* 25 (2012): www.flowjournal.org/2012/09/it%E2%80%99s-not-in-his-kiss-gay/ (accessed September 11, 2020).

Marx, Nick, and Matt Sienkiewicz, eds. *The Comedy Studies Reader*. Austin: University of Texas Press, 2018.

Mather, Nigel. *Tears of Laughter: Comedy-Drama in 1990s British Cinema*. Edinburgh: Edinburgh University Press, 2006.

May, Elaine Tyler. "Explosive Issues: Sex, Women, and the Bomb." In *Homeward Bound: American Families in the Postwar Era*, 89–108. New York: Basic Books, 1988.

———. *Great Expectations: Marriage and Divorce in Post-Victorian America*. Chicago: University of Chicago Press, 1980.

McCallum, Ellen. "Mother Talk: Maternal Masquerade and the Problem of the Single Girl." *Camera Obscura* 42 (1999): 71–94.

McGilligan, Patrick. *George Cukor: A Double Life*. New York: St. Martin's, 1991.

McRobbie, Angela. "Postfeminism and Popular Culture." *Feminist Media Studies* 4, no. 3 (2004): 255–64.

McWilliam, Kelly. "Girl Meets Girl: Sexual Sitings in Lesbian Romantic Comedies." In *Intimate Relationships in Cinema, Literature, and Visual Culture*, edited by Gilad Padva and Nurit Buchweitz, 145–55. London: Palgrave Macmillan, 2017.

Mellencamp, Patricia. "Situation Comedy, Feminism, and Freud: Discourses of Gracie and Lucy." In *Studies in Entertainment: Critical Approaches to Mass Culture*, vol. 7, edited by Tania Modleski, 80–95. Bloomington: Indiana University Press, 1986.

Meriwether, Liz. "Sex Is Funny. Love Is Funny. So Where Are All Our Great Romantic Comedies?" The Cut, September 8, 2016. www.thecut.com/2016/09/where-are-all-the-great-new-romantic-comedies.html.

Meyer, Richard. "Rock Hudson's Body." In *Inside/Out: Lesbian Theories, Gay Theories*, edited by Diana Fuss, 258–88. London: Routledge, 1991.

Mirza, Candace. "The Collective Spirit of Revolt: An Historical Reading of *Holiday*." *Wide Angle* 12, no. 3 (July 1990): 98–116.

Mizejewski, Linda. "Queen Latifah, Unruly Women, and the Bodies of Romantic Comedy." *Genders* (October 2007): https://www.colorado.edu/gendersarchive1998-2013/2007/10/01/queen-latifah-unruly-women-and-bodies-romantic-comedy (accessed September 11, 2020).

———. *Pretty/Funny: Women Comedians and Body Politics*. Austin: University of Texas Press, 2014.

Mizejewski, Linda, ed. *Hysterical!: Women in American Comedy*. Austin: University of Texas Press, 2017.

Moddelmog, Debra A. "Can Romantic Comedy Be Gay? Hollywood Romance, Citizenship, and Same-Sex Marriage Panic." *Journal of Popular Film & Television* 36, no. 4 (2009): 162–73.

Modleski, Tania. "An Affair to Forget: Melancholia in Bromantic Comedy." *Camera Obscura* 29, no. 2 (2014): 119–47.

———. *Feminism without Women: Culture and Criticism in a "Postfeminist" Age*. London: Routledge, 1994.

———. *Loving with a Vengeance: Mass-Produced Fantasies for Women*. London: Routledge, 1999.

Morris, Wesley. "Rom-Coms Were Corny and Retrograde. Why Do I Miss Them so Much?" *New York Times Magazine*, April 24, 2019. www.nytimes.com/2019/04/24/magazine/romantic-comedy-movies.html.

Morrison, Aimée. "Newfangled Computers and Old-Fashioned Romantic Comedy: *You've Got Mail*'s Futuristic Nostalgia." *Canadian Journal of Film Studies* 19, no. 1 (March 2010): 41–58.

Morrissey, Katherine E. "From Crazy Rich Asians to Netflix: The 'Rebirth' of Romantic Comedies, Parts I and II." Flow, November 4, 2019, www.flowjournal.org/2019/11/rebirth-of-romantic-comedies/; and February 3, 2020, www.flowjournal.org/2020/02/from-crazy-rich-asians-to-netflix/.

Mortimer, Claire. *Romantic Comedy*. London: Routledge, 2010.

Moss-Wellington, Wyatt. "The Emotional Politics of Limerence in Romantic Comedy Films." NECSUS: *European Journal of Media Studies* 8, no. 1 (2019): 191–209.

Mulvey, Laura. *Visual and Other Pleasures*. Basingstoke.: Palgrave Macmillan, 1989.

Mundy, John, and Glyn White. "The Romantic Comedy Film." In *Laughing Matters: Understanding Film, Television, and Radio Comedy*, 65–80. Manchester: Manchester University Press, 2012.

Musser, Charles. "Divorce, DeMille, and the Comedy of Remarriage." In *Classical Hollywood Comedy*, edited by Kristina Brunovska Karnick and Henry Jenkins, 282–313. London: Routledge, 2015.

Napier, Susan J. "Carnival and Conservatism in Romantic Comedy." In *Anime from Akira to Princess Mononoke: Experiencing Contemporary Japanese Animation*, 139–56. Basingstoke: Palgrave Macmillan, 2001.

Nash, Meredith, and Imelda Whelehan, eds. *Reading Lena Dunham's* Girls: *Feminism, Postfeminism, Authenticity, and Gendered Performance in Contemporary Television*. Basingstoke: Palgrave Macmillan, 2017.

Neale, Steve. "The Big Romance or Something Wild? Romantic Comedy Today." *Screen* 33, no 3 (Autumn 1992): 284–99.

———. "Masculinity as Spectacle: Reflections on Men and Mainstream Cinema." In *Screening the Male: Exploring Masculinities in Hollywood Cinema*, edited by Steven Cohan and Ina Rae Hark, 9–20. London: Routledge, 1992.

Negra, Diane. "Age Disproportion in the Post-Epitaph Chick Flick: Reading *The Proposal*." In *Cross-Generational Relationships and Cinema*, edited by Joel Gwynne and Niall Richardson, 55–77. Cham, CH: Palgrave Macmillan, 2020.

———. "Structural Integrity, Historical Reversion, and the Post-9/11 Chick Flick." *Feminist Media Studies* 8, no. 1 (March 2008): 51–68.

———. "Where the Boys Are: Postfeminism and the New Single Man." *Flow* 4, no. 3 (2006): flowtv.org/?p=223 (accessed September 11, 2020).

Negra, Diane, and Yvonne Tasker, eds. *Gendering the Recession: Media and Culture in an Age of Austerity*. Durham, NC: Duke University Press, 2014.

———. *Interrogating Postfeminism: Gender and the Politics of Popular Culture.* Durham, NC: Duke University Press, 2007.

———. "Neoliberal Frames and Genres of Inequality: Recession-era Chick Flicks and Male-Centred Corporate Melodrama." *European Journal of Cultural Studies* 16, no. 3 (2013): 344–61.

Ng, Kenny K. K. "The Romantic Comedies of Cathay/MP&GI in the 1950s and 60s: Language, Locality, and Urban Character." *Jump Cut* 49 (Spring 2007): www.ejumpcut.org/archive/jc49.2007/Ng-Cathay/ (accessed September 11, 2020).

Nicholson, Amy. "Who Killed the Romantic Comedy?" *L.A. Weekly*, February 27, 2014. www.laweekly.com/news/who-killed-the-romantic-comedy-4464884.

Nochimson, Martha P. *Screen Couple Chemistry: The Power of 2.* Austin: University of Texas Press, 2002.

The Numbers. "Box Office History for Romantic Comedy." Accessed September 11, 2020. www.the-numbers.com/market/genre/Romantic-Comedy.

Oria, Beatriz. "'I'm Taken . . . by Myself': Romantic Crisis in the Self-Centered Indie Rom-Com." *Journal of Film and Video* 72 (2020): forthcoming.

———. "Love Is a Man's Thing: Hollywood and the Spanish 'Homme-com.'" *Journal of Popular Film and Television* 43, issue 1 (2015): 28–38.

———. "Love on the Margins: The American Indie Rom-com of the 2010s." *Atlantis: Journal of the Spanish Association for Anglo-American Studies* 40, no. 2 (2018): 145–67.

———. *Talking Dirty on* Sex and the City: *Romance, Intimacy, Friendship*. Lanham, MD: Rowman & Littlefield, 2014.

———. "Television to the Rescue of Romantic Comedy: *Sex and the City*'s Revitalisation of the Genre at the Turn of the Millennium." *International Journal of Interdisciplinary Social Sciences* 5, no. 11 (2011): 127–38.

Ostrowska, Elżbieta. "Corporations of Feelings: Romantic Comedy in the Age of Neoliberalism." In *Contemporary Cinema and Neoliberal Ideology*, edited by Ewa Mazierska and Lars Kristensen, 185–201. London: Routledge, 2017.

———. "Emotional Investments: Contemporary Polish Romantic Comedy and Neoliberalism." *Literatura i Kultura Popularna* 24 (2018): 143–53.

Paul, William. *Ernst Lubitsch's American Comedy.* New York: Columbia University Press, 1983.

———. "The Impossibility of Romance: Hollywood Comedy, 1978–99." In *Genre and Contemporary Hollywood*, edited by Steve Neale, 117–29. London: BFI, 2002.

———. *Laughing Screaming: Modern Hollywood Horror and Comedy*. New York: Columbia University Press, 1994.

Petersen, Anne Helen. *Too Fat, Too Slutty, Too Loud: The Rise and Reign of the Unruly Woman*. New York: Plume, 2017.

Pinazza, Natália. "Self-referentiality and Neoliberalism in Contemporary Argentine Cinema." *New Review of Film and Television Studies* 17, issue 3 (2019): 315–30.

Poague, Leland A., and Karyn Kay. "A Short Defense of Screwball Comedy." *Film Quarterly* 29, no. 4 (Summer 1976): 62–64.

Pomerance, Murray, ed. *The Last Laugh: Strange Humors of Cinema*. Detroit: Wayne State University Press, 2013.

Potter, Cherry. *I Love You But . . . : Romance, Comedy, and the Movies*. London: Methuen, 2002.

Povinelli, Elizabeth. *The Empire of Love: Toward a Theory of Intimacy, Genealogy, and Carnality*. Durham, NC: Duke University Press, 2006.

Prado, Ignacio M. Sánchez. "Humorous Affects: Romantic Comedies in Contemporary Mexico." In *Humor in Latin American Cinema*, edited by Juan Poblete and Juana Suárez, 203–22. Basingstoke: Palgrave Macmillan, 2016.

———. "Publicists in Love: Romantic Comedy, Cinema Privitization, and the Aesthetics of the Middle Class." In *Screening Neoliberalism: Transforming Mexican Cinema, 1988–2012*, 61–104. Nashville: Vanderbilt University Press, 2015.

Preston, Catherine L. "Hanging on a Star: The Resurrection of the Romance Film in the 1990s." In *Genre 2000*, edited by Wheeler Winston Dixon, 227–44. Albany, NY: SUNY Press, 2000.

Quinn, Emelia Jane. "No Country for Queer Dogs: Veganism in the Contemporary Hollywood Romantic Comedy." *Society & Animals* 24, no. 5 (2016): 507–21.

Rabin, Nathan. "I'm Sorry for Coining the Phrase 'Manic Pixie Dream Girl.'" Salon, July 15, 2014. www.salon.com/2014/07/15/im_sorry_for_coining_the_phrase_manic_pixie_dream_girl.

Radner, Hilary. *Neo-Feminist Cinema: Girly Films, Chick Flicks, and Consumer Culture*. London: Routledge, 2011.

———. "'Pretty Is as Pretty Does': Free Enterprise and the Marriage Plot." In *Film Theory Goes to the Movies*, edited by Jim Collins, Hilary Radner and Ava Preacher Collins, 56–76. New York: Routledge, 1993.

———. *Shopping Around: Feminine Culture and the Pursuit of Pleasure*. New York: Routledge, 1995.

Radner, Hilary, and Rebecca Stringer, eds. *Feminism at the Movies*. London: Routledge, 2011.

Radway, Janice A. *Reading the Romance: Women, Patriarchy and Popular Literature*. Chapel Hill: University of North Carolina Press, 1984.

Rayns, Tony. "Funny Valentines: Mating Rituals and Alternate Realities in the Films of Hong Sangsoo." *Film Comment* 51, no. 3 (May–June 2015): 54–57.

Rennett, Michael. "Bros, BFFs, and the New Romantic Foil: Homosocial Relationships in the Emerging Adult Film." *Quarterly Review of Film and Video* 32, no. 6 (2015): 568–83.

Rickman, Gregg, ed. *The Film Comedy Reader*. New York: Limelight, 2004.

Ritrosky-Winslow, Madelyn. "Colin & Renée & Mark & Bridget: The Intertextual Crowd." *Quarterly Review of Film and Video* 23 (2006): 237–56.

Ross, Sheryl Tuttle. "*(500) Days of Summer*: A Postmodern Romantic Comedy?" *Aesthetics and Gender* 41, no. 2 (2016): 155–76.

Rubinfeld, Mark D. *Bound to Bond: Gender, Genre, and the Hollywood Romantic Comedy*. New York: Praeger, 2001.

Rubinstein, Eliot. "The End of Screwball Comedy: *The Lady Eve* and *The Palm Beach Story*." *Post Script* 1, no. 3 (Spring–Summer 1982): 33–47.

Ruiz, Manuela. "Addicted to Fun: Courtship, Play, and Romance in the Screwball Comedy." *Revista alicantina de estudios ingleses* no. 13 (November 2000): 153–60.

———. "Cosmopolitan Spaces and Generic Boundaries in Hollywood Overseas Romances." In *Culture, Space, and Power: Blurred Lines*, 139–60. Lanham, MD: Lexington, 2016.

———. *Hollywood Romantic Comedies of the Fifties: A Critical Study of a Film Genre*. Lewiston, NY: Edwin Mellen, 2013.

Ruti, Mari. *Feminist Film Theory and* Pretty Woman. New York: Bloomsbury Academic, 2016.

Rybin, Steven. *Gestures of Love: Romancing Performance in Classical Hollywood Cinema*. Albany, NY: SUNY Press, 2017.

San Filippo, Maria. "More Than Buddies: *Wedding Crashers* and the Bromance as Comedy of (Re)Marriage Equality." In *Millennial Masculinity: Men in Contemporary American Cinema*, edited by Timothy Shary, 181–99. Detroit: Wayne State University Press, 2013.

———, ed. "Radical Romantic Comedy," special issue of *New Review of Film and Television Studies* 18, no. 1 (2020): www.tandfonline.com/toc/rfts20/18/1?nav=tocList.

Saraiya, Sonia. "The Rise of the Rom-Sitcom." AV Club, September 11, 2014. tv.avclub.com/the-rise-of-the-rom-sitcom-1798271986.

Scala, Elizabeth. "Pretty Women: The Romance of the Fair Unknown, Feminism, and Contemporary Romantic Comedy." *Film & History: An Interdisciplinary Journal of Film and Television Studies* 29, nos. 1–2 (1999): 34–45.

Scharff, Christina. *Repudiating Feminism: Young Women in a Neoliberal World.* Burlington, VT: Ashgate, 2012.

Schreiber, Michele. *American Postfeminist Cinema: Women, Romance, and Contemporary Culture.* Edinburgh: University of Edinburgh Press, 2014.

———. "'Misty Water-Colored Memories of the Way We Were . . .': Postfeminist Nostalgia in Contemporary Romance Narratives." In *Reclaiming the Archive: Feminism and Film History*, edited by Vicki Callahan, 264–83. Detroit: Wayne State University Press, 2010.

Schweitzer, Dahlia. "*The Mindy Project*: Or Why 'I'm The Mary, You're The Rhoda' Is the RomComSitCom's Most Revealing Accusation." *Journal of Popular Film and Television* 43, issue 2 (2015): 63–69.

Scodari, Christine. "Possession, Attraction, and the Thrill of the Chase: Gendered Myth-Making in Film and Television Comedy of the Sexes." *Critical Studies in Mass Communication* 12 (1995): 23–39.

Seidman, Steven. *Romantic Longings: Love in America, 1830–1980.* London: Routledge, 1991.

Sennett, Ted. *Lunatics and Lovers.* New York: Limelight, 1985.

Seppälä, Jaakko. "Contesting Marriage: The Finnish Unromantic Comedy." In *Nordic Genre Film: Small-Nation Film Cultures in the Global Marketplace*, edited by Tommy Gustafsson and Pietari Kääpä, 159–72. Edinburgh: Edinburgh University Press, 2015.

Shary, Timothy. "Buying Me Love: 1980s Class-Clash Teen Romances." *Journal of Popular Culture* 44, no. 3 (2011): 563–82.

Shearer, Martha. "Frances Doesn't Live Here Anymore: Gender, Crisis, and the Creative City in *Frances Ha* and *The Giant Mechanical Man*." In *The City in American Cinema: Film and Postindustrial Culture*, edited by Johan Andersson and Lawrence Webb, 351–73. London: Bloomsbury, 2019.

Shields, Meg. "The Romantic Comedy Ideology." Film School Rejects, July 17, 2018. filmschoolrejects.com/romantic-comedy-ideology/.

Shumway, David R. *Modern Love: Romance, Intimacy, and the Marriage Crisis.* New York: New York University Press, 2003.

———. "Screwball Comedies: Constructing Romance, Mystifying Marriage." In *The Film Genre Reader*, 3rd ed., edited by Barry Keith Grant, 396–416. Austin: University of Texas Press, 2003.

Sickels, Robert C. "'We're in a tight spot!': The Coen Brothers' Screwy Romantic Comedies." *Journal of Popular Film and Television* 36, no. 3 (2008): 114–22.

Siede, Carolyn. "When Romance Met Comedy." AV Club, September 28, 2018. www.avclub.com/romantic-comedies-briefly-came-out-of-the-closet-with-1829155199.

Siegel, Carol. "Two Funerals and a Wedding: Not So Nice Jewish Girls in *Transparent* and *Broad City*." In *Intercourse in Television and Film: The Presentation of Explicit Sex Acts*, edited by Lindsay Coleman and Carol Siegel, 157–78. Lanham, MD: Lexington, 2017.

Siegel, Tatiana. "R.I.P. Romantic Comedies: Why Harry Wouldn't Meet Sally in 2013." *Hollywood Reporter*, September 26, 2013. www.hollywoodreporter.com/news/rip-romantic-comedies-why-harry-634776.

Sikov, Ed. *Screwball: Hollywood's Madcap Romantic Comedies*. New York: Crown, 1989.

———. *Laughing Hysterically: American Screen Comedy of the 1950s*. New York: Columbia University Press, 1994.

Sinowitz, Michael. "Elmore Leonard and the Romantic Comedy, or 'Get Some Love into It.'" In *Critical Essays on Elmore Leonard: If It Sounds Like Writing*, edited by Charles J. Rzepka, 27–39. Hoboken, NJ: John Wiley & Sons, 2020.

Smith, Frances. *Rethinking the Hollywood Teen Movie: Gender, Genre, and Identity*. Edinburgh: Edinburgh University Press, 2017.

———. "'Time of My Life?' The Afterlife of *Dirty Dancing* in the Contemporary Romantic Comedy." *Soundtrack* 7, no. 2 (October 2014): 67–78.

Smith, Richard. "The 'tedious yammering of selves': The End of Intimacy in Spike Jonze's *Her*." In *ReFocus: The Films of Spike Jonze*, edited by Kim Wilkins and Wyatt Moss-Wellington, 175–92. Edinburgh: Edinburgh University Press, 2019.

Soles, Carter. "Team Apatow and the Tropes of Geek-Centered Romantic Comedy." *Bright Lights Film Journal* (2013): brightlightsfilm.com/team-apatow-and-the-tropes-of-geek-centered-romantic-comedy/#.XtVihcZ7ldg.

Spicer, Andrew. "The Reluctance to Commit: Hugh Grant and the New British Romantic Comedy." In *The Trouble with Men: Masculinities in European and Hollywood Cinema*, edited by Phil Powrie, Ann Davies, and Bruce Babington, 77–89. London: Wallflower, 2004.

Stacey, Jackie. "Desperately Seeking Difference." *Screen* 28, no. 1 (January 1987): 48–61.

Stacey, Jackie, and Lynne Pearce, eds. *Romance Revisited*. London: Lawrence & Wishart, 1995.

Staff, "Romantic-Comedy Behavior Gets Real-Life Man Arrested." *Onion*, April 7, 1999. local.theonion.com/romantic-comedy-behavior-gets-real-life-man-arrested-1819565117.

Straayer, Chris. "Redressing the 'Natural': The Temporary Transvestite Film." In *Film Genre Reader IV*, edited by Barry Keith Grant, 417–42. Austin: University of Texas Press, 2012.

Sweeney, Gael. "Beyond Golden Gardenias: Versions of Same-Sex Marriage in *Queer as Folk*." In *Queer TV in the 21st Century: Essays on Broadcasting from Taboo to Acceptance*, edited by Kylo-Patrick R. Hart, 41–61. Jefferson, NC: McFarland, 2016.

———. "The Man in the Pink Shirt: Actor Hugh Grant and British Masculinity." *CineAction* (Spring 2001): 57–67.

Symons, Alex. "The Problem of 'High Culture' Comedy: How *Annie Hall* (1977) Complicated Woody Allen's Reputation." *Journal of Popular Film & Television* 41, no. 3 (July 2013): 118–27.

Tasker, Yvonne. *Working Girls: Gender and Sexuality in Popular Cinema*. London: Routledge, 1998.

Taylor, Aaron. "New Media and the Solipsistic Romantic Comedy." IndieWire, May 30, 2014. www.indiewire.com/2014/05/new-media-and-the-solipsistic-romantic-comedy-133439/.

Taylor, Anthea. *Single Women in Popular Culture: The Limits of Postfeminism*. Basingstoke: Palgrave Macmillan, 2012.

Thoma, Pamela. "Buying Up Baby: Modern Feminine Subjectivity, Assertions of 'Choice,' and the Repudiation of Reproductive Justice in Postfeminist Unwanted Pregnancy Films." *Feminist Media Studies* 9, no. 4 (2009): 409–25.

Thomas, Deborah. *Beyond Genre: Melodrama, Comedy, and Romance in Hollywood Films*. Galloway: Cameron & Hollis, 2000.

Thompson, Kristin. "Lubitsch, Acting, and the Silent Romantic Comedy." *Film History* 13, no. 4 (2001): 390–408.

Thumim, Janet. "'Miss Hepburn Is Humanized': The Star Persona of Katharine Hepburn." *Feminist Review* 24 (Autumn 1986): 71–102.

Todd, Drew. "Decadent Heroes: Dandyism and Masculinity in Art Deco Hollywood." *Journal of Popular Film & Television* 32, no. 4 (Winter 2005): 168–81.

Traister, Rebecca. *All the Single Ladies: Unmarried Women and the Rise of an Independent Nation*. New York: Simon & Schuster, 2016.

Tropiano, Stephen. *The Prime Time Closet: A History of Gays and Lesbians on TV*. New York: Applause Theatre & Cinema, 2002.

VanDerWerff, Emily. "Why Romantic Comedies Matter." Vox, August 29, 2018. www.vox.com/culture/2018/8/29/17769168/romantic-comedies-crazy-rich-asians-all-the-boys-set-it-up.

Wanzo, Rebecca. "Precarious-Girl Comedy: Issa Rae, Lena Dunham, and Abjection Aesthetics." *Camera Obscura* 31, no. 2 (2016): 26–59.

Webb, Lawrence. "When Harry Met Siri: Digital Romcom and the Global City in Spike Jonze's *Her*." In *Global Cinematic Cities: New Landscapes of Film and Media*, edited by Johan Andersson and Lawrence Webb, 95–118. London: Wallflower, 2016.

Wexman, Virginia Wright. *Creating the Couple: Love, Marriage, and Hollywood Performance*. Princeton, NJ: Princeton University Press, 1993.

White, R. S. *Romantic Comedy in Shakespeare's Cinema of Love: A Study in Genre and Influence*. Manchester: Manchester University Press, 2020.

Willett, Cynthia, Julie Willett, and Yael D. Sherman. "The Seriously Erotic Politics of Feminist Laughter." *Social Research* 79, no. 1 (Spring 2012): 217–46.

Wilkie, Ian, ed. *The Routledge Comedy Studies Reader*. London: Routledge, 2019.

Winch, Alison. "We Can Have It All: The Girlfriend Flick." *Feminist Media Studies* 12, no. 1 (2012): 69–82.

———. *Girlfriends and Postfeminist Sisterhood*. Basingstoke: Palgrave Macmillan, 2013.

Wolf, Susan, and Christopher Grau, eds. *Understanding Love: Philosophy, Film, and Fiction*. Oxford: Oxford University Press, 2014.

Wood, Robin. "Screwball and the Masquerade: *The Lady Eve* and *Two-Faced Woman*." *CineAction* 54 (2001): 12–19.

———. *Sexual Politics and Narrative Film: Hollywood and Beyond*. New York: Columbia University Press, 1998.

Woods, Faye. "*Girls* Talk: Authorship and Authenticity in the Reception of Lena Dunham's *Girls*." *Critical Studies in Television* 10, no. 2 (Summer 2015): 37–54.

———. "Too Close for Comfort: Direct Address and the Affective Pull of the Confessional Comic Woman in *Chewing Gum* and *Fleabag*." *Communication, Culture, and Critique* 12, no. 2 (2019): 194–212.

Yahr, Emily. "The Rom-Com Is Dead. Good." *Washington Post*, October 8, 2016. www.washingtonpost.com/lifestyle/style/the-rom-com-is-dead-good/2016/

10/06/6d82a934-859c-11e6-ac72-a29979381495_story.html?utm_term= .d635325b91b2.

York, Ashley Elaine. "From Chick Flicks to Millennial Blockbusters: Spinning Female-Driven Narratives into Franchises." *Journal of Popular Culture*, 43. no. 1 (2010): 3–25.

Young, Kay. "Hollywood, 1934: 'Inventing' Romantic Comedy." In *Look Who's Laughing: Studies in Gender and Comedy*, edited by Gail Finney, 257–74. Langhorne, PA: Gordon & Breach, 1994.

Yusoff, Norman. "Genre and Pleasure: The Case of Malay(sian) Romantic Comedy." *Jurnal Skrin* 1 (2004): 23–38.

Zarum, Lara. "Trendspotting: Old-Age Romance on TV." Flavorwire, August 4, 2016. flavorwire.com/584832/trendspotting-old-age-romance-on-tv.

Contributors

JOHN ALBERTI is professor of English and chair of the English Department at Northern Kentucky University, where he teaches classes on cinema studies, writing studies, and American literature. He has published on the pedagogy of multicultural literature, class issues in higher education, the crisis of gender in relation to the contemporary romantic comedy, *The Simpsons* as oppositional culture, and writing in the digital age. He is the author of *Masculinity in the Contemporary Romantic Comedy: Gender as Genre* (Routledge, 2013) and *Screen Ages: A Survey of American Cinema* (Routledge, 2015), and a coeditor of an essay collection on the adaption of the *Harry Potter* series, *Transforming Harry: The Adaptation of Harry Potter in the Transmedia Age* (Wayne State University Press, 2018).

ELIZABETH ALSOP is assistant professor of communication and media at the CUNY School of Professional Studies. Her essays have previously appeared in *Feminist Media Studies*, the *Journal of Film and Video*, the *Velvet Light Trap*, *Adaptation*, and the *Quarterly Review of Film and Video*, and she has also written about film and television for the *Atlantic*, *Los Angeles Review of Books*, and *New York Times Magazine*. Her current book project explores American television aesthetics in the postnetwork era.

TOM CUNLIFFE is an early career researcher and has taught film studies at SOAS University of London; Goldsmiths, University of London; and King's College London. He is currently working on a monograph titled *Lung Kong and a Cinema of Ethical Imagination* and is co-editing a special issue of the *Journal of Chinese Cinemas* on the topic of the politics of Hong Kong leftwing cinema, 1950s–1970s. His essays have appeared in journals including *Framework* and *Screen*.

Ash Kinney d'Harcourt completed their PhD in cognitive psychology at the University of Texas at Austin and is currently pursuing a doctorate in the department of Radio-Television-Film. Their writing has appeared in *Flow*, the university's online media and culture journal, and their research interests include queer and feminist media studies, media representation of identity, television genre, and celebrity culture.

Alice Guilluy is course leader of the BA (Hons.) in Filmmaking at the London Film Academy. Her research interests include audience studies and research methods, popular cinema, and gender and representation. She is currently working on *Guilty Pleasures? European Audiences and Contemporary Hollywood Romantic Comedy* (Bloomsbury Academic, forthcoming) and has recently published in the *Bulletin of Sociological Methodology* and the edited collection *Love Across the Atlantic* (Edinburgh University Press, 2020).

Mary Harrod is associate professor in French studies at the University of Warwick. Much of her research to date has focused on gender- and cultural-studies approaches to popular (trans)national genres, especially in France and Hollywood. Complementing numerous journal articles and book chapters, her book publications comprise the monograph *From France with Love: Gender and Identity in French Romantic Comedy* (I. B. Tauris, 2015), and the coedited collections *The Europeanness of European Cinema* (I. B. Tauris, 2015) and *Women Do Genre in Film and Television* (Routledge, 2017), which won the BAFTSS Best Edited Collection prize in 2019. She is currently working on the monograph *Heightened Genre and Women's Filmmaking in Hollywood*, for Palgrave Macmillan.

Tamar Jeffers McDonald is reader in film at the University of Kent. She is the author of *Romantic Comedy: Boy Meets Girl Meets Genre* (Columbia University Press, 2007) and *Hollywood Catwalk: Exploring Costume and Transformation in American Film* (I. B. Tauris, 2010). *Virgin Territory: Representing Sexual Inexperience in Film*, her edited collection on filmic presentations of virginity, was published in 2010 by Wayne State University Press. Her research interests include film costume, romantic comedy, performance and movie magazines, topics that coalesced in her 2013 publication, *Doris Day Confidential: Hollywood, Sex and Stardom* (I. B. Tauris), which explored the myth of the "forty-year-old virgin" attached to Day, locating its origins in the very movie magazines that condemned her for playing the role. Her most recent monograph is an in-depth analysis of *When Harry Met Sally . . .* published by the British Film Institute (2015).

DEBORAH JERMYN is reader in film and television at the University of Roehampton. She is the author or editor of eleven books and has published widely on romantic comedy, with a particular interest in aging and gender in the genre. Her last monograph, *Nancy Meyers*, was published by Bloomsbury in 2017, and most recently she is coeditor, along with Barbara Jane Brickman and Theodore Louis Trost, of *Love Across the Atlantic: U.S.-U.K. Romance in Popular Culture* (Edinburgh University Press, 2020).

BETTY KAKLAMANIDOU is a Fulbright scholar and an associate professor in film and television history and theory at Aristotle University, Thessaloniki, Greece. She is the author of *Easy A: The End of the High-School Teen Comedy?* (Routledge, 2018), *The "Disguised" Political Film in Contemporary Hollywood* (Bloomsbury, 2016), *Genre, Gender, and the Effects of Neoliberalism* (Routledge, 2013), and two books in Greek on adaptation and the history of the Hollywood romcom. She is also the coeditor of *Contemporary European Cinema: Crisis Narratives and Narratives in Crisis* (Routledge, 2018), *Politics and Politicians in Contemporary U.S. Television* (Routledge, 2016), *The Millennials on Film and Television* (McFarland, 2014), *HBO's Girls* (Cambridge Scholars, 2014), and *The 21st-Century Superhero* (McFarland, 2010). Her articles have appeared in *Television & New Media*, *Literature/Film Quarterly*, *Celebrity Studies*, and the *Journal of Popular Romance Studies*.

JAMES MACDOWELL is associate professor of film and television studies at the University of Warwick. He is the author of *Happy Endings in Hollywood Cinema: Cliché, Convention, and the Final Couple* (Edinburgh University Press, 2013), and *Irony in Film* (Palgrave Macmillan, 2016).

BEATRIZ ORIA is associate professor of film studies at the University of Zaragoza, Spain. Her essays have been published in the *Journal of Popular Culture*, *Journal of Popular Film and Television*, *Journal of Popular Romance Studies*, and *Journal of Film and Video*. She is the author of *Talking Dirty on Sex and the City: Romance, Intimacy, Friendship* (Rowman & Littlefield, 2014), and a coeditor of *Global Genres, Local Films: The Transnational*

Dimension of Spanish Cinema (Bloomsbury, 2015). Her current research focuses on the contemporary chick flick.

SUEYOUNG PARK-PRIMIANO is assistant professor of English and film studies at Kennesaw State University. She is a contributing author to *Cinema's Military Industrial Complex* (University of California Press, 2018), *American Militarism on the Small Screen* (Routledge, 2016), and *Popular Culture in Asia: Memory, City, Celebrity* (Palgrave Macmillan, 2013).

MANUELA RUIZ received her Ph.D. in English in 2005 from the University of Zaragoza, Spain, where she is a Senior Lecturer of English. Since 2004, she has been a member of the research team *Cinema, Culture, and Society* (ccs.filmculture.net). Her most recent publications include chapters in international collections including *Culture, Space and Power: Blurred Lines* (Lexington, 2016), and the monograph *Hollywood Romantic Comedies of the Fifties: A Critical Study of a Film Genre* (Edwin Mellen, 2013). As part of the university research project in progress "Between Utopia and Armageddon: The Spaces of the Cosmopolitan in Contemporary Cinema," she is currently exploring the cinematic construction of a global narrative of intimate encounters across the boundaries of romantic comedy and melodrama from the perspective of cosmopolitan theory.

MARIA SAN FILIPPO is associate professor in the Department of Visual and Media Arts at Emerson College and editor of *New Review of Film and Television Studies*. She has authored two monographs, the Lambda Literary Award–winning *The B Word: Bisexuality in Contemporary Film and Television* (2013), and *Provocauteurs and Provocations: Screening Sex in 21st-Century Media* (2021), both published by Indiana University Press. She is currently at work on a *Queer Film Classics* volume on Desiree Akhavan's *Appropriate Behavior* (2014) to be published by McGill-Queen's University Press.

MARTHA SHEARER is assistant professor of film studies and Ad Astra Fellow at University College Dublin. She is the author of *New York City and the Hollywood Musical: Dancing in the Streets* (Palgrave Macmillan, 2016). Her work has also been published in *Screen* and the *Soundtrack* and in the edited collections *The City in American Cinema* (Bloomsbury, 2019), *The Oxford*

Handbook of Musical Theatre Screen Adaptations (Oxford University Press, 2019), and *Love across the Atlantic* (Edinburgh University Press, 2020). She is currently coediting two books: *Musicals at the Margins: Genre, Boundaries, Canons*, with Julie Lobalzo Wright, and *Women and New Hollywood*, with Aaron Hunter.

MAYA MONTAÑEZ SMUKLER is head of the UCLA Film & Television Archive's Research and Study Center. She is the author of *Liberating Hollywood: Women Directors and the Feminist Reform of 1970s American Cinema* (Rutgers University Press, 2018), winner of the 2018 Richard Wall Memorial Award.

Index

abject cosmopolitanism, 185–86, 193
abjection, 170, 171
abortion, 33, 142, 166, 170, 172, 173, 174, 261
action films, 146
addiction, 261, 262–63, 265, 267, 268, 269
adulthood, delayed, 40–42
age, and cinema audiences, 88–89. *See also* third-act romances
Ahmed, Sara, 278, 284, 288
Akhavan, Desiree, 275–76, 287, 293, 297–98; *Appropriate Behavior*, 275, 276, 279, 286–90; *The Bisexual*, 275, 293–97; *The Slope*, 275, 279–83; uncoupling narratives of, 277, 278–79
Alberti, John, 4, 17, 208, 315
alcohol, in Hong films, 251–52
Allen, Woody: *Annie Hall*, 8, 16, 241, 264–65, 277, 286–90; Hong compared to, 241, 244; *Manhattan Murder Mystery*, 290, 291
Allynne, Stephanie, 106
al-Mansour, Haifaa, *Nappily Ever After*, 75
alternative plotlines, 244
Always Be My Maybe, xiv–xvi

ambiguity, and double voice in Austen works, 71
Ames, Melissa, 301–2
An Jinsoo, 249
Annie Hall, 8, 16, 241, 264–65; *Appropriate Behavior* compared to, 277, 286–90
antielitism, 197
anxious romance, 4
Apatow, Judd: and bromance, 27, 37, 261–62; *Knocked Up*, 138, 312; *This Is 40*, 311–13; utopian project of, 263, 265
Appiah, Kwame, 189
Appropriate Behavior, 166, 275, 276, 279, 286–90
Arfin, Leslie, 260; *Love*, 257–71
L'Arnacœur, 210, 211
Aroesti, Rachel, xviiin18
Asian romantic comedy: *Crazy Rich Asians*, 1–2, 235n2, 261; *Don't Go Breaking My Heart 1*, 145, 146–55, 159–60; *Don't Go Breaking My Heart 2*, 145, 146–47, 155–60. *See also* Hong Sang-soo
Astaire, Fred, 145
audience: female, 6, 15, 137–38; of romcoms, 137–38; of stoner films, 138; for third-act romances, 88–90

Austen, Jane: and critical undervaluing of romantic comedy, 78; *Emma*, 78; influence on Ephron, 74; influence on Kaling, 77; narration in works of, 69–71; *Pride and Prejudice*, 67, 69, 77, 78–79
auteurs, 8, 14, 146, 200, 203, 241, 257, 270, 279. *See also* Apatow, Judd; Ephron, Nora; Meyers, Nancy

Badinter, Élisabeth, 206
Baker, Gideon, 186–87
Barbecue, 206
Barr, Rosanne, 101, 102
Barthes, Roland, 90
Basinger, Jeanine, 305
Beck, Ulrich, 31, 181
Beck-Gernsheim, Elisabeth, 31, 181
Bee, Samantha, 102
Before Midnight, 47, 49, 52–62
Before Sunrise, 47, 48–49, 50–51, 58–62
Before Sunset, 10, 47, 50, 51–52
Berger, John, 147
Berlant, Lauren, 29, 172, 278
Best Exotic Marigold Hotel, The, 99n11
beta males, 209–10
Bisexual, The, 275, 293–97
Blockbuster, 211–12
blockbusters, 1–2
Bloom, Rachel. See *Crazy Ex-Girlfriend*
Bonos, Lisa, 3
books and bookshops: in *Obvious Child*'s romantic narrative, 166–75; in romcom genre, 163–64; and shift in romcom genre, 165–66; unstable position of, in New York, 164–65, 167–70
Booth, Molly, 107, 108
borders, and creation of meaning in globalized world, 180

Bordwell, David, 222, 244
Bowler, Alexia L., 301
Brabazon, Tara, 164
break-ups. *See* uncoupling narrative(s)
Bridesmaids, 3, 37–38
Bridget Jones's Diary, 70, 238n29
Brittany, France, 202–3
Broad City, 102, 141–43
Brodesser-Akner, Claude, 108
Brody, Richard, 312–13
bromances: French, 206–10; and gender performance in 21st-century romcom, 261–62; as offshoot of romcom genre, 124, 250; and visibility of same-sex friendship, 37. See also *Harold & Kumar Escape from Guantanamo Bay*; *Harold & Kumar Go to White Castle*; *Up in Smoke*
Brook, Heather, 305
Brooks, Peter, 222
Brownstein, Rachel, 72
buddy films. *See* bromances
Burcon, Sarah, 301–2
Bush, George W., 136, 140
Butcher, Rhea, 102–3, 109, 112, 115–16, 117n12. See also *Take My Wife*

capitalism: in *Don't Go Breaking My Heart 1*, 147–55, 159–60; in *Don't Go Breaking My Heart 2*, 155–60; romantic comedy and interrogation of ethics of, 145; in To films, 146–47; and unstable position of New York bookshops, 164–65, 167–70. *See also* consumerism; neoliberalism
Cavell, Stanley, 5, 156, 248, 251, 259–60. *See also* comedy of remarriage
Célérier, Stéphane, 201
Cheech & Chong, 129–33
Chic!, 202–3

Chong, Tommy, 129–33
Christian, Aymar Jean, 257
Claire's Camera, 246
class distinction: in Hong films, 250–51; and South Korean romantic comedies, 249
Clinton, Kate, 101
Clueless, 71
Cohen-Shalev, Amir, 87
Collins, Jim, 164
comedy of remarriage, 5, 248, 259–60, 304. See also Cavell, Stanley
conscious uncoupling, 276–79. See also uncoupling narrative(s); wrong-coms
consumerism: in *Don't Go Breaking My Heart 1*, 147–55, 159–60; in *Don't Go Breaking My Heart 2*, 155–60; and romance in United States, 247; in To films, 146–47. See also capitalism
Corkin, Stanley, 166
corporeal comedy, in wrong-coms, 311–12
cosmopolitanism, 179–80; abject, 185–86, 193; cosmopolitanism-from-below, 186; and hospitality and openness in *Samba*, 185–91; in *Samba*, 180–84; and unconventional formulations of traditional romcom, 191–94; visceral, 188
cosmopolitanism-from-below, 186
Couples Retreat, 304, 312, 313
Cover, Rob, 277
Crazy, Stupid, Love, 306–7, 313, 314
Crazy Ex-Girlfriend, 219–20; friendship plots in, 229–34; paradiegetic spaces in, 220–21; as post-conventional, 108, 221–22; "uncertain middle" as space of ambiguity and ideological possibility in, 225–26

Crazy Rich Asians, 1–2, 235n2, 261
Crossing Delancey, 164
cross-sex friendship, 35–36, 38–39
Crouch, Ian, 266
Curtin, Michael, 104, 272n1
Curtis, Richard, *Love Actually*, 74
cynicism, toward romance, 19–20, 29–31

Date Night, 307–8, 310–11
dating apps, 30
DeGeneres, Ellen, 104, 105
Deleyto, Celestino: on borders and creation of meaning, 180; on cosmopolitan approach to film studies, 179; on evolution of romcom, 107; on friendship in romcoms, 35; on romcom genre, 5, 15, 50, 65n36, 260, 271, 304; and romcom happy ending, 222, 302, 303
Denby, David, 138
Dido and Aeneas (Purcell), 59
difficult subjects, addressed in romcoms, 16, 32–34
divorce comedies, 259. See also uncoupling narrative(s); wrong-coms
Dolan, Josephine, 89
Donalson, Melvin, 132
Don't Go Breaking My Heart 1, 145; capitalism and consumerism in, 147–55, 159–60; themes shared in *Life Without Principle* and, 146–47
Don't Go Breaking My Heart 2, 145; capitalism and consumerism in, 155–60; themes shared in *Life Without Principle* and, 146–47
Doty, Alexander, 106, 114
double voice, in Austen works, 71
Douthat, Ross, 31

drinking scenes, in Hong films, 251–52
Dunham, Lena, 263, 276

egalitarianism, in *Before Sunrise*, 48–49, 60
Ehrenreich, Barbara, 31
Ellen, 104
Emera, Louane, 200, 201
emerging adulthood, 40–42
Emma (Austen), 73, 78
Emma (film, 1995), 73
enemies-to-lovers trope, 67–68
English, Deirdre, 31
Ephron, Nora, 7–8, 74
Épouse-moi mon pote, 209, 213
Esposito, Cameron, 102–3, 109, 112–13, 115–16. See also *Take My Wife*
Eternal Sunshine of the Spotless Mind, 10
ethics as hospitality, 186–87
ethnicity, in French romcoms, 213–14

Fadina, Nadi, 305
Famille Bélier, La (*The Bélier Family*), 200–202
family: in French romcoms, 200–202; in Hong films, 250; influence of, in *Love*, 264, 268; and South Korean romantic comedies, 249
fantasy, 32
Female Boss, The, 248
feminism, 8–10; and *Broad City*, 142–43; and French romcoms, 213–14; ideological disconnects between romcom and, 301; and rejection of romcoms, 13–14; as undermining heteronormative marriage plot, 258–59
financial crisis of 2008, 165
flashbacks: and alternative plotlines, 244; in *Appropriate Behavior*, 288;

in *The Bisexual*, 294–95; in *Jane the Virgin*, 229; in *27 Dresses*, 70
Fletcher, Anne, *27 Dresses*, 70, 224, 301–2
Fonda, Jane, 97. See also *Grace and Frankie*; *Our Souls at Night*
Forever, 317n27
forking-path narratives, 244
40-Year-Old Virgin, The, xii
free indirect discourse, 69–71, 77
French, Philip, 312
French romcoms, 197–98; ethnicity in, 213–14; evocations of global culture in, 211–13; family in, 203–6; heterosexual masculinity in, 206–10; popularity and success of, 197–200; renewed nationalism characterizing, 200–202. See also *Samba*
Friedberg, Anne, 148, 153
friendship: in *The Bisexual*, 297; in *Crazy Ex-Girlfriend*, 229–34; cross-sex, 35–36, 38–39; girlfriend flicks, 9–10; in post-romantic age romcoms, 35–39. See also bromances
friends with benefits, 35–36
Friends with Benefits, 77–78
Frugiuele, Cecilia, 294
F to 7th, 283–86
Fullerton, Susannah, 69
fumerists, 101
functions, as unit in narrative, 90
Furst, Lilian, 72

Ganatra, Nisha, *Late Night*, 79
Gardies, André, 90–91
gaycoms, 103. See also queerness
gender: gendered conflict in *Before Midnight*, 52–55, 56–58, 60, 62; gendered conflict in *Before Sunrise*, 60–61; in Hong films,

252–53; intersection of race and, 75–76; performance of, in 21st-century romcom, 260–61, 264–65; and South Korean romantic comedies, 249; and stoner films, 138–43; and subversion through comedy, 101–2; suspicion regarding tropes of, in *Love*, 263. See also *Take My Wife*
generic hybridity, 31–35, 183, 184, 191, 192, 305, 306
genre, and gender performance in 21st-century romcom, 260–61
genre cinema, and expression of zeitgeist, 29
gentrification, 167–71, 174, 175
Genzlinger, Neil, 108
Gilbert, Joanne, 102
Gilda, 224–25
Gilleard, Chris, 86–87
girlfriend flicks, 9–10
Girls, 169–70
Glazer, Ilana, 141–43
Glitre, Kathrina, 67, 222, 223–24
globalization, 180, 211–13
Gluck, Will, *Friends with Benefits*, 77–78
Go Fish, 292
Going in Style, 99n11
Grace and Frankie, 86, 92, 93, 94–95
Graduate, The, 289
Gray, Francine du Plessix, 231–32
Grindon, Leger, 10, 107
grit, in consumer culture, 169, 170, 171
Gunning, Tom, 151–52

Haag, Pamela, 16
Hahaha, 250
Hair, Melissa, 171, 174
Halberstam, Jack, 278, 284
Haley, Brett, 97
Half Baked, 138

happy endings: as characteristic of romcom, 222, 236n8, 258–59, 260–61, 301–3; in television romcoms, 257; unconventional formulations of traditional, 191–94, 220, 234
Harold & Kumar Escape from Guantanamo Bay, 123–24; race and ethnicity in, 133–34; romance in, 127–29; striver-slacker romantic dynamic in, 138–40; wedding-crashing trope in, 134–37
Harold & Kumar Go to White Castle, 123–24; race and ethnicity in, 133–34; romance in, 125–27
Harris, Mark, 97
Harrod, Mary, 17
Hastie, Amelie, 173
Hello, My Name Is Doris, 89, 91–92
Henderson, Brian, ix–xi, xii, 7, 258, 264–65
Her, 1, 34–35
Higgs, P., 86–87
Hockley, Luke, 305
Holiday in Seoul, 247
hommecom, xi–xii
homophobia, in French romcoms, 206–10
Hong Kong film: *Don't Go Breaking My Heart 1*, 145, 146–55, 159–60; *Don't Go Breaking My Heart 2*, 145, 146–47, 155–60
Hong Sang-soo, 241–46, 250–54, 255n9; *Claire's Camera*, 246; *Hahaha*, 250; *Hotel by the River*, 250; *Like You Know It All*, 245; *Oki's Movie*, 253; *On the Occasion of Remembering the Turning Gate*, 242–43; *Right Now, Wrong Then*, 245–46, 252; *Tale of Cinema*, 241–42, 250; *Woman on the Beach*, 253

Hope Springs, 308
hospitality, and cosmopolitanism in *Samba*, 185–91, 193–94
Hotel by the River, 250
Huppert, Isabelle, 255n9
Hurwitz, Jon, 133
Hyperbola of Youth, 247

Ibiza, 8–10, 12, 13
I Do . . . Until I Don't, 308
I Know Where I'm Going!, 151–52
Illouz, Eva, 247
I'll See You in My Dreams, 89, 91, 94, 97
immigration. See *Samba*
indices, as unit in narrative, 90–91
indirect discourse, in Austen works, 69
individualism: and contemporary lack of engagement with traditional romance, 30–31; and self-centered romcoms, 39–42
Insecure, 115, 220, 283
interracial buddy comedies, 132–33. See also *Harold & Kumar Escape from Guantanamo Bay*; *Harold & Kumar Go to White Castle*; *Up in Smoke*
ironic pretense, comic effect in *The Mindy Project* though, 72–74
Isn't It Romantic, 2, 77
It Happened One Night, 135

Jacobson, Abbi, 141–43
James, P. D., 78
James, Robin, 173
Jane the Virgin, 219–20; diversity of writers of, 235–36n4; paradiegetic spaces in, 221; as post-conventional, 221–22; self-reflexivity of, 226–29, 237n23; "uncertain middle" as space of ambiguity and ideological possibility in, 226

Jeffers McDonald, Tamar, 2, 7–8, 17, 19, 219, 233
Jermyn, Deborah, 17
Johnson, Susan, *To All the Boys I've Loved Before*, 76–77
Jonze, Spike, *Her*, 33–34
Julian, Kate, 19–20, 45n27
Jungermann, Ingrid, 275–76, 291, 297–98; *F to 7th*, 283–86; *The Slope*, 275, 279–83; uncoupling narratives of, 277, 278–79; *Women Who Kill*, 275, 276, 279, 290–93

Kaklamanidou, Betty, 3, 17, 21n7, 107, 301, 304
Kaling, Mindy: on enemies-to-lovers trope, 67; *The Mindy Project*, 71–76, 115; on romantic comedies, 77, 78
Karlyn, Kathleen Rowe, 53, 101, 182
Karnick, Kristine Brunovska, 135
Kasman, Daniel, 156
Kauffman, Marta, 97. See also *Grace and Frankie*
Kim Min-hee, 245–46
Klinenberg, Eric, 309–10
Knocked Up, 138, 312
Kohan, Jenji, 239n36
Kozloff, Sarah, 68, 70, 72
Kristeva, Julia, 172
Krizan, Kim, 59
Krutnik, Frank, 236n8, 258

Lady Eve, The, 136
Laggies, 41–42
Last Vegas, 99n11
Late Night, 75
learning process, as romcom narrative element, 182–83, 190
Lees, Loretta, 169
Letter from an Unknown Woman (Ophüls), 59

Levine, Elana, 223, 235
Levine, Judith, 277
Le Vine, Lauren, 108
Lidofsky, Mia, *Strangers*, 11–13
life expectancy, 309
Life Without Principle, 146–47, 150
lighting, in Hong films, 253–54
Like You Know It All, 245
Limon, John, 170–71
Linklater, Richard: *Before Midnight*, 47, 49, 52–62; *Before Sunrise*, 47, 48–49, 50–51, 58–62; *Before Sunset*, 10, 47, 50, 51–52
List, Christine, 131
literary culture, romanticization of, 163–64. *See also* books and bookshops
living alone, 309–10
Loofbourow, Lili, 15
loss: feeling of, in *Before* series, 60; in third-act romances, 90–93. *See also* uncoupling narrative(s)
Lotz, Amanda D., 237–38n27
louts, 209–10
Love, 257–71
love: cosmopolitanism and differing patterns of intimacy versus, 183–84; in romantic comedies versus melodramas, 50, 51; and unconventional formulations of traditional happy endings, 191–94, 220, 234
Love, Heather K., 278
Love Actually, 5, 74
Love Marriage, The, 247–48
luxury, 156

MacDowell, James, 17, 70, 72, 146, 302
Manhattan Murder Mystery, 290, 291
Marcus, Esther-Lee, 87
marijuana. *See* stoner comedies
Marin, Richard "Cheech," 129–33

marriage: changing attitudes toward, in romcom, 302–4; fluctuating social contexts of, 309–11; and heteronormative romcom formula, 258–60, 267, 269–71, 301–3; as inertia in wrong-com, 306–8; among millennials, 46n35; and structural uncertainty of serial TV romcom, 268. *See also* wrong-coms
marriage equality, 311
marriage movies, 305
Martel, Lucrecia, 14
Martin, Adrian, 4, 146, 235, 236n5, 236n7
Martin, Alfred L., 106
Marvelous Mrs. Maisel, The, 176–77n16
masculinity: in French romcoms, 206–10; in U.S. romcoms, 208
masturbation, 36, 95, 99n18, 142, 285
matrix media, 272n1
McCormick, Casey, 223
McGrath, Douglas, *Emma*, 73
McKenna, Brosh, 231, 238n31. *See also Crazy Ex-Girlfriend*
McWhorter, Ladelle, 278
Mernit, Billy, 31
#MeToo movement, 38, 105
Meyers, Nancy, 8; *Something's Gotta Give*, 96
"middle, uncertain," as space of ambiguity and ideological possibility, 222–26
migration. *See Samba*
Mildred Pierce, 224–25
millennials: and individualism, 39–42; marriage among, 46n35
Miller, Laura, 163–64, 168
Miller, Nancy, 67
Mindy Project, The, 71–76, 108, 115
Mittell, Jason, 223

Modleski, Tania, 225
Morrison, Sarah M., 69–70
Mortimer, Claire, 302
Moss, Jeremiah, 168
Mr. & Mrs. Smith, 307, 313, 315, 317n37
multilinear narrative films, 244
multiprotagonist films, 27–28
musicals. See *Crazy Ex-Girlfriend*

Nachumi, Nora, 69–70
Nagel, Joanne, 210
nail-cutting, 292
Nakache, Olivier. See *Samba*
Nappily Ever After, 75
narrative control: in contemporary romantic comedy, 67–79; in *Jane the Virgin*, 221, 228
nationalism, 197; characterizing French romcoms, 200–202; and heterosexual masculinity in French romcoms, 209–10. See also right-wing populism
Nava, Mica, 188
Neale, Stephen, 51, 236n8, 260
Negra, Diane, 29, 164–65
neoliberalism, 3, 8, 31, 173, 190, 204, 212–13, 278, 279, 310. See also capitalism
neotraditional romcoms, xi, 7–10, 13
nervous romance, 264–65
Netflix: *Ibiza*, 8–10; *Isn't It Romantic*, 2, 77; *Love*, 257–71; and resurgence of romantic comedy, xiii–xvi; and rhetorical functionality of television endings, 223; romantic comedies released on, 3, 6; and success of French romcoms, 200
Neumann, Anne Waldron, 71
Newman, Michael, 223
Nicholson, Amy, 1, 263

nonlinear films, 244
Notaro, Tig, 106

Obvious Child, 165, 166–75, 261
Oki's Movie, 253
older protagonists: defining, 86–87; increased visibility of, in post-romantic age, 28–29. See also third-act romances
One Mississippi, 106
On the Occasion of Remembering the Turning Gate, 242–43
openness, and hospitality in *Samba*, 185–91
Ophüls, Max, *Letter from an Unknown Woman*, 59
Orange Is the New Black, 106, 112, 239n36
Ostrowska, Elżbieta, 3
otherness: and hospitality and openness in *Samba*, 186–88; normalization of, in *Take My Wife*, 102–4
Our Souls at Night, 85, 89, 92, 94
overseas romances, 180–81. See also *Samba*

Papa ou Maman 1, 204–5
Papa ou Maman 2, 205–6
parenthood, in French romcoms, 204–6
Park, Randall, xv
passivity, in *Obvious Child*, 172–73
Payet, Manu, 209, 213
people of color protagonists, xv, 10–13, 28. See also *Always Be My Maybe*; *Appropriate Behavior*; Asian romantic comedy; *Harold & Kumar Escape from Guantanamo Bay*; *Harold & Kumar Go to White Castle*; Hong Kong film; *Jane the Virgin*; *Mindy Project, The*; South Korean film; *Strangers*; *Up in Smoke*

pessimism, toward romance, 19–20, 29–31
Philadelphia Story, The, 135–36
Pillow Talk, 259, 269
point-of-view shots, 57, 74, 152
populism. *See* right-wing populism
post-romantic age, 16; cynicism toward romance in, 29–31; friendship in, 35–39; genre hybridity in, 31–35; individualism in, 39–42; reinvention of romcoms in, 27–29, 42–43
Powrie, Phil, 201
Pretty Woman, 8, 13, 16, 30
Pride and Prejudice (Austen), 67, 69, 77, 78–79
Pryor, Richard, 133
Purcell, Henry, *Dido and Aeneas*, 59

queerness: increased visibility of queer characters in post-romantic age, 28; and marriage equality, 311; and normalization of otherness in *Take My Wife*, 102–4; queer characters in *Always Be My Maybe*, xv–xvi; queer ethics, 278; romcoms featuring queer characters, 10–13; sociocultural and TV industry contexts of representations of, 104–6; *Strangers*, 11–13; in *Toute première fois*, 206–8; and uncoupling narratives, 276–79. See also *Appropriate Behavior*; *Bisexual, The*; *F to 7th*; *Slope, The*; *Take My Wife*; *Women Who Kill*

race and racism: in *Harold & Kumar Escape from Guantanamo Bay*, 123–24; in Kaling works, 75–76; in *Up in Smoke*, 131–33
radicalism, and evocations of global culture in French romcoms, 212–13

radical romcoms, xi, 8, 17, 19, 40
Rayns, Tony, 242–43
rebels, protagonists of stoner films as, 134–37
remarriage, comedy of, 5, 248, 259–60, 304
resilience, 173–75
Resnais, Alain, 242–43, 255n9
Rich, B. Ruby, 20
Right Now, Wrong Then, 245–46, 252
right-wing populism: and ethnicity in French romcoms, 213–14; and evocations of global culture in French romcoms, 211–13; and family in French romcoms, 203–6; in French romcoms, 197–98, 202–3; and heterosexual masculinity in French romcoms, 206–10
Ritchie, Michael, *Semi-Tough*, x–xi
Rizvi, Fazal, 188
Robespierre, Gillian, 168
Rogers, Ginger, 145
Rohmer, Eric, 241, 255n9
romance: and consumption in United States, 247; cosmopolitanism and differing patterns of intimacy versus, 183–84; cross-sex friendship as alternative to, 38–39; cynicism toward, 19–20, 29–31; fractured, in Hong films, 241–46, 250–54; versus friendship in *Crazy Ex-Girlfriend*, 229–34; in *Harold & Kumar Escape from Guantanamo Bay*, 127–29; in *Harold & Kumar Go to White Castle*, 125–27; in Korean comedies, 247–48; nervous, 264–65; suspicion regarding tropes of, in *Love*, 263; in *Take My Wife*, 111–13; and unconventional formulations of traditional happy endings, 191–94, 220, 234

romantic comedies: Austen's influence on contemporary, 77; auteurs, 8, 14, 146, 200, 203, 241, 257, 270, 279; box office performance of, 1–3, 146; central narrative elements of, 182–83; death of, ix–xi, 1, 7, 258, 264–65; decline of traditional formula for, 29–30; as defense against cultural and generational pessimism, 19–20; development of genre, 3–7; embracing, 13–16; featuring queer and/or people of color protagonists, 10–13, 102–6, 108–16, 119n45, 166, 275, 276, 279–83, 286–93; happy ending as characteristic of, 222, 236n8, 258–59, 260–61, 301–3; ideological disconnects between feminism and, 301; intersection between other genres and, 31–35; Kaling on, 77, 78; neotraditional, xi, 7–10; Netflix and resurgence of, xiii–xvi; politics of narrative control in contemporary, 67–79; radical, xi, 8, 40; real-life challenges in, 16, 32–34; reinvention of, in post-romantic age, 27–29, 42–43; released on streaming platforms, 2–3; resurgence of, 8; versus romantic melodramas, 49–50, 182; romantico-sexual, 93–94; scholarship on, 16–17, 68; self-centered, 39–42; shift in, 165–66, 302–4; stigmatization of, 5–6, 14–15, 146; subdivision of, xi–xii, 4; television and evolution of, 219–20, 234–35; and women viewers, 6, 15, 137–38

romantic irony, 72–74

romantic melodrama: *Before Midnight* as, 62; *Before* series as, 48–55; versus romantic comedy, 49–50, 182; *Samba* as, 181–82

romantico-sexual romcom, 93–94

rom-sitcom, 107–11. See also *Take My Wife*

Roseanne, 101, 102

Rowe, Kathleen. See Karlyn, Kathleen Rowe

Rowlson-Hall, Celia, 11

Ruiz, Manuela, 17

Russo, Mary, 102

Rust, Paul, 263; *Love*, 257–71

Samba: cosmopolitanism in, 180–84; ending of, 191–94; hospitality and openness in, 185–91; success of, 200

same-sex marriage, 311

Sardou, Michel, 202

Schlossberg, Hayden, 133

Schor, Hilary, 73

Schreiber, Michele, 8–9

Schumer, Amy, 102; *Trainwreck*, 1, 224

science fiction, 32

screwball comedies, x, 124–25

Second Best Exotic Marigold Hotel, The, 99n11

Seeso, 105. See also *Take My Wife*

self-centered romcoms, 39–42

self-help, 264–66, 267, 269–70

Semi-Tough, x–xi

seriality. See television

Set It Up, xviiin18

sex and sexuality: and affirmative uncoupling narratives, 277; in *The Bisexual*, 293–97; decline in, among young people, 45n27; and friends with benefits, 35–36; romantico-sexual romcom, 93–94; in *Take My Wife*, 111–13; in third-act romances, 93–97; as unacknowledged in romantic comedies, xi–xii; in wrong-coms, 308. See also queerness

Shelton, Lynn, 41–42, 271
Shumway, David R., 314
Silverman, Sarah, 102
single-occupancy households, 309–10
single women, 310
Situation amoureuse: c'est compliquée (Relationship Status: It's Complicated), 209–10, 211
Skrbiš, Zlatko, 179, 189
Sleeping with Other People, 36
Sleepless in Seattle, 7, 30, 107
Slope, The, 275, 279–83
Smiley Face, 138
soap operas, 226–29. See also *Jane the Virgin*
social embarrassments, in Hong films, 243–44
social media, 6, 10–11, 30, 105
Something's Gotta Give, 96
South Korean film, 241–54
stand-up comedy, 102–3, 105, 109, 170–71, 173, 176–77n16
Stevens, Kyle, 107
stoner comedies: audience of, 138; combining of romcoms and, 123–24; gender and, 138–43; genre conventions in screwball comedies and, 124–25; quest for love in, 125–29. See also *Harold & Kumar Escape from Guantanamo Bay*; *Harold & Kumar Go to White Castle*; *Up in Smoke*
Stout, Janis, 79
Strangers, 11–13
streaming platforms, 2–3. See also Netflix
striver-slacker romance, 138–40
Subramanian, Janani, 75, 77
Sucsy, Michael, 42
supergentrification, 169
Swift, Taylor, 169–70

Take My Wife, 113–16, 119n45; normalization of otherness in, 102–4; and queerness in changing television landscape, 104–6; romance and sexuality in, 111–13; rom-sitcom conventions in, 108–11
Tale of Cinema, 241–42, 250
Tasker, Yvonne, 29, 165
teenage audiences, 88–89
telenovelas, 226–29. See also *Jane the Virgin*
television: and evolution of romcom, 219–20, 234–35; friendship plots in *Crazy Ex-Girlfriend*, 229–34; gender in, 101–2; as matrix medium, 272n1; and maximization of ideological possibility, 220; preference for episodic versus serialized programs, 237–38n27; productive pathology in *Love*, 257–71; queerness in changing landscape of, 104–6; romantic comedy genre in, 107–8; self-reflexivity of *Jane the Virgin*, 226–29, 237n23; "uncertain middle" as space of ambiguity and ideological possibility in, 222–26; wrong-coms in, 317n27. See also *Bisexual, The*; *Broad City*; *Ellen*; *Grace and Frankie*; *Mindy Project, The*; Netflix; *Roseanne*; *Take My Wife*
therapy, 264–66, 269–70
third-act romances, 85–88; and increased visibility of older protagonists in post-romantic age, 28–29; loss in, 90–93; and rise of 50–60+ viewers, 88–90; sex in, 97
This Is 40, 311–13

Thomas, Deborah, 50, 51, 58, 60, 182
To, Johnnie, 160nn5–6; *Don't Go Breaking My Heart 1*, 145, 146; *Don't Go Breaking My Heart 2*, 145, 146; *Life Without Principle*, 146–47, 150
To All the Boys I've Loved Before, 76–77
Toledano, Eric. See *Samba*
Toute première fois (*I Kissed a Girl*), 206–8
Trainwreck, 1, 224
Traister, Rebecca, 310
transnational romantic comedy. See overseas romances; *Samba*
Transparent, 106
Tropiano, Stephen, 103
"troubled-marriage" cycle, 304
27 Dresses, 70, 224, 301–2

"uncertain middle," as space of ambiguity and ideological possibility, 222–26
uncoupling narrative(s), 276–79, 297–98; in *Appropriate Behavior*, 286–90; in *The Bisexual*, 293–97; in *F to 7th*, 283–86; in *The Slope*, 279–83; in *Women Who Kill*, 290–93. See also divorce comedies; wrong-coms
Up in Smoke, 129–33
Urman, Jenny Snyder, 235–36n4. See also *Jane the Virgin*

VanDerWerff, Emily, 14
violence, palimpsests of, in wrong-coms, 312–13
visceral cosmopolitanism, 188
Vishnevetsky, Ignatiy, 148
voice-over: in contemporary romantic comedy, 67–79; in *Jane the Virgin*, 221, 228

von Arendonk, Kathryn, 228, 235–36n4
Vulture, ix

Walker, Alexander, 15
Wanzo, Rebecca, 170
Warshow, Robert, 15
web series: *F to 7th*, 283–86; *The Slope*, 279–83; *Strangers*, 11–14
Wedding Crashers, xii
wedding-crashing trope, 134–37
wedding movies, 305
When Harry Met Sally . . . , 35, 74, 163, 164
Wicker Park, 169
Wilder, Gene, 133
Williams, Linda, 235
Williamsburg, 168–69
Winch, Alison, 9
window-shopping, in *Don't Go Breaking My Heart*, 148–49, 153, 154–55
womances, 37–38
Woman on the Beach, 253
Women Who Kill, 275, 276, 279, 290–93
Wong, Ali, xv
Wood, Robin, 49, 58, 59–60, 145
Woodward, Ian, 179, 189
Working Girl, 9
wrong-coms, 301–4, 314–15; humor in, 311–14; identifying, 305–6; marriage as inertia in, 306–8; rise of, 309–11. See also divorce comedies; uncoupling narrative(s)

Yahr, Emily, 30
York, Ashley Elaine, 3
You, 175
You've Got Mail, 163, 164–65, 172

Zarum, Lara, 97
Zukin, Sharon, 169